Kissinger the Negotiator

Kissinger
the
Negotiator

Lessons from Dealmaking

at the Highest Level

James K. Sebenius

R. Nicholas Burns and Robert H. Mnookin

Foreword by Henry A. Kissinger

HARPER

An Imprint of HarperCollins*Publishers*

HarperCollins books may be purchased for educational, business, or sales promotional use. For information, please email the Special Markets Department at SPsales@harpercollins.com.

FIRST EDITION

Designed by William Ruoto

Library of Congress Cataloging-in-Publication Data has been applied for.

ISBN 978-0-06-269417-1

18 19 20 21 22   LSC   10 9 8 7 6 5 4 3 2 1

Contents

Contents

Part III: "Zooming In"

Foreword

by Henry A. Kissinger

Among the tools of statecraft, strategic negotiation occupies a prime position. Over my career, I have conducted many negotiations and made numerous observations on this vital subject. I have not, however, methodically reviewed the many negotiations in which I was involved to determine the most effective strategies and tactics to address different challenges at the table. To my knowledge, none of the many books written about my foreign policy record as secretary of state and national security advisor seriously analyzes this central topic. This book, therefore, is unique. It is the first to delve deeply into my philosophy and method of negotiation. James K. Sebenius, as lead author, along with his Harvard colleagues R. Nicholas Burns and Robert H. Mnookin, has produced a superb and practical analysis of how to forge worthwhile agreements in complex situations.

This book was not my idea. Until a few years ago, I did not know Jim or Bob. And while I knew Nick well, his years of government service began after my time as secretary of state. I have no institutional connections with any of the authors. This effort originated when the three professors invited me to Harvard in 2014 as part of their ambitious project to interview all former American secretaries of state about their toughest negotiations. Thus far, they have conducted in-depth interviews with seven men and women who have occupied that office. They plan to draw on these extraordinary discussions to write a major book on the American diplomatic experience over the last forty years, to serve as the basis for a three-part public television series.

The book you now hold, however, explores a more focused question: what analysis and action consistently lead to success (or failure) in complex, high-level negotiations? Beyond platitudes and well-known principles such as the importance of credibility, I expressed skepticism during our Harvard interviews about whether robust answers to this question could be extracted from the written record. I wondered aloud whether it would be possible to come up with systematic advice given the diverse contexts, distinctive personalities, and unique features of individual negotiations.

Subsequent conversations with Jim, Nick, and Bob increasingly persuaded me that useful, nonobvious prescriptions could be identified. To do this, the authors have concisely recounted a number of episodes in which I was involved. They have brought the negotiating aspects to the foreground, with just enough historical and policy context to make their analysis accessible. Some of these cases are broadly familiar, such as the opening to China and the disengagement agreements between Egypt and Israel after the 1973 Arab-Israeli War. Other challenging cases, such as negotiating for black-majority rule in Rhodesia in 1976 with Britain and key African states, though widely discussed at the time, have faded into relative obscurity. Yet viewing these episodes primarily through a negotiation lens yields fresh understandings. While I disagree with some of their policy judgments, especially on the Vietnam talks, the authors have done outstanding work in researching these complex negotiations and generating actionable insights from them.

I am often struck by the ad hoc approach to vital negotiations taken by otherwise experienced public officials and private executives. For example, one courts failure by concentrating on process and tactics divorced from a strategic conception of one's fundamental interests and objectives. Another common error is to expend the bulk of one's energies getting the parties to the table, hoping that once they engage face-to-face, a deal will somehow follow. In fact, the more important challenge can be to act, often beforehand and away from the table, to shape the situation to one's advantage. This can mean putting in place strong penalties for failure to agree and arranging appealing incentives for agreement. It can mean carefully building supportive coalitions and neutralizing potential blockers. Jim, Nick, and Bob draw on my record to catalogue many other such snares—and offer useful advice on avoiding and escaping them.

This book's importance does not lie mainly in telling the stories of my negotiations, however colorful or historically intriguing. Instead, readers will find its true value in its distillation of the valuable principles and practices that were largely implicit during and after my tenure, occasionally even to me. Given his familiarity with the relevant academic research plus extensive personal experience in high-stakes dealmaking, Jim, along with his coauthors, Nick and Bob, possesses a deep understanding of complex negotiations. This has enabled them to interpret my experience and to extract thoughtful generalizations from it.

In undertaking this project in the spirit of applied history, Sebenius, Burns, and Mnookin have made a major contribution to our understanding of negotiation and diplomacy at a time when the utility and promise of these activities are often overlooked. When employed with skill and thorough knowledge of the issues at stake, their analysis promises genuine improvement in diplomatic support. Every CEO, diplomat, and dealmaker facing complex negotiation challenges will benefit from reading this book.

Preface

Who are the world's best negotiators? What makes them effective? When colleagues, students, and clients ask us these questions, Henry Kissinger's name inevitably arises. Some remember his secret negotiations to open U.S.-Chinese relations after years of mutual hostility. Others recall détente with the Soviets, the first nuclear arms control deal, the Egyptian and Syrian disengagement accords with Israel, or the controversies over Cambodia or Chile. Even for those who know few details of Kissinger's record, the former secretary of state regularly features in conversations about great negotiators.

This widespread perception of Kissinger's negotiating prowess has deep roots. According to a June 1974 Harris poll, an astonishing 85 percent of Americans judged that Kissinger was doing a "splendid" job, while 88 percent considered him to be a "highly skilled negotiator."[1] This represented "the highest approval rating for anyone in government since the polls were begun."[2] Forty years later, in 2014, a survey of 1,615 international relations scholars in 1,375 colleges and universities overwhelmingly ranked Henry Kissinger as the most effective U.S. secretary of state in the last fifty years. This top ranking held among most subgroups of the expert respondents: liberal, middle-of-the-road, and conservative; male and female; and so on.[3] Even Walter Isaacson, Kissinger's often critical biographer, judged him to have been "the foremost American negotiator of [the twentieth] century."[4]

Millions of words have been written both by and about Kissinger the influential secretary of state, diplomatic historian, and foreign policy analyst. Along with countless commentators, both sympathetic and critical, Kissinger has himself chronicled his role in dozens of particular negotiations. Yet, to our surprise, a serious overall examination of an important aspect of Kissinger's record as negotiator does not appear to exist.[5] By looking *across* Kissinger's most significant negotiations to ferret out common characteristics, this book represents our critical exploration of Kissinger's approach to negotiation and its underlying logic, strategies, and tactics. Our goal is to generate the prescriptive insights that are essential to understanding and addressing today's conflicts and dealmaking challenges, whether international or domestic, public or private.

Our quest to learn from Kissinger's approach has its origins in a larger ongoing project. Since 2001, the Program on Negotiation, a Harvard-MIT-Tufts consortium, has annually sponsored a "Great Negotiator" event to honor men and women from around the world who overcame significant barriers to reach worthy agreements.[6]

Faculty and graduate students do substantial research and case writing before bringing each year's Great Negotiator honoree(s) to Harvard for a public program of intensive videotaped interviews about each of their toughest negotiations: What were its most challenging elements? How did you handle them? What would you have done differently? Why? What insights do you draw from these experiences? What advice would you give someone facing a similar situation?

Our 2012 honoree was former secretary of state James A. Baker III, for his central role in negotiations leading to the unification of Germany within NATO, actions to forge the Gulf War coalition to eject Saddam Hussein from Kuwait, and the diplomacy paving the road to the Madrid Conference, the first time Israelis and Arabs had engaged in a multilateral setting. That year's events were so stimulating that we decided to adapt this "Great Negotiator" methodology between 2014 and 2016 to conduct lengthy interviews with all former U.S. secretaries of state.

As part of the resulting American Secretaries of State Project, we conducted wide-ranging research on and lengthy interviews with Henry Kissinger, in addition to George Shultz, Madeleine Albright, Colin Powell, Condoleezza Rice, and Hillary Clinton.[7]

Our initial conversations with Henry Kissinger, which marked his first time in a Harvard classroom in forty-five years, proved intellectually engaging and represented a deeply emotional "homecoming" for the former Harvard student and professor. Kissinger turned out, in the words of Drew Gilpin Faust, Harvard's president, to be a ninety-two-year-old "rock star" in the eyes of the three hundred or so students in attendance, who asked very tough questions of the former secretary of state.

During these conversations, Jim Sebenius cited George Shultz's insightful essay "The 10 Commandments of Negotiation," and noted several generalizations we had drawn from James Baker's approach to diplomacy.[8] We queried Kissinger: "If you were to formulate your version of Shultz's Ten Commandments of negotiation, what would be on your list?" He chose not to give us his prescriptions, suggesting that general advice of this type would be unlikely to apply across the variety of negotiating situations one encountered.[9]

This skeptical answer gave us pause: would it really be impossible to encapsulate the essence of "Kissinger the negotiator" into a set of broadly applicable prescriptive insights? Intrigued by this challenge, Jim decided to carefully analyze hours of personal interviews and reread all three volumes of Kissinger's memoirs—*White House Years*, *Years of Upheaval*, and *Years of Renewal*—plus *Diplomacy*, *On China*, and *World Order*; all told, roughly six thousand pages bristling with accounts of various negotiations. Jim then took a first cut at a prescriptive synthesis in a lengthy draft essay, which he sent to Dr. Kissinger in New York with a simple query: did the analysis accurately capture Kissinger's approach across a wide range of negotiations?[10]

After meeting and discussing the draft, Kissinger responded affirmatively, offered suggestions, and urged that we delve more deeply into several of his negotiations, noting that our work was the first of its kind. Of course, plenty of studies have been done on specific negotiations, such as the opening to China or the Paris talks to end the Vietnam War, but not on this general topic. Nor had the insights of current negotiation theory been systematically brought to bear on Kissinger's approach. Believing this to be an important subject from which we could learn a great deal to advance both the theory and practice of negotiation, we decided to collaborate on this book, with Jim taking the analytical and editorial lead as first author.

In this work, we have sought to accurately capture and illustrate the precepts underlying Henry Kissinger's approach to negotiation; we think of this task as characterizing "the mind of the negotiator." After studying the great nineteenth-century statesman Klemens von Metternich, Kissinger applauded "Metternich's marvelous diplomatic skill," observing that "diplomacy can achieve a great deal through the proper evaluation of the factors of international relations and by their skillful utilization."[11]

In part, Kissinger studied Metternich to understand (and, later, employ) the most effective strategies and tactics of negotiation. It is in that spirit that we study Kissinger. Yet technical virtuosity in a negotiator has a fundamental limitation: it is blind to the purposes that are to be negotiated and the worldview that informs those purposes. Technique says nothing about whether the objectives of the negotiator are good or evil, wise or foolish.

So, when we study Kissinger's negotiations, we take *his* objectives and his worldview as givens for our analysis, at least as a point of departure. To ensure American security during his time in office from the late 1960s through the mid-1970s, Kissinger pursued at least three overarching objectives: (1) preventing the great evil of nuclear war, while (2) restraining Soviet expansion and managing Cold War conflicts to American advantage and (3) building a more stable "structure of peace" among China, the USSR, and the United States. When we analyze a specific negotiation, such as the Paris Peace Accords over the Vietnam War, we highlight (and often question) how Kissinger's assumptions about that particular conflict influenced his negotiation strategy.

Today's challenges differ sharply from those of the Cold War era: the dominant bipolar U.S.-Soviet rivalry has given way to a more multipolar world, with emerging powers such as China and India increasingly influential. Nonstate actors and cross-border issues are on the rise: from global warming and international financial flows to transnational crime and airplane-borne viruses. Interconnected webs enmesh the geopolitical chessboard.[12] Yet effective negotiation remains vital. Harnessed to wise purposes and adapted to changing circumstances, carefully chosen lessons extracted from Kissinger's experience offer an enduring source of invaluable guidance to those in the public and private spheres who understand the value of successful negotiation in human affairs.

★ ★ ★

We are three experts in different disciplines, with diverse backgrounds, yet our intellectual and professional lives revolve around negotiation. One of us, Nick Burns, teaches diplomacy and international politics at Harvard's Kennedy School of Government, following a twenty-seven-year career as a diplomat in the U.S. Foreign Service. Bob Mnookin, with significant experience in legal mediation and negotiation, teaches negotiation at Harvard Law School. Completing our trio, Jim Sebenius, who spent years on Wall Street and decades advising clients worldwide on deals and disputes, teaches negotiation at Harvard Business School. In

2010, the three of us sponsored the visit of a remarkable negotiator, former Finnish president and Nobel Laureate Martti Ahtisaari, to Harvard as part of the Great Negotiator Award program. We found the experience so mutually stimulating that we began to bring our distinct perspectives and experiences together in research and teaching across our three professional schools.

While this book and our larger American Secretaries of State Project are collaborative efforts among the three of us, Jim Sebenius conceived the idea of writing about Henry Kissinger's negotiating philosophy and record. He took the analytical lead, wrote the first draft of every chapter, and shepherded what turned out to be a substantial research effort. Nick and Bob are thankful to Jim for his unstinting belief in this book and for his leadership in our joint effort to extract the right lessons from Kissinger the negotiator.

A word on methodology: We have sought accuracy throughout this book concerning the historical events under discussion. Yet our main purpose has been to extract useful prescriptions for effective negotiation rather than to set the historical record straight or provide the last word on policy disputes.

Capturing the "mind of the negotiator" is an inherently subjective undertaking. To succeed in doing so, we have relied heavily on our conversations with Henry Kissinger. Given the importance of how *he* explains the rationale for his negotiating strategy and tactics, we quote extensively from these conversations and from his many books. We also draw on his memos and interviews, often those from the time of the given negotiation under discussion. Because we seek to capture how Kissinger himself reasons about the process, the quotations we weave into the text, mostly without indentation, are often lengthy.

Because recollection and writing after the fact inevitably color accounts of earlier events and can generate self-serving rationalizations, we have searched for independent, and sometimes conflicting, sources about such events, as our bibliography and many notes attest. These include the many primary source documents, interviews, and excellent interpretive summaries undertaken by the Digital National Security Archive (in particular, its invaluable compilation the Kissinger Telephone Conversations: A Verbatim Record of U.S. Diplomacy, 1969–1977), the Association for Diplomatic Studies and Training, the Nixon and Ford Presidential Libraries, and the U.S. State Department Office of the Historian.[13] Where possible, we include the perceptions of those who negotiated with Kissinger.

We have been privileged to enjoy Dr. Kissinger's cooperation in multiple conversations and interviews, especially to ensure that we have accurately represented his views on negotiation strategy and tactics. Yet he has neither requested, nor would we have approved, any editorial control on his part. For better or worse, the text and conclusions are our own.

Kissinger the Negotiator

A Story That Should Be Told

Every U.S. president since John F. Kennedy has sought Henry Kissinger's counsel, as have CEOs and political leaders worldwide. His insights into foreign policy, statecraft, and world order have enjoyed broad influence. Yet his impressive overall record as a negotiator has somehow escaped systematic analysis.[1]

After studying Kissinger's negotiating experience and writings, plus lengthy interviews with him on this subject, we have found remarkable levels of sophistication and consistency in his approach. This has motivated us to achieve two goals in this book.

First, we seek to characterize "Kissinger the negotiator" by looking back across the many important negotiations, involving China, the Soviet Union, Vietnam, the Middle East, and Southern Africa, in which he played central roles as national security advisor and secretary of state in the Nixon and Ford administrations. We then crystallize a set of characteristics that underpin his approach.

Our second purpose is forward looking: while Kissinger's conception of effective negotiation derives largely from the diplomacy of earlier decades, we seek to assess the value, and limits, of his approach as a source of guidance for today's diplomats and others who negotiate in business, finance, public policy, and law. Throughout the book, we endeavor to extract negotiating principles and techniques of enduring value and wide relevance. Three examples suggest what readers may expect to learn from studying Kissinger the negotiator:

First, while the term *strategic* is often bandied about, a closer look at Kissinger's approach clarifies what strategic negotiation actually means in practice and why this orientation can be such a powerful tool.

Second, Kissinger's negotiations consistently illustrate the back-and-forth process by which he "zoomed out" to a broader strategy and then "zoomed in" to become highly persuasive with a specific counterpart. We have seen a number of top-flight negotiators develop this "zoom-out, zoom-in" approach to the strategic and interpersonal aspects of challenging deals.[2] Exposure to this distinctive aspect of Kissinger's dealmaking has helped many of our students and executive program participants, often in the middle of successful careers, become far more effective in their public and private negotiations.

Third, examining Henry Kissinger's behavior across his many negotiations shows how his extensive actions "away from the table" often dramatically improved outcomes in tandem with his more familiar tactics "at the table." Put more simply, watching a particularly effective negotiator at work unshackles our minds from thinking of negotiation mainly in terms of persuasive interpersonal dealings. Getting to the right "yes" in the face of formidable obstacles requires a much broader and more robust conception of negotiation than is often the case.

In his ninety-fifth year as we complete this book, Henry Kissinger remains in the global spotlight as a senior statesman, global strategist, and active commentator on foreign affairs. Beyond authoring a regular stream of articles, he has seen his recent books, *On China* (2011) and *World Order* (2014), make the best-seller lists, and a new volume on statesmanship is in the works.[3] And he remains controversial. For example, some *thirty-nine years* after Kissinger left public office, an "intense confrontation" over his record erupted during the 2016 Democratic presidential primary debates. Hillary Clinton's praise and Bernie Sanders's condemnation sparked a clash of columnists in the *New York Times* under the headline "Henry Kissinger: Sage or Pariah?"[4] In the twelve months alone before this very public conflict, the publication of the first volume of Niall Ferguson's generally sympathetic two-part biography of Kissinger has contrasted with a scathing assessment of Kissinger's record in a new book by historian Greg Grandin.[5]

Like their innumerable predecessors dating back to the 1970s, such books, related articles, and media episodes (admiring, dispassionate, or critical) do not generally highlight Kissinger's approach to negotiation, though this aspect of his record is often very much in the background. Rather, such accounts tend to emphasize Kissinger's complex analyses of international relations and his extensive record as a practitioner of statecraft in the realist tradition.[6]

Across these and other events in which he was involved, Kissinger's negotiations are described mostly in the context of specific episodes, not examined in depth across a range of situations. Kissinger's own writing is suffused with observations on the art and science of negotiation, though mainly with respect to particular instances. This vital but relatively neglected aspect of Kissinger's work deserves explicit focus and analysis, largely as a function of his remarkable strength as a negotiator.

While he is almost universally judged to have been highly effective, Kissinger's record has attracted a number of severe critics, especially with respect to human rights, covert actions, undemocratic secrecy, and support for authoritarian regimes, with special focus on his actions in Cambodia, Laos, North Vietnam, Argentina,

Chile, East Pakistan (now Bangladesh), and East Timor. As such, our analysis of his approach to negotiation could quickly devolve into an evaluation of his actions while in office. Yet trying to judge whether he was a saint or a sinner (in effect, relitigating well-worn controversies) is not the purpose of this book. Moreover, we would have little comparative advantage for such a task (though interested readers may consult the voluminous debates among his various detractors and defenders).[7]

Our purpose is neither to judge the man nor to set the historical record straight. Instead, by plumbing and evaluating a career of impressive accomplishment in some of the world's most challenging negotiations, we seek to *learn* as much as possible from Kissinger about this vital subject. If successful, we will have extracted actionable insights into the art and science of negotiation at the highest levels.

Who Is Henry Kissinger?

The outlines of Kissinger's life and career are generally familiar.[8] He was born in 1923 to a German-Jewish family. Sensing the impending Holocaust at the hands of the Nazis, they emigrated to the United States in 1938, only a few months before the violent anti-Jewish rampage of Kristallnacht. Kissinger became a naturalized United States citizen in 1943 and served with the U.S. Army in the European theater from 1943 to 1946. After completing his undergraduate and graduate education at Harvard, he was appointed to the school's faculty, and rose in academic rank to tenured professor. He was active in Harvard's Department of Government and its Center for International Affairs from 1954 to 1969.

Kissinger acted as an advisor on foreign policy to New York governor Nelson Rockefeller, who three times sought the Republican nomination for president and was a political rival to Richard Nixon. Despite Kissinger's support for Rockefeller, Nixon selected the Harvard professor to serve as his advisor for national security affairs. While in this role, Kissinger was also sworn in as the fifty-sixth secretary of state, on September 22, 1973. After the Watergate scandal led to Nixon's resignation, Kissinger continued to serve as secretary of state, under President Gerald Ford, until January 20, 1977.

Even given Kissinger's elevated public profile at this writing (2018), it can be difficult to recall the extent of his national and global celebrity. While in office, he appeared on no fewer than fifteen covers of *Time* magazine and, jointly with Richard Nixon, was named *Time*'s "Man of the Year" in 1972.[9] He was awarded the Nobel Peace Prize in 1973, along with Le Duc Tho, for their negotiations to end the Vietnam War (though Kissinger later tried to return the prize); he was also honored, in 1977, with the Presidential Medal of Freedom, the nation's highest civilian award.

Following his terms as secretary of state, Kissinger founded a global consulting firm and served on a number of prominent public and private boards and commissions.[10] Through his nineties, he remains a prolific commentator and analyst, consulted by world leaders ranging from Barack Obama to Donald Trump, and from Vladimir Putin to Angela Merkel and Xi Jinping.

In tandem with his prominent public persona, Kissinger is the author of seventeen books, along with innumerable articles, speeches, and opinion pieces.[11] Two of his early books, *A World Restored: Metternich, Castlereagh, and the Problems of Peace, 1812–22*, and *Nuclear Weapons and Foreign Policy*, both published in 1957, when he was a young academic, were widely regarded as pathbreaking, both conceptually and for their policy implications.[12] Following his government service, he is especially notable for his three-volume set of memoirs, which chronicles his time in office. The first volume, *White House Years*, won the National Book Award in 1980.[13]

His 1994 book, *Diplomacy*, offers a panoramic view of international relations and diplomacy, with special concentration on the twentieth century and the West. The book articulates Kissinger's "realist" orientation and argues for the importance of the balance of power and the concept of "national interest." In it, Kissinger critiques an overly idealistic foreign policy while insisting that actions abroad must at least be consistent with a nation's moral views.[14] *On China* (2011) examines Chinese history and Kissinger's long negotiating experience in that country, especially with its leaders ranging from Mao Zedong to Xi Jinping, and makes a forward assessment of U.S.-Chinese relations in the twenty-first century.[15] More recently, *World Order* (2014) offers a more global and historical perspective on Kissinger's traditional themes, including war, peace, and the balance of power in the international system.[16]

Why Study "Kissinger the Negotiator"?

Given Kissinger's experience and extensive written work, studying his foreign policy thinking and statesmanship makes evident sense. But what, exactly, is the case for analyzing Kissinger the negotiator? What did his major negotiations actually demonstrate or achieve to merit careful analysis so many years after the fact? And beyond historical interest, what might such episodes teach us that will be of value to present and future negotiators?

Our answer to these questions calls for glancing back at the world that confronted Richard Nixon and Henry Kissinger (and, later, Gerald Ford) mainly between 1969 and 1976. By design, the thumbnail sketches that follow are not full accounts of events during this period, but they should help readers recall key challenges that set up the critical negotiations we later analyze in this book.[17] The sketches only highlight what Kissinger and his colleagues accomplished in each negotiation; in subsequent chapters, we explain *how* he did it and discuss the broader lessons.

The Cold War

Appointed in 1969 as President Nixon's national security advisor, Kissinger confronted a potentially existential threat: The United States and the Soviet Union had for decades been locked in a simmering and dangerous Cold War. More than thirty-seven thousand nuclear weapons, many on hair-trigger alert, were aimed at each other. Europe was divided, as was Berlin, in a hostile stand-off between Eastern and Western blocs linked to rival military alliances, the Warsaw Pact and NATO. At the same time, the Soviets were supplying North Vietnam with extensive armaments used to kill thousands of Americans during the bitter Vietnam War.

Against this menacing backdrop, Kissinger made major contributions to negotiating improved relations with the Soviet Union through a policy of "détente," that is, a lessening of U.S.-Soviet tensions across a broad front, and forged the first major nuclear arms control deal (SALT I) between the superpowers.

A Hostile United States–China Relationship

For twenty years, the United States had neither recognized nor had meaningful contact with the People's Republic of China, whose troops had fought American soldiers in Korea, a nation that later supported North Vietnam with war matériel and advisors. As Kissinger put it, "For twenty years, US policymakers considered China as a brooding, chaotic, fanatical, and alien realm difficult to comprehend and impossible to sway."[18] China routinely validated such impressions with fire-breathing rhetoric. For instance, in May 1969, during Nixon's first year in office, an article by Chairman Mao Zedong was entitled "People of the World, Unite and Defeat the U.S. Aggressors and All Their Running Dogs."[19]

Working closely with President Nixon, Kissinger secretly opened negotiations with Chinese leaders Mao Zedong and Zhou Enlai in 1971.[20] Though bitterly controversial at the time, especially among American conservatives, this process was key to developing an opening to China in 1972 that paved the way toward American recognition of and increasing engagement with over a billion Chinese citizens of the People's Republic.

The War in Vietnam

By 1969, the bloody war in Vietnam had already cost some 36,000 American lives, led to a far larger number of Vietnamese deaths, and effectively ended Lyndon Johnson's presidency. Widespread campus demonstrations and antiwar protests across the country, sometimes violent, underscored the views of nearly two-thirds of Americans polled in August 1968 who had come to believe that sending troops to Vietnam had been a mistake.[21] Under intense domestic pressure, Nixon was committed to rapidly drawing down American forces in Indochina. From almost 550,000 troops when he took office, more than 200,000 were withdrawn between 1969 and 1970. In 1972, total U.S. troop strength in Vietnam fell by 95 percent below its peak to less than 25,000.[22] As Kissinger began negotiating, the pace of the American military withdrawal accelerated—and North Vietnam knew it. The North's unalterable negotiating position during a process that began in 1969 was that the United States itself had to topple the South Vietnamese government (its putative ally) and then withdraw. During the negotiations, U.S. Army general Vernon Walters observed the main North Vietnamese negotiator, Le Duc Tho, "standing at the top of the [Paris] villa steps, smiling triumphantly down at Kissinger [saying,] 'I really don't know why I am negotiating anything with you. I have just spent several hours with Senator [George] McGovern and your opposition will force you to give me what I want.'"[23] Meanwhile, South Vietnam's leaders would staunchly oppose any deal in which American troops returned home.

A complex of factors led to the end of the Vietnam War, including what we analyze as a "multifront negotiation campaign" that was orchestrated by Henry Kissinger and Richard Nixon. Kissinger dealt directly with Le Duc Tho, his North Vietnamese counterpart, in Paris. Kissinger also negotiated to improve American relations with the Soviets and Chinese, pressing both Communist giants directly and indirectly to curtail their support for North Vietnam. These talks came to involve West Germany and Western Europe, too. The resulting Paris Peace Accords in 1973 meant that fighting would cease, prisoners of war would be released, U.S. troops would be withdrawn, and the South Vietnamese government would remain, ultimately to take part in new elections. (Of course, with Watergate, Nixon's resignation, and the U.S. unwillingness and/or inability to enforce the deal, North Vietnam soon violated this agreement and South Vietnam fell to the North in April 1975.)

The 1973 Arab-Israeli War

In October 1973, surprise attacks by Egypt and Syria on Israel on the holiest day of the Jewish year (and in the Muslim holy month of Ramadan) unexpectedly showed Israeli military vulnerability. Arab forces made unprecedented advances, which included the Egyptian army's crossing of the Suez Canal. With Kissinger as secretary of state, an emergency U.S. effort resupplied the Israel Defense Forces, enabling Israel to regain its balance and to counterattack. Up to that time, the Soviet Union had enjoyed a strong position in the Middle East, with important Arab states as clients, among them Egypt and Syria. The Soviets also resupplied their allies, threatening direct intervention and sharp escalation if Israel continued its march toward Cairo and Damascus. A superpower confrontation loomed.

Through sustained shuttle diplomacy, Kissinger was instrumental in negotiating disengagement accords between Egypt and Israel and Syria and Israel in late 1973 and early 1974. These agreements have, for the most part, held to this day. Kissinger undertook these negotiations with the conscious objective of severely curtailing Soviet influence in the Middle East, a result that largely continued for more than forty years (until Russia's September 2015 entry into Syria's civil war).

Southern Africa

With Soviet support and an influx of Cuban troops into Angola in the mid-1970s, the mineral-rich countries of Southern Africa seemed at risk of falling into the Soviet orbit and becoming a major front in the Cold War. Given the searing American experience in Vietnam, there was no stomach for countervailing U.S. military action or even aid; Congress had quickly outlawed a covert U.S. response to the Cuban and Soviet actions. Deeply complicating matters, both Rhodesia and South Africa, likely important to countering the Soviet and Cuban moves, were governed by white-minority regimes with significant American political support, especially in conservative quarters. After Rhodesia had illegally declared its independence from Britain in 1965, the United Kingdom had tried over several years, but utterly failed, to persuade Ian Smith, leader of Rhodesia's white-minority government, even to consider majority rule for the six million black Africans under the control of fewer than three hundred thousand whites. (For example, the Rhodesian constitution mandated that the legislative assembly have fifty European members and sixteen African members, only half of whom could be directly elected.[24])

In a little known 1976 initiative—one we analyze in some detail in the chapters that follow—Henry Kissinger negotiated with a range of African states, both radical and moderate. In so doing, he persuaded a deeply recalcitrant Rhodesia finally to accept the principle of black-majority rule within a two-year period. In particular, he convinced South Africa to exert powerful pressure on Rhodesia for this purpose—despite South Africa's own white-minority rule and the fact that such pressure would surely boomerang. These negotiations were carried out in a manner that significantly helped contain the Cuban and Soviet presence in Angola, ultimately paved the way for Rhodesia (later Zimbabwe) to gain its independence, helped to avert a feared "race war" in the region, and arguably moved South Africa a significant step closer to black–majority rule.

Looking back at this substantial record of diplomatic accomplishment (with respect to détente, arms control, China, Vietnam, the Middle East, and Southern Africa), we were intrigued at what a closer examination might reveal: *How* did Kissinger prepare, design, and conduct these complex high-wire negotiations? What aspects of his approach to negotiation (its underlying logic, strategies, and tactics) could be valuable in meeting today's negotiation challenges, both public and private?

Naturally we do not claim that negotiation by itself, in the narrow sense of the term, produced these results; many complementary policies and actions were involved. Nor would we claim that one man's actions were fully responsible. Other parties, as well as chance, plainly influenced outcomes.[25] Given these caveats, we explore Kissinger's actions and writings for insights into overcoming high barriers to desirable agreements. With these insights, we aim to develop better analysis and more potent prescriptions to help individual negotiators realize superior results.[26]

What Do We Mean by "Negotiation"?

In shorthand, we might characterize bilateral or multilateral "negotiation" in the context of international relations as the dealmaking subset of diplomacy and foreign policy. To fall into this category, a negotiator must, at a minimum, have a target agreement in mind among parties that often see things differently and have conflicting interests.

Caveat: common usage and the bulk of contemporary academic work on negotiation often have a narrow focus on the purely "talking part" of the process, or interpersonal moves mainly "at the table." This typically means face-to-face communication, empathy, assertiveness, persuasive argument, body language, dealing with cross-cultural and personality differences, patterns of offers and counteroffers, and the like.[27] Consistent with a more expansive tradition of negotiation research, however, Kissinger's negotiating strategy and tactics also encompass moves "away from the table" taken to enhance the odds of a better outcome.[28] For example, such moves can entail actions to include or exclude parties from the process, to build or break coalitions, and to enhance or worsen the consequences of impasse.

Seeking to cleanly distinguish this broader conception of negotiation from "statecraft" or "diplomacy" can quickly become a pointless exercise in semantics. The lines among these closely related activities become blurry at best, and usage varies widely. As a result, and in line with Kissinger's writings and practice, we consistently adopt an expansive view of "negotiation," including actions taken both at and away from the table intended to induce agreement on desirable terms. In many books and articles, Kissinger's negotiations constitute a necessary subplot of the larger statecraft-focused story; in this book, we invert the perspective, focusing on his negotiations, broadly construed, with the larger story as backdrop.

The Plan of This Book

Our quest, then, is to crystallize, learn from, and evaluate the relevance of Kissinger's approach to negotiation. To do so, we draw mainly on accounts of the episodes just sketched out, filling in context as needed, but mostly without presenting detailed case studies.

To convey a more granular sense of Henry Kissinger as negotiator, however, we begin the next section by exploring his negotiations in Southern Africa toward the end of the Ford administration, in 1976. Though celebrated at the time, these complex talks we've briefly referenced here are much less well known today than his dealings with the Soviets, Chinese, North Vietnamese, or various players in the Middle East. Initially spurred by Cold War concerns with Soviet and Cuban moves into Angola, Kissinger's diplomacy in Southern Africa was directed at ending firmly entrenched white-minority rule in what became Zimbabwe and Namibia—a perhaps surprising initiative for a Republican administration.

We use these negotiations in Southern Africa, intriguing in themselves, to introduce and illustrate a number of prescriptive insights suggested by Kissinger's strategy and tactics. At several points during the next three chapters, we step outside the narrative, by means of shaded boxes containing broader observations about Kissinger's approach to negotiation. After analyzing the Southern Africa talks, we develop and generalize most of these insights in separate chapters, with illustrations from a range of Kissinger's other dealings. Finally, we evaluate these generalizations for their relevance to current negotiations in diplomacy and other realms.

By the end of this book, readers will have encountered a range of dauntingly complex and often fascinating negotiations. Learning how Kissinger cracked many of these cases provides insights that can sharply improve negotiated results in challenging situations. Such insights include:

- what it actually means to be "strategic" in negotiation;
- how to realistically assess whether an agreement potentially exists;
- how a "wide-angle lens" and game-changing moves *away* from the negotiating table can create the space for a deal and enable favorable outcomes at the table;
- how careful sequencing, coalition building, and handling those who would block a deal are keys to multiparty effectiveness;
- the importance of truly understanding, reading, and building rapport with your counterparts;
- how assertiveness and empathy can be productively combined;
- how to act opportunistically as circumstances shift while maintaining a strategic perspective;
- how dogged persistence rather than blinding insights is often the essential ingredient for success; and
- effective, and ineffective, ways to make proposals, frame concessions, build credibility, utilize "constructive ambiguity," embark on shuttles among the parties rather than deal with them together, and opt for open versus secret talks.

Throughout this book, readers will see the value of Kissinger's practice of repeatedly zooming out to the strategic and zooming in to the interpersonal. Yet underlying our exploration of these many facets of negotiation will be a sobering truth: the techniques of reaching agreement, however creative, depend for their ultimate success on the accuracy of underlying assumptions about the world, judgments about the parties' real interests, and in-depth knowledge of history, politics, economics, and culture. Process insights in the service of flawed objectives or divorced from an understanding of the true situation are unlikely to yield much of value. By studying a great negotiator like Kissinger, however, we can learn to be far more effective in the business, legal, and government negotiations we conduct in our professional lives.

I

How Kissinger Negotiates: The Forgotten Case of Southern Africa

1

Crafting a Negotiating Strategy*

It would not have been predicted by any observer of American politics that a Republican administration would take the lead in bringing about the breakthrough to majority rule in Southern Africa. Majority rule had been a liberal cause, never translated into an operational policy.[1]

—HENRY KISSINGER

"I don't believe in black majority rule ever in Rhodesia, not in a thousand years." Thus vowed Ian Smith, Rhodesia's white prime minister, on March 20, 1976.[2] Outnumbered twenty-two to one in that Southern African country, some 270,000 whites had defiantly ruled over 6 million blacks since Smith unilaterally declared Rhodesia's "independence" from Great Britain just over a decade earlier.

Since "independence," which no other country in the world had recognized, intensive British diplomatic efforts at the highest levels had utterly failed to persuade the intransigent Smith to

---

* This chapter relies heavily, with great appreciation, on extensive research by and the suggestions of Alex Green.

3

accept black-majority rule. (At the time, the Rhodesian constitution effectively gave full legislative control to the small white,
European minority.) Despite this history, Henry Kissinger had
initiated complex coalitional negotiations in the region during
the waning years of Gerald Ford's administration. Scarcely six
months after Smith's "not in a thousand years" declaration,
Kissinger had orchestrated an about-face by the Rhodesian prime
minister. Stunning his white countrymen, and a world audience,
Smith made a televised announcement accepting the principle of
majority rule for his country, to take effect within two years.[3]

More surprising was *how* Kissinger had engineered Smith's
turnabout. By delicately working with both moderate and radical
black African states, he had persuaded a most reluctant South Africa, that "citadel of apartheid," to apply decisive pressure on neighboring Rhodesia to abandon its policy of white-minority rule.[4]
Remarkably, South Africa agreed to bring this pressure despite the
plain fact that, if Rhodesia capitulated, antiapartheid forces would
(and later did) shift their energies toward South Africa, the major
remaining white-ruled state in the region.

At the time, this was big news. *Time* magazine's cover story on
October 11, 1976, lauded Henry Kissinger's "dazzling diplomatic
foray into Southern Africa," which had "raised the possibility that
Rhodesia, as well as much of the rest of Southern Africa, might be
poised on the brink of peace instead of a race war that was once
thought inevitable."[5] Along with much of the world's press, the
British *Observer* gushed that this intricately choreographed process
represented "a staggering diplomatic coup" in a "seemingly intrac-
table crisis."[6]

Though Ian Smith's reversal would prove pivotal, black-
majority rule in Rhodesia would not come on Kissinger's watch.
When Gerald Ford lost the 1976 presidential election soon after
Smith's announcement, Kissinger became a lame duck, depart-

ing as secretary of state in 1977. This effectively ended his role in the negotiations, which stalled, triggering an upsurge in guerrilla fighting and diplomatic activity. Majority rule in Rhodesia, later known as Zimbabwe, became a reality only with a 1979 agreement that largely followed the Kissinger blueprint and was forged under British leadership at London's Lancaster House.

Many of us remember the worldwide celebration and 1993 Nobel Prize when Nelson Mandela, with F. W. de Klerk, ended apartheid in South Africa and launched black-majority rule in that country. Yet Kissinger's diplomatic push some seventeen years earlier to achieve majority rule in neighboring Rhodesia has mostly been forgotten, perhaps as a result of his higher profile actions elsewhere or since the disastrous thirty-seven-year reign of Robert Mugabe, Zimbabwe's first president, has eclipsed that long-ago moment of hope when democratic principle triumphed over white-minority rule. As some suggest, however, Kissinger's prior negotiations helped set the stage for the ultimate end of apartheid in South Africa.

By the start of his negotiations over Rhodesia, Henry Kissinger had confronted a range of negotiating challenges over almost eight years under two presidents. These included the opening to China, the end to the Vietnam War, détente and arms control with the Soviets, and lasting disengagement accords among Egypt, Israel, and Syria following their 1973 war. Yet, in the last volume of his memoirs, *Years of Renewal*, Kissinger startled the authors of this book by declaring, "Of all the negotiations I conducted, by far the most complex was the one over majority rule in Southern Africa."[7] Indeed, the book devotes 157 pages over five chapters to these events.[8] After studying Kissinger's own account, interviewing him, and delving into many other descriptions and analyses of this case, we reached two conclusions.[9]

First, while these negotiations remain far less familiar than many of Kissinger's other dealings, a highly abbreviated version makes for a captivating story today: historically significant, populated by memorable characters, and worth telling for its intrinsic interest.

Second, and at the heart of this book, the Rhodesia episode serves as an excellent vehicle to introduce and illustrate key characteristics of the Kissinger negotiation approach that we analyze more deeply in later chapters. Press accounts cite Kissinger's "splendid diplomatic skill in loosely assembling the black and white pieces of the Rhodesian puzzle" (*Washington Post*), his "uncanny understanding of the realities of power," and "his shrewd timing" (*Time*).[10] Yet such fulsome praise tells us absolutely nothing about the actual logic, strategy, and tactics of his negotiation approach, which we seek to illuminate in the analysis that follows.

★ ★ ★

We have already referred to Southern Africa, the region, and to South Africa, the country. To clarify, Kissinger's negotiations focused on *three* white-ruled entities. (See Figure 1.1.) In 1975, these included:

- **South Africa**—an increasingly isolated but regionally dominant country in which some 4 million whites, among a population of roughly 22 million at the time, had instituted apartheid, a policy of harsh and brutal segregation by race that imposed severe civil, legal, and economic restrictions on nonwhites and denied them many rights afforded to white citizens.
- **Rhodesia**—a former British colony later known as Zimbabwe, in which, as noted, some 270,000 whites controlled some 6 million black Africans. Rhodesia had illegally declared independence in 1965 under the leadership of Ian Smith, a Royal Air Force fighter pilot in World War II. No other country had recognized this defiant pariah state, which was subject to com-

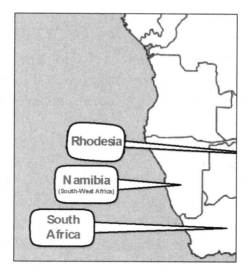

Figure 1.1

prehensive UN economic sanctions and under increasing military pressure from guerrilla forces seeking to topple its white supremacist regime.

- **Namibia**—a former German colony known earlier as South West Africa. Namibia was administered by South Africa under a limited mandate from the League of Nations after World War I. While the United Nations revoked this mandate in 1966, South Africa continued to govern this large territory of fewer than a million inhabitants as its de facto "fifth province."

Fears of an African Front in the Cold War, Crisis in Angola, and the Failure of a Covert Response

Dramatic photos of helicopters evacuating desperate Vietnamese and Americans from Saigon on April 29, 1975, dominated U.S.

front pages as a brewing crisis in Southern Africa began to engage the White House. Relatively neglected by American diplomacy, this region assumed a new importance during the final eighteen months of the (Republican) Ford administration in 1975 and 1976 as Angola and Mozambique, both newly independent from Portugal, began to fall under Marxist sway.

The first indication that the Cold War might be coming to Southern Africa occurred in 1974, when a left-wing coup in Portugal spurred the demise of that country's colonial domination of Mozambique. An indigenous Marxist group rapidly gained power in that East African country, which declared independence in 1975. On an April state visit to Washington, Zambian president Kenneth Kaunda warned of a growing Marxist insurgency in neighboring Angola as the Portuguese colonial power departed that nation. This Angolan insurgent group had increasingly been supported by significant military aid from the Soviet Union and what would ultimately amount to some twenty thousand Cuban combat troops. In some sense, these movements were merely part of a larger pattern; many other African countries had been ousting their former European colonial masters since Ghana gained its independence in 1957. But through Washington's Cold War eyes, by early 1976, two important coastal nations in Southern Africa, Angola on the west coast and Mozambique on the east, were fast falling under Soviet and Cuban influence.

In the contest for influence and resources that characterized the Cold War, a Soviet-sponsored Cuban alliance with African Marxists alarmed Kissinger and Ford as well as many leaders of newly decolonized African nations in this region from Tanzania and Zambia to the white regimes of Rhodesia and South Africa. Unless effectively opposed, Soviet-Cuban insurrections could spread via direct intervention and the support of favored guerrilla groups in different countries. (See Figure 1.2, which also shows the

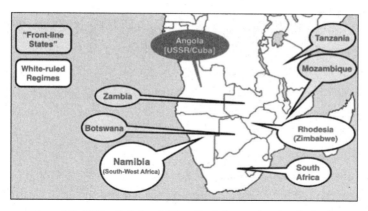

Figure 1.2: White-Ruled and "Frontline" States, plus Angola (1975)

"Frontline States" that surrounded white-ruled Rhodesia.) Even if the prime targets of such guerrilla groups were the white-ruled regimes, their presence in neighboring countries, such as Zambia and Tanzania, could destabilize and even overthrow such fragile "host" governments. U.S. inaction could cede dominant influence over this mineral-rich region to the Soviets. More broadly, Ford and Kissinger judged that an ineffectual U.S. response would vividly demonstrate the post-Vietnam loss of American will, in the midst of the Cold War that then dominated geopolitics.

Beyond geopolitics, there was widespread, almost fatalistic, talk about a coming "race war" in Southern Africa, especially in Rhodesia. For example, a 1976 Associated Press dispatch stated, "Most worrying to whites is the prospect that Soviet arms and Cuban troops in Angola might be used in Rhodesia to back militant black movements in a conflict that could spill over borders to engulf the entire region. Neighboring black-ruled states—Tanzania, Angola, Mozambique, and Zambia—all have warned a racial 'bloodbath' is imminent in Rhodesia."[11] Even with respect to the prospect of black rule in that country, the normally sober diplomat George Kennan raised the specter "of some form of genocide" for whites and "a cost in bloodshed so appalling as to rock the stability of international life."[12]

As will increasingly become evident, Kissinger had multiple, entangled motives for acting in Southern Africa: to prevent Cold War rivals from dominating the region, to advance democratic principles by promoting black-majority rule, and to avert a race war. There is little doubt that his early actions prioritized Cold War geopolitics: to counter the Soviets and Cubans in Angola, he orchestrated a covert military operation with French help. While he kept Congress quietly informed, public revelation of these covert plans rapidly led to a U.S. law banning them entirely. With Watergate, Nixon's resignation, and the searing Vietnam experience fresh in American minds, such a congressional response should hardly have been surprising. In any event, with the covert route firmly blocked and military options effectively off the table, Kissinger was left to ponder how the United States could use diplomatic power to achieve its objectives in Southern Africa.

An Alternative Strategy: Negotiation to Hasten Majority Rule

Kissinger came to believe that the Soviet/Cuban threat could be weakened if American diplomacy persuaded the nations of Southern Africa to rebuff *any* foreign intervention in the region. As he observed, "If we wanted to resist future Soviet and Cuban adventures in Southern Africa and to reduce and expel Soviet and Cuban influence there—as we had in the Middle East—our policy would have to reflect the aspirations of the vast majority of the continent."[13] These strongly held aspirations included the end of white-minority rule in Rhodesia, South West Africa/Namibia, and eventually in South Africa itself.

Existing moderate American policy toward Rhodesia and South Africa had been (insensitively) dubbed the "Tar Baby option."[14] The secret Nixon administration document that adopted this policy in

1969 noted that "We would maintain public opposition to racial repression but relax political isolation and economic restrictions on the white [ruled] states."[15] Kissinger's new approach (persuading states in the region to rebuff foreign intervention) would require abandoning the "Tar Baby option"—insensitively named for the Uncle Remus story about an approach that ensnares an adversary—in favor of actively supporting black-majority rule in Rhodesia and Namibia.[16]

To further this goal, Kissinger hoped to orchestrate negotiations that would put Rhodesia and Namibia on a clear path to black-majority rule on fixed timetables. Apart from South Africa, all states in the region passionately desired this outcome. Yet it had long seemed completely out of reach, despite the fact that by the 1960s, Britain, the United States, and other global powers firmly supported an end to white-minority rule in Africa. Since 1965, in line with its policy of not granting independence to its colonies until the white colonial minority ceded electoral power to the majority, Britain had actively sought to persuade the white Rhodesian regime not to declare independence and to accept black-majority rule. Dramatizing British power, Prime Minister Harold Wilson twice summoned Ian Smith, in 1966 and 1968, to the decks of two British warships, the *Fearless* and the *Tiger*, for direct, high-level negotiations. These talks utterly failed, leading the British to largely abandon their efforts and want nothing more to do with Smith.[17] Whether from conviction or bluster, Rhodesian prime minister Smith's uncompromising position—no black-majority rule in Rhodesia "in a thousand years"—reflected the reality that, if the black majority ruled in Rhodesia, the political, judicial, and economic power enjoyed by the white minority would inevitably suffer. (As late as March 22, 1976, British prime minister James Callaghan unveiled a new proposal whose principal feature was a "precise timetable for majority rule within eighteen to twenty-four months." Though

Kissinger supported the proposal as "constructive," Ian Smith rejected it within twenty-four hours.)[18]

How to Negotiate with Ian Smith

Pause with us for a moment, and imagine how one might most effectively negotiate with Ian Smith, Rhodesia's white leader, to persuade him to accept majority rule within two years. Naturally, one would look into Smith's background, finding that he was born in 1919 to Scottish immigrants on a farm in Rhodesia; that he preferred sports to academics in school; that he was downed twice and injured as a British Royal Air Force pilot in the Second World War, his face partially paralyzed into what many observers saw as a permanently stern expression. Smith entered politics, declared Rhodesia independent from British colonial rule, styled his renegade government as a "front line against international Communism," and professed that "The white man is master of Rhodesia. He has built it, and he intends to keep it."[19] And, as Kissinger observed, the British "detested Ian Smith, believing he had deceived and embarrassed them, first by declaring independence and then in the course of a number of stalemated negotiations."[20]

Assuming one enriched this skeletal profile of Smith with deeper psychological and background research, what negotiating approach would offer the best chances for success? Following the lead of British diplomats and the prime minister himself over the decade since Rhodesia declared independence, a merely competent negotiator facing this challenge might start by setting up a high-stakes meeting with Ian Smith in a carefully chosen location. Then, face-to-face with Smith, by some combination of flattery, a steely gaze, vague warnings or threats, historical argument, and a silver tongue, our negotiator might seek to persuade the defiant leader to offer some form of majority rule to Rhodesia's black citizens.

Not Henry Kissinger. During a news conference on September 5,

1976, when asked about even the "possibility of meeting" with Smith, Kissinger replied, "I have no present plans to meet with Mr. Smith and this would depend entirely on assurance that a successful outcome of the negotiations will occur."[21] His blunt assessment: "All previous efforts had failed because they had started with negotiations with this representative of a white minority that had no conceivable incentive to abandon its dominance."[22]

COMMON APPROACH: To this day, even experienced dealmakers often see the essence of negotiation as carefully setting up a meeting and persuasively making the best case for their desired deal. This is the "direct" approach—adopted by the British and rejected by Kissinger in many situations. It will often fail if the parties lack incentives to say yes to the deal you seek.

BROADER NEGOTIATION INSIGHT: Decide when and under what circumstances you should meet with your counterpart. Assess key barriers to agreement and consider direct versus indirect approaches to overcoming those obstacles. Equating negotiation with merely "talking at the table" often risks failure, depending on the barriers to agreement. These can take many forms: economic (e.g., your counterpart has a better offer), psychological (e.g., there exists distrust, dislike, poor communication, or egotism), tactical (e.g., one party makes hardball moves, tells lies), setup related (e.g., key allies are not involved, self-interested agents selectively filter information), and so on.[23] A fundamental barrier to Smith's agreement: A "yes" to majority rule meant a grave loss of power and wealth for his white constituents, while a "no" gave whites a fighting chance to preserve their privileged status. Given this barrier, any successful negotiating strategy had to make "yes" more attractive to Smith, "no" costlier, or both. To accomplish this, Kissinger chose an "indirect" approach, acting "away from the table" to favorably orchestrate incentives and penalties. While direct persuasive efforts play a vital role, Kissinger, like other highly effective negotiators, often looks imaginatively beyond the table to set up more promising situations before even meeting with counterparts.

Assessing the Situation: Parties, Interests, Resources, and Barriers

Mindful that his would be the first substantive (non-ceremonial) visit to Southern Africa by a U.S. secretary of state in American history, Kissinger pragmatically assessed the situation, especially the interests of the varied stakeholders, his resources in a potential negotiation, and the barriers to be overcome. Here in the next six paragraphs in his own words, is his assessment:

"Before launching ourselves into Africa, we needed to distill a strategy from the partially overlapping, partially incompatible objectives of the various parties. Our principal asset was that the African states themselves were urging us to become involved while the white minority governments trusted us more than any other country or, for that matter, any alternative leadership group in the United States. As for the other parties or potential parties:

- The "Frontline States"—that is, the countries bordering or close to Rhodesia: Mozambique, Zambia, Tanzania, and Botswana—on whose territory the guerrillas were organizing, were the conduit for arms from outside the continent and for foreign advisers or Cuban troops. [See map on page 9.] But their leaders also knew that the Rhodesian forces were well armed and tough. A war would be costly and might well end with the guerrilla forces ceasing to be guests and instead dominating the host country.

- The other African states, less immediately engaged, supported majority rule in principle but were prepared to cooperate in preventing the continent from becoming a battleground of the Cold War.

- South Africa [longtime supporter of Rhodesia] feared that armed struggle in Rhodesia might turn into the prelude to an assault against South Africa itself. At the same time, all the Frontline States recognized that South African assistance was indispensable to a Rhodesian solution, for, without it, the transition would be bloody, the outcome uncertain, and the radicalization of the whole region inevitable.

- For Britain, Rhodesia represented a painful reminder of the diminution of its international status. Britain's inability to force Rhodesia into submission weakened its effort to develop a new African role based on cooperation with its former colonies. It explains as well the personal hatred many British leaders felt for Ian Smith, which complicated and often frustrated British dealings with him.

- As for the Rhodesian authorities, they had the least to gain. . . . Whatever guarantees of minority rights might be associated with majority rule, the position of the European population would inevitably atrophy. . . . The Ian Smith authorities could be induced to settle only by having it brought home to them that the policy we were fashioning was the least distasteful of the painful choices before them."[24]

From this assessment of the African and British parties, Kissinger crystallized a key part of the negotiating challenge: "This maze of incommensurables—that those with power had no legitimacy and those with legitimacy no power, that the passions of the parties were matched by their distrust of each other—defined both the limits of our African strategy and its prospects."[25]

Finally, Kissinger had to consider the politically treacherous division on the home front. In the United States, the hard-fought advancement of civil rights over the previous fifteen years made minority-white-ruled regimes and apartheid especially controversial. Believing that the increased pressure of sanctions would hasten the demise of apartheid, one group in Congress and beyond, generally liberal in political orientation, advocated more isolation and pressure. An opposing group, generally conservative, strongly opposed any U.S. efforts to weaken white-minority regimes in Southern Africa. Some members of this group believed that the normalization of relations with South Africa would over time moderate the white-minority government's policies. Sanctions and excessive pressure on these regimes, this more conservative group argued, risked abandoning whites to what could easily devolve into a bloody race war, the emergence of countries hostile to the West, and regional anarchy.

This long-standing divide in U.S. politics took on new intensity as imminent Republican primaries in 1976 pitted conservative icon Ronald Reagan against Gerald Ford, the incumbent president who had succeeded Richard Nixon. Already suspicious of Kissinger, détente with the Soviets, and the opening to China, many Republican primary voters opposed policies that seemed to favor black-majority rule in Rhodesia and South Africa. Yet Kissinger had a stalwart backer in President Ford, who consistently took the high ground: "I cannot judge whether the political impact will be good or bad. But we must do this because it is the right thing to do."[26]

BROADER NEGOTIATION INSIGHT: To craft a strategy, employ a "wide-angle lens" to assess the full set of potentially relevant

Figure 1.3: Some key leaders in the Southern Africa negotiations[27]

parties. Many negotiators think too narrowly about the parties to a negotiation, limiting their focus to those people necessary to sign an agreement or their direct agents. By contrast, before Kissinger settled on a negotiating strategy, he thoroughly assessed the situation, especially the full set of potentially involved and influential parties from key nations (Rhodesia, South Africa, the Frontline States, and elsewhere in Africa, and from Britain, France, and the United States, both in and outside the government). Even if his target deal was with the Rhodesians, his party assessment was much broader. Not only did it include "external" parties, but also "internal" U.S. parties. In particular, Kissinger made sure that his boss, the president, was part of the assessment and was fully behind his efforts.

From this assessment of the parties and their interests, Kissinger needed to craft a strategy that would overcome the reason for prior failures: "Previous efforts had failed because they could not generate the balance of rewards and penalties to reconcile the conflicting motivations comprising the cauldron of Southern Africa."[28] (For reference, Figure 1.3 on page 17 displays key parties in this negotiation.)

A Seven-Part Negotiation Strategy

To generate the favorable balance of rewards and penalties that had eluded prior negotiators, Kissinger began to develop "a coherent strategy for breaking the deadlock once and for all."[29] The strategy to guide his actions (in close concert with his handpicked team) encompassed seven broad elements, which Kissinger outlines:[30]

1. It would offer "the front-line states a shortcut to majority rule by throwing the weight of American diplomacy behind their goals. They would be spared the destruction attendant on a prolonged struggle and the risk to their domestic stability of establishing large guerrilla units on their soil." In return, Kissinger would insist "that they keep foreign forces out of the conflict, assume responsibility for the negotiating positions of the Rhodesian liberation movements, and guarantee [white] minority rights."

2. Kissinger would work "closely with moderate African leaders, especially in Kenya, Zaire, Senegal, and the Ivory Coast, to help shape a consensus in the [Organization of African Unity] OAU supportive of our policies and to protect the frontline Presidents from radical African and international pressures."

3. Kissinger would count "on Britain to reenter the diplomacy in Southern Africa and to play an important role in the constitutional conference that would be the culmination of the breakthrough we hoped to achieve."

4. To South Africa's leaders, Kissinger would convey "that they would be given a responsible role in helping shape an Africa of peace, stability, and racial justice. South Africa would be treated as a valuable interlocutor and given a breathing space in dealing with its own problems provided it helped move Southern Africa toward a new political dispensation." But, Kissinger emphasized, we would make "it very clear that our support of majority rule did not stop at the borders of South Africa."

5. As just noted with respect to Rhodesian leader Ian Smith, Kissinger observed, "All previous efforts had failed because they had started with negotiations with this representative of a white minority that had no conceivable incentive to abandon its dominance. We therefore proposed to deal with Smith only after the other parties' commitments had been agreed. We could do nothing about the reality that Smith and his European minority had little to gain from our diplomacy. But we proposed to ease the transition by treating him with respect. I had no record with him either for good or ill and considered him a problem to be dealt with rather than an enemy to be overcome."[31]

6. Kissinger planned to engage France, the "European country with perhaps the strongest continuing involvement in Africa . . . The French President [Giscard d'Estaing] strongly supported [this] policy . . . The task of relating Africa to the West, Giscard argued, was too great for the United States acting alone; there should be a division of labor. The United States should handle the diplomacy leading toward

19

majority rule in Southern Africa. Britain should make itself responsible for the . . . [final and formal] negotiations; and he, Giscard, was prepared to put forward a joint Western program for the economic development designed to rally the moderate states, the program's principal beneficiaries."[32]

7. Finally, throughout this process, Kissinger would maintain a focus on the domestic front: "As we ventured into heretofore uncharted territory, we made a major effort to build domestic support."[33] This involved extended consultations with Congress, meetings with influential African American leaders, and, critically, nurturing and relying on support from the most important relationship of all for a U.S. secretary of state: the president.

This is hardly a case of "making it up as you go along." Indeed, Kissinger's carefully conceptualized strategy for an ultimate deal with Smith leading to all-party talks involves what we might describe as a "multifront negotiation campaign" implicitly designed to overcome the barriers he had identified in his assessment.[34] Subsidiary negotiations involving many different parties and interests would be carefully sequenced to culminate in a powerful de facto coalition that Smith could not ultimately resist. If Kissinger's approach played out as planned, "no" would cease to be a viable option for Rhodesia's Ian Smith. Time and again, we observe Kissinger "zooming out" to this strategic conception even as he "zooms in" to his individual counterparts.

A simplified version of how Kissinger intended to sequence several key elements of the strategy detailed above would be to:

1. obtain a domestic mandate for the approach;
2. consult with Britain and secure agreement on its provisional role in the negotiations;

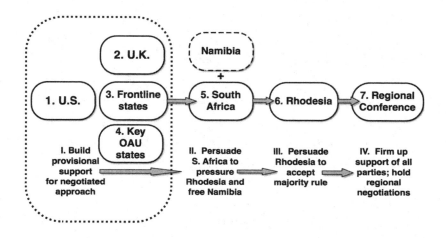

Figure 1.4: Planned Negotiation Strategy (simplified)

3. bring Frontline States on board;

4. pitch the more distant African states;

5. persuade South Africa to pressure Rhodesia;

6. negotiate with Rhodesia to accept the principle of majority rule with a timetable; and

7. finalize British support and rely on the United Kingdom to orchestrate a conference at which all the relevant parties would negotiate the full regional terms of accompanying black-majority rule in Rhodesia and the creation of its newly independent successor state, Zimbabwe.

Figure 1.4, in which we have somewhat arbitrarily divided the planned negotiation into four major phases, underscores the importance to Kissinger of careful sequencing and coalitional sophistication.

BROADER NEGOTIATION INSIGHT: "Map backward" from your target deal to design a sequential "negotiation campaign."[35] With a target agreement in mind between you and a key party, decide whether a direct or indirect approach would be more promising. If you opt for an indirect approach, consider orchestrating a sequence of negotiations that puts in place the most promising possible setup for your ultimate negotiation with the key party. To help determine that sequence, "map backward" from the key party to figure out whose prior support would be most valuable to have when you negotiate with that key party. Then map backward from that next-to-last stage to determine how best to put that support in place—and so on. In the case of Ian Smith, an indirect approach was required that would worsen the consequences of his saying "no to majority rule." To set up the most promising ultimate negotiation with Smith, consider "mapping backward" from that final stage to determine what conditions would have to be in place to maximize the chances of his saying "yes." For Kissinger, this meant getting the South Africans, the Frontline States, Britain, and the United States on board in order to put meaningful pressure on Smith. South Africa was the key to this sequence. Thus, Kissinger in effect also mapped backward from South Africa (specifically, its prime minister John Vorster) to determine what conditions would ideally be in place to induce a "yes" from South Africa to pressure Smith—and so on, until the most promising sequential campaign was clear.

While Kissinger would be the principal soloist and conductor for this sequential negotiation campaign, orchestrating such a complex strategy required a skilled ensemble. Following the failure of his covert Angola initiative, Kissinger had rebuilt the State Department's Bureau of African Affairs, staffing it with trusted diplomats.[36] He regularly consulted and traveled with Winston Lord (then with the State Department's Policy Planning Bureau) and William Schaufele Jr. (assistant secretary for African Affairs, later ambassador), whom he regularly dispatched to the capitals of Southern African states to gather information and convey sensitive messages.[37] To travel with Schaufele, Kissinger recruited longtime friend Undersecretary of State for Economic Affairs William D. Rogers (no relation to the former secretary of state), whose involvement in Rhodesian diplomacy extended back to the Johnson administration.[38] Beyond his longtime assistant, Peter Rodman, Kissinger also turned to younger career Foreign Service Officers. Frank Wisner joined Ambassador William Bowdler in South Africa (and, later, the regional conference), Stephen Low was brought in to report on the Frontline States from Zambia, and John E. Reinhardt accompanied Kissinger on his visit to Pretoria.[39] Almost continuously, in cables and in person, Kissinger relied on his team to provide him with information and updates, to convey messages to the various players, and to help maintain momentum on multiple fronts.[40]

GENERAL NEGOTIATION INSIGHT: While the "captain" is key, complex negotiation is a team sport. It is easy shorthand to describe such events as if they were conceived and carried out by the most visible player. Yet, whether a cross-border merger, a complex sale, or a diplomatic campaign, such negotiations in reality inevitably involve the carefully coordinated efforts of a skilled team.

2

From Strategy to Execution

Kissinger's Original Strategy

The first steps of Kissinger's original approach were to gain at least provisional support from the United States, Britain, and the Frontline States. This approach developed with President Ford's concurrence, rested on a fundamental U.S. reorientation of its policy toward Southern Africa. As Kissinger wrote, "On March 13, Ford for the first time committed the United States to unequivocal support for majority rule in Southern Africa: [in the president's words] 'The United States is totally dedicated to seeing to it that the majority becomes the ruling power in Rhodesia.'"[1] Ford later underscored a key motive: "Political stability [in Southern Africa] was crumbling everywhere and it was imperative to send Henry Kissinger to the continent to see if he could head off a race war."[2]

Although this African initiative posed an extreme challenge, Kissinger approached it at the apex of his diplomatic credibility, having enjoyed signal successes in China, with the Soviet Union, with North Vietnam, and in the Middle East. His global reputation for overcoming formidable obstacles to agreement ensured that even suspicious, skeptical African parties would take his actions seriously.

Kissinger closely aligned his specific goals with conditions set forth by the British in a speech given nine days after Ford's remarks

24

on majority rule. As the former colonial power in Rhodesia, the British had been frustrated by years of unproductive attempts to get Smith to relinquish power. Wary of overinvolvement, reluctant to be drawn into a possible military entanglement, and grappling with an economic downturn at home, they had nonetheless kept a watchful eye on events in the region.[3] The news had not been good.

In 1974, Zambian president Kenneth Kaunda and South African prime minister Johannes "John" Vorster had led a regional effort intended to get Smith to negotiate with the black Rhodesian opposition. As he had done with the British before, Smith had first scuttled the resulting talks and then dragged out subsequent negotiations. Two years later, in a March 22 speech, with any chance of productive talks stalemated and a likelihood of escalating violence, James Callaghan publicly outlined the four conditions by which the United Kingdom would support a revived attempt to reach a peaceful settlement in the region:

"[F]irst, acceptance of the principle of majority rule; secondly, elections for majority rule to take place in 18 months to two years; thirdly, agreement that there will be no [recognized] independence [for Rhodesia] before majority rule; fourthly, the negotiations must not be long drawn out."[4]

Kissinger felt that securing British backing and adopting elements of Callaghan's framework would be a political and legal asset. Britain's role as the former colonial power would add international support and give Kissinger insights into the region beyond those that the State Department's newly reformed African Bureau could provide. In addition, any Rhodesian agreement would have to conclude with the creation of a constitution and a legal transfer of power. Because Smith's regime had no international standing, Kissinger believed that the British would have to formally oversee that effort to ensure an agreement's legitimacy.

After reaching a general understanding with the British on the role they would play in the process, Kissinger planned an unprecedented visit during April 1976 to meet with African leaders face-to-face, shoring up support with powerful members of the Organization for African Unity.[5] The focal point of his trip would be a speech in Lusaka, Zambia, that would publicly unveil the new U.S. policy of support for majority rule. Kissinger intended his remarks to go far beyond simply expressing shared values with the leaders of the Frontline States. He would outline specific steps and conditions (aligned with Callaghan's four conditions) that he believed were necessary to usher in black African leadership in Rhodesia and Namibia.[6]

The Africa Trip and "Zooming In" on Julius Nyerere

First, Kissinger visited Kenya, to describe his initiative to Jomo Kenyatta, its widely respected president, and to seek Kenyatta's support. From Kenya, he flew to meet with President Julius Nyerere of Tanzania, a key member of the Frontline States and a central figure in the Non-Aligned Movement of developing countries that sought a political path independent of East and West.

As an example of how Kissinger "zooms in" on his negotiating counterparts as individuals, we consider his interactions with Nyerere in greater detail than will be the case with several other figures (such as Kenyatta), simply because it serves as a good case study of his dealings with a pivotal African leader. Kissinger described Nyerere as "a slight, wiry man, [who] invited me to his modest private residence. . . . He was graceful and elegant, his eyes sparkling, his gestures fluid. With an awesome command of the English language (he had translated *Julius Caesar* into Swahili), Nyerere could be a seductive interlocutor. But he was also capable of steely hostility. . . . He took pride in his chosen role as 'Mwalimu' (the 'teacher') of his people."[7]

A supporter of the militant rebel faction led by Robert Mugabe in Rhodesia and the South West Africa People's Organization (SWAPO) guerrilla movement, Nyerere was also thought to be allied with Mozambique's radical Marxist president, Samora Machel, and opposed to the moderate Kenneth Kaunda in Zambia. Despite these ideological differences and Nyerere's ingrained suspicion of American policy, Kissinger developed a rapport with the Tanzanian president, who was, he wrote, "his own man. His idiosyncratic blend of Western liberal rhetoric, socialist practice, nonaligned righteousness, and African tribalism was driven, above all, by a passionate desire to free his continent from Western categories of thought, of which Marxism happens to be one. His ideas were emphatically his own." Kissinger continues: "I got along with the front-line Presidents, including and especially Nyerere, because I took them seriously. I met them on their own terms and did not treat them—as did so many of their admirers in the West—as extensions of Western preconceptions."[8]

Nyerere proved to be an adept sparring partner for Kissinger. As David Martin, the *Observer*'s longtime Africa correspondent, wryly commented, "One began a quote from Shakespeare . . . or a Greek philosopher and the other would end the quotation. Then Nyerere quoted an American author. Kissinger laughed: Nyerere knew Kissinger had written the words."[9]

The two soon found a shared pragmatism and a desire for stability. Despite his radical leanings, Nyerere concurred with Kissinger's regional assessment that recent Cuban success in Angola might lead to the involvement of Cuba's troops elsewhere in the region, potentially destabilizing existing regimes. While the Frontline States' presidents agreed on the imperative of ending minority rule in Rhodesia, significant disagreements existed among them about how this should be accomplished. Nyerere agreed to advocate for an American-backed peace initiative, later commenting,

"We want the two greatest sources of power on our side—God and Kissinger."[10]

Kissinger did not take Nyerere's support as unconditional. "To Nyerere, the United States was a weapon to be employed to accelerate the liberation struggle. For this, he was prepared to pay some price in moderating his colleagues. More reluctantly, he was prepared to grant some rights to the white minorities, and, even more reluctantly, to exclude Cuban participation in the struggle."[11]

As Kissinger departed, he believed he had found in Nyerere an important ally and the key to gaining the support of the Frontline States. Nyerere would be, he wrote, "the bridge between such moderates as Zambia's Kenneth Kaunda and Botswana's President Seretse Khama on one side, and the radicals . . . in the former Portuguese colonies of Mozambique and Angola on the other."[12]

Yet the American secretary of state offered a measured report to President Ford. "I have no illusions," he said: "[Nyerere] will remain ideologically opposed and watch our future actions very strictly. On the other hand, he certainly has a better comprehension of our motives and intentions; sees the opportunity for parallel actions; is smart enough to take my points about American public opinion; understands that it is in his own self-interest to ease matters for us; and should use his considerable influence with others on Southern African issues."[13]

As Kissinger negotiated further with Nyerere, he refined his psychological understanding and consciously catalogued the Tanzanian president's characteristic tactics, including different messages for different audiences. For example, Kissinger once reported to Ford that Nyerere was privately "giving us the green light on most of our proposals for both Rhodesia and Namibia while beating us over the head publicly."[14] At another point, Kissinger observed, "I had grown sufficiently familiar with Nyerere's methods to understand that I was watching a virtuoso performance, which, in effect, endorsed our diplomacy while hedging against its failure."[15]

BROADER NEGOTIATION INSIGHT: "Zoom in" on your counterpart while "zooming out" to your strategy. In tandem with "zooming out" to his overall strategy—think of a grandmaster craftily moving the pieces on a regional or global chessboard—Kissinger consistently "zoomed in" to his counterparts as individuals. This is a valuable practice: to determine the most effective approach to each person with whom you deal, research and pay close attention to his or her characteristics, psychology, history, interests, motivations, relationships, potential breadth of influence, political context, and style. In our experience, negotiators tend toward being either "strategists" or "people focused," but they rarely make a conscious effort to bring the micro and macro perspectives consistently into alignment. To keep your negotiation on track, practice continually zooming out and zooming in.[16]

The Lusaka Speech

Arriving in Lusaka, Zambia, after his negotiations with Nyerere, Kissinger met with President Kenneth Kaunda. There, as planned, the U.S. secretary of state made a major speech to regional leaders outlining his intention to jump-start negotiations in the region. Declaring Smith's regime and the South African occupation of Namibia illegal, he urged both governments to present timetables for handing over power and establishing majority rule.

Kissinger described measures by which the United States

would further isolate Smith while assisting the Frontline States. He would commit the United States to tripling its funding for development initiatives in sub-Saharan Africa. Financial support would be arranged for Mozambique. Efforts would be made to provide aid to refugees displaced by the increasing violence that stemmed from Smith's refusal to abdicate power. Kissinger urged American citizens to leave Rhodesia immediately and avoid travel to the country. He announced that he would seek the repeal of the 1971 Byrd Amendment, which had allowed the United States to circumvent the UN embargoes on key Rhodesian products (e.g., chrome), and had drawn sustained international condemnation.[17] (Chrome was considered a strategically important metal; some 40 percent of U.S. chrome had come from Rhodesia while the United States depended on the Soviet Union, its Cold War adversary, for another 40 percent of its needs for this vital material.[18])

Referring to Rhodesia as "Zimbabwe," the name preferred by black Africans, Kissinger assailed the separation of races and called for equal rights in an independent nation. "So let it be said," he concluded, "that black people and white people working together achieved on this continent, which has suffered so much and seen so much injustice, a new era of peace, well-being, and human dignity."[19]

Widely covered internationally, the Lusaka speech expressed a momentous shift in American policy that was immediately evident to those present. When Kissinger finished speaking, Zambian president Kenneth Kaunda embraced him. "Some of us," he said "were so emotionally charged when you were speaking. We could not believe this was a Secretary of State from Washington, D.C."[20] Kaunda delivered an immediate, impromptu response on behalf of the Frontline State leaders, telling Kissinger to "assure President Ford of our support."[21]

From Lusaka to Nairobi

"With the Lusaka speech," Kissinger observed, "our African strategy was falling into place: first, agreement with front-line states on an overall strategy for Southern Africa; next, a visit to key Central and West African countries to reassure them about America's staying power and to enlist their support in African forums."[22] He sought backing for his efforts across the entire continent, especially given the close connections between many African leaders, forged during their shared struggles for independence from colonial rule.[23] As Kissinger reached out to the leaders of former French colonies, he found French president Valéry Giscard d'Estaing to be especially helpful.[24]

On his first post-Lusaka stop, Kissinger found longtime U.S. ally Mobutu Sese Seko of Zaire to be receptive, as he shared Kissinger's concerns about potential Soviet intervention. Although he was controversial for his authoritarian rule, a "succession of American administrations maintained a working relationship with Mobutu because none of them wanted to add turmoil in Central Africa to an already excessive list of foreign crises." Kissinger departed the meeting with an understanding that Mobutu would support his efforts.[25]

Following a visit to Liberia, Kissinger met with Léopold Senghor, president of Senegal, a "poet and philosopher" who turned out to be sympathetic to the proposed U.S. diplomatic initiative. Kissinger later wrote that Senghor was among the most remarkable leaders he had encountered on the trip. He saw the Senegalese leader as "an intellectual who had taught himself the grammar of power." Kissinger noted that Senghor "interpreted what had happened in Angola [Soviet and Cuban intervention] as a defeat for all of moderate Africa."[26] He recalls, "Deeply impressed, I told Senghor: 'If you feel strongly about something—if you feel we're wrong, or if you feel we can do something better—get in touch with me or directly with President Ford. I'll see it.'"[27]

Kissinger ended his trip at the fourth United Nations Conference on Trade and Development, held in Nairobi, Kenya, with promises of American economic commitments to Africa, putting them in the context of global growth.[28] By the time Kissinger arrived in the Kenyan capital, Tanzanian president Nyerere had gained initial support among the Frontline States for the American initiative.[29]

The Domestic Front

Four days after the Lusaka speech, Ronald Reagan catastrophically defeated Gerald Ford in the Texas Republican primary on May 1, 1976. Kissinger's efforts had inflamed conservatives. As CBS News Radio reported, "Reagan quickly picked up Kissinger's new theme in Africa, and accused the secretary of preparing a bloodbath in Rhodesia."[30] A later article in *Diplomatic History* colorfully declared that the "Republican right . . . howled with indignation at Kissinger's intended betrayal of fellow whites."[31] More soberly, Kissinger observed, "Some political experts subsequently claimed that it was our support of majority rule—interpreted as abandonment of the white populations of Southern Africa—that had transformed Ford's probable setback into a debacle."[32]

Along with the sentiments expressed in primary voting, the State Department received seventeen hundred letters opposing Kissinger's speech and only twenty-three in support of it.[33] Kissinger redoubled his efforts to blunt domestic criticism of his initiative by meeting with as many U.S. stakeholders as possible and regularly briefing key members of Congress.[34]

For example, he consulted with about thirty African American leaders to explain his goals, better understand their concerns, and seek their support.[35] The Rev. Jesse Jackson concluded one of four such meetings by stating that "No other Secretary of State has accorded such respect to the black American community . . . We support the African policy that you have enunciated. You have our support on this. Other Secretaries of State would not have met with us as you have."[36]

Most important for the initiative of an American secretary of state, Kissinger cultivated and enjoyed unwavering support from President Ford, despite the political consequences for his reelection prospects.[37] During Kissinger's mission, Ford issued the following statement to the press: "The President makes foreign policy, and Dr. Kissinger carries out and enunciates that foreign policy, and that is what he has done on the African trip."[38] Upon Kissinger's return to Washington, Ford held, and made a point of publicizing, high-profile meetings with his secretary of state about the African initiative, one with the National Security Council and another at the White House with bipartisan congressional leadership.[39]

Gaining South African Agreement

As Figure 2.1 suggests (with provisionally completed phase one shaded), Kissinger had by May 1976 obtained a U.S. mandate for

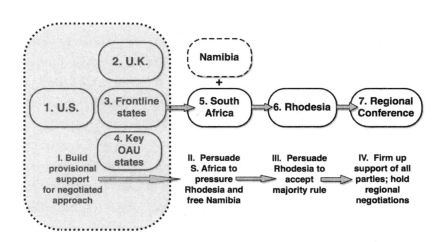

Figure 2.1: Negotiation Strategy—phase I (shaded portion completed)

his Southern African strategy along with at least provisional support from the Frontline States, other key African nations, and from the United Kingdom. The next vital ingredient in his strategy was to negotiate for South African pressure on Ian Smith in order to induce the Rhodesian leader to agree to black-majority rule on a tight timetable. South Africa had provided vital economic and military support to Rhodesia as well as key transport links and access to the rest of the world, which were especially valuable when Mozambique closed its border to Rhodesia in March 1976. "Incongruously," Kissinger observed, "pariah South Africa, the citadel of apartheid, was emerging as the key to progress toward majority rule in Southern Africa. All black African leaders castigated it, and all of them urged us into a dialogue with South Africa's leaders."[40]

At first blush, the prospect of white-minority-ruled South Africa pressing white-minority-ruled Rhodesia to accept black-majority rule must have seemed inconceivable. If the white regimes in Rhodesia and Namibia lost power, South Africa would stand "alone without any buffer to face an Africa united in its demand for an end to apartheid. . . . [S]ooner or later such demands were bound to become irresistible."[41]

Despite the almost certain prospect that South African pressure on Rhodesia for majority rule would boomerang, Kissinger crafted his persuasive appeal to South African prime minister Vorster on the basis of at least four related factors: First, South Africa was becoming far more isolated internationally, partly as a result of international opprobrium and sanctions and partly due to U.S. actions. For example, in January 1976, the United States voted in favor of a UN resolution demanding that South Africa set a timetable for ending its illegal occupation of Namibia.[42] Two months later, another resolution passed—again, with American support—this time condemning South Africa's military involvement in Angola.[43] Weeks later, Kissinger's Lusaka speech set forth explicit demands that South Africa take steps to dismantle apartheid. If, in sharp contrast to its growing reputation as a pariah state, South Africa were to assist the United States, Britain, and the Frontline States in bringing black-majority rule to Rhodesia, Pretoria's international reputation might improve and its isolation ease.

Second, South Africa faced rising threats of domestic instability and a deteriorating military outlook on its borders.[44] These were exacerbated by international isolation and sanctions, and an economy in steep decline, suffering from the combined effects of a worldwide energy crisis and the loss of regional trade resulting from the recent closure of the Mozambique border.[45] Demands for military support were outpacing the government's ability to pay for it, depleted as it was by the increasing costs of fighting guerrillas in Namibia, securing the borders, managing internal state security, and supporting Ian Smith's regime.[46]

Third, from South Africa's standpoint, an agreement for majority rule in Rhodesia, if under relatively moderate black leadership, might forestall yet worse outcomes if more radical elements took power. Kissinger made a fundamental judgment: "Rhodesia and Namibia had turned into liabilities for South Africa internationally and a drain on its resources. . . . What South Africa's leaders sought to avoid was to be obliged to stand by while the white minority in Rhodesia was being overrun militarily by black guerrillas. And no doubt they hoped to create successor regimes in both Rhodesia and Namibia which, though black, would stem the radical tide before it could reach South Africa's borders."[47] Rather than see the guerrilla forces of Robert Mugabe ultimately take over, the South African government felt that early action in support of Kissinger's initiative might increase the leadership chances of the more moderate Joshua Nkomo, who was committed to regional dialogue rather than violence.[48]

Fourth, we observe that because Vorster himself had promoted a kind of regional détente over the last few years, he was at least somewhat predisposed to accept Kissinger's arguments. One element of Vorster's prior initiative had been to press Rhodesia into giving greater voice to its black citizens, perhaps in the form of a qualified and less restrictive franchise than was then the case.[49] His efforts were overshadowed, however, by South African military incursions into Angola, which had shattered a long-standing claim by the white regime that it would remain uninvolved in the affairs of neighboring African countries. The framing used to justify Angolan intervention (Cold War–driven anticommunism) had only galvanized the region in ways that increased pressure on South Africa.[50] Moreover, Ian Smith's refusal to admit to Rhodesia's worsening outlook weakened Vorster's ability to facilitate a regional détente. In private, Vorster had made clear his frustrations with Smith, especially during the earlier regional talks that Smith had ultimately scuttled.[51] Nor could Vorster easily take public steps that would reveal any divide between the Rhodesian and South African positions without facing outraged opposition from various South African political constituencies.[52] So, while Vorster's prior détente initiative had been stymied, for Kissinger to take up a stronger version of this cause was not altogether unwelcome to the South African prime minister.

Mindful of these four factors, Kissinger offered the South Africans an unprecedented meeting in Europe, leaving open the possibility of a later visit to South Africa. He underscored the significance of U.S. willingness to visibly lessen South Africa's deepening isolation: "No American Secretary of State had been prepared to meet South African leaders in over thirty years, much less to negotiate with them—even in world forums like the U.N. I was, in effect, offering South Africa a role in shaping the future of Southern Africa in return for a commitment to majority rule in the neighboring countries and ultimately in their own."[53] Boosting the appeal of

Kissinger's offer, President Ford publicly indicated that "[I]f at some point it would seem wise to meet with the two heads of Rhodesia and South Africa, I certainly would."[54]

Vorster agreed to a June 16, 1976, meeting, but as the date approached, the South African authorities viciously cracked down on a protest by blacks in the South African township of Soweto, killing more than four hundred civilians. This brutality by the regime sparked months of protests in the black townships.[55] The United States joined the United Nations in condemning the South African government's violent and disproportionate crackdown.

In the face of this sharply intensified international criticism, Kissinger's continued willingness to meet Vorster in Germany, despite the virtual certainty of thousands of antiapartheid protesters, became even more valuable to the South African leadership.

Finally, on June 23, face-to-face with Vorster "in a smallish sitting room, I began—as was my habit in almost all negotiations—with a philosophical discussion of what we were trying to achieve."[56] For both geopolitical and moral reasons, the United States was seeking peaceful transitions to majority rule in the region. But, Kissinger argued, "If Vorster identified the future of his country with the fate of Rhodesia and Namibia, the outcome would be complicated and surely considerably delayed. But in the end, majority rule was unavoidable in Rhodesia . . . Violence would increase; radicals would gain control of the armed struggle, aided probably by foreign forces, at which point South Africa would face the dilemma of holding still while the European populations of Rhodesia and Namibia were expelled[,] or joining the conflict."[57]

However, by working with the Americans, Kissinger made the case that Vorster could draw "a distinction between his northern neighbors and South Africa based on the reality that South Africa was considered[,] even in Africa[,] as an African, not a colonial, country—however resented its domestic institutions were. This point had been stressed by every African leader I had encountered. . . . The opportunity I was offering Vorster was to achieve a certain breathing space in which his country might solve its problems peacefully, not a means for escaping them."[58]

Kissinger neither threatened the South Africans nor lectured them. The Ford administration was not "waging a crusade against them as individuals; indeed, . . . we had compassion for the agonizing dilemmas bequeathed them by preceding generations . . . We were not out to punish them for their fathers' sins or even their own—as were so many of their critics in the West. Rather, our goal was to bring them face-to-face with their realities and lead them as gently as possible to the acceptance of the fact that these [realities] dictated change both on moral and on political grounds."[59] As such, Kissinger "presented these views more in sorrow than in anger, not as a debate over South Africa's past so much as an option for its future."[60]

South African prime minister Vorster, with a notably hard-line record, proved responsive to this combination of tone and arguments. His "entire bearing suggested that, faced with a superpower which treated them with some consideration, the Afrikaners were not circling their wagons as they had been obliged to do too often in their difficult history."[61]

In general terms, Vorster agreed to help promote change in Rhodesia and Namibia based on self-determination. Kissinger concluded that "Provided he was not being asked to abandon Rhodesia's European population without any rights, he would support our efforts to produce majority rule in Rhodesia. He agreed that a moderate outcome in Rhodesia was possible only if the armed struggle was brought to an early end."[62]

"It was a measure of both their isolation and [their] sense of foreboding that the South Africans should have accepted so readily the only quid pro quo I could offer in exchange for their coopera-

tion on Rhodesia and Namibia: time in which to solve their problems. . . . 'I think history is against you,' I informed South African
Ambassador Roelof "Pik" Botha . . . 'but we want to buy time at
least . . . If we can separate the South African issue from Rhodesia,
it will give more time to deal with South Africa—unless Rhodesia
is settled in a way that accelerates the problem.' '"[63]

BROADER NEGOTIATION INSIGHT: Empathy and assertiveness can be a potent combination.[64] Many negotiators act as if
one can be either empathetic or assertive but not both. Kissinger's
approach to the South Africans (and, later, as we show, the Rhodesians) combined these two supposedly incompatible elements.
An empathetic understanding gave him insight into South Africa's
most acute interests: reversing the country's increasing pariah status, avoiding the high costs of supporting Rhodesia and Namibia,
and preventing a worse outcome. An empathetic style in negotiation is not the same as one expressing agreement or sympathy, but
instead involves showing the other party your understanding of its
perspective. This approach may have softened reflexive South African defensiveness. At the same time, Kissinger's actions and requests (U.S. denunciation of South African policies, U.S. backing of
harsh UN resolutions condemning South Africa, and U.S. demands
for Vorster to put serious pressure on Rhodesia) were highly assertive in substance—even though, during face-to-face negotiations,
delivered "softly."

Under steady pressure from Kissinger, Vorster also made
several concessions with regard to negotiations over Namibian

independence that had thus far been subject to restrictive South African conditions. At least in principle, the South Africans had agreed that the Namibian independence talks could be held in Geneva, that a deadline of the end of 1978 could be put in place, that there could be a formal UN role, and, in effect, that the door could be open for the SWAPO guerrillas, led by Sam Nujoma, to play a central role in these future negotiations.[65]

These potentially major shifts in South African policy, if deployed carefully as Kissinger negotiated with other African states, could enhance his credibility and build momentum toward Smith's acceptance of majority rule. As Figure 2.2 suggests, with the provisionally completed parts of the strategy shaded, phases one and two of Kissinger's approach were playing out as planned.

Kissinger worried that if the Frontline States learned about these unprecedented South African agreements on Rhodesia and Namibia, they would simply pocket the concessions and press for more. So, during the next phase of the strategy, he would insist on

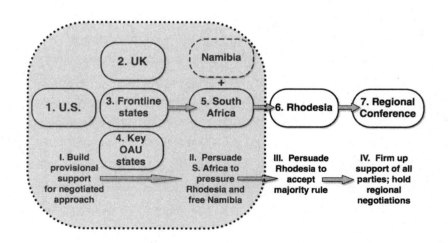

Figure 2.2: Negotiation Strategy—phase II (shaded portion completed)

secrecy regarding the results of his negotiations with Vorster. At the right time, he and his team planned to visit countries in the region and dangle the *prospect* of South African flexibility, which he privately knew to be virtually assured, in order to firm up Frontline State support for the American and British plan.

More generally, Kissinger's negotiations sometimes relied on secrecy, back channels, and the selective revelation of information. Such choices could keep the process moving forward, an essential objective. (In chapters 11 and 13, we analyze such choices in detail.) Yet such tactics could also raise grounds for suspicion and damage trust, especially if a tactic were revealed or a party felt duped; indeed, critics would later characterize this and similar tactics as "mendacious."[66]

Provisional British and Frontline State Support Erodes

Britain's active support was essential to success. Kissinger's plan was for Britain, the governing power displaced by Smith's unrecognized "declaration of independence," to return to Rhodesia temporarily while a new constitution was being drafted and then to preside over a legitimate transfer of power. Kissinger articulated the double negotiation challenge that this situation presented: "Britain would never agree to undertake the task unless requested to do so by the black frontline states, if then. It fell on us, therefore, to embark on the ironic dual mission of persuading reluctant Britain to reassume for a brief period the imperial mantle it had been shedding for three decades and to convince its former colonial subjects to invite their erstwhile rulers to return so that imperial rule could be abandoned properly and legitimately."[67]

Unfortunately for this "dual mission," the British appeared to be increasingly conflicted about a more active role in the negotiations. British prime minister Callaghan and Foreign Secretary Crosland were nominally committed to Kissinger's diplomacy, but proved maddeningly vague on their alignment with American thinking on vital issues. These included the white/black balance of senior roles during a Rhodesian transition, the extent of property and political protections, and any compensation for white Rhodesians. The British had serious economic troubles at home, were concerned about military entanglement in Rhodesia, and had been double-crossed by Ian Smith too many times to be confident in mere assurances that the various parties were committed to a negotiation.

Support by the Frontline States was also becoming more tenuous by the day, with backsliding in all quarters. British hedging and the ongoing ambivalence of the Frontline States reinforced each other. Kissinger also surmised that Nyerere expected guerrilla pressures on Rhodesia to mount; delaying the talks would thus weaken the bargaining position of the white regime. Whatever the precise causes, with his strategy eroding in Africa and Britain, and coming under intense domestic pressure from Republicans to desist, Kissinger ruminated that the "temptation to abandon the negotiation at this point was overwhelming."[68] Yet the tantalizing prospect of success seemed so close and the consequences of stopping seemed so awful that Kissinger decided to persist, but to completely rethink his strategy and tactics.

Sharply Revised Negotiating Strategy

In a nutshell, "the original strategy had been to work out a common position with the Frontline States, take it to Vorster, and then impose it on Smith."[69] In light of British ambivalence, which was driven in part by the increasing evasions of the Frontline State lead-

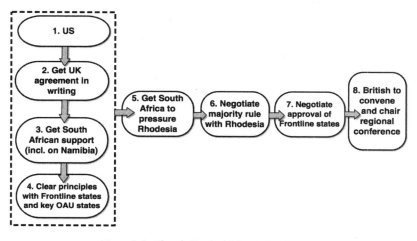

Figure 2.3: Sharply Revised Negotiating Strategy

ers, Kissinger dramatically altered his approach, upending the careful sequence by which his negotiations had originally proceeded. To build a supportive coalition that would pressure Smith, he now decided to "reverse the procedure. . . . [He] would try to work out a detailed proposal with Callaghan [in writing], obtain Vorster's support, clear the principles of it with the front-line Presidents, convince Smith with Vorster's help, and then bring it back to the front-line Presidents for their final approval."[70] (See Figure 2.3.)

This resequencing and tactical shift would require great finesse and a measure of luck. "It was a complicated scenario," Kissinger observed, "depending crucially on our stage-managing it in such a way as to have the final breakthrough emerge as Smith's acceptance of terms proposed by Britain and the United States to which the front-line states were invited to respond, and not as African concessions to Smith."[71] By this time, Kissinger knew that if the proposal were seen to come from South Africa or Rhodesia, it would have no chance of regional acceptance.

BROADER NEGOTIATION INSIGHT: Think strategically but act opportunistically. Many negotiators stick to a strategy or, worse, a fixed script even as circumstances change, new information surfaces, or moves by the other side undercut their original strategy. By contrast, Kissinger, time and again, appears to follow the maxim to "think strategically but act opportunistically." Much as was the case when his plans for covert action in Angola were blocked and he shifted to a diplomatic course, his strategic rationale was clear, but circumstances had changed. Thus, his approach to the negotiations had to adapt. With his original sequential concept falling apart, his revised strategy called for a radically different sequence to build a de facto coalition that could successfully pressure Smith and secure British involvement.

To preempt future British waffling or backsliding, Kissinger pressed for Britain's proposal in writing. By the end of August, a joint UK–U.S. working group produced the desired document. Prime Minister Callaghan and Foreign Secretary Crosland presented it to Kissinger in the Cabinet Room in London. Now Kissinger could use this text to firm up South African commitments and nudge the hesitant Tanzanian president (Nyerere) back on board, gaining his agreement to convene the Frontline State leaders to persuade them to support a deal.

On Saturday, September 4, 1976, Kissinger met Vorster for the second time in two months. This meeting was, "in itself, a major event for the South Africans, for whom it spelled a symbolic end to their isolation."[72] The South Africans more firmly committed themselves to pressuring Rhodesia and became more specific and forthcoming on Namibia. Again, Kissinger planned to hold back this information in his next negotiations with the Frontline States, as he explained to Ford: "I do not—repeat, not—plan to surface these papers with anyone at this stage, because it is essential that we not reveal South Africa's forthcoming position until the black Africans commit themselves more concretely."[73]

Such selective revelation helped to advance the process, at least to the next stage. Deeply skeptical that Kissinger could secure such commitments from the South Africans or British, Julius Nyerere remarked, "Supposing a miracle took place—I really think of it as a miracle—and Vorster gets Smith to say 'Majority rule must come; it's better that it come peacefully, so I accept Mr. Callaghan's position.' . . . I'd be happy if . . . the British call a constitutional conference."[74] Of course Kissinger "knew from [Foreign Secretary] Crosland that Britain would agree to call such a conference. And I knew from Vorster—though Nyerere did not—that the 'miracle' of Smith's acceptance of majority rule was awaiting me in [South Africa's capital] Pretoria."[75] Nyerere, Kissinger went on, "in effect, endorsed our diplomacy."[76] Generally successful meetings with other African leaders followed; the shaded portion of Figure 2.4 indicates the progress so far with Kissinger's revised strategy.

Getting Ian Smith to Say "Yes" and Dealing with an Unwelcome London Surprise

When South Africa publicly committed to greater flexibility on Namibian independence and British support was shored up, Kissinger and his team made a second African trip. They arranged to meet Vorster again, this time in Pretoria—but only if Vorster could deliver an Ian Smith who would be open to majority-black rule in Rhodesia within two years. This would be a tough sell. Even with a worsening military outlook and collapsing regional trade, Ian Smith had remained defiant, convinced that the United States and South Africa would be forced to come to his aid or the

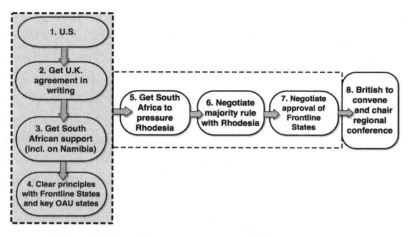

Figure 2.4: Revised Negotiating Strategy (shaded portion completed)

entire region would be ceded to the Cubans and Soviets.[77] Un-flinching, he had refused to accommodate any South African requests that he moderate his course. In a virtual rebuke to Vorster and a shock to the international community, Smith's troops carried out an early August raid into neighboring Mozambique, where they massacred some one thousand men, women, and children in a guerrilla camp.[78]

VORSTER DELIVERS AN ULTIMATUM

Exasperated with Smith, the South Africans pulled their long-standing military helicopter crews and signalers from Rhodesia at the end of August.[79] Vorster sent a message: he was finished dealing with Smith's hard-line defense minister and wished to hold conversations with the more moderate minister of finance.[80] Following Mozambique's closure of the border in March, Rhodesia had become increasingly reliant on South Africa for access to the outside world. Most essential imports and exports that sustained Rhodesia's economy and Smith's war effort (including produce, oil, weapons, and minerals) now had to travel through South Africa.[81] So when, prior to his meeting with Kissinger, Vorster delivered an ultimatum to Smith to accept the principles in the Anglo-American memorandum "or else," the Rhodesian leader was cornered.

MEETING WITH IAN SMITH

Ian Smith contemplated his upcoming negotiations with Henry Kissinger with a sense of foreboding, if not dread, having just experienced another dose of "Vorster's arm-twisting" and the South African's explanation of "the kind of plan Kissinger would bring."[82] Long having viewed white-ruled Rhodesia as a Western bulwark against communism, Smith recounted in his 1997 book (tellingly entitled *The Great Betrayal*) the "Hobson's choice" he would soon face and lamented "what a desperate position [it was] for the poor Rhodesians." (Oddly, Smith remembered receiving "a book from some interested person in America entitled *Kissinger—Communist Agent!*)[83]

As Kissinger planned to meet with Ian Smith and his Rhodesian colleagues in Pretoria on September 19, 1976, the American remarked that "Even though it had been my diplomacy which had closed off Smith's every escape route, I nevertheless did not relish having to tell my interlocutors that their way of life was coming to an end."[84] A lengthy, though respectful, negotiation ensued, with Kissinger finally bringing matters to a head after offering to support (in line with the U.S.-British document that had been shown to Vorster) provisions to protect white-minority property and political rights and to discuss the prospects for compensation for those forced off their land. In return, Kissinger's conditions crystallized: Smith would have to take part in all-party negotiations, publicly accepting the talks with the precondition that majority-black rule would prevail in Rhodesia within two years.

The Rhodesian prime minister later reflected at length about the somber, even empathetic, approach Kissinger took during these daylong negotiations, which in effect delivered a brutal ultimatum to the white regime. In Smith's words, "Kissinger admitted that the package he had to offer was unattractive, but it was the best he could extract from the other parties, the British government and the front-line states, who had to be taken along." Smith lamented that even the conservatives in the U.S. Congress, who could be expected to act forcefully against any Communist threat, had backed down on the issue of covert action in Angola, and would not reliably back Rhodesia in the future. Smith continued: "[Kissinger] did not see the free world lifting a finger to help us, and, with the passage of time, he only saw our position deteriorating. On the evidence now available it looked as if Gerald Ford would lose the presidential election at the end of the year, and with [Jimmy] Carter in office then the Lord help us . . . Once again . . . [Kissinger] stressed that his heart was heavy for us . . . If we rejected this offer, there would be understanding and sympathy, never recrimination from him . . . The decision was for us to make."[85]

Smith recalled that "[Kissinger] spoke with obvious sincerity, and there was great emotion in his voice. For awhile, words escaped him . . . If we agreed that day, he would fly off immediately to reconfirm the plan with Kaunda and Nyerere. If we rejected it, he would be off to the other side of the world for his business there, and Rhodesia would be behind him. . . . All of us were impressed by Kissinger's sincerity and straightforward approach."[86] Ken Flower, longtime chief of Rhodesia's intelligence service and a participant in these talks, wrote in his diary, "Most impressed with K's grasp of the situation. He was well ahead of his staff in providing answers on debating points as they cropped up . . . As we broke for lunch Kissinger kept saying how much he appreciated Rhodesia's position: how he would not know what decision to make if he were in Ian Smith's shoes."[87]

BROADER NEGOTIATION INSIGHT: The message may be harsh, but the delivery may be soft. While the content of Kissinger's message to Vorster and, especially, Smith was quite tough, his style was low key and empathetic, not accusatory or demanding. This approach was more likely to elicit the agreement Kissinger sought than a more confrontational manner, which often evokes defensiveness and rejection. Kissinger later told us that, in his judgment, a blunt approach to Vorster or Smith "would have blown up the process." As we note in an earlier "negotiation insight," less effective negotiators often see a tradeoff between empathy and assertiveness when, in fact, one can be both empathetic in style and assertive in substance.[88] Yet there is a risk to an empathetic approach: when an external audience (in this case, the more ardent opponents of apartheid) observes what appears to be conciliatory negotiating behavior, that audience may infer approval and vociferously object.

However the message was delivered, Smith bitterly reflected on the deciding factor (engineered, of course, by Kissinger's earlier negotiations): "South African eagerness to throw us to the wolves in their desperate panic to try to buy time and gain credit for solving the Rhodesian problem . . . [W]e were confronted by the one country in the world [South Africa] that controlled our lifeline, and which had now issued an ultimatum leaving us no alternative."[89] Cornered, the Rhodesian prime minister agreed to the framework.

It is worth noting how Kissinger's methodical moves "away from the table" to worsen Smith's no-deal options achieved the result that had eluded a decade of British diplomacy, including two high-profile attempts by Prime Minister Harold Wilson to negotiate directly with Ian Smith on the decks of British warships. Reflecting on the negotiations, Smith ruefully stated that Kissinger "made un-equivocally clear that this was a package deal tied up by the British, Americans and South Africans on the one side and the black presidents (Kaunda and Nyerere) on the other, and that there could be no going back over all that ground again. Our option was to accept or reject. If we rejected, the next offer would only be worse."[90]

BROADER NEGOTIATION INSIGHT: Effective negotiation often requires more than persuasive verbal exchange; actions away from the table to orchestrate incentives and penalties can be crucial to induce the desired "yes." Many people conceptualize "negotiation" as equivalent to talking at the table. Kissinger's carefully orchestrated actions (with respect to the United States, the British, the Frontline States, key OAU members, and the South Africans) made the cost for Rhodesia of continuing to say "no" far too high. In our view, actions of this kind, either to make the deal sweeter to the target and/or the consequences of impasse costlier, should be understood as inherently part of an effective negotiator's tool kit.

Implicitly reinforcing Kissinger's diplomatic maneuvers, Bishop Abel Muzorewa, one of Rhodesia's black leaders (cofounder of the United African National Council and briefly interim prime minister) underscored the effects on the negotiations of the "militants'" decision to intensify the armed struggle against the white regime: "Our militancy seemed only to drive Dr. Kissinger to redouble his peace initiative. In fact, our action may have strengthened his hand with Vorster and Smith, since they both abhorred the alternative to a settlement—a prolonged guerrilla war."[91]

While Smith returned to Rhodesia, Kissinger met once again with Nyerere and Kaunda, carrying news of Smith's agreement and of Vorster's commitment to move forward on Namibia.[92] Given the Frontline presidents' earlier expectations that nothing would result from Smith—recall Nyerere's description of this potential outcome as a "miracle"—Kissinger anticipated that news of his breakthrough would be received with delight. In Lusaka and Dar es Salaam, the presidents welcomed the deal, but they indicated their support only privately and held back on ringing public endorsements. Although Kissinger was sure that they would join all-party talks, he understood that both had hard-line constituents and allies. They would need to proceed cautiously.

As Kissinger traveled, it became clear that Nyerere and Kaunda viewed the "details" of the British-American framework as something to be worked out through negotiation by all parties. In contrast, ahead of any negotiations, Smith worked on Kissinger's associates to tie down, favorably to Rhodesia, details beyond the written framework itself. Such "details" included institutional protection for whites during a transition, a possible compensation fund for white Rhodesians, and the racial composition of the two-year transition regime. Resisting anything in addition to what was actually written, the American team would not go beyond Kissinger's verbal commitments to explore various aspects of the agreement on the Rhodesians' behalf. Precisely what had been agreed upon and by whom would prove controversial in the coming negotiations.

A BRITISH SHOCK

Kissinger judged that all-party talks were now a virtual certainty. Yet, as he traveled back through Zambia, he was shocked to learn that the British were poised to back out of their agreement to support the deal and participate in a conference.[93] How, Kissinger wondered, might a written agreement (worked out between him, the UK prime minister, and the foreign secretary, and presented throughout Africa as a U.S.-British proposal) now be unacceptable to the British government?

After unsuccessfully attempting to reach his British counterparts, Kissinger hurriedly flew to London, where Callaghan and Crosland greeted him awkwardly.[94] Fearful that a deal committing Britain to negotiations with the unreliable Smith would have been scuttled by members of his governing coalition, *the prime minister had not shared the document with his own cabinet.* To recover, Callaghan made a highly unorthodox request: would Kissinger himself present the proposal directly to the British cabinet for its approval? Somehow, he had finessed the fact that Kissinger had been portraying the document throughout Southern Africa as an official U.S.-British proposal. Kissinger was persuasive; the British cabinet approved the approach.[95]

SMITH PUBLICLY CONCEDES

Five days after his talks with Kissinger, on Friday, September 24, Smith made a televised announcement, publicly confirming his acceptance of the principle of majority rule within two years, and his agreement to participate in the negotiations.[96] He characterized this statement as a "savage blow."[97] On a plane at the time, the American team cheered at the news.[98] Close observers record the "stunning effect of Smith's broadcast on the Rhodesian white population."[99] For Smith's intelligence chief, Ken Flower, the announcement "turned the world upside down for most Rhodesians."[100] In the words of Bishop Abel Muzorewa, Smith's broadcast "electrified the world."[101]

Barely six months before, Smith had defiantly declared that black-majority rule would not come for "a thousand years." Kissinger's assistant secretary of state, William Schaufele, wryly commented that with their one meeting in Pretoria on September 19, "we reduced this period . . . by 98.9 percent."[102]

In a "fighting statement," the Frontline presidents publicly hailed Smith's statement as the "collapse" of the illegal, racist Rhodesian regime, framing it as a victory for the guerrilla freedom fighters without mentioning U.S.-British diplomacy. Privately, however, Kissinger confirmed that the presidents accepted the framework and plan for negotiations. At the same time, he stressed how frequently firm understandings between negotiators clash with public pronouncements intended to keep key behind-the-table groups on board—at least for the next stage of the process.[103] True to the form that Kissinger had often observed, Nyerere explained, "You and I, Dr. Kissinger, have very different 'political constituencies' to take account of, and inevitably, there is a danger that in dealing with them we shall each appear insensitive to the problems of the other . . . I hope that through frank and friendly contact we can reduce misunderstandings between us to the minimum."[104]

GENERAL NEGOTIATION INSIGHT: At a minimum, effective negotiators are sensitive to, and often actively help with, the other side's "behind-the-table" constituency issues.[105] It is easy to believe that the actual terms of an agreement determine its acceptance or rejection. Yet how each side's constituencies view it can be vital to a deal's acceptability. Less effective negotiators often assume that it is strictly "the other side's problem" to sell the deal internally and with key stakeholders. Yet, if internal or constituent opposition blocks a deal, it becomes both sides' problem.[106] Kissinger and Nyerere each understood the importance of differentiating between the private and public sides of the negotiation. As Kissinger observed with respect to some delicate negotiations, it is often important to "stage-manage" the process so all sides appear to achieve a victory or at least an acceptable outcome.

A "Spectacular Climax"

Globally, this shocking and unexpected turnabout by the Rhodesian government drew banner headlines heralding "Kissinger's amazing diplomatic triumph . . . Television and newspaper photos showed him announcing the agreement while holding a ceremonial tribal sword and shield presented to him by President Jomo Kenyatta in Kenya . . . [Kissinger] . . . was featured on the covers of the newsmagazines, and *Time* proclaimed it the 'spectacular climax of a carefully and astutely planned push for peace.' "[107] The *Washington Post* deemed getting the parties on track for regional talks to be a "minor miracle."[108] As shown in Figure 2.5, but one phase remained to bring Kissinger's revised strategy to completion.

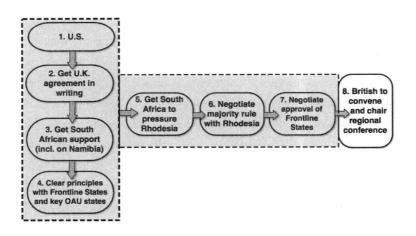

Figure 2.5: Revised Negotiating Strategy (shaded portion completed)

The Outcome of the Southern Africa Campaign and Insights into Effective Negotiation

Intended as the capstone of Kissinger's negotiation campaign to achieve majority rule in Rhodesia, the Geneva conference soon fizzled. While a complex of factors delayed the result for three years, many well-placed observers credit Smith's announcement as a turning point in the region's long path to shaking off white-minority rule.[1]

The path proved to be bumpy and indirect. On November 2, 1976, scarcely after the British had convened the negotiations without the participation of their foreign secretary, Jimmy Carter beat Gerald Ford in the U.S. presidential election. Though Ford had defeated Ronald Reagan's Republican primary challenge, Ford's election loss transformed Kissinger into a lame-duck secretary, unable to hold the process together. With Kissinger on the way out, British confidence in and commitment to the Geneva process sharply declined. Carter would soon take office with an uncompromising antiapartheid stance that quickly eroded Vorster's incentives to keep up the pressure on Rhodesia.[2]

Over the next few years, guerrilla violence sharply increased as Smith unsuccessfully sought to negotiate with Rhodesia's black leaders. When the Conservative Party's Margaret Thatcher became British prime minister, she convened negotiations in London's Lancaster House over the conditions for Rhodesian independence. Many white Rhodesians felt more comfortable with Thatcher than they had with previous Labour governments. Even so, the negotiations largely followed the Kissinger script, concluding in December 1979, with a new constitution for Zimbabwe that ensured black-majority rule.

Majority rule in Zimbabwe was a victory for democratic political principle, but in practice, it would usher in a disastrous regime. In 1980, Robert Mugabe won a landslide election to become the first black prime minister of a newly independent Zimbabwe.[3] Ian Smith remained on his farm even as one hundred thousand whites fled the country, until ailing health took him to Cape Town, where he died in 2007.[4] Repression, violence, corruption, and economic failure increasingly characterized Mugabe's tenure as he ruthlessly consolidated power over the government and military.[5] In global rankings of per capita GDP, World Bank and International Monetary Fund estimates placed Zimbabwe at the 45th percentile in 1976, when Smith made his announcement; by 2016, its economy had plummeted to the bottom 15 percent.[6] Its economy in tatters, corruption rife, much of its population destitute, and an HIV/AIDS pandemic raging, Zimbabwe had once again become a pariah state, this time under the near-dictatorial rule of the ninety-three-year-old Mugabe, who had displaced the white regime headed by Ian Smith some forty years before.[7]

As Kissinger had expected, the demise of minority rule in Rhodesia bought time for South Africa but not stability. John Vorster was succeeded by the harder-line P. W. Botha, who presided over increasing civil unrest, violence, and boycotts until his rival, F. W.

de Klerk, took power.[8] The South African experience with eventual black-majority rule, ushered in by negotiations between Nelson Mandela and F. W. de Klerk, had far happier results than had been the case in Zimbabwe.[9] Like South Africa, Namibia struggled toward majority rule amid worsening violence, until 1990, when SWAPO leader Sam Nujoma was elected the country's first president.[10]

Evaluating the Results of Kissinger's Negotiations

If persuading the seemingly immovable Ian Smith to accept the principle of black-majority rule is the test of Kissinger's diplomatic campaign, the glowing headlines of the day attest to its apparent success—as do the previously mentioned assessments from the heads of Rhodesian Central Intelligence (Ken Flower) and the United African National Council (Bishop Abel Muzorewa). After years of British failure to achieve this result, Prime Minister James Callaghan graciously lauded Kissinger's "remarkable contribution," stating, "Without the decisive intervention of the United States, I do not believe there would have been a turnabout in the attitude of Mr. Smith."[11]

Yet the Geneva conference that Kissinger designed to build on Smith's landmark concession failed to produce regional agreement on black-majority rule in Rhodesia; that result would await the Lancaster House talks three years hence. As such, some scholars have labeled, even condemned, Kissinger's negotiations in Southern Africa as a "failure" or worse.[12] A veritable cottage industry has sprung up to pin blame on someone for Kissinger's falling short of his goal.[13] In brief, here are the contending culprits:

FORD DID IT: Ford's electoral loss ended Kissinger's influence, which had been vital to hold the fractious parties together and herd them toward agreement. In particular, with Kissinger soon to be out of the picture, the British judged the odds of success to have sharply declined, and they took their role in Geneva much less seriously.

CARTER DID IT: The Carter administration's uncompromising line toward South Africa removed key incentives offered by Kissinger for that country to exert pressure on Rhodesia to accept a deal. Without South African pressure, Rhodesia could and did resume its defiant posture.

THE BRITISH DID IT: Continuing British reluctance to become involved, exacerbated by Kissinger's sudden lack of relevance, led the British to halfhearted support for the Geneva conference and for the terms they had only reluctantly endorsed. For example, instead of tasking Foreign Secretary Anthony Crosland with chairing the negotiations, they sent a lower-ranking diplomat, Ivor Richard, who enjoyed little high-level backing and had scant experience in African affairs.

SMITH DID IT: With his disingenuous ploy of making a dramatic declaration that he had no intention of following through on if circumstances changed, Ian Smith succeeded in taking South African pressure off Rhodesia.

THE FRONTLINE STATES DID IT: The Frontline States nominally endorsed the UK-U.S. framework for reasons of tactical expediency, only to abandon it (at least in principle) after Smith caved.

THE GUERRILLAS DID IT: By failing early on to bring enough military pressure on the white regime, the guerrillas provided no "hurting stalemate" in Rhodesia, which meant that the dispute wasn't truly "ripe" for resolution in Geneva.

KISSINGER DID IT: Kissinger's lack of deep understanding of Africa, his Cold War–based geopolitical interpretation of what was actually a regional affair, plus his "tactical ambiguity," even "lies," induced the parties to go to Geneva under false pretenses, with incompatible expectations and no real basis for agreement.[14] Or perhaps he failed by commencing this initiative too late: had he begun the process earlier, well before the U.S. elections, would his negotiations have had a better chance of success?

And so on. Fortunately, we need not act as the jury in the trial over "who/what killed Geneva" or "why Kissinger failed." Geneva was inconclusive, but declaring Kissinger's negotiations a failure misses their signal contribution. What we can say, with confidence, is that the process leading to Smith's declaration, as well as the declaration itself, *mattered*.

Twenty years after the fact, Stephen Low, then American ambassador to Zambia, observed that "Kissinger had completely changed U.S. policy, taken over the negotiations between the independent but illegal white Southern Rhodesian government and the Africans, introduced the principle of majority rule as the basis for world recognition of the independence of Southern Rhodesia and gotten it accepted by the Smith white ruled government of the country."[15] Winston Lord, director of policy planning at the State Department and later U.S. ambassador to China, concluded in 1998 that "Rhodesia became independent eventually as a result of Kissinger diplomacy . . . [This was] one of Kissinger's major diplomatic achievements, and least heralded."[16] Jeffrey Davidow, American diplomat and author of a widely cited study on the Lancaster House negotiations that finally brought black-majority rule to Rhodesia, observed that the "unsuccessful" negotiations prior to the Lancaster House agreement nonetheless "helped change the Rhodesian scene dramatically. Smith, in accepting the Kissinger plan, had at least acknowledged the possibility of majority rule within a few years."[17]

Frank G. Wisner (whose later diplomatic career included ambassadorships to India, the Philippines, and Egypt) fleshed out the conclusions articulated by Low, Lord, and Davidow: "Kissinger's plan was to create a set of propositions around which a transition to elections and a transition to majority rule would take place, over a period of time: a set of propositions that he would sell first to the Africans, then having already started working on John Vorster, finish the job with the South Africans and then get them to help him sell it to the Rhodesians, then get the two parties together—the white minority regime and the cantankerous and divided nationalist side together in a final conference and put it back under British authority and then have Britain hold the brass ring. Kissinger's conception was brilliant, and his execution was admirable. That he failed to reach 100 percent is not to gainsay the fact that he got us well along that path and opened the door for what ended up later, an independent Zimbabwe . . . [These efforts helped] set the stage for Maggie Thatcher to come on board and to kick-start Lancaster House, get an agreement and bring Rhodesia to independence."[18]

With the end of white-minority rule in both Namibia and Zimbabwe, South Africa alone maintained its increasingly vulnerable undemocratic status. Though Pretoria did buy some time by its cooperation with Kissinger, the Rhodesian transition heightened its political vulnerability. Indeed, Ambassador William Schaufele, assistant secretary of state for African affairs during this initiative, in effect argued that the Kissinger mission could be interpreted as the beginning of the end of apartheid.[19]

Perhaps. Even calibrating for the fact that they worked with and generally admired Kissinger, we are inclined to agree with Low, Lord, Davidow, Wisner, and Schaufele. Still, at a minimum, Kissinger's complex negotiations in Southern Africa can be said to reflect Talleyrand's famous maxim that "the art of statesmanship is to foresee the inevitable and to expedite its occurrence."[20]

In this spirit, Walter Isaacson observed that the Lancaster House negotiations that completed the process were based largely on Kissinger's plan. He notes that "[e]ven though Kissinger's shuttle did not immediately produce the solution that was celebrated in September, it succeeded in its larger aims. The nations of black Africa, whose attitude toward the U.S. had ranged from wariness to hostility, began to trust Washington as a force for majority rule. The growing appeal of the Soviet Union was countered."[21]

Some twenty-three years after these events, Kissinger rendered his own verdict: "From the geopolitical perspective, we had achieved the purpose of our African diplomacy. Six months after the debacle of Angola, the United States was demonstrating a continuing capacity to shape events in Africa . . . Rhodesia and Namibia became independent, implementing principles and procedures agreed during the African shuttles—though more slowly and with the emergence of more radical governments, especially in Rhodesia, than we would have liked. International war in Southern Africa was avoided . . . there were to be no other Cuban adventures in the independence struggles of Southern Africa."[22]

Insights from Kissinger the Negotiator Through the Prism of the Southern Africa Campaign

Without doubt, Henry Kissinger undertook this initiative primarily for Cold War–related reasons, though his ultimate motives also entailed promoting democracy and avoiding a potential race war in Southern Africa. And as with all his negotiations, he was hardly unmindful of its effect on his reputation. However one judges the motives for this initiative or its longer-term impact, we recount the saga in Southern Africa mainly to highlight many of the broader negotiation principles that underpin his approach. These negotiations exhibit several characteristics that we repeatedly observe and elaborate upon (some that we highlighted in boxes as the story unfolded) as we analyze his dealings with China, the Soviet Union, Vietnam, the Middle East, and elsewhere. Summarizing these principles, we observe that:

- *His negotiations were strategic* in their nuanced and far-reaching understanding of how the parties and interests in each aspect of the process potentially related to others. Kissinger crafted a multifront negotiation campaign, with direct and indirect elements, one that linked a series of actions with desired results. His strategic plan, to which specific tactics were subordinate, looked well beyond a target "negotiation table" (in this case, his ultimate direct dealings with Smith) to involve a range of other parties and issues in a carefully sequenced process that enhanced the odds of a superior target outcome.

- Kissinger did not treat negotiating strategy as a static blueprint to be methodically executed, but rather, as a concept that evolved and adapted as other players took actions, as information surfaced, as other parties reacted, and as circumstances changed. *He thought strategically, but acted opportunistically.* (Recall his shift to a diplomatic course when covert options were blocked or his radically revised sequence as the British got cold feet late in the process and the Frontline States wavered in their support for his plan.)

- *His approach was realistic* in that negotiations were seen neither as ends in themselves nor as formalities for ratifying one side's overwhelming superiority over another. Instead, they were designed for specific ends around an understanding of all potentially relevant factors—in this case, the United States, Britain, the Frontline States, the OAU, South Africa, Namibia, as well as Rhodesia—to judge where a desirable agreement might lie and what levers might exist. Only by assessing how the other side(s) compared the value of "no deal" with a proposed "deal" could strategy and tactics be formulated to open up a zone of possible agreement.

- *Kissinger treated incentives and penalties as inherent to the negotiation process.* A distressingly large number of people limit their effectiveness by conceptualizing "negotiation" as the "talking at the table" part of the process, as purely verbal exchange. Not Kissinger. To induce the desired "yes," he acted both at and away from the table to favorably shape the parties' incentives. Previous negotiation attempts had failed, he averred, "because they could not generate the balance of rewards and penalties to reconcile the conflicting motivations comprising the cauldron of Southern Africa."[23]

- *His negotiations displayed deep coalitional sophistication with respect to the full set of actual and potential parties to agreement.* By careful choice of parties and artful sequencing among them, Kissinger effectively built a multiparty coalition that pressured Ian Smith and then continued on to an all-party conference. This sequence was implicitly determined by "mapping backward" from the target deal to the starting point: Kissinger saw that Smith was the key to the ultimate deal, South Africa was the key to Smith, and a combination of the United States, Britain, and the Frontline States were keys to South Africa.

- To complement his emphasis on "zooming out" to a larger strategy, *Kissinger "zoomed in" on his individual counterparts*: their personalities, experiences, motivations, and political contexts.

Recall his insightful characterizations, for example, of Julius Nyerere and Ian Smith. Far from only acting as the geopolitical grandmaster dispassionately moving regional chess pieces to advantage, Kissinger also saw a keen understanding of individuals as keys to negotiating success. When "zooming in" on individuals, *Kissinger demonstrated that empathy and assertiveness could be effectively combined* rather than treated as opposites.

- Building on psychological insight, *Kissinger saw the importance of developing relationships with the key parties*—certainly with Nyerere and Vorster, but especially with his boss, President Gerald Ford. While such relationships were useful conduits for information, Kissinger clearly understood their limitations: though potentially vital in negotiations, good personal relations with a national leader will not override that country's national interest.

- While there was never any doubt that Kissinger himself headlined these complex negotiations, *his was a team effort* with handpicked members who were continually central to the process. They variously describe working for Kissinger as both exhilarating and exhausting. As a boss, he was sparing with direct praise but genuinely respected team members who could say no to him and back it up.[24]

Beyond these broad characteristics of Kissinger's approach to negotiation, many specific tactics from the Southern Africa story will occupy us in subsequent chapters: opening negotiations with a philosophical discussion of the broad objectives at stake, the choice of tone, wordsmithing, secrecy, "constructive ambiguity," and so on. Next, however, we turn to a deeper exploration of what Kissinger means by "negotiating strategy."

II

"Zooming Out"

4

Strategic: Big-Picture
Negotiating

We use the term *strategic* as shorthand for the most distinctive aspect of Kissinger's approach to negotiation. Looking across several cases, we highlight five factors that characterize this strategic orientation:

1. Setting clear, long-term objectives—not having a short-term focus;

2. Emphasizing the broader context and possible links among parties, issues, and regions over time—not treating each negotiation on its "independent" merits;

3. Devising a careful plan to achieve negotiating objectives by acting directly "at the table" and, often, indirectly "away from the table" to create incentives and penalties for maximum influence—not primarily relying on an improvisational approach limited to verbal persuasion;

4. Adapting the plan to new information, moves by others, and changing circumstances, while firmly maintaining long-term objectives—not sticking to a fixed blueprint for action, to be methodically executed; and

5. Fostering a reputation for credibility across negotiations and over time—not neglecting the influence of actions in one negotiation on expectations elsewhere.

Loosely speaking, Kissinger the strategic negotiator "zooms out" to these factors to determine where and how to concentrate his efforts. We saw this clearly enacted in his negotiations for majority rule in Rhodesia, and we will shortly flesh out what this means in practice with his plans for peace in the Middle East and opening up China.

Strategic Negotiation to Enhance Regional Stability and Reduce Soviet Influence in the Middle East

Kissinger stressed how a strategic negotiation concept, articulated well in advance, could offer a useful framework for negotiating specific issues in relation to one another. Such issues could arise unpredictably. When a crisis hit, Kissinger stated that "it was not a question ever of saying 'now, we deal with Russia, now, we deal with China.' We tried to have a coherent policy."

For example, of war in the Middle East in 1973, following attacks by a coalition of Arab states (led by Egypt and Syria), Kissinger notes: "[W]e hadn't expected the Middle East war. But we had thought about it. What we had thought about was how do we solve—the dilemma we had on the Middle East was that the Soviets were pouring arms into Egypt and encouraging a number of other countries. How could we make progress towards a negotiation that does not look as if it had been produced by Soviet blackmail? And so we had a strategy. . . . when the [1973] war started, we had two problems. One was how to handle the day, the hour-by-hour crisis. And secondly, how do we put it into a bigger framework? But we had thought about it."[1] By a "bigger framework," Kissinger meant an approach that would end the war and serve long-term U.S. objectives, namely, to create a more stable regional situation and dramatically reduce Soviet influence in the Middle East—a goal he articulated well before the 1973 war broke out. He explained: "If the United States played its cards carefully, either the Soviet Union would be obliged to contribute to a genuine solution or one of its Arab clients would break ranks and begin moving toward the United States. In either case, Soviet influence among the radical Arab states would be reduced. This was why, early in Nixon's first term, I felt confident enough to tell a journalist that the new administration would seek to expel Soviet influence from the Middle East.

"Though that incautious remark created a furor, it accurately described the strategy the Nixon administration was about to implement . . . the best strategy was to demonstrate that the Soviet Union's capacity to foment crises was not matched by its ability to resolve them."[2]

With respect to those "incautious" remarks, a sample (alarmed) headline from the *Washington Post* in July 1970, years before a version of Kissinger's contemplated strategy would take effect in 1973 and 1974, read, "U.S. Seeking to Oust Soviet Units in Egypt: U.S. Seeks Soviet Pullback in Mideast," followed by a skeptical editorial "On 'Expelling' the Russians from the Mideast."[3]

A less strategic perspective might have focused on the specific, nominally separate negotiations that then dominated the news. For example, following the 1973 war, Kissinger conducted dramatic disengagement negotiations with Egypt in 1974 and with Syria through 1975 with respect to Israel. Both sets of shuttle talks led to stabilizing agreements among these countries, agreements that have endured to the present (2018). In the same time frame as these shuttles, Kissinger undertook negotiations with the Soviets over Berlin and European security aimed at a general reduction in tensions ("détente") and an opening to the Soviets of a range of trade and other possibilities. But observe how Kissinger framed these multiple negotiations with respect to the larger strategy of reducing Soviet influence in the Middle East and moderating Soviet behavior in the context of détente: "In pursuit of this goal, the United States . . . blocked every Arab move that resulted from Soviet military support or involved a Soviet military threat; and it took charge of the peace process once frustration with the stalemate had brought some key Arab leaders to dissociate from the Soviet Union and turn to the United States.

"American strategy was based on the proposition that the Soviet Union should be faced with the choice of either separating itself from its radical Arab clients or accepting a reduction of its influence. In the end, this strategy curtailed Soviet influence and placed the United States into the pivotal position in Middle East diplomacy. The Nixon Administration pursued two courses to achieve this goal. During the Middle East War, it kept open an almost daily channel of communication with the Kremlin to avoid permitting decisions to be taken in the heat of the moment or on the basis of inadequate information. . . .

". . . Simultaneously we conducted negotiations on a range of issues in order to give the Soviet leaders a stake they would be reluctant to jeopardize. The Berlin negotiations contributed to Soviet restraint in the Middle East until well into 1973. Afterward, the European Security Conference helped to moderate the Soviet reaction during the various diplomatic shuttles that moved the Soviet Union to the fringes of Mideast diplomacy. . . . Détente not only calmed the international situation, it created inhibitions which caused Soviet leaders to accept what amounted to a major geopolitical retreat."[4]

Other analysts have confirmed the significant economic effects on the Soviets of these nominally separate negotiations. Absent Moscow's expectation of greatly enhanced trade with the West, these linked talks would not have played such a significant role in the diplomacy surrounding the Middle Eastern conflict.[5]

Kissinger's success in limiting Soviet and then Russian influence in the Middle East largely endured for more than forty years, until September 2015, when Russian president Vladimir Putin launched military actions in Syria following President Obama's pullback of American engagement.

This example highlights the characteristics of Kissinger the strategic negotiator: clear long-term objectives (ensure regional stability, enhance détente, reduce Soviet influence in the Middle East), a focus on the broader context and possible connections among parties and issues rather than treating them as independent (forge linkages among negotiations over disengagement with those over détente involving Berlin and European security that included the Soviets, Europeans, Egyptians, Syrians, and Israelis), as well as a clear plan with direct and indirect elements, enhanced American credibility, and flexibility of means while firmly maintaining ends.

Strategic Versus Tactical Negotiation

Kissinger described the tactical orientation of the "lawyerly" secretary of state William Rogers, whom he credited with having "a shrewd analytical mind and outstanding common sense. . . . [Yet Rogers's] perspective was tactical; as a lawyer he was trained to deal with issues as they arose 'on their merits.' "[6]

By comparison, Kissinger saw himself as a strategic negotiator. We concur with this assessment. When he envisioned a desirable agreement that would advance broader interests but that was currently out of reach, he would conceive of moves he might make ahead of time and across different issues or regions. Such moves would often generate a more promising setup for achieving his target deal. In his words, "I attempted to relate events to each other, to create incentives or pressures in one part of the world to influence events in another. Rogers was keenly attuned to the requirements of particular negotiations. I wanted to accumulate nuances for a long-range strategy. Rogers was concerned with immediate reaction in the Congress and media, which was to some extent his responsibility as principal spokesman in foreign affairs. I was more worried about results some years down the road."[7] In tandem with the long view, Kissinger's negotiations were also often initiated with stability as a major focus. As he told *Atlantic* editor Jeffrey Goldberg in 2016, "The challenge, then, is to devise a system in which change can be accommodated without producing chaos."[8]

Other sophisticated observers underscored Kissinger's strategic orientation and its relationship to how he approached negotiation. Typical of such assessments would be that of Brent Scowcroft, national security advisor to both Gerald Ford and George H. W. Bush. Scowcroft judged that Kissinger had "the finest strategic mind I have ever come across. He could balance a whole lot of disparate issues and interrelate them all a year or two on. That was very rare. Several years later, all the strands would come together."[9] In Kissinger, the roles of strategist, tactician, and negotiator entwined.

Some may interpret Kissinger's "strategic orientation" toward negotiation as limited to his overarching objectives related to the Cold War during the 1970s. In our judgment, this view would be too narrow and time bound. Read carefully, Kissinger's comparison of his negotiating approach to that of William Rogers (just given) and Scowcroft's judgment about Kissinger's strategic sense both point to a more general meaning of "strategic negotiation." The five factors we have isolated—a long-term focus, a wide-angle lens on the broader context, a plan with direct and indirect elements, an adaptable blueprint, and a reputation for credibility—transcend particular foreign policy objectives at any given time and extend to business, legal, and any other subjects characterized by complex negotiations.

A Relentless Focus on a Strategy to Guide Negotiations

During his years as a Harvard academic, prior to serving in government, Kissinger harshly criticized negotiations that were not pursuant to a clear set of larger interests and thus, in his view, that were consumed with largely meaningless tactical choices. For example, with respect to arms control, he argued that "because we lack a strategic doctrine . . . it is inevitable that our proposals . . . are fitful . . . developed as a compromise between competing groups and without an overall sense of purpose . . . typically we have been forced to assemble a set of hasty proposals because we have agreed to go to a conference under the pressure of world opinion. . . . [A]ttention has been focused . . . on a fruitless controversy over whether we should be 'conciliatory' or 'tough,' 'flexible' or 'rigid.' "[10] In later faulting President Obama's foreign policy for its lack of long-term strategic initiative, especially with respect to China and Iran, Kissinger echoed his earlier critique: "We must take care lest the Obama Doctrine become an essentially reactive and passive foreign policy."[11] More broadly, he argued that "Too much of our public debate deals with tactical expedients. What we need is a strategic concept and to establish priorities."[12]

More operationally and with respect to his team, he emphasized the importance of a continual and explicit focus on larger strategic objectives: "I have always put great stress on getting my associates to analyze where they are, where they want to go, where our country should go, and then work back from that to practical solutions. . . . [W]hen I came to Washington, I assembled a group . . . [of] . . . really young, able, dedicated people. I would meet with them several times a week, preferably daily, asking the question, what are we trying to do? What is our strategy in the world?"[13]

Kissinger's staff clearly internalized the importance of a strategic perspective. For example, Harold Saunders, who would later play key roles in the 1978 Camp David Accords and the Iran hostage crisis, stressed that "we always lived with the long-term strategy, regardless of the short-term efforts that we might be making." In preparation for each of the twenty-six Tel Aviv–Damascus trips during the grueling shuttle diplomacy between Syria and Israel, Saunders "would write a memorandum analyzing the situation then in existence, the long-term goals we were trying to achieve and how that particular trip was to move the negotiations forward along the long range path . . . The detail agreement was another step down the road."[14]

To Kissinger and his associates, a strategic concept was not merely an abstract guide; it could also play a critical tactical role. Facing adamant but incompatible Israeli and Syrian positions over how many artillery pieces and tanks would be permitted in a buffer zone, Saunders related a tense moment with Israeli prime minister Golda Meir. Kissinger "stopped being the Secretary of State of the United States who was trying to mediate an agreement" and became "an American professor serving as a consultant to the State of Israel who, incidentally, had shared the Jewish experience." According to Saunders, Kissinger "said that for a moment he wanted to leave the number issue aside. He then began to remind all in attendance of the fundamental strategy that he was pursuing. He noted that the interim agreements were designed to acquire control over the peace process, to push the Soviets out of their involvement in the area and to obtain European support for the peace process by getting the oil embargo lifted. . . . He laid out all of these goals and by doing so, he pushed back the Israeli gloom. He reminded them gently that what was at stake that day was the basic strategy and the long-range goals. . . . The number of artillery pieces and tanks was only incidental to the general direction and final goals to be achieved. Kissinger painted that big picture exquisitely."[15] After consulting with her team, Golda Meir gave Kissinger permission to get the best number he could from the Syrians, and Israel would go along.

An Expansive View of Negotiating Interests: Potential Links Among Parties and Interests over Time

Phrases such as *bigger framework* or *strategic perspective* can sound weighty but risk having little real content. Kissinger, however, had quite precise meanings in mind. Recall the Rhodesian case in which a target deal between Kissinger and Ian Smith required a wider scope. The most promising possible Kissinger–Smith meeting could be set up only by a prior sequential negotiation campaign involving the Americans, British, French, Tanzanians, Zambians, South Africans, and others. Similarly, it is instructive to examine the connections that Kissinger saw and forged in negotiating across major regions—China and Vietnam, the Soviet Union, the Middle East, and Europe. "So our attempt was to get a perspective for American foreign policy that . . . opened up the possibility of a broader perspective of peace. And therefore . . . we . . . began, wherever we could, a dialogue with the Soviet Union and an opening to China and various Middle East initiatives . . . So when I had the good fortune of being selected by President Nixon to be the first American emissary [on a secret mission to China], so on that July 9th [when I embarked on this mission], I did not look at it from the point of view of settling the immediate issues, [but rather] as an opportunity for opening a canvas on which we were going to paint as it developed."[16]

Kissinger judged that improved Sino-American relationships were a vital component of the Nixon administration's approach to the Soviet Union.[17] Moreover, he stressed that "we also always had in mind that we wanted to settle the Vietnam War at the same time. And we didn't want little victories. What we wanted was a structural improvement."[18] While Kissinger and Nixon were seeking détente with the USSR, especially with respect to arms control and summit talks, the Soviets were increasingly posing a direct threat to China (a situation that involved actual military clashes, as we later describe in greater detail). This threat made the Chinese far more receptive to American overtures, which Kissinger nurtured.

The American opening to China was important not only on its own terms but as a method for nudging forward détente with the Soviets, who had been stalling its progress, likely seeking greater American concessions. When the Soviets suddenly became aware of the secret Nixon-Kissinger initiative on China, they sought to avoid the formation of a Chinese-U.S. axis by moving toward the United States. U.S.-Soviet détente and arms control gained new life. The so-called triangular relationship negotiated among the United States, China, and the Soviet Union was coming into being, with the United States at the pivot point. In this setting, the potential interconnections among the three powers, perceived by Kissinger and Nixon well before many others, turned out to be decisive for years.

As Kissinger's parallel but linked negotiations with these two Communist giants progressed, both China and the Soviet Union separately began to see much greater value in improved relations with the United States. In turn, as we later detail in chapter 6, Kissinger sought to use this carefully choreographed prospect (of more valuable relationships with the United States) to persuade China and the Soviets to reduce their diplomatic and material support for North Vietnam, their ally—thus enhancing American leverage in the Paris peace negotiations to end the Vietnam War. (Unlike the triangular U.S.-Soviet-Chinese connections, which proved potent in practice, analysts are divided on the effect of Kissinger's efforts at linkage with Vietnam, though the negotiating logic was clear.[19])

Looking beyond Vietnam and détente, the larger question for negotiators contemplating issue linkage is the extent and nature of potential connectedness among issues, parties, and regions. While the strategic negotiator should be alert to such potential, whether an attempted linkage or separation of issues (including the relative importance to the parties of the issues at stake) will succeed is an empirical matter.[20]

Think Strategically, Act Opportunistically

Given that situations often shift unpredictably, Kissinger's approach to a given negotiation could involve flexibly responding to such changes while still pursuing the same larger purposes and interests. We have characterized this aspect of his approach with the aphorism "think strategically but act opportunistically."[21] For example, in the Southern Africa negotiations, when British and Frontline State support unexpectedly eroded in the middle of the process, Kissinger opportunistically reversed his original coalition-building sequence (with British agreement in writing now, at the start of the revised sequence, rather than as its capstone, as he had originally planned).

Harold Saunders offered another example of strategic firmness combined with tactical flexibility. Saunders accompanied Kissinger in his efforts, just described, to negotiate Egyptian and Syrian disengagement accords with Israel following their 1973 war. As a staff member, Saunders stressed that they always "had a fundamental analysis, a long-term strategy and a myriad of details [sic] to be negotiated. The resolution of each detail would eventually achieve our long-term objectives. . . . The details never drove our strategy, but would occasionally require mid-course corrections." He illustrated this point by noting that Kissinger's team would never have contemplated stationing American monitors in the Sinai passes as was suggested by the Israelis in June 1974. "Our strategy didn't change," Saunders observed, but U.S. willingness to acquiesce in this new idea made the deal "more acceptable to the Israelis without foreclosing the possibility of the whole Sinai being returned to Egypt as was later done."[22]

Fostering Credibility

Kissinger's focus on the potential interdependencies among parties and issues over time also helps explain the central role he gave to a reputation for "credibility" in his negotiations. Simply put, one's credibility is the belief by others that one's threats and promises will be carried out. To many people, fostering credibility seems a matter of common sense, though the concept has long been a controversial preoccupation both for those involved in foreign policy and for those who analyze it. Derided as the "credibility addiction" by some who believe that the United States has made costly mistakes by overemphasizing this aspect of its policies, Kissinger sharply disagreed: "no serious policymaker" could debunk or ignore U.S. credibility, as "scores of countries and millions of people relied for their security on our willingness to stand by allies."[23] Seemingly separate negotiations were, in Kissinger's view, tightly connected by the beliefs of counterparts that the United States would (or would not) act in accord with its words. Such beliefs in one negotiation heavily depended on U.S. actions elsewhere. For example, Kissinger was concerned that too rapid a withdrawal from Vietnam would damage China's respect for American power.

After all, such power was a major factor that impelled China, facing Soviet threats, to seek rapprochement with the United States. Kissinger reflected, "Peking had no interest in a demonstration that the United States was prepared to dump its friends; in its long-range perspective of seeking a counterweight to the Soviet Union, Peking in fact had a stake in our reputation for reliability."[24] Yet, after years of fighting in Southeast Asia, it was unclear to many observers how heavily U.S. credibility should have been weighed relative to the costs and prospects of military success, domestic cohesion, and other elements of America's international reputation, prestige, and judgment.

Although hardly an absolute, maintaining the credibility of one's words, promises, and threats is clearly an important factor in negotiation. As Kissinger stressed, "The one general rule I would apply for consideration is I tried never to leave Washington for a negotiation unless I had an 80 percent assurance it would succeed. . . . [O]ne shouldn't risk it as Secretary of State, because you use up your prestige too easily."[25]

The importance of maintaining a reputation for U.S. credibility in negotiations and foreign policy more generally continues to be an issue. For example, President Obama famously declared in 2012 that a "red line" for U.S. intervention in Syria would be crossed if that regime used chemical weapons. When his administration subsequently failed to act after Syria used sarin gas in an attack that killed fifteen hundred people, its inaction was widely cited as having damaged U.S. credibility in Moscow, Tehran, and Beijing.[26] Similarly, the proclivity of President Trump to frequently contradict his international and domestic pronouncements on important matters, thereby damaging his credibility more broadly, has attracted widespread criticism from analysts and practitioners alike.[27] In 2016, Kissinger compared credibility on the part of nation-states to a key quality for individuals: "Credibility for a state plays the role of character for a human being. It provides a guarantee that its assurance can be relied upon by friends and its threats taken seriously by adversaries."[28]

★ ★ ★

In short, we see Henry Kissinger's approach to negotiation as "strategic" in its consistent connection to long-term objectives, in its expansive conception of the interests at stake in specific interactions and possible linkages elsewhere, in its development of tactical plans that can include both direct and indirect elements, in its capacity to maintain core purposes while adapting to changing circumstances, and in its stress on the importance of credibility.

Our emphasis on a strategic concept to guide negotiations has much wider applicability in international relations—think of nuclear negotiations over North Korea and Iran—and in business situations. For example, in the so-called browser wars during the mid- to late 1990s, a fledgling Netscape, with superior technology, vied with incumbent Microsoft over whose Internet browser would be chosen by AOL. Yet the strategic stakes in the early Internet era went well beyond which firm would capture AOL as a customer. While Netscape missed the strategic significance of what it merely regarded as a large sale, Microsoft believed that if it lost the competition, its "core assets were at risk." As such, Microsoft deployed what some saw as disproportionate resources toward winning the sale.[29] (It won, and Netscape did not last as an independent entity.) Yet many other negotiations (buying a building, selling a peripheral division, working out a supply contract for embassy food service) are mainly transactional, with little or no strategic significance. An effective strategic negotiator has the discipline to assess the broader significance of the issues to be worked out, and to bargain accordingly.

When we began to research Kissinger's negotiations, we sensibly divided the work by regions: the Soviet Union, the Middle East, and China/Asia. As we deepened our understanding, though, we realized that, in Kissinger's strategic approach to negotiation, ours was an artificial and even misleading division of labor. Indeed, it ran counter to the essence of his strategy, which sought out and exploited powerful potential connections among negotiations in each of these regions and over time to shape outcomes elsewhere. The implication? Don't just focus on the negotiation that presents itself over this or that issue. When warranted, "zoom out" to a larger strategic framework as a guide, and negotiate to advance that strategic conception.

5

Realistic: Tracking the Deal/No-Deal Balance

What we call Kissinger's "realistic" approach to negotiation becomes clearest in contrast to what he, somewhat tongue in cheek, caricatured as "theological" and "psychiatric" views of the process. Absolutist "theologians" see negotiation mainly as a useful tool for virtually imposing "terms" when one side has completely dominated the other. "Psychiatrists" are true believers in negotiation for its own sake in nearly all circumstances.

In a Cold War context, "theologians" were those who counseled achieving overwhelming military and economic superiority before even turning to negotiation, which would then, more or less automatically, by some mystical process, ratify this asymmetrical power relationship. Kissinger observed, "Since [the 'theologians' such as John Foster Dulles] deemed the Soviet proclivity for world domination to be congenial, they did not consider Soviet leaders as suitable negotiating partners until the Kremlin had abandoned its ideology. And since the principal task of American foreign policy was seen as achieving the overthrow of the Soviets, comprehensive negotiations, or even a diplomatic blueprint for them, were pointless (if not immoral) until 'positions of strength' had brought about a change in Soviet purposes."[1]

At the time that Kissinger and Nixon were pursuing negotiations toward an opening to China and détente with the Soviet Union, many Americans were aligned with the "theologians." They rejected the idea of negotiating with "godless Soviet Communists" and the "fanatic Chinese ideologues." How could one deal with parties who spouted fearsome anti-American rhetoric, who espoused ideologies antithetical to core Western values, and whose policies badly damaged or destroyed even their own traditional societies (e.g., Mao's Cultural Revolution or Stalin's actions to cause dreadful famine in Ukraine)? Beyond ideological or rhetorical considerations, both China and the Soviets were major allies and weapons suppliers to North Vietnam. By 1969, more than thirty-six thousand Americans had died in that still-raging Southeast Asian war. Despite these obstacles, Kissinger saw realistic possibilities for each side's interests to be met more fully, on balance, by carefully designed agreements than continued hot or cold conflict.

Each era has its version of the Cold War "theologians," who see little use for negotiation except to deliver ultimatums accompanied by credible, overwhelming consequences should the target say no. In Vice President Dick Cheney's famous phrase (variously applied to North Korea, Iran, terrorists, and elsewhere), "We don't negotiate with evil. We defeat it." In bitter business or legal disputes, a too-quick refusal to consider negotiation may have analogous "theological" roots—for example, if one side insists from the start that "the only language they understand is power," or if the issue is reflexively defined as "on principle," or if a willingness to negotiate "signals weakness." This viewpoint animated many of the opponents of President Obama's 2015 negotiations with Iran over that country's nuclear program.

At the other end of the spectrum, Kissinger's realistic approach to negotiation contrasts with the views of those he termed the "psychiatrists." Also present in some form in every era, these often naïve idealists regularly urge negotiation largely for its own sake, see disagreements mainly as unfortunate misunderstandings or purely failures of process, and relegate tangible and strategic factors to the background.

Kissinger observed that "According to the 'psychiatric school,' the Soviet leaders were not so different from the American in their desire for peace. They acted intransigently partly because the United States had made them feel insecure. The 'psychiatric school' urged patience in order to strengthen the peace-loving segment of the Soviet leadership, which was said to be divided between hawks and doves in much the same way that the American government was."[2]

Eschewing both "theology" and "psychiatry," Kissinger and Nixon articulated a realistic approach to negotiation with the Soviets that would "weave together all the many elements of the superpower relationship into an overall approach that was neither totally confrontational (like that of the 'theologians') nor totally conciliatory (like that of the 'psychiatrists'). The idea was to emphasize those areas in which cooperation was possible, and to use that cooperation as leverage to modify Soviet behavior in areas in which the two countries were at loggerheads."[3]

In this vein, one of us (Mnookin) wrote a book, entitled *Bargaining with the Devil*, that analyzed analogous approaches to negotiating with a counterpart that one regards as evil.[4] While some would *never* bargain with the devil (theologians), others would *always* do so (psychiatrists). À la Kissinger, much better advice is to make a realistic assessment of the context to decide whether it does or does not make sense to bargain with the devil—and if it does, how.

When we use the term *realistic* to describe Kissinger's approach to negotiation, we thus refer to a context-driven approach that is deeply informed by the interests of the parties, as they see them, rather than by ideologies about the role of the negotiation process. At bottom, "realistic" negotiation is pragmatic in the sense that Kissinger describes: "[Y]ou are trying to affect the conclusions of the other side, and you are trying to find something that both sides find sufficiently in their interest to adopt. That's the essence of negotiation."[5] (In characterizing Kissinger's approach to negotiation as "realistic," we thus have a much narrower meaning than that in the full-blown school of "realism," or *realpolitik*, in international relations, which posits rational state actors jockeying for and/or applying power in a perpetual state of conflict with one another.)[6]

While Kissinger never argued for negotiation as a universal conflict solvent, he had a very clear "criterion for progress" in negotiation, which would be substantive, "expressed in precise agreements reflecting mutual interests and not atmospherics. Above all, relaxation of tensions had to proceed on a broad front: We will regard our Communist adversaries first and foremost as nations pursuing their own interests as they perceive these interests, just as we follow our own interests as we see them. We will judge them by their actions as we expect to be judged by our own. Specific agreements, and the structure of peace they help build, will come from a realistic accommodation of conflicting interests."[7]

The concept of interests is core to a realistic approach to negotiation. For Kissinger, a sophisticated interest assessment calls for carefully probing not only the views of one's counterpart, but also the historical context shaping those views. This "requires a sense of history, an understanding of manifold forces not within our control, and a broad view of the fabric of events."[8]

Interests can certainly consist of territorial, military, economic, or other tangible assets, but the concept is broader. In fact, *whatever* the parties genuinely care about that is at stake in a negotiation, tangible or intangible, can be understood as an interest.[9] Considerations as varied as mutual recognition, a cease-fire, one's reputation, or your future credibility can all qualify as interests in a negotiation. As such, acting as a "realistic" negotiator need not imply indifference toward moral or ethical concerns. Indeed, Kissinger believes that a negotiator can, and should, be highly realistic about how best to negotiate to advance idealistic objectives.[10]

Writing in 2014, Kissinger emphasized this point, but sharply critiqued a focus on advancing principles or ideals by rhetorical means without a realistic strategy: "If the old diplomacy sometimes failed to extend support to morally deserving political forces, the new diplomacy risks indiscriminate intervention disconnected from strategy. It declares moral absolutes to a global audience before it has become possible to assess the long-term intentions of the central actors, their prospects for success, or the ability to carry out a long-term policy . . . Order should not have priority over freedom. But the affirmation of freedom should be elevated from a mood to a strategy."[11]

Ingredients for the Realistic Negotiator: Parties, Interests, Possible Deals, and Alternatives to Negotiated Agreements

As in the Rhodesian case, to prepare for negotiations with Ian Smith, Kissinger characteristically assessed the full set of parties, actual and potential, along with the full set of their interests and the implications of impasse, which he frequently manipulated. For a deal to be realistically possible, its signatories must judge it to be preferable, in terms of their interests, to the consequences of failure to agree. This is a minimum necessary condition for any deal to be struck, and it accounts for the focus of modern negotiation analysts on the vital importance of each side's "best alternative to negotiated agreement" (or, in the jargon, its BATNA).[12]

Kissinger continually sought to evaluate and influence both sides of the "deal-versus-no deal" equation, emphasizing (a) the value of his target deal to his counterparts relative to (b) the cost of no deal.[13] He often argued that for a deal to be attractive and sustainable, each party had to have a stake, or to see real value, in it relative to no-deal. And value, for Kissinger, is measured in terms of the parties' interests as *they* judge them.

In tandem with stressing how a proposed deal could serve the parties' interests, Kissinger frequently emphasized the high costs to his counterpart of a failure to agree. To Rhodesia's Ian Smith, saying no to majority rule came to mean a Kissinger-engineered cutoff of rail lines and an end to vital military support by South Africa plus escalating guerrilla action. To the Chinese, no-deal with the United States meant facing an increasingly aggressive Soviet Union alone. And Kissinger could be quite forceful in describing the consequences of no-deal. In pressing the Israelis to be more forthcoming with respect to the Syrians, Walter Isaacson somewhat dramatically recounts Kissinger's "doomsday" argument: "Conceding territory in the Golan was bad [for Israel], Kissinger admitted, but letting the negotiations fail would be worse. 'I think it is essential that the gravity of a failure be understood,' he said. . . . If that happened, the U.S. (and Kissinger) would no longer be willing to act as a mediator, he warned. The pro-Israel coalition in Washington, which was based on 'an odd combination,' would quickly fall apart. Israel would find itself alone, helpless."[14]

When Success Is Unrealistic:
Fruitless Negotiations When "No" Dominates "Yes"

To a realistic negotiator, in the sense we use the term, one fundamental reason for a negotiation to stall or fail is simple: in terms of the interests at stake, refusing to agree looks more attractive to one or more sides than saying yes. For example, when the British prime minister arranged to negotiate with Rhodesia's Ian Smith on the warships HMS *Fearless* and HMS *Tiger*, the talks did not fundamentally fail as a result of a faulty process, an inauspicious venue, poor communication, cross-cultural miscues, personality clashes, or lack of preparation. Instead, they went nowhere because, for Smith, acceding to a deal meant a crushing loss of white power and position, while a "no" meant a chance for their continuation. (Kissinger's approach to the negotiations, by contrast, ultimately confronted Smith with a situation in which the dire consequences of a "no" to majority rule were worse than the merely bad ones for a "yes.") When one or both sides prefer "no" (or no-deal) to "yes" (or a deal), for any plausible deals, we describe the situation as having an adverse deal/no-deal balance; simply put, there is no zone of possible agreement.

While we have thus far cited a number of examples of Kissinger's successful negotiations, we now examine two episodes in which he was unsuccessful at reaching the deal he sought. These cases (first, a failed effort to gain Pakistani agreement to halt its nuclear weapons program; second, a failed effort at Jordanian-Israeli disengagement) offer useful insights into the minimum conditions for deal prospects to be realistic. (Of course, Kissinger had a number of other negotiation "failures": some, because no zone of possible agreement existed; others, due to a faulty approach or other factors. When it is instructive for our purposes, we later delve into some of these cases.)[15] Such insights can help one assess the likelihood that a potential negotiation will succeed and determine when one should abandon the effort to reach agreement. In both the Pakistani and Jordanian cases, as we will soon show, it became increasingly evident that Kissinger's counterparts saw no deal as superior to any agreement that the American could plausibly offer.

At such a point in the process, a realistic negotiator will abandon the effort unless other factors, such as domestic politics, compel a continuation of the talks.

Failed Effort: To Persuade Pakistan to Halt Its Nuclear Weapons Program

In 1976, as President Ford's term neared its end, Kissinger attempted to halt the proliferation of nuclear weapons in Pakistan. Five years earlier, as national security advisor to President Richard Nixon, Kissinger had developed close ties with Pakistan, which played a crucial role in facilitating the negotiated opening to China. Now he hoped to prevent Pakistan from pursuing an already dangerous arms race with neighboring India and undermining the global nuclear nonproliferation regime. Despite Kissinger's arduous efforts, his negotiations with Pakistan failed. Probing the reasons for this failure helps clarify the importance of the deal/no-deal balance as a diagnostic tool.

Following humiliating defeat in its 1971 war with India, Pakistan accelerated its covert nuclear weapons program.[16] These efforts were ramped up in 1974, after India successfully tested a nuclear bomb in May of that year.[17] From Pakistan's perspective, only its own nuclear weapons could counter India's massive conventional military edge and developing nuclear capability.[18] By 1976, however, the Ford administration and the U.S. Congress were determined to stop the potential global spread of nuclear weapons, including to Pakistan.[19] Yet Pakistan was resolutely intent on obtaining such weapons, with its prime minister, Zulfikar Ali Bhutto, having famously and publicly promised, "If India builds the bomb, we will eat grass or leaves, even go hungry, but we will get one of our own."[20]

Some members of the Ford administration, including Dick Cheney and Donald Rumsfeld, proposed the idea of supporting nuclear energy programs in Iran, and offering Pakistan access to the energy, but Kissinger attempted a more direct approach.[21] In order to obtain nuclear components, the Pakistani government had turned to France in 1974 to purchase a nuclear reprocessing facility.[22] In June 1976, U.S. pressure, via the Nuclear Suppliers Group, failed to persuade the French to cancel the agreement.[23] (It is intriguing to speculate whether commencing an earlier, more intensive negotiation campaign à la Kissinger's Rhodesian effort might have built sufficient leverage to dissuade France from the sale. For example, might Kissinger have earlier and more forcefully enlisted Britain or West Germany's help with the French?)

In any case, Kissinger flew to Pakistan in August 1976 to negotiate directly with Prime Minister Bhutto, strongly encouraging him to halt the nuclear program. At stake was over $100 million in annual aid from the United States. If Bhutto agreed to halt the program, Kissinger offered, aid would continue and the United States would provide Pakistan with 110 A-7 military aircraft and additional military aid.[24] This was a potent incentive; the Pakistani air force supported the deal, but Bhutto refused.[25]

Though not independently verified, a colorful account of the discussion has widely circulated, with a smiling Bhutto asking Kissinger what would happen if he [Bhutto] refused the deal. Temper rising, Kissinger is alleged to have replied, "Then we will make a horrible example of you!" Bhutto responded that Pakistan could survive without support from the United States, but that the United States would then have to find some other ally in the region. He then promptly walked out of the room, leaving Kissinger without an agreement.[26] Regardless of the details of the account, Bhutto was in a difficult position. Having taken a strong public stance in favor of a nuclear weapons program for Pakistan, for both strategic parity with India and national prestige, and with an election upcoming, he was unable to retreat without facing a catastrophic loss of public support.[27] Kissinger, too, was in a tough spot; India seemed to be moving closer to the Soviet Union, and Pakistan was a valuable regional ally.

In September, Kissinger began a revived effort to reach an agreement with an enhanced offer. Beyond the financial and military lure of his new proposal, he predicted that a Pakistani "no" would be damaging to that country's interests, especially if Jimmy Carter won in the upcoming November elections. He stressed the likelihood that the more liberal Carter would sever *all* U.S. aid to Pakistan, including vital defensive military hardware.[28] Hence, Kissinger urged Pakistan to make a deal now, with the Ford administration.

Kissinger's effort had been given a boost in August 1976, with the resignation of French prime minister Jacques Chirac, who had been handling that country's nuclear export policy. French president Valéry Giscard d'Estaing now took over this file. In September, Kissinger met with Giscard, who was receptive to prioritizing nonproliferation over commercial concerns. The French president also suggested that Kissinger turn to the Shah of Iran to exert additional pressure on Bhutto. Once again, however, setbacks soon followed. The French quietly informed Kissinger that they could not halt their sale of nuclear equipment to the Pakistanis, despite their support for nonproliferation, as no one could prove that the supplies would be used for weapons. Similarly, efforts with Iran faltered.[29]

In November, Carter defeated Ford. Kissinger undertook one last effort at a negotiated resolution, putting together even greater incentives to propose to Pakistan. In January 1977, he offered Bhutto substantial military and economic aid and U.S. support to obtain the basic infrastructure for a nuclear energy program, all in return for an "indefinite postponement" of Pakistan's nuclear weapons program. He made the case that Bhutto should agree now or confront far harsher terms from the incoming Carter administration. Facing upcoming elections, however, Bhutto refused at least until after the vote.[30] On January 20, Jimmy Carter took office. Kissinger was out of time, and no deal was reached.

This was a case of an adverse deal/no-deal balance from Pakistan's perspective. Virtually no agreement that Kissinger could have plausibly offered would have exceeded the strategic and political value to Bhutto of no deal (which meant continuing Pakistan's pursuit of nuclear weapons). In short, while making the attempt was clearly worthwhile, the odds were stacked against success.[31]

Subsequent events strengthen this conclusion. Later that year, the Carter administration failed to gain Bhutto's agreement to a sweetened economic deal. In July 1977, Bhutto was deposed and ultimately executed. The United States severed all economic and military aid to Pakistan in September 1977. Aid was restored in subsequent years, but Pakistan's overt and clandestine pursuit of a nuclear bomb was undeterred. The country carried out five successful nuclear tests in 1998 and now has many nuclear weapons in its arsenal.[32]

Failed Effort: To Close the "Jordanian Deal" After Egyptian and Syrian Disengagement Agreements with Israel

On October 6, 1973, the holiest day of the Jewish year, Egypt and Syria led Arab armies in a surprise attack on Israel, in part to avenge their humiliation in the 1967 war. Although the Arabs were strikingly successful in the early days of the war, Israel, heavily resupplied by the United States, eventually pushed each army well back into its home territory. Angry at U.S. and allied support for Israel during the war, Arab oil producers imposed an oil embargo on the United States and its allies (Canada, Japan, the Netherlands, and the United Kingdom), causing a fourfold spike in world oil prices and economic distress.

As the 1973 war concluded, Kissinger envisioned three potential agreements among Israel and its neighboring states that could dramatically stabilize the region: an Egyptian-Israeli disengagement accord, a Syrian-Israeli disengagement deal, and a Jordanian-Israeli pact, though Jordan was not among the attacking armies. As an immediate benefit, such agreements should result in the lifting of the oil embargo against the United States and its allies.

Each of these diplomatic initiatives was audacious to contemplate, especially given that none of the Arab countries even recognized the State of Israel. By May, however, to an admiring world, disengagement accords had been struck on the Egyptian and Syrian fronts—after challenging mediations by Henry Kissinger (as we see in chapter 4). Yet a deal with Jordan, the smallest and weakest of the Arab parties, eluded American efforts. As such, this was a "failed" deal. What led to this outcome and what might we learn from it, especially about the deal/no-deal balance as a diagnostic tool?

In 1950, the Kingdom of Jordan annexed the West Bank (including East Jerusalem), but later lost the territory to Israel during the 1967 Six-Day War. In subsequent years, Jordan's king Hussein privately took pains to ease relations with the Israelis. While the two countries remained publicly at odds, Hussein's interest in negotiations was strong enough for Kissinger to propose in December 1973, *before* the Egyptian and Syrian agreements, that Israel enter into talks to return at least some of the West Bank to Jordan.[33] The Israeli government, however, nixed the idea, rejecting any such territorial concessions.[34]

Undeterred, Hussein and Kissinger discussed making a new offer in January 1974, following the successful conclusion of the Sinai Disengagement Accords with Egypt. Yet the two ultimately agreed that the planned talks would have to wait. In the wake of the 1973 war, the Organization of Arab Petroleum Exporting Countries

(OAPEC) had initiated an oil embargo against the United States and its allies. At the same time, skirmishes along the Israeli-Syrian border threatened to break out into renewed warfare. Regional leaders, including Jordan's king Hussein, concurred that an agreement would have to be struck between Israel and hard-line Syrian leader Hafez al-Assad before any Jordanian-Israeli accord moved into the realm of possibility.[35]

Kissinger returned to the Jordanian capital of Amman in early March 1974 (before he began the Israeli-Syrian shuttle in April). He judged that Israel could reasonably negotiate only one agreement at a time (with Syria next in line), but he hoped to set the stage for a Jordanian-Israeli deal over the West Bank. Controlled and occupied by Israel but overwhelmingly populated by Palestinians, the West Bank had become a focus for Palestinian statehood by the Palestinian Liberation Organization (PLO). At that time, Israel, the United States, and Jordan vigorously opposed giving the PLO a role in any future talks, considering it a terrorist organization, one committed by charter to the destruction of Israel and hostile to the Jordanian government. Although interpretations of his real views of the PLO range widely, Kissinger himself held that "the PLO's principal weapon was terror against individuals or groups identified with peace negotiations. Its policies were radical and pro-Soviet."[36]

This American-Israeli-Jordanian opposition to a PLO role ran counter to the growing prestige of the PLO, in part as a function of its "heroic" resistance to Israel, in much of the Arab world, which increasingly saw the PLO as the true representative of the Palestinian people.[37] (Kissinger saw this view emerging elsewhere as well: "more and more bystanders—European governments, American intellectuals—were putting forward the PLO as the fashionable key to unlock the West Bank. I was sure that it would bolt the door to a settlement."[38]) As a result, he consistently stressed the view that "everybody's interest would be served best by establishing as rapidly as possible a Jordanian presence on the West Bank. This would make moderate Jordan the negotiator for the Palestinian phase of the peace process."[39] Kissinger's emphasis on speed was derived from his judgment that the Jordanian option was a rapidly fading opportunity as the PLO's appeal for formally representing the Palestinians grew.

He saw the stakes for potential talks as high because, when appropriately structured, an Israeli-Jordanian agreement could preempt future PLO claims to West Bank territory and enhance the prospect that moderate Jordan (and not the PLO) would represent the Palestinians in future Arab-Israeli peace negotiations (if and when a Geneva conference took place). As he stressed, "we think the best way to handle the Palestinian issue is through negotiations between Israel and Jordan. That is what we've said publicly many times; that's our real policy. Therefore, we see a Jordanian negotiation as important."[40] If successful, such a negotiation would "turn the debate of the Palestinians into one between the Jordanians and the Palestinians rather than between the Palestinians and Israelis."[41]

With the end of Egyptian-Israeli hostilities, the Arab oil embargo against the United States and its allies was lifted in March 1974. However, to keep the pressure on the United States to broker an Israeli-Syrian accord, the embargo-lifting move was made subject to an oil ministers' review on June 1. When the Syrian disengagement deal was concluded on May 31, and oil continued to flow, Kissinger's negotiating activities refocused on Jordan.[42] High-level American attention was almost immediate: in June 1974, President Nixon traveled to the Middle East and, in Jerusalem along with Kissinger, pressed Israeli prime minister Yitzhak Rabin to negotiate an agreement with Jordan over the West Bank.[43]

Kissinger sought to create a sense of urgency for the Israeli-

Jordanian negotiations. To Israeli defense minister Moshe Dayan, he highlighted the fading opportunity: "There are two possible strategies—to bring the Jordanians into the West Bank, or to stonewall with Jordan and sooner or later all hell will break loose with the Palestinians."[44] To Yigal Allon, Israel's foreign minister, Kissinger essentially said that the Jordanian option was now or never: "Israel did not have the option of freezing the status quo on the West Bank in expectation that a Jordanian negotiation would always remain available later on. If Israel did not deal with Hussein now, PLO leader Yasser Arafat would be recognized as the spokesman for the West Bank within a year."[45]

So why, with direct presidential backing and with the widely heralded Egyptian and Syrian disengagement agreements with Israel to his credit, was Kissinger unable to broker what he regarded as an important deal with smaller and weaker Jordan, a deal that would have involved only a modest Israeli territorial withdrawal (likely ten to twelve kilometers immediately west of the Jordan River)? Much of the answer can be found by realistically comparing how attractive "no" increasingly looked to the key parties (Israel and Jordan) relative to the consequences of "yes."

A contributing factor involved government turmoil in Israel and the United States. Having failed to anticipate the near-disastrous 1973 war, Golda Meir had stepped down as Israeli prime minister in June 1974, to be replaced by Yitzhak Rabin. Following President Richard Nixon's June tour through the Middle East, the Watergate scandal forced him to resign on August 9, 1974. Vice President Gerald Ford took over and kept Kissinger as both his secretary of state and national security advisor. Hence both the new Israeli and U.S. administrations were coping with recent national traumas.

Emphasizing the vital importance of a Jordanian-Israeli deal, King Hussein was the first head of state to visit Washington after

Ford became president (soon followed by other Middle Eastern leaders). The Ford-Hussein communiqué affirmed that the "discussions between his majesty and the President and the Secretary of State were a constructive contribution . . . [toward] addressing at an appropriately early date . . . a Jordanian-Israeli disengagement agreement."[46]

From August to October, Kissinger and Ford attempted to revive the Jordanian-Israeli negotiations. Yet Prime Minister Yitzhak Rabin, Golda Meir's successor, faced a sharply divided cabinet and country. His coalition government held but a one-vote majority in the Israeli Knesset, and he had pledged that no changes to the status of the West Bank would be made without an election or plebiscite.[47] Both the Egyptian and Syrian disengagement agreements, heavily pushed by the Americans as well as the Israeli government, were quite unpopular, especially among some segments of conservative and religious Israeli groups.[48] With respect to a possible Jordanian deal, many Israelis strongly opposed reestablishing any Arab authority on the West Bank.[49]

To counter this, Kissinger was said to have "put the United States' full diplomatic support" behind the plan for an Israeli-Jordanian accord, ordering "scheduled shipments of tanks and other arms to be held up, their release to be linked directly to Israel's acceptance of the disengagement plan."[50] To no avail: for Rabin, the political risks of saying "yes" to a Jordanian deal were too heavy. Fearful of an electoral backlash that would bring down the government, the Israeli cabinet was not even prepared to open negotiations with Jordan.[51] Kissinger's intensive shuttle from October 9 to 15 (with multiple stops in Israel, Jordan, Egypt, Syria, Saudi Arabia, Algeria, and Morocco) also failed to produce any movement. (Kissinger was later reported to have admitted to the king that he had miscalculated "our manipulative capabilities."[52] And he acknowledged ambivalence over how hard to press for the

Jordanian option or a second Israeli withdrawal from Sinai. Others offer more devious interpretations.[53])

Although King Hussein had pressed for a deal, Arab heads of state assembled at a summit in Rabat, Morocco, on October 28 and unanimously endorsed the PLO as "the sole legitimate representative of the Palestinian people." For Hussein to defy his Arab peers by undertaking any West Bank negotiation with Israel was now unthinkable; as he proclaimed, "when my tribe goes astray, I follow it." To Kissinger, the realistic negotiator, "Hussein was [now] out of the picture. . . . [G]iven the PLO's vociferous rejection of Israel's right to exist and its active use of terrorism as an instrument of policy, the Rabat decision guaranteed a nineteen-year impasse on West Bank negotiations."[54]

For Kissinger, pursuing negotiations toward an Israeli-Jordanian disengagement deal may have been a decent bet early on. At the point, however, when it became clear, in terms of the interests at stake for both Rabin and Hussein, that "no" decisively dominated "yes," thus violating the minimum condition for agreement prospects to be realistic, it made sense for Kissinger to abandon the attempt and to shift his negotiating attention elsewhere.

Suppose, however, that Kissinger had somehow been able to reach a disengagement deal making Jordan responsible for representing the Palestinians. Given the sustained swell of support for the PLO in the Arab world and elsewhere as the real voice of the Palestinians, a good case can be made that such a Jordanian agreement would have proved unsustainable. Some go even further, arguing that "what was achieved in 1993 [the Oslo agreement] might have been achieved in 1974, and much bloodshed prevented, had [Kissinger] not worked against the Palestinians."[55] Such speculative judgments, of course, are less about Kissinger's negotiating approach than about the accuracy of the assumptions that underlay and drove his actions. As we will again see with respect to American policy in Indochina, a negotiation strategy and tactics can be no better than the substantive premises on which they are based.

★ ★ ★

The Jordan negotiation "failed" in the sense that the agreement sought by Kissinger eluded him, at least during the time frame under consideration. Yet, as with failed efforts to negotiate a halt to Pakistan's nuclear program, our examination highlighted the crucial importance of the "deal/no-deal balance" as a key tool for realistically analyzing the prospects for a negotiation to succeed or fail. In each instance, a strong case can be made that there was no zone of possible agreement: for different reasons, no-deal was a better option than any plausible deal for at least one crucial party. Yet does this kind of "failure" mean that it was a mistake for Kissinger to have entered the Jordanian or Pakistani talks at all or to have persevered when deal prospects looked bleak?

In general, the greater the potential value of a deal appears relative to the cost of impasse for each of the parties (as well as any costs of engaging in negotiation), the greater the odds of success and the more it makes sense to engage. By contrast, when success odds appear low and/or the costs of negotiating are high, entering or prolonging a negotiation may be ill-advised and counterproductive. This could be the case, for example, if the other side simply used negotiation as a delaying tactic to rearm, get reinforcements, or watch the costs to its counterpart mount ruinously during the process. And the costs of entering negotiation can include setting a bad precedent, activating potent opposition from key groups "behind the table," and risking greater "deal fatigue" for future negotiation attempts.

Yet, even where the deal/no-deal balance appears adverse, entering a negotiation may make sense for at least four reasons. First, the alternative to a negotiation (for example, war) may be much costlier, and even low odds of a deal may be worth testing. Second, by entering a negotiation, one may glean new information that may shift the perceived odds of success. Third, the deal/no-deal balance may not be static; for example, changes in the underlying situation may influence these odds while negotiation is ongoing. Fourth, as we soon explore in more detail, one may act away from the table to tilt the deal/no-deal balance favorably.

In our judgment, therefore, Kissinger's decision to test a Jordanian negotiation made good sense. Yet the Israelis showed no interest in a deal (for clear electoral reasons). When the Arabs made the PLO the sole legitimate representative of the Palestinians, King Hussein was clearly out of the game. At that point, the chances of a deal vanished and Kissinger wisely abandoned the effort to negotiate an Israeli-Jordanian agreement. Similarly, in our view, it was worth seeking a negotiated halt to Pakistan's nuclear program.

In sum, steering between the poles of what Kissinger caricatured as the "theologians" (for whom negotiation is generally useless except to ratify overwhelming superiority) and the "psychiatrists" (for whom negotiation is ever and always desirable for mutual understanding), the "realistic" negotiator seeks to craft agreements that serve each party's interests better than if no deal were struck.

A realistic orientation provides a systematic way to size up the potential of a situation to support a deal (or not). One should scan widely for all relevant factors: the actual and potential parties; a nuanced understanding of how each sees its interests; possible accords and the value they offer; and an appraisal of the consequences of impasse. Only when the deal-versus-no-deal (or the "yes-no" or "deal/no-deal balance") can potentially be favorable does the realistic negotiator see the possibility of agreement.

We see the deal/no-deal balance as fundamental to a "realistic" negotiation approach: when no-deal appears irrevocably superior to the value of a deal in the eyes of one or more parties critical to agreement, the necessary condition for a deal is not met. At that point, attempting different tactics, venues, or negotiation process choices will prove futile. Unless other reasons for negotiating appear compelling (to delay, to hope for an exogenous event to shift the balance, to placate a key constituency), the realistic negotiator will focus efforts elsewhere.

Kissinger's ideal negotiator, therefore, is both strategic and realistic. This carries powerful implications, as the next chapter illustrates, for negotiating not only "at the table" but also away from it to change the game and favorably tilt the odds of success.

6

Game Changing: Shaping the Deal/No-Deal Balance*

Beyond "zooming out" to a larger strategic concept and adopting a realistic stance, Kissinger counsels negotiators to embrace what we call a "wide-angle" view of the process that seeks sources of influence that may reach well beyond persuasive arguments in the conference room. In Kissinger's words, as a negotiator, "you are trying to affect the conclusions of the other side, and you are trying to find something that both sides find sufficiently in their interest to adopt. That's the essence of negotiation. . . . [I]n an international negotiation, the panoply of pressures and incentives that you can marshal is crucial."[1] The idea is to tilt the deal/no-deal balance in favor of a target agreement.

To identify potential incentives and pressures that could "affect the conclusions of the other side," Kissinger often looks for moves *outside* the negotiation at hand, or "away from the table." Faced with a reluctant counterpart to whom "no" looks superior to "yes," Kissinger often *changes the game* to induce agreement. Instead of drawing a circle around yourself and your direct counterpart and

---

* Eugene Kogan provided extensive assistance with this chapter, for which we are grateful.

simply defining your interaction as two-sided, change the game. This can mean involving or excluding parties, altering the set of issues under consideration, and/or enhancing your own no-deal option or worsening that of the other side. More conventional negotiators often focus on directly persuading a counterpart; by contrast, Kissinger often reshapes the negotiating setup itself in order to enhance the value of agreement, raise the costs of impasse, or both.

Recall the Rhodesian case study (in chapters 1–3), in which Kissinger diagnosed the fundamental reason that even the British prime minister twice failed to negotiate successfully, mano a mano, black-majority rule with Ian Smith on the decks of two British warships. Implicitly, the prime minister equated "negotiation" with the interpersonal dealings between two parties. The plain, realistic reason for the British failure: to Smith, a "no" to the British demand maintained at least some chance of preserving white power and privilege, while a "yes" meant that Rhodesian whites would soon be subordinate to blacks in that country.

Given this diagnosis, Kissinger was able to elicit a "yes" from Smith by changing the negotiating game itself to tilt the deal/no-deal balance toward the American's preferred agreement. Kissinger undertook complex coalitional moves *away* from his ultimate meeting with Smith. He actively brought Britain, Tanzania, Zambia, other OAU states, and South Africa into the process in a manner that resulted in putting decisive South African pressure on Rhodesia. While giving key transitional political and economic reassurances to whites, Kissinger deployed an empathetic yet assertive style in dealing with Vorster and, especially, Smith. Within a few months, Smith's blunt declaration that black-majority rule would not come to Rhodesia for "a thousand years" was transformed into black-majority rule "within two years."

The inseparability of negotiation and consequences via game-changing moves will seem self-evident to many people. Yet, while there are important exceptions, nowhere does Kissinger's approach to negotiation differ more from much current scholarship on the subject.[2] This is especially true for research based on laboratory experiments in well-specified setups whose elements (e.g., the parties, issues, walkaway alternatives), by design, cannot be changed by the subjects/participants. Modern behavioral investigations into negotiation tend to focus almost exclusively on the effects on negotiated outcomes of varying one at-the-table factor at a time, while holding all else constant. Such factors might include the number of issues, the time limits, ultimatums versus an offer-counteroffer dynamic, the patterns of concession, and the attributes of the negotiators (e.g., competitive or cooperative orientation, national culture, gender).[3] In a fairly typical academic view, the first editor of Harvard's *Negotiation Journal*, a distinguished psychologist, characterized negotiation "as the settlement of differences and the waging of conflict *through verbal exchange*"[emphasis supplied].[4]

Kissinger stresses the narrowness and practical limitations of this view. "Historically, negotiators have rarely relied exclusively on the persuasiveness of the argument," he averred. "A country's bargaining position has traditionally depended not only on the logic of its proposals but also on the penalties it could exact for the other side's failure to agree."[5] For Kissinger, artificially separating actions at and away from the table is almost analytically, and practically, incoherent: "One fundamental principle that I have learned in diplomacy is you cannot separate diplomacy from the consequences of action. The idea that you can have a diplomacy that is conducted like a graduate seminar without the rewards and penalties that attach to actions, it's a fantasy."[6]

The Special Case of Changing the Game via Coercive Moves

While changing the game can involve many elements such as parties, issues, and no-deal alternatives, Kissinger pays special attention to the close relationship of force and negotiation. In *The Necessity for Choice*, he notes that "Even at the Congress of Vienna, long considered the model diplomatic conference, the settlement which maintained the peace of Europe for a century, was not achieved without the threat of war."[7]

In Kissinger's experience, an overly narrow view of negotiation, as a purely verbal exchange, extends well beyond the academy: "The prevalent view within the American body politic sees military force and diplomacy as distinct, in essence separate, phases of action. Military action is viewed as occasionally creating the conditions for negotiations, but once negotiations begin, they are seen as being propelled by their own internal logic."[8]

Elaborating this general point, Kissinger goes on to highlight how, in his view, this common fallacy (of separating negotiation from incentives) has worked against the effectiveness of many U.S. negotiations in practice: "[I]n America, we found it very hard to understand this . . . because we tend to present diplomacy as there's a period of pressure and then there's a period of negotiation, and they're separate. . . . So in the Korean War, we stopped military operations at the beginning of negotiations. . . . So therefore you remove one of the incentives."[9]

While a military pause during negotiation, in the form of a bombing halt or cease-fire, does temporarily remove an incentive for the other side to agree, it can make sense for other reasons. It can lend credibility to your willingness to call a halt to violence if a final agreement is reached, while giving the other side a taste of peace. It may strengthen a pro-deal faction on the other side or mollify one of your key domestic constituencies. Also, it may simply be the right thing to do for ethical reasons, such as damaging effects on civilians. Of course, Kissinger is often right: a pause may simply provide breathing space for one or both sides to rearm, recruit allies, and regroup.

With respect to Kissinger's larger point about the relationship between force and negotiation, it would be hard today to find many professionals who see force and diplomacy as separate and opposite activities. The vast majority of senior officials in U.S. career services and among political appointees holds the belief that diplomacy and negotiations are most effective when joined with other instruments of national power, including economic sanctions as well as the threat and use of force. While maintaining the key role of game-changing moves, Kissinger warns bargainers not to crudely deploy sticks and carrots to influence behavior: "you have to be careful not to marshal [them] in such a way that it looks like a demand for surrender, because then you are creating an additional incentive for resistance."[10] He broadened this point in a 2016 interview: "Diplomacy and power are not discrete activities. They are linked, though not in the sense that each time negotiations stall, you resort to force. It simply means that the opposite number in a negotiation needs to know there is a breaking point at which you will attempt to impose your will. Otherwise, there will be a deadlock or a diplomatic defeat."[11]

Once coercion and negotiation are explicitly linked, however, two sets of questions immediately arise. First, under what conditions are coercive measures effective as part of a negotiating strategy? Second, even if potentially effective, under what conditions are coercive moves *ethical*? We highlight these issues as they arise in Kissinger's negotiations, especially with respect to military action in Vietnam and Cambodia, which we will soon examine in some depth. With the Indochina (i.e., Vietnam, Cambodia, and Laos) example in mind, we will revisit this important topic more fully in a separate section at the end of this chapter, "Force and Diplomacy: Considerations of Ethics and Effectiveness."

While moves to worsen the other side's no-deal options may involve military force, such cases are extreme; most negotiations do not involve B-52s. Rather, if the other side won't agree, more normal consequences include economic costs, competitive disadvantages, or legal risks. No-deal can mean forging a countervailing alliance or giving a huge order to an alternative supplier. And, of course, while it is preferable to have an attractive no-deal option, sometimes your no-deal option is poor. This can give an edge to your counterpart—unless you can change the game by improving your walkaway and/or worsening theirs. Analytically, however, the core point remains: effective negotiation often involves *both* words at the table and deeds away from it.

Lessons from the Vietnam Negotiations

What can we learn from a reexamination of Kissinger's arduous talks that produced the Paris Peace Accords in January 1973? After all, this agreement scarcely lasted two years before North Vietnam conquered the South. We are neither historians nor experts on this war; nor are we likely to add to the controversial "lessons of Vietnam" (a phrase that turns up no fewer than 184,000 times in a 2017 Google search).

Despite these limitations, we see taking a fresh look at the Vietnam negotiations as worthwhile because, first, they represent a challenging case of how to strengthen a weak bargaining position; second, they highlight the potential role of creative game-changing moves in such situations, including the ethics and effectiveness of coercive actions; and third, they underscore how even highly skill-ful negotiation ultimately depends for success on the quality of basic assumptions about the situation.

It may surprise some readers that we will characterize Kissin-ger's early bargaining position with the North Vietnamese as weak. After explaining this judgment, we focus on the complex of actions that he took (often not obvious and often away from the table) to transform a poor hand into a better one. Military action certainly mattered, but so did other, less familiar factors that suggest a fairly creative approach to very tough negotiations. In various forms, this challenge of bargaining from weakness is common, important, and difficult. All things considered, despite the pain of revisiting Vietnam and the ultimate failure of the Paris Peace Accords, a fresh look can yield worthwhile insights.

Background to the Vietnam War

Countless books have been written about the polarizing war in Vietnam; the full story and its implications are complex and fraught with enduring disagreements.[12] Rather than enter this debate or seek to be at all comprehensive, we will try to offer essential con-text and highlight aspects of the Vietnam saga that are most rele-vant to our focus on game-changing moves in the negotiations.[13]

Occupied by Japan during the Second World War, Indochina had been a French colony of some forty-two million people. With postwar Vietnam back nominally under French rule, Communist guerrillas waged an anticolonial struggle for independence with support from Communist China.

After the onset of the Korean War in 1950 and following dis-cussions of what came to be known as the "domino theory," Pres-ident Harry Truman began aiding France in the war in Indochina.

In the context of the Cold War, this theory suggested that once one country fell under Communist control, other "dominoes" in the region would fall and communism would spread. The implication was that the expansion of Communist influence had to be resisted even in areas that did not otherwise have significant strategic importance to the United States. Following its defeat at Dien Bien Phu, France withdrew from Vietnam with the signing of the July 20, 1954, Geneva Accords, which divided the country at the seventeenth parallel into northern and southern entities.[14] (In fact, given the Soviet and Chinese Communist threats of that era, Truman and his successors were not wrong to worry about the aggressive campaigns of both Communist powers to undermine existing democracies and to sow divisions in the West. The issue for Indochina, however, was whether the domino theory was applicable.) Worried by the French defeat, the United States effectively recognized South Vietnam in 1955. By the end of its term, the Eisenhower administration had provided over a billion dollars in assistance, with 692 U.S. "military advisors" helping to train the South Vietnamese Army.[15] Seeking to contain the spread of communism, then the guiding principle of U.S. foreign policy, President John F. Kennedy increased the U.S. presence in Vietnam from 900 to 16,263 military advisors.[16] By 1963, South Vietnamese president Ngo Dinh Diem, whose policies clashed with Washington's preferences, had been deposed and killed in a coup that the United States at least passively condoned. General Nguyen Van Thieu, one of the coup leaders, became president of South Vietnam in 1967, and remained in that position throughout the Nixon years.[17]

Following John F. Kennedy's assassination, Lyndon Johnson was elected president in 1964 in a landslide. Continuing to espouse the domino theory, Johnson's defense secretary, Robert McNamara, articulated a common view among American policy makers: "Hanoi's victory [in South Vietnam] would be a first step toward eventual Chinese hegemony over the two Vietnams and Southeast Asia and toward exploitation of the new [wars of liberation] strategy in other parts of the world."[18]

In August 1964, Congress passed the Gulf of Tonkin Resolution after the North Vietnamese were said to have attacked two American destroyers. Later the subject of controversy over the accuracy of reports about the attack, including whether it even happened, the Tonkin Resolution authorized President Johnson to use force to repel aggression and, in effect, to dramatically expand the war in Indochina.[19]

The Soviet and Chinese Connections

Although the U.S. public and policymaking community had generally regarded Communist countries as monolithic during the 1950s and '60s, relations between the USSR and China had become increasingly tense through the 1960s. This "Sino–Soviet split" generally worked in Hanoi's favor as the Soviet Union and China competed to be North Vietnam's primary supporter.[20] For a decade after the French defeat in 1954, China provided Hanoi with an estimated $670 million in aid, and increased support from $110 million in 1965 to $225 million in 1967. China's aid averaged between $150 and $200 million per year during the remaining years of the war.[21]

After the Gulf of Tonkin Resolution was passed, Chinese premier Mao Zedong personally assured Ho Chi Minh, North Vietnam's leader, of China's support. From 1965 to 1969, Beijing is estimated to have sent 320,000 personnel to Vietnam to help operate military equipment and to build and repair transportation links.[22]

The Soviet Union's support (estimated at $365 million from 1954 to 1964) was more modest than Beijing's, reflecting Soviet general secretary Nikita Khrushchev's belief that Indochina was a low strategic priority compared to postwar German issues and the emerging China challenge.[23] Leonid Brezhnev's assumption of power in October 1964 marked a change in Moscow's approach.[24] As the Sino-Soviet split deepened, it became "critically important [for Moscow] to reverse the pro-Chinese trend in Hanoi."[25] Embroiling the United States in a protracted, divisive struggle that drained its resources was an added advantage that the Soviet leadership sought to exploit.[26]

In 1965, Hanoi rejected Chinese premier Zhou Enlai's request that North Vietnam dissociate itself from Moscow, and accepted some $550 million in Soviet military assistance.[27] In short, North Vietnam was able to secure substantial support from both the Soviets and Chinese. The forces deployed against South Vietnam included North Vietnamese troops and the Vietcong, a closely allied force of guerrillas and some regular army units, based mostly in the South.[28]

That same year, reassured of continued Soviet and Chinese support, Vietcong forces attacked an American air base near the South Vietnamese city of Pleiku, killing 8 Americans and wounding 126 more.[29] This led President Lyndon Johnson to order the rapidly intensifying "Rolling Thunder" bombing campaign, which began in March 1965 and included targets in North Vietnam. Though smaller skirmishes involving U.S. personnel and advisors had earlier taken place, Rolling Thunder marked the beginning of major direct U.S. military engagement. Later that month, the first U.S. combat troops, consisting of 3,500 marines, landed in Vietnam.[30] American involvement escalated rapidly: by the end of 1965, U.S. military forces exceeded 180,000. Over the next two years, the totals exceeded 385,000 and 485,000, respectively, growing to 536,100 U.S. troops deployed in Vietnam by 1968.[31]

On January 30, 1968, the Vietnamese New Year, or Tet, North

Vietnamese and Vietcong troops launched massive surprise attacks throughout South Vietnam. These forces captured several cities, including Hué, Vietnam's ancient imperial capital. They assaulted targets ranging from military command centers to the U.S. embassy in Saigon, which Vietcong troops briefly occupied. Over the next month, American and South Vietnamese forces beat back the attacks, inflicting heavy losses on North Vietnamese and Vietcong forces during what became known as the Tet Offensive.

Despite the adverse military outcome for the North and the Vietcong, the Tet Offensive shocked U.S. political and defense officials, many of whom had judged the enemy incapable of mounting such an ambitious operation. More important, it stunned the American public, which generally believed that the war was being won. CBS news anchor Walter Cronkite, widely regarded as "the most trusted man in America," exclaimed, "What the hell is going on? I thought we were winning the war." While a clear military defeat for the North, the Tet Offensive proved to be a great symbolic and political victory. It became the turning point in U.S. attitudes toward the war, decisively shifting the objective from winning the war militarily to finding an acceptable way out.[32]

Increasing waves of domestic antiwar protests had accompanied the escalation of the U.S. military role in Vietnam.[33] Frustrated by his inability to bring the conflict to an end and facing a huge domestic backlash against the war, President Johnson announced in March 1968 that he would not seek reelection. Though the Vietnam War had claimed one U.S. presidency, Johnson actively pursued negotiations with the North Vietnamese, which included a bombing halt and offers of economic aid. These talks apparently came very close to fruition, but ultimately failed (likely due to interference by then-candidate Nixon, who evidently persuaded the South Vietnamese to reject the deal since they would get better terms under his administration).[34]

The New Nixon Administration:
Interests and Target Agreement

It is important to understand that, especially given the U.S. domestic situation, neither Richard Nixon nor Henry Kissinger believed that the Vietnam War could now be won militarily in the manner sought by previous administrations. As a candidate, Nixon promised that the "first priority foreign policy objective of our next Administration will be to bring an honorable end to the war in Vietnam."[35] Elsewhere, he bluntly articulated one of the "fundamental premises" with which he began his presidency: on Vietnam, "total military victory was no longer possible."[36] In 1968, Kissinger wrote, "The Tet Offensive marked the watershed of the American effort. Henceforth, no matter how effective our actions, the prevalent strategy could no longer achieve its objectives within a period or with force levels politically acceptable to the American people."[37] Not surprisingly, both men early on focused on finding a negotiated solution.

An Overview of Key Parties' Interests

American and South Vietnamese Interests

Making sense of the negotiations that followed calls for at least a basic understanding of how each side saw its most important interests. Inspired by the "lessons of Munich" and the domino theory, American policy makers during the 1950s and '60s had envisioned the Vietnam War primarily as part of a larger global pattern of Soviet- and Chinese-sponsored Communist aggression. When the Nixon administration took office, China and the USSR continued to support the North Vietnamese and Vietcong against the South. Yet, although outside Communist patrons played important roles, the war was increasingly seen as being fought among and between the Vietnamese themselves.

Given this understanding and the vanishing U.S. prospects for winning the war militarily, Nixon and Kissinger had shifted from the earlier goal of outright victory. They identified several key U.S. interests: to give the anticommunist South Vietnamese a solid chance to fend off the North militarily, to let the different Vietnam parties determine their own political fate more or less peacefully, to withdraw American troops from Indochina, and to bring home U.S. prisoners of war. These interests would be served by a withdrawal of North Vietnamese forces from the South and incorporation of the Vietcong into a peaceful political process.

More broadly, from the outset of the Nixon administration, the divisive Vietnam War had dominated U.S. foreign policy and interfered with the United States' larger geopolitical goals, principally détente with the Soviet Union and rapprochement with China. Ending American involvement in this bloody war would enable more effective diplomacy on other, more strategically critical fronts. Yet Nixon and Kissinger were determined that Vietnam should be handled in a way that maintained the credibility of U.S. security commitments worldwide.

The Thieu regime in South Vietnam clearly saw its core interest in retaining power by preventing a takeover by the powerful North and the Vietcong. From its viewpoint, this would require the withdrawal of North Vietnamese forces from the South and continued American military involvement at a significant level. This latter preference would conflict with the U.S. interest in its forces returning home. Yet, in a critical respect, Thieu's interests dovetailed with Kissinger's conviction that abandoning South Vietnam, an ally of the United States through four presidencies, both was wrong in itself and would irreparably damage U.S. prestige and credibility across the globe. Indeed, Kissinger emphasized the extent to which countries ranging from Germany and the NATO allies to Japan and South Korea depended for their security on belief in American promises.[38]

Kissinger was especially concerned that rapidly withdrawing from Vietnam and in effect abandoning Saigon would damage Chinese respect for American power. The prospect of countervailing American force was a major factor that led China, facing a threatening Soviet Union massing troops on its border, to seek rapprochement with the United States. "Peking had no interest in a demonstration that the United States was prepared to dump its friends," Kissinger stated; "in its long-range perspective of seeking a counterweight to the Soviet Union, Peking in fact had a stake in our reputation for reliability."[39]

North Vietnamese and Vietcong Interests

For decades, North Vietnamese and Vietcong interests had included expelling foreigners (Chinese, French, and then American) from Vietnamese territory. By the time Nixon and Kissinger took power, the prime interest of the North was to ensure the withdrawal of American forces, while leaving its own forces in position. In tandem with the Vietcong guerrillas, it sought to take over the remaining noncommunist parts of South Vietnam.

In its December 31, 1968, message, Hanoi called for the "replacement of . . . the 'Thieu-Ky-Huong' clique," the disparaging epithet by which the North Vietnamese regularly referred to South Vietnam's leadership.[40] At one point, North Vietnamese negotiator Le Duc Tho helpfully advised Kissinger that South Vietnamese president Thieu did not have to be removed publicly; it could be done secretly—for example, through assassination.[41]

The strength of the opposing North Vietnamese versus American interests on this issue, in overthrowing versus maintaining the Saigon government in the South, can be gauged from Kissinger's unequivocal declaration on this point. He stated that "our refusal to overthrow an allied government [in Saigon] remained the single and crucial issue that deadlocked all negotiation until October 8, 1972, when Hanoi withdrew the demand.[42] The North Vietnamese foreign minister explicitly and emphatically corroborated this point from his government's viewpoint.[43]

As later events underscored, the North wanted to impose a Communist form of government throughout the (unified) country. While a North Vietnamese and Vietcong victory would have pleased their Soviet and Chinese patrons, the Vietnamese combatants' focus was on Indochina, not mainly on the advance of global communism.

In this context, Nixon and Kissinger sought to negotiate an agreement with the North Vietnamese that would see all sides withdraw their forces from the South with the political future of the South determined peacefully by the key Vietnamese parties— and with American prisoners of war brought home. This had to be done in a manner that preserved the credibility of American foreign policy commitments. As should be evident even from this cursory examination of the interests of the major parties to the conflict, this would prove to be a tough sell.

As we launch into an analysis of the Vietnam talks, we step back briefly to emphasize a point that is basic to any effective negotiation: an accurate assessment of your interests. It drives the target agreement you seek to reach and often influences your strategy and tactics. If the assumptions underlying your interest assessment are deeply flawed, even a superb negotiation strategy and tactical brilliance cannot be truly successful. For purposes of the negotiation analysis that follows, we provisionally take as givens the American interests and target agreement as they were expressed at the time. Toward the end of this chapter, we revisit the assumptions underlying Kissinger's conception of the American interests at stake in this conflict.

Negotiations Begin

On December 20, 1968, soon after Richard Nixon's election, but before he took office, his incoming administration expressed readiness to negotiate.[44] While there were numerous detailed military and political issues, the essential questions involved the terms of a cease-fire and bombing halt, the extent and timing of North Vietnamese and American troop withdrawals from the South,[45] the fate of prisoners of war, and the basis for a settlement between Saigon and the Vietcong on the political future of the South. On May 14, 1969, in his first televised speech on Vietnam, Nixon presented an eight-point peace proposal, the central feature of which was a mutual pullout of each side's forces within a year (at least the "major portions" of U.S. and allied forces[46]).

The North Vietnamese and Vietcong remained steady with their ultimatum: all U.S. forces had to leave Vietnam, and the United States had to depose the South Vietnamese government, with which it was allied.[47] Nixon and Kissinger refused, judging that acceding to Hanoi's demands would not only betray an ally but also deal a severe blow to U.S. credibility worldwide, putting other crucial foreign policy objectives at risk.

While inconclusive public talks (among the Americans, the North and South Vietnamese, and the Vietcong) took place in Paris, Kissinger met and negotiated secretly with his North Vietnamese counterpart, Le Duc Tho. Kissinger judged that private talks could not be used for North Vietnamese propaganda and that any willingness to settle on the part of the North would more likely be revealed in secret talks.[48] (Later, and especially in chapter 13 we further explore the ramifications of secrecy in these and other negotiations.) Beginning on February 20, 1970, Kissinger and Tho met three times through April 4, 1970. During the last of these sessions, Kissinger proposed a mutual U.S.–North Vietnamese withdrawal from South Vietnam on a precise schedule over sixteen months.[49] Le Duc Tho turned down this proposal.

In March 1969, Nixon had ordered the launch of a U.S. secret bombing campaign against North Vietnamese sanctuaries and supply lines in Cambodia. On April 20, 1970, partly to shore up public support for the war, and in line with his campaign pledge to end the war, Nixon announced the withdrawal of one hundred fifty thousand Americans from Vietnam within a year. Ten days later, he announced a ground "incursion" into Cambodia, consisting of tens of thousands of American and South Vietnamese troops. With public revelation of this escalation into a formally neutral country, ongoing demonstrations against the war mounted to a tidal wave of protest that washed over the United States. At Ohio's Kent State University, on May 4, 1970, National Guardsmen shot and killed four unarmed protesting students, further convulsing the country. On May 8, almost a hundred thousand marchers converged on the White House.[50] Events and proposals moved more quickly. On June 24, the Senate repealed the Gulf of Tonkin Resolution, though the House did not follow suit.

Hanoi, unmoved by various American proposals during this period, continued to insist that the United States withdraw its forces and effect regime change in Saigon. During 1970, the war continued to rage, with more than 6,100 American deaths in Vietnam during that *single* year (and many times that number of Vietnamese war fatalities). For comparison, total American deaths in Iraq during the *seven* years between 2003 and 2010 were 4,424.[51]

Barriers to Agreement

Why were these talks stuck? From a realistic perspective (evaluating the deal/no-deal balance), it is hardly surprising that these negotiations and subsequent talks went nowhere for some time. Consider three related factors—we might call them barriers to agreement—influencing how North Vietnam weighed accepting American proposals relative to saying no, stonewalling, and continuing to fight:

1. In August 1965, 61 percent of Americans believed that the United States was right in sending troops to fight in Vietnam. That belief had dwindled to 41 percent by the time Lyndon Johnson announced on March 31, 1968, that he would not seek a second presidential term, due largely to the unpopular Vietnam War. By May 1971, this figure had dropped to 28 percent, meaning that 72 percent of the public thought that sending U.S. troops had been a mistake (although public support for Nixon's Vietnam policies were significantly higher).[52]

2. Domestic pressures rapidly mounted on the new Nixon administration to withdraw. Numerous public and congressional critics had been demanding prompt disengagement from Vietnam in return only for the release of American prisoners of war. On October 15, 1969, massive demonstrations took place around the country—twenty thousand strong in New York, thirty thousand in New Haven, and one hundred thousand in Boston (where a skywriting plane drew a huge peace sign overhead).[53] The Cambodian incursion in May 1970 triggered even more intense protests. In 1971, Congress passed seventy-two (nonbinding) resolutions demanding U.S. withdrawal.[54] These pressures continued to escalate, as did international condemnation of the U.S. role.

3. Responding to public opposition, protests, and Congressional actions—in large part to shore up public support for its Vietnam policies and given its campaign promise to extricate the United States from Vietnam—the Nixon administration unilaterally withdrew American forces at a strikingly

rapid pace. From approximately 536,000 American troops in Vietnam in 1968, when Nixon won the presidency, the total force level dropped by 70 percent, to about 157,000 troops by 1971, and to fewer than 25,000 in 1972.[55]

Given these factors, what incentive did a militarily confident Hanoi conceivably have to agree during those first years of negotiation, in light of its relatively appealing no-deal alternative: a fast-diminishing American military presence linked to mounting public and congressional opposition? The North Vietnamese, Kissinger observed, "coolly analyzed the withdrawal [of U.S. troops], weighing its psychological benefits to us in terms of enhanced staying power against the decline in military effectiveness represented by a shrinking number of American forces. Hanoi kept up incessant pressure for the largest possible withdrawal in the shortest possible time. The more automatic our withdrawal, the less useful it was as a bargaining weapon; [our] demand for mutual withdrawal grew hollow as our unilateral withdrawal accelerated."[56]

Given this situation, Le Duc Tho "tormented" Kissinger with the seemingly unanswerable military question: "Before, there were over a million U.S. and puppet [South Vietnamese] troops, and you failed. How can you succeed when you let the puppet troops do the fighting? Now, with only U.S. [air] support, how can you win?"[57] Kissinger's evaluation of the early years of the negotiation was bluntly realistic: the North Vietnamese would draw out the negotiations while seeking a military victory.[58]

Recall the September 1971 image of U.S. Army general Vernon Walters hearing Le Duc Tho say to Kissinger, "I really don't know why I am negotiating anything with you. I have just spent several hours with Senator [George] McGovern and your opposition will force you to give me what I want."[59]

Kissinger's assessment: "To them [the North Vietnamese] the

Paris talks were not a device for settlement but an instrument of political warfare. They were a weapon to exhaust us psychologically, to split us from our South Vietnamese ally, and to divide our public opinion through vague hints of solutions just out of reach because of the foolishness or obduracy of our government."[60] He concluded: "No negotiator, least of all the hard-boiled revolutionaries from Hanoi, will settle so long as he knows that his opposite number will be prevented from sticking to a position by constantly escalating domestic pressures."[61]

Figure 6.1 offers a highly simplified description of one core barrier to an acceptable agreement. In the figure, the two-headed arrow shows the direct U.S.–North Vietnamese negotiations; the single-headed arrows indicate one party exerting pressure on another, whether political, public relations, diplomatic, or military. The relative sizes of the two rounded figures to the right of "North Vietnam" suggest the fundamental and seemingly obvious implication: for Hanoi in 1970, "no" powerfully dominated "yes." If this observation is accurate, just what approaches to this negotiation might Kissinger (and Nixon) have adopted that could conceivably

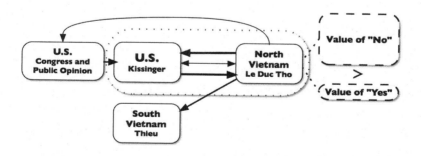

Figure 6.1: Fundamental Barrier, 1970–

North Vietnam Strongly Prefers "No" to "Yes"

Note: Two-headed arrows imply direct negotiations; single-headed arrows imply pressure

(political, PR, diplomatic, military).

have borne fruit in such unpromising circumstances, which we have characterized as "negotiating from a weak position"?

Along with President Nixon, Kissinger confronted three broad challenges as he sought to transform a North Vietnamese "no" into an acceptable "yes" that would end the war, at least for the United States:

- First, he would have to overcome unrelenting military efforts by the North Vietnamese and Vietcong to vanquish South Vietnam, persuading Hanoi that genuine negotiations leading to an acceptable deal were in its interest relative to no-deal options—despite the rapidly diminishing U.S. military presence.
- Second, he would somehow have to respond to increasingly insistent pressure from the Congress and domestic antiwar protesters to withdraw entirely and unilaterally from Indochina.
- Third, for any U.S.-Hanoi agreement short of the military victory the South Vietnamese fervently pursued, Kissinger would have to persuade a most reluctant South Vietnamese president Thieu to accept it.

In confronting these challenges, one can imagine trying different negotiation styles or venues. Would a cooperative or competitive orientation toward Le Duc Tho be best? Greater cultural understanding and sensitivity? An exquisitely tuned ability to listen to Tho, read his body language, or formulate genuinely creative options? Tune up the persuasiveness and charm of American rhetoric? Even listing these various tactical and process options should make clear how inadequate they would likely be in the face of the barriers to agreement we have identified. So, what might work?

Nixon and Kissinger's actions to surmount these barriers, to transform a weak hand into a stronger one, can be analyzed as a "negotiation campaign."[62] When we speak of a negotiation campaign, as we briefly did in analyzing the Rhodesian talks, we have in mind a *target agreement*—in this case, getting Le Duc Tho to say yes to an acceptable deal. (Although, if he did, further tough negotiations would be required with the South Vietnamese.) Mapping backward from that target "yes" will typically involve highlighting a required series of other agreements and actions on multiple fronts, thus maximizing, once those other agreements are in place, the chances of realizing the target agreement. As we will soon see, direct negotiations with Le Duc Tho (the North Vietnamese front) would be inadequate for success. Beyond these direct talks, Kissinger and Nixon changed the game by altering the parties, the issues, and the consequences of impasse. A simplified listing of these other campaign fronts that had been put in place by 1973 would include:[63] the military contest with the North Vietnamese and Vietcong that came to involve neighboring Cambodia and Laos; U.S. domestic and congressional opinion; the Chinese; the Soviet Union; West Germany and other European countries; and President Thieu of South Vietnam.

Yet, before analyzing this multifront negotiation campaign designed to strengthen an arguably weak hand, we pose a more basic question—especially in the face of such daunting barriers to agreement that had already claimed one president, convulsed the country, and led to militarily questionable withdrawals of U.S. forces. Instead of negotiating from this unpromising position in the hope of achieving a more ambitious deal, would it have been wiser for Kissinger and Nixon to have sought an earlier agreement (say, in 1969) that would simply have provided for the return of American prisoners of war and permitted a U.S. exit from the conflict?

This question is especially apt given that, scarcely two years after the Paris Peace Accords were signed in January 1973, South Vietnam fell to the North. Agreeing earlier to the same ultimate result would, to a first approximation, have saved many of the tens of thousands of lives lost between 1969 and 1973.[64] After analyzing the actual negotiations, we return to this pointed question toward the end of this chapter in a separate section entitled "Underlying Judgments: Why Not Simply Withdraw from Vietnam in 1969?"

Negotiating, Responding Militarily, and Seeking Domestic Support

Prior to our analysis of barriers to negotiated agreement, we recounted the Nixon administration's military and diplomatic actions through the May 1970 Cambodian "incursion" ("invasion" to critics). Both Nixon and Kissinger had become convinced that a strong military response to North Vietnam was required. In Kissinger's words, "An enemy determined on protracted struggle could only be brought to compromise by being confronted by insuperable obstacles on the ground."[65] In the language we've been using, to make a deal more appealing to Hanoi, military action was intended to make no-deal worse. However, if such actions were seen mainly as escalating and expanding the war, they would trigger powerful protests and cost vital domestic support.

Partly on the merits and partly to maintain adequate public backing for their Vietnam policies, Nixon and Kissinger pursued three related sets of actions. First, as we have indicated, they rapidly accelerated U.S. troop withdrawals. Second, as U.S. troops went home, the fighting shifted from American ground forces to the South Vietnamese army, increasingly backed by American air and naval power (which involved comparatively few Americans and did not "count" against troop ceilings). Dubbed "Vietnamization," this policy shift required a rapid increase in the size and training of South Vietnam's army.[66] Third, in seeking an acceptable negotiated outcome in Paris, the administration sought to "write an impeccable record of reasonableness."[67] This was intended to persuade both domestic and key foreign audiences that the United States was forthcoming in the negotiations while North Vietnam was intransigent. Being seen as flexible in negotiation would also make a tough U.S. military response more palatable if it were later required.

On September 7, 1970, in the secret Paris talks, Kissinger enhanced his earlier proposal (which Hanoi had rejected): the United States was now prepared to leave after a year (versus the prior offer of sixteen months) with no residual presence in South Vietnam (without residual forces, bases, or U.S. advisors, as the previous proposal had envisioned), provided that free and internationally supervised elections took place in the South.[68]

At first blush, this proposal might be seen as Kissinger making the Negotiation 101 mistake of "bidding against himself," as the North Vietnamese had not budged before he made a better offer. Yet two factors work against this interpretation. First, a critical objective in these negotiations was to establish for domestic and other audiences (when the American concessions became public) just how reasonable and forthcoming the United States had been relative to Hanoi. Second, the American position on the ground was steadily weakening as U.S. troops rapidly withdrew; the negotiating position reflected this reality—and both sides knew it.

On October 7, in a major television speech that was generally well received, Nixon proposed a "standstill" cease-fire across Indochina, including a bombing halt, until a broader agreement could be reached. Along with troop withdrawals and increasing Vietnamization, this speech was intended in part to open up more domestic political space for stronger military action against North Vietnam and the Vietcong, which both Kissinger and Nixon expected to be necessary. Referring only to the public negotiations in

Paris, Nixon positioned the United States as accommodating and persistent in seeking a negotiated settlement while accusing Hanoi of being unreasonable and uncompromising.[69] Nixon kept the Kissinger-Tho talks secret, hoping that this channel might prove more promising. The North Vietnamese quickly turned down his proposals.[70]

The United States took much more extensive steps to cut off the Vietcong insurgency's supply lines and sanctuaries in neighboring Cambodia and Laos. Hanoi had been using these routes and locations since the late 1950s to supply the Vietcong guerrillas and to attack and kill South Vietnamese and American troops.[71] As we've just described, following the secret bombing that started in March 1969, thousands of U.S. and South Vietnamese troops had invaded North Vietnamese sanctuaries in Cambodia in May 1970 (which led to massive U.S. antiwar demonstrations). In January 1971, U.S. fighter-bombers launched heavy airstrikes intended to hit North Vietnamese supply camps in Laos and Cambodia. During the first few months of that year, an all–South Vietnamese force, aided by American airpower, attacked North Vietnamese positions in Laos, taking very heavy casualties and calling into serious question the effectiveness of the Vietnamization program.[72]

In the context of the Vietnam War, Nixon and Kissinger, along with others, saw Cambodia in particular as a key front where the North Vietnamese had been massively involved for years, independent of American actions. The Americans regarded the ground invasions and bombing of Cambodian and Laotian sanctuaries as militarily necessary to starve the Vietcong insurgency of support and to reduce Vietcong attacks on American and South Vietnamese soldiers. Kissinger indicated that within weeks of the Nixon administration's taking office, "[t]he Vietnamese communists started an offensive that killed four to six hundred Americans a week, so that after a month we had lost more people in the Vietnamese offensive than we were to lose in 10 years of war in Afghanistan. Many of these casualties came from four North Vietnamese divisions that had occupied a part of Cambodian territory."[73] Kissinger and Nixon saw the Cambodian operations as signaling to the North Vietnamese and their patrons in Moscow and Beijing that the United States had the will and capacity to resist Hanoi.[74] As Kissinger argued more broadly, "We needed a strategy that made continuation of the war seem less attractive to Hanoi than a settlement."[75]

This military strategy triggered extensive domestic protests about U.S. military moves in Cambodia and Laos. Critics condemned these sometimes secret actions as militarily ineffective, democratically illegitimate, and representing an unjustified expansion of the war into neutral countries with dire long-term consequences for the region. (We revisit these critiques in a separate section toward the end of this chapter, when we explicitly examine the effectiveness and ethics of imposing costs, especially the use of force, as a means of inducing agreement in negotiation.)

In the meantime, American troop withdrawals continued. The last U.S. Marine combat units left Vietnam in April 1971, ending major marine participation in the war. In the ensuing period, Kissinger offered a series of increasingly significant concessions. While previous offers envisioned a mutual U.S.–North Vietnamese withdrawal from South Vietnam, Kissinger told Le Duc Tho on May 31, 1971, that the United States was prepared to withdraw unilaterally in return for an end to North Vietnamese infiltration of Cambodia and Laos, which at least implicitly meant leaving intact the existing Vietcong and regular North Vietnamese formations in the South.[76] On August 16, he offered to withdraw U.S. troops at the same time as the prisoners were released, as long as this did not involve the United States removing Saigon's government on the way out.[77] Hanoi continued to say no.

Henry Kissinger had developed a more granular view of his consistently intransigent North Vietnamese counterpart. In later reflections, he observed that "Le Duc Tho's profession was revolution, his vocation guerrilla warfare. He could speak eloquently of peace but it was an abstraction alien to any personal experience. He had spent ten years of his life in prisons under the French. In 1973 he showed me around an historical museum in Hanoi, which he admitted sheepishly he had never visited previously."[78]

Kissinger's assessment of Le Duc Tho and the North Vietnamese leadership he represented had straightforward implications for the negotiation approach that had a chance of succeeding: "I grew to understand that Le Duc Tho considered negotiations as another battle. Any settlement that deprived Hanoi of final victory was by definition in his eyes a ruse. He was there to wear me down. As the representative of the truth[,] he had no category for compromise. Hanoi's proposals were put forward as the sole "logical and reasonable" for negotiations. . . . As a spokesman for the 'truth,' Le Duc Tho had no category for our method of negotiating; trading concessions seemed to him immoral unless a superior necessity supervened, and until that happened he was prepared to wait us out indefinitely. He seemed concerned to rank favorably in the epic pantheon of Vietnamese struggles; he could not consider as an equal this barbarian from across the sea who thought that eloquent words were a means to deflect the inexorable march of history."[79]

Of course, whether it was personality or ideology that induced Le Duc Tho toward intransigence, it was also a plain fact that a North Vietnamese waiting game seemed likely to pay off given the steadily weakening American position.

As 1972 approached, however, a number of signs pointed toward a major North Vietnamese offensive that was taking shape against the South. Especially in view of his assessment of Le Duc

Tho and the Hanoi regime behind him, Kissinger argued that such an offensive must be blunted in order for him to make progress in the Paris talks: "In the final analysis we cannot expect the enemy to negotiate seriously with us until he is convinced nothing can be gained by continuing the war."[80]

Nixon and Kissinger sought to further prepare the diplomatic and domestic ground for the powerful U.S. military response (primarily via airpower) that they felt would be necessary to complement the South Vietnamese ground defense.[81] To accomplish this, Nixon felt that he needed to greatly strengthen his administration's public record of reasonableness in negotiations and to bring home more soldiers. Although a reduced U.S. force would be less effective in thwarting a North Vietnamese offensive, and would certainly diminish Kissinger's bargaining leverage, Nixon continued to withdraw American troops, bringing the level down to 156,800 soldiers by the end of 1971 (from half a million only two years prior—and that total would rapidly fall to fewer than 25,000 by year's end 1972).

At the same time, to strengthen the U.S. military posture even as troops were being withdrawn, Kissinger noted that "by early March, with a decisive [North Vietnamese] offensive clearly approaching, we found ourselves in the anomalous position of augmenting with forces that did not count against the troop ceiling—B-52s, aircraft carriers—while continuing the promised withdrawals of ground troops and planning the announcement of the next round of withdrawals, which would be expected about May 1."[82]

In a January 25, 1972, address to the nation, President Nixon for the first time revealed the secret talks between Kissinger and Le Duc Tho, publicizing an eight-point peace plan. Disclosure of these talks was not unanticipated by Kissinger, who later wrote, "To be sure, our exchanges with the North Vietnamese were secret. But I always conducted them with their ultimate public impact in mind. If pressed too far, we had the option to disclose them."[83] After criticizing Hanoi for earlier rejecting the increasingly forthcoming American peace proposals, Nixon offered to withdraw the balance of U.S. troops within six months.[84] However, he once again refused to overthrow the government in Saigon.[85]

Kissinger shared the text of Nixon's January 25 speech with Moscow and Beijing, warning that U.S. patience with North Vietnam was running low.[86] As expected, Hanoi launched a major Spring Offensive on March 30, 1972, employing as many as two hundred thousand troops in an all-out effort to vanquish South Vietnam, largely by conventional rather than guerrilla forces.

In Nixon and Kissinger's view, this represented one last (massive) throw of the dice by North Vietnam. In Kissinger's words, "Now, as before, we were given only one way out of the war [in the Paris negotiations]—to dismantle our ally and withdraw unconditionally. We had rejected surrender at the conference table; we would refuse it on the battlefield."[87] He continued: "I had reckoned all along that Hanoi's offensive would culminate in a serious negotiation, whatever happened. If Hanoi were to prevail on the battlefield, Nixon would be forced to settle on Hanoi's terms; if the offensive were halted and the probable Democratic candidate, Senator George McGovern, looked as if he was winning the election, Hanoi would wait; it would gamble on the extremely favorable terms he was offering. . . . If the offensive were blunted and Nixon looked like the probable winner, Hanoi would make a major effort to settle with us."[88]

Nixon and Kissinger decided to respond forcefully to the huge Spring Offensive, by mining North Vietnam's Haiphong harbor, thus depriving Hanoi of Soviet military supplies (especially oil) that arrived by sea. They also undertook a massive bombing campaign both of North Vietnamese forces and in North Vietnam, especially of the roads and rail lines from China, which would be the preferred alternative route for supplies.[89] As the fierce fighting in the South subsided, it appeared that North Vietnam suffered more than one hundred thousand casualties and lost more than half its tanks and heavy artillery. It would take more than three years for it to regroup for its next major conventional assault on the South (which took place *after* the Peace Accords and succeeded in conquering the South).[90] Yet, as the broader failure of its Spring Offensive sank in, Hanoi began to soften its stance in the talks.[91]

This U.S. campaign of bombing and mining generated major protests in the United States. Still, contrary to widespread later impressions, careful tracking of polls measuring overall public support for Nixon's Vietnam policies shows this support starting to climb steadily from the 1972 Spring Offensive onward. At that time, support for Nixon's policies stood at about 50 percent, then climbed through the signing of the Paris Peace Accords, when that figure approached 80 percent.[92] In part, the positive public reaction was informed by two historic and widely popular U.S. diplomatic initiatives (except among many conservatives) that sandwiched North Vietnam's Spring Offensive (launched March 1972) between President Nixon's highly publicized trip to China to meet with Mao Zedong and Zhou Enlai (February 21–28) and his high-profile summit in Moscow with Leonid Brezhnev (May 22–30).

Thus far we have discussed Kissinger's campaign for "yes" from Hanoi in terms of direct negotiation with the North Vietnamese, the use of force, and moves to manage strenuous domestic and congressional opposition (including troop withdrawals and seeming reasonableness in the Paris talks). Yet the negotiations, from an American point of view, were still stuck, though the North Vietnamese position showed signs of softening after the North's costly 1972 offensive. How else might Kissinger strengthen his position in these talks by raising the cost of impasse to Hanoi?

Beyond direct military action to counter the North Vietnamese offensive, Nixon and Kissinger had consistently been seeking new sources of pressure on Hanoi in Paris. Specifically, they attempted to reduce or eliminate at least some of the significant diplomatic and military support for North Vietnam that Moscow and Beijing had provided. To do so, Nixon and Kissinger had consciously linked U.S. policy in Vietnam to the developing détente with Moscow and the nascent rapprochement with Beijing—which represented two additional "fronts" in the negotiation campaign. Indeed, focusing well beyond the U.S.-Hanoi "table," Kissinger consistently stressed the priority the United States attached to obtaining Soviet and Chinese help with the Vietnam negotiations. "Every statement [we made]," Kissinger declared, "was part of an effort to persuade Moscow and Peking to acquiesce in our course and thus to move Hanoi, by isolating it, to meaningful negotiations."[93]

Seeking Chinese Assistance on Vietnam

From early in the Nixon administration, Kissinger had sought better relations and an arms control agreement with the USSR. While professing interest, however, the Soviets appeared to be going slow, even stalling progress, perhaps hoping that American eagerness would produce concessions. Yet, soon after coming into office, President Nixon and Kissinger acted on a historic opportunity to explore positive relations with Beijing, hoping to overcome the U.S.-Chinese mutual hostility of the preceding years.[94] Not only did better relations with China promise independent benefits for the United States, but the prospect of a closer U.S.-Chinese relationship would likely prod the Soviets into a more forthcoming approach with the United States (discussed at length in the next chapter).

This dynamic would capitalize on the deteriorating Sino–Soviet relationship, which had continued to sour since the mid-1960s, with the Soviets increasing troop numbers from twelve to forty divisions along the Sino–Soviet border.[95] Not only had the rhetoric between Moscow and Beijing become more strident, but serious border clashes had broken out along the Ussuri River in 1969, with dozens killed and perhaps hundreds of casualties on each side.[96]

We pause for a moment to reflect on the role that luck can play in negotiation—if the potential of an unexpected opportunity is recognized and developed. Kissinger explains: "[B]y March 1969, Chinese-American relations seemed essentially frozen in the same hostility of mutual incomprehension and distrust that had characterized them for twenty years. The new Administration had a notion, but not yet a strategy, to move toward China. *Policy emerges when concept encounters opportunity.* Such an occasion arose when Soviet and Chinese troops clashed in the frozen Siberian tundra along a river of which none of us had ever heard. From then on ambiguity vanished, and we moved without further hesitation toward a momentous change in global diplomacy [emphasis added]."[97]

To move forward, it was important to signal to a suspicious China that the United States had a genuine interest in better relations. At a National Security Council meeting in August 1969, Nixon expressed the view that, given the tense circumstances between the two Communist giants, the Soviet Union was the more dangerous party and it would be against U.S. interests for China to be "smashed" in a Soviet-Chinese war. Kissinger underscored the significance of this shift: "It was a revolutionary moment in U.S. foreign policy: an American President declared that we had a strategic interest in the survival of a major communist country with which we had had no meaningful contact for twenty years and against which we had fought a war and engaged in two military confrontations."[98]

Nixon and Kissinger made a major decision to the effect that, in a Sino-Soviet conflict, the United States would adopt a posture of neutrality but "tilt to the greatest extent possible toward China."[99] Various U.S. officials conveyed versions of this message in different forums. These moves were intended to dispel Mao's fears that the United States would cooperate with the USSR against China.

Even as the United States began to interact directly with Beijing—Kissinger's first secret visit took place in July 1971 and Nixon's initial state visit in February 1972—Kissinger needed to confirm that China's close links to North Vietnam would not preclude a U.S.-Chinese rapprochement. As the relationship developed, Kissinger went further: he increasingly made clear to his Chinese interlocutors that U.S.-Chinese strategic cooperation was partially linked to China's assistance in reining in its North Vietnamese client, a point that was not lost on the Chinese. During the first meeting between Zhou Enlai and Kissinger, Zhou remarked of North Vietnam, "[W]e still feel a deep and full sympathy for them." Kissinger noted afterward, "Sympathy, of course, was not the same as political or military support; it was a delicate way to convey that China would not become involved militarily or press us diplomatically."[100]

This Chinese shift shook Hanoi. In an interview, Nguyen Co Thach, an aide to Le Duc Tho during the Paris talks and later North Vietnam's foreign minister, strikingly characterized Chinese support of his country after Kissinger's July 1971 trip to the Middle Kingdom: "I must say that we have realized that step by step they have reduced their support. And in '71 we see that it is a turning point. It is not only to reduce aid, but *it is a betrayal . . .* after the visit of Kissinger, they advised us to accept the position of the USA. So, we see that it was . . . *betrayal* [emphasis added]."[101]

Nixon and Kissinger judged that negotiating better U.S.-

Chinese relations would be intrinsically worthwhile, independent of any consequences for the Vietnam talks. Yet American diplomacy with China had three direct and indirect effects on efforts to negotiate a settlement to the Vietnam conflict. First, unlike with the Korean War, in which Chinese troops directly fought American forces, China gave tacit (and true) assurances to Kissinger that its forces would not have a combat role in Vietnam. Second, to an extent that is still debated but that certainly mattered, China moderated its material support for Hanoi and helped isolate North Vietnam diplomatically.[102] Third, the threat of a developing U.S.-China axis led the Soviets to moderate their support for Hanoi.

Seeking Soviet Assistance on Vietnam

Kissinger had earlier sought to reduce U.S.-Soviet tensions through a policy of détente. While somewhat receptive, the Soviets had been playing hard to get. The surprise opening to China apparently jolted Moscow and worried the Kremlin about a possible U.S.-China alignment. Building on the developing American rapprochement with China, Kissinger turned to the Soviet front with renewed emphasis. Results were not long in coming. Kissinger noted that "Prior to my secret trip to China, Moscow had been stalling for over a year on arrangements for a summit between Brezhnev and Nixon . . . [T]hen, within a month of my visit to Beijing, the Kremlin reversed itself and invited Nixon to Moscow."[103]

In this new situation, Kissinger sought to persuade the Kremlin to sharply reduce its diplomatic and military support for North Vietnam, in part by threatening Moscow with abandoning détente and risking its potential benefits.[104] Kissinger calculated that the prospect of deeper détente had already built up the Soviet "stake" in the USSR's bilateral relationship with the United States—which,

Kissinger recognized, Moscow cultivated in part to counterbalance the burgeoning U.S. relationship with China. That improvement had whetted Moscow's appetite for further progress.[105]

Opening a German Front to Induce Further Soviet Pressure on Hanoi

Yet how might this Soviet appetite for enhanced trade be useful with respect both to Vietnam and to the Strategic Arms Limitation Talks, or SALT? Kissinger saw a potential source of U.S. leverage in the United States' ability to offer, or block, progress toward resolving the long-simmering dispute between the Soviets and the Western Allies over wartime claims and the status of Germany. This dispute had hampered Soviet efforts to expand valuable trade and diplomatic efforts, especially with Western Europe.[106] Hence, Kissinger envisioned yet another front, this time a German one, in the campaign to persuade Moscow to lean on North Vietnam in its Paris talks with the United States.

The essential background: in 1969, West German prime minister Willy Brandt had begun an intensive effort (*Ostpolitik*), largely independent of Washington, to break the Cold War impasse with the Soviets that had persisted for years. Brandt proposed a series of treaties to reduce tensions with the USSR by opening trade agreements, resolving disputed territorial claims, and clarifying military arrangements. His initiative was motivated largely by his goal of keeping alive the dream of a unified German state (through engendering Soviet flexibility on this issue).

Brandt's *Ostpolitik* would earn him the Nobel Peace Prize, but Washington had been deeply concerned that this policy might lead toward a neutral, possibly nationalist Germany. Now Kissinger realized that, in order to gain U.S. leverage on Vietnam (and arms control), it might be an opportune time to carefully soften American reservations about Brandt's *Ostpolitik*, which the Soviets had eagerly sought to advance.

A tangible opportunity for such leverage flowed from the so-called Eastern treaties, which would help Moscow relax its tensions with West Germany and, more broadly, Western Europe.[107] Under the Eastern treaties championed by Brandt (notably, the 1970 Treaty of Moscow between West Germany and the USSR), the signatories would normalize relations and renounce the use of military force. While West Germany and the USSR signed the Moscow treaty on August 12, 1970, Germany had not yet ratified it. Given Brandt's somewhat shaky political situation, Moscow sought U.S. help in pressing Bonn for prompt ratification (which Kissinger linked to a separate deal on Berlin).[108] In a preparatory decision memo, Kissinger's top staff explicitly raised the option of using these issues to obtain Soviet help with the Vietnam talks.[109]

Privately, Kissinger doubted how effectively the United States could be in intervening in West Germany's domestic politics. Nevertheless, seeking leverage that could lead to Soviet help on Vietnam, he took advantage of Moscow's assumption that American support was crucial to achieving German ratification. According to the U.S. State Department Office of the Historian, shortly after Kissinger's meeting with Brezhnev, Kissinger reported back to Nixon, " 'Brezhnev and his colleagues displayed obvious uneasiness over the outcome of the German treaties,' he reported, 'and made repeated pitches for our direct intervention. The results of Sunday's election and the FDP defection have heightened their concern, and the situation gives us leverage. I made no commitment to bail them out . . . We will see to it that we give them no help on this matter so long as they don't help on Vietnam.' "[110]

Beyond the China factor, economic considerations offered

Kissinger considerable potential leverage. From the time of Soviet premier Alexei Kosygin through Leonid Brezhnev, increased trade with the United States in particular and the West in general became a major Soviet objective, both to boost the USSR's sagging economy and to close a widening technological gap. A number of economists and security analysts have traced the evolution of this priority; drawing on their work, one summary concludes that "Western trade was emerging as the panacea for Brezhnev's problems: it would revitalize the economy, allowing it to compete with [the] West; and it would do so without requiring a fundamental restructuring of the economy."[111] During 1971 and 1972, an increasing number of large trade deals (e.g., grain, trucks) between the two countries were inked, and Most Favored Nation trading status was promised to the Soviet Union, along with extensive trade credits. If détente could be made irreversible, expectations were for this trend in trade to accelerate. Soviet academic and theoretical institutes as well as the Central Committee endorsed the value of this development. Brezhnev stressed its importance in his visits to America and West Germany. He was "staking the success of his revitalization program" on stable U.S.-Soviet relations and making détente "irreversible."[112]

During a conversation with Soviet ambassador Anatoly Dobrynin, Kissinger accused Moscow of "complicity" in Hanoi's March 1972 offensive against South Vietnam, and stated explicitly that Soviet support for North Vietnam now posed grave difficulties for Washington to cooperate with Moscow on the Eastern treaties.[113] Lest the Soviets fail to get the seriousness of this message, Kissinger communicated the same point to Egon Bahr, Brandt's advisor, with the expectation that Bahr would pass the message to the Soviet ambassador in Bonn.[114]

With respect to the talks in Paris over Vietnam, Nixon's public revelations about American negotiating flexibility and major concessions had pointedly contrasted with North Vietnamese intransigence. This was not lost on the Soviets. On May 8, Nixon had publicly offered the North Vietnamese the most generous terms so far (while still mining the Haiphong harbor and bombing transportation links to China in response to the North Vietnamese Spring Offensive). As Kissinger described it, Nixon's proposal offered "a standstill cease-fire, release of prisoners, and total American withdrawal within four months. The deadline for withdrawal was the shortest ever. The offer of a standstill cease-fire implied that American bombing would stop and that Hanoi could keep all the gains made in its offensive. We were pledged to withdraw totally in return for a cease-fire and return of our prisoners."[115]

Kissinger used the impending May 1972 Soviet-American presidential summit in Moscow (which would include the signing of the SALT agreement) as another forcing point. Though warning Moscow about its support for Hanoi, Kissinger explicitly emphasized to the Soviet leader a major American concession he had been signaling to Le Duc Tho: the United States would not demand a complete withdrawal of the regular North Vietnamese forces from South Vietnam in return for the North Vietnamese relinquishing their demand for the Americans to forcibly remove Thieu from power.[116]

During a presummit meeting with Soviet leader Leonid Brezhnev in Moscow, Kissinger pointedly complained about the continued stalling tactics by the North Vietnamese and ended with a stern warning: "If this process is maintained we will act unilaterally at whatever risk to whatever relationship."[117] At one point, Kissinger told Soviet ambassador Dobrynin that "the Soviets had put themselves into the position where a miserable little country [North Vietnam] could jeopardize everything that had been negotiated for years."[118] Despite the tough talk, Kissinger himself did not think that Moscow could "halt the war by *ukase* [edict], or be expected to turn openly against its ally [North Vietnam]." But Moscow's acquiescence could "ease our job."[119]

On the Soviet diplomatic front, however, major progress was made. While rhetorically condemning U.S. policy in Vietnam, the Soviets did not meaningfully act in response to the massive American bombing and mining during the Spring Offensive. The Moscow Summit took place, the SALT I treaty was signed, and the USSR assumed a more restrained public posture vis-à-vis Hanoi. The absence of a significant Soviet reaction to the major American escalation in Vietnam (e.g., the summit, SALT), a real concern to many American officials, offers a measure of Kissinger's success in his efforts to boost the importance to the Soviets of their relationship with the United States relative to their commitment to North Vietnam.

The extent of Soviet pressure on North Vietnam has been the subject of debate, but it was certainly a factor in Hanoi's calculations. For example, Marvin and Bernard Kalb offered a relatively positive assessment: "On June 15 [1972], [Soviet] President Podgorny flew to Hanoi. The North Vietnamese, feeling betrayed by Russia's hospitality to Nixon, were nevertheless dependent on Moscow as the chief supplier of their war matériel, and they listened carefully to Podgorny's message. It was simple but fundamental: he suggested it was time to switch tactics, time for serious negotiations with the United States. The risk, he argued, would not be critical; after all, Nixon seemed serious about withdrawing, and the new U.S. position no longer demanded a North Vietnamese troop pullout from the [S]outh. . . . It was a new vocabulary for the Russians—the first time they had so openly committed their prestige to a resumption of negotiations. It clearly reflected the Soviet conclusion that the advantages of dealing with Washington on such matters as trade, credits, and

SALT were important enough for Moscow to lend Nixon a hand in settling the Vietnam War."[120]

In contrast to the Kalbs, others, such as Winston Lord (who participated in the Moscow, Beijing, and Hanoi talks with Kissinger), judged the effects of Soviet pressure on the North to be more psychological than material.[121] And as just noted, Kissinger himself expected Soviet pressure to be helpful, but not decisive, in the Paris talks.

It is hard to sort out whether Soviet pressure on Hanoi resulted from the U.S. opening to China, American actions on the Soviet-German front, or the broader risk to the Soviets that benefits of détente would be lost. Opinions vary, but the implication is similar: the Kremlin, mindful of its developing relationship with America, exerted some pressure on North Vietnam to settle. For example, in the view of Georgy Arbatov, a leading Soviet expert on American politics who advised five general secretaries of the Soviet Union, "Kissinger thinks it was China that played the decisive role in getting us to feel the need to preserve our relationship with the U.S.A." Arbatov reflected, "But Berlin actually played a much bigger role, almost a decisive one. Having the East German situation settled was most important to us, and we did not want to jeopardize that."[122]

Independent of the magnitude of pressure on Hanoi that resulted from Kissinger's actions away from the table in Beijing, Moscow, and Berlin, we pause to note how these rather creative moves were designed to improve the fairly weak hand that Kissinger was originally dealt. As game-changing moves (relative to purely at-the-table tactics in Paris), they opened new fronts in Kissinger's negotiation campaign. The extent to which his actions on these new fronts actually furthered American objectives at the table (for which the evidence is mixed) stands as an important related question.

Breakthrough in the Paris Talks

The combination of U.S. actions on multiple fronts (blunting Hanoi's Spring Offensive on the ground and with the bombing and mining of the North; securing Chinese agreement to moderate China's support for North Vietnam; inducing greater Soviet cooperation as a function of the U.S.–China initiative and linked German-Soviet talks) appeared to produce the result in the Paris talks that Kissinger deemed essential. On October 8, 1972, Le Duc Tho dropped North Vietnam's long-standing demand for the United States to force regime change in Saigon as a condition for the deal. The provisional agreement included a cease-fire, the withdrawal of American forces, cessation of North Vietnamese infiltration of South Vietnam from Laos and Cambodia, and the release of the American prisoners of war.[123] Kissinger and his associates were privately jubilant at what finally appeared to be the breakthrough they had sought. Kissinger reflected, "I turned to Winston [Lord] and said 'we've done it' and shook hands with him. So it was a great moment."[124]

Persuading South Vietnamese President Thieu to Agree

Expecting a turning point in the negotiations, Kissinger had kept in contact with President Nguyen Van Thieu in Saigon.[125] He had not, however, revealed the full extent of American concessions to Hanoi. He indicated that Thieu "had authorized such secret talks" and that he "was kept thoroughly briefed on my secret negotiations from the beginning."[126] How fully Thieu was informed or consulted is a matter of considerable disagreement.[127] In any case, Alexander Haig, Kissinger's military assistant, briefed Thieu in

Saigon on August 17 on the emerging agreement and gave him a letter of reassurance from Nixon, who pledged continued support for Saigon after the war.[128] Still, it was not clear whether the South Vietnamese leader would eventually accept the agreement. In fact, Thieu was adamant in his opposition.

Almost immediately, persuading President Thieu (using both threats and assurances) to accept the negotiated outcome became Kissinger's top priority. The threats, delivered orally and in writing, centered on the possibility of the complete cutoff of American aid in case Saigon refused to go along with the negotiated framework.[129] Along with the threats, Kissinger frequently communicated Nixon's assurances, which revolved around the president's stated determination to stand by its ally in Saigon in response to violations of the agreement by the North Vietnamese.[130]

Reelected to the presidency in a November 1972 landslide against the antiwar candidate George McGovern, Nixon saw his rising political standing seem to enhance the credibility of these promises and threats. With the election, he appeared to enjoy a significant popular mandate.[131] "Our thinking," Kissinger remembered, "was that the agreement could be preserved unless the North Vietnamese launched another all-out offensive, in which case we believed that a combination of American air power and existing South Vietnamese ground forces could repeat the experience of '72 [the successful military response by South Vietnamese forces and American airpower to the spring 1972 North Vietnamese offensive]."[132]

From early October until mid–November 1972, Thieu artfully postponed his acceptance of the agreement, requesting a number of changes.[133] In Kissinger's view, it was becoming increasingly clear that Saigon was not interested in *any* negotiated compromise, but, understandably, in keeping a major U.S. military presence in the South and ensuring a total victory over Hanoi.[134]

This apparent revelation of Thieu's deeper interests and fundamental opposition may have surfaced only late in the process for Kissinger, but the latter may well have earlier sensed South Vietnam's fundamental reluctance to accept an agreement that involved American withdrawal. Perhaps this was a factor in setting up the secret negotiations that, unlike the public ones, did *not* include Saigon. The North Vietnamese certainly expected Thieu to block any progress in the talks. As former North Vietnamese foreign minister Thach indicated, his government "decided to accept the secret talks because we see that the official one in the Kléber Avenue could not lead to the settlement. Because there is the Thieu government there. And we think that the problem of South Vietnam, or Vietnam War, could be settled only between USA and Vietnam. . . . [T]he Thieu government[,] they would like to drag on the war and to have American troops in South Vietnam. And . . . the Nixon government would like to withdraw. So there are contradictions. And it could not help the settlement with the presence of the Thieu government."[135]

Nonetheless, Kissinger negotiated with Le Duc Tho from November 20 to 25 and from December 4 to 13, in order to achieve the changes Thieu sought.[136] Le Duc Tho dragged out the negotiations without any substantive shifts.[137] To force Hanoi's hand and help persuade Thieu of American resolve to settle the war and enforce an agreement, Kissinger and Nixon decided on a short but powerful military response: the United States again mined the Haiphong harbor and, from December 18 to 29, heavily bombed North Vietnam. While "monstrously brutal" and a "Stone Age tactic," in the words of its critics, this operation arguably achieved its objectives, though the image of a giant lashing out against a smaller nation cost the United States dearly in terms of national and global opinion.[138] The same day that this "Christmas Bombing" began, Washington proposed renewed negotiations amid intensified war protests at home. Kissinger met Tho on January 8 to urge that he accept the agreement; they finally negotiated a series of relatively modest changes.[139] From January 14 to 21, there were final efforts, including both promises and harsh American threats, to persuade a deeply reluctant Thieu to sign the accord, which he did, and that came into effect on January 27, 1973.[140]

The Aftermath

Hanoi proceeded "immediately and grossly" to violate the Paris Peace Accords, continuing the infiltration and attacks against South Vietnam.[141] (And the case can be made that South Vietnam also violated the agreement.[142]) Years later, Kissinger reflected: "[H]ad Nixon stayed in office, we would surely have attacked their [North Vietnamese] supply lines [through Cambodia and Laos]."[143] Instead, the United States responded with focused but very limited bombing campaigns on March 22–23 and April 16–17, 1973. However, it was clear to Kissinger that President Nixon was too preoccupied by the Watergate scandal to react as forcefully as he had previously done.

Amid Watergate investigations and with the American public largely sick of the seemingly endless involvement in Vietnam, Congress voted in June 1973 to prohibit further U.S. military involvement in Indochina after August 15.[144] Kissinger lamented that the "stick of bombing was lost by our own domestic incapacity. . . . [T]he 'window' we had in those few months of early 1973 [before the June cutoff] was closed by Watergate's enfeeblements."[145]

Blaming the U.S. failure to enforce the deal on a feckless congress neglects the power of public opinion. Even absent the loss of presidential authority due to Watergate, it is doubtful that the public would have supported actions to enforce the Paris Agreement (which, of course, would have influenced the congress). After the

Agreement was signed in January 1973, a Gallup poll reported that an overwhelming 79 percent of the public opposed the reintervention of American military troops in Vietnam even "if North Vietnam were to try to take over South Vietnam."[146]

On September 22, 1973, Kissinger was sworn in as the fifty-sixth secretary of state of the United States, and on October 16, 1973, he and Le Duc Tho were awarded the Nobel Peace Prize for the negotiation of the Paris Peace Accords. Le Duc Tho refused to accept the prize. Kissinger donated the monetary proceeds of the award to a scholarship fund for the children of American soldiers killed or missing in Vietnam, and later sought, unsuccessfully, to return the prize.

Amid Watergate, Nixon resigned in August 1974—the first U.S. president to do so. Three years after its thwarted spring 1972 offensive, North Vietnam conquered South Vietnam on April 30, 1975. After the last U.S. and South Vietnamese personnel were helicoptered out of Saigon, Kissinger lamented that "only a feeling of emptiness remained."[147] According to Alistair Horne, one of Kissinger's biographers, the failure in Vietnam is "the outstanding disappointment of his [Kissinger's] life—a source of never-ending regret."[148] "It was, to me," Kissinger reflected, "the saddest point in my governmental experience."[149]

The Negotiation Campaign as a Whole

The negotiation campaign failed in its broader aims, leaving South Vietnam to years of brutality as the North Vietnamese unified the country following the collapse of the Thieu regime. The negotiations did, however, serve to largely end U.S. involvement in the war. And this episode vividly illustrates the inherent inseparability of tactics "at the table" and game-changing negotiation moves "away from the table."

For purposes of analyzing Kissinger's overall approach to negotiation, this case complements the *strategic* and *realistic* aspects we have developed thus far. In the last chapter, we stress how a realistic negotiator constantly monitors the deal/no-deal balance. For example, there came a point in the Israeli–Jordanian negotiations (discussed in the previous chapter) when it was clear that this balance would remain adverse. Given that assessment, Kissinger abandoned those talks and focused elsewhere; a similar point occurred in the talks over Pakistan's nuclear program. As we have demonstrated in this chapter, the Vietnam negotiations looked almost hopeless during their first years, when Hanoi clearly saw rejecting any American proposal as preferable to accepting it. For Hanoi, "no" dominated "yes," and Kissinger had few cards to play at that stage.

Making sense of the actions and underlying principles by which he arguably strengthened his hand has occupied this chapter (although the South Vietnamese and Americans were certainly the losers in the longer term). In doing so, we have illustrated the next steps beyond tracking and assessing the deal/no-deal balance. If this balance appears adverse, reaching agreement requires that a negotiator act, often away from the table, to tilt the balance to support a "yes." This is possible only by worsening the consequences of no-deal and/or enhancing the value of a deal. When doing so entails altering the parties, issues, or consequences of impasse, we say that the "game has been changed." As illustrated in this chapter, had one focused exclusively on Kissinger and Le Duc Tho in Paris, proclaiming that to be "the negotiation," one would have missed the essence of the negotiating strategy.

In confronting what he regarded as an intransigent North Vietnam, Kissinger looked across the larger context to discern possible links and connections, the "panoply of pressures and incentives," that might enable him to tilt Hanoi away from "no" and toward "yes." He did so via what we have called a multifront negotiation

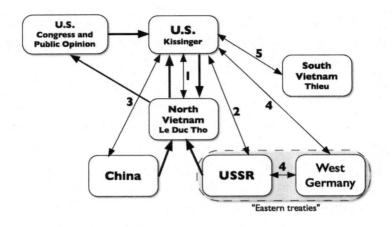

Figure 6.2: Negotiation Campaign v. North Vietnam

Note: *Two-headed arrows imply direct negotiations; single-headed arrows imply pressure (political, PR, diplomatic, military).*

campaign. Figure 6.2 offers a simplified schematic of this campaign. For Kissinger, the primary front was North Vietnam, with the negotiations (indicated by the "1" and the double-headed arrow) heavily conditioned by the military situation and by U.S. domestic and congressional opinion (which itself was influenced by the state of the war and by North Vietnam—represented by the single-headed arrows).

Meanwhile, Kissinger opened an initially unrelated second negotiation front ("2" in Figure 6.2) with the Soviets, in an effort to advance détente and arms control. With slow progress, apparently stalled by Moscow, and with the Chinese perceiving an acute Soviet threat, Kissinger opened up a third negotiation front ("3" in Figure 6.2) with China. As the Chinese came to see more value in a relationship with the United States, they confirmed that they would not intervene on behalf of North Vietnam and would help press their client toward a more forthcoming negotiating stance.

As these events proceeded, the Soviets became acutely concerned about the developing U.S.-Chinese axis and, independently saw greater benefits in improved relations with the United States. Kissinger then forged a fourth negotiation front ("4" in Figure 6.2), involving West Germany and the "Eastern treaties," a front the USSR eagerly sought but that the United States could appear either to foster or frustrate.

Kissinger sought to translate the growing Soviet interests ("stakes" he often called them) in better relations with the United States, magnified by the Chinese and German negotiations, into Soviet pressure on North Vietnam to be more reasonable in the Paris talks. As Kissinger not so subtly warned, it would be a shame if that "miserable little country" [North Vietnam] were to block the potential value to the Soviets of the better relations with the United States that were being negotiated in many forums.

Note the importance, to multiple fronts, of the public perception that Kissinger and Nixon sought to foster: that in Paris, the United States was relatively reasonable and forthcoming with the North Vietnamese (e.g., accelerating offers to withdraw troops and reduced insistence on mutual withdrawal of North Vietnamese forces from the South), while Hanoi remained stubborn and unyielding. With respect to the U.S. domestic and congressional fronts, this perception, if genuinely held, would have made strong U.S. military responses to North Vietnamese offensives seem more justified and less politically costly (although these military responses still generated enormous domestic protests). Relative U.S. negotiating flexibility vis-à-vis Hanoi also made it easier for the Soviets and Chinese to pressure a stubborn North Vietnam. (This Chinese and Soviet pressure is shown in Figure 6.2 by the single-headed arrows emanating from the two Communist giants toward North Vietnam.)

When, on October 8, 1972, Hanoi dropped its long-standing

demand for the United States to force regime change in Saigon as a condition for the deal, a fifth front ("5" in Figure 6.2) took shape vis-à-vis South Vietnam's president Thieu. The provisional agreement included a cease-fire, the withdrawal of American forces, cessation of North Vietnamese infiltration of South Vietnam from Laos and Cambodia, and the release of American prisoners of war. With this agreement largely in place, Kissinger and Nixon won Thieu's acquiescence by offering reassurances of American support; demonstrating, by means of the Christmas Bombing, that this support was real; and threatening to sign the deal without Saigon. Of course, in part due to Watergate along with adverse public opinion, Nixon and Kissinger were ultimately unsuccessful in sustaining enough U.S. support to enforce the Paris Agreement.

Broader Observations

With the Vietnam talks as an illustrative backdrop, we return to Kissinger's emphatic contention that "One fundamental principle that I have learned in diplomacy is you cannot separate diplomacy from the consequences of action."[150] And "[d]iplomacy and power are not discrete activities. They are linked, though not in the sense that each time negotiations stall, you resort to force."[151]

Specifically with respect to Vietnam, he explained, "My aim was to weave a complex web that would give us the greatest number of options. Though favoring a strong military reaction, I never wanted to rely on power alone or, for that matter, on negotiation by itself. In my view diplomacy and strategy should support each other. I always favored preceding or at least accompanying a military move with a diplomatic one, even when I rated the chances of success as low. If it were accepted, we would achieve the goal of our diplomacy. If rejected, a conciliatory offer would help sustain our military effort with our public."[152]

Kissinger consistently stresses how the fallacy of separating negotiation from incentives and pressures has worked against the effectiveness of many U.S. negotiations in practice. A more general concept than applying "force" or "pressure," however, involves the range of parties and actions that can be deployed to favorably tilt an adverse deal/no-deal balance. Facing an unfavorable balance with seemingly few good cards to play, effective negotiators often look (as illustrated by the Paris talks) quite imaginatively and entrepreneurially "beyond" the immediate negotiation table to change the game. In other words, it is not just how skillfully you play the hand you are given, but also your ability to come up with a better hand and play your improved cards masterfully.

So, in conjunction with "zooming out" to a strategic understanding, Kissinger counsels realistic negotiators to adopt a "wide-angle view," beyond the purely interpersonal aspect of negotiations "at the table," one that includes the possibility of changing the game by finding and arraying the most effective combination of incentives and penalties. As he stressed, to maximize the chances of success in negotiation, "first of all, [we should] analyze correctly what the pressures are and the incentives and then . . . deploy them in an integrated way."[153]

Whether the semantics suggest that this broad approach corresponds to what is often called "negotiation," "diplomacy," or "statecraft" is largely immaterial for our purposes. The strategic, realistic negotiator does not regard the game as fixed. Such a negotiator scans panoramically for potential incentives and penalties. These will then be integral to the process, not artificially separate, separable, or even the opposite of "negotiation."

With this sense of how Kissinger and Nixon sought to transform an initially weak hand into a stronger one, we return to two fundamental issues with implications well beyond the Indochinese case study that has occupied the bulk of this chapter. The first pertains to the accuracy of the assumptions underlying your negotiation strategy and tactics; given the intimate relationship between force and diplomacy, the second deal with the ethics and effectiveness of coercion and negotiation.

Underlying Judgments: Why Not Simply Withdraw from Vietnam in 1969?

Before Nixon and Kissinger undertook a lengthy negotiation campaign to achieve their ambitious target agreement, did they properly explore whether another course of action would have been more promising? Kissinger does not see one. In the case of Vietnam, he reminisced in 2014, "[In Vietnam] we did the best we could in a war we inherited. People forget that. The one condition that we would not yield to was to replace the government that our predecessors had established with a communist-style government. The only thing I misjudged was the possibility of a negotiated compromise. But even if I [had] judged it correctly, how could we have acted in any other way?"[154]

Alternatively, faced with daunting barriers to the kind of agreement they sought, one that had already defeated Lyndon Johnson's efforts, why not simply withdraw in 1969 subject only to American prisoners of war being released? If a narrower deal of this kind could have been negotiated in 1969, proponents argue, many of the additional 21,194 American and countless Vietnamese deaths between 1969 and 1973, when the Paris Peace Accords were finally signed, could have been prevented. After all, North Vietnamese forces conquered South Vietnam in April 1975, so holding out in negotiations for four years against the North Vietnamese demand that the United States depose the Saigon regime did not change the ultimate political result.

Books such as *Vietnam Settlement: Why 1973, Not 1969?*, by Morton Kaplan and Abram Chayes, sharply posed these questions and continued the debate.[155] Along with various journalists and politicians, some officials who participated in these talks passionately argued that such an agreement was indeed available.[156] Kissinger, however, strongly disagreed with the view that such a course was even possible, given Hanoi's stance and interests. He further argued that "It was not even logistically possible to withdraw 500,000 men instantaneously; the Pentagon estimated that a minimum of twelve to eighteen months would be required to remove the numbers that had gone to Vietnam over a period of four years. They would have to be extricated amidst the disintegration and panic our collapse was certain to produce; the South Vietnamese army of close to a million might well turn on the ally that had so betrayed it."[157]

However one estimates the magnitude of the bloodshed that would have been averted by an earlier end to the war, there is a broader point: sometimes, the wisest course of action is to abandon the field to prevent further losses. Still, we need to distinguish between decision making at the outset of a challenge and later. For example, knowing *after the fact* that you lost a lawsuit need not imply that you should have preemptively settled at the outset if your initial decision was driven by an informed and favorable assessment of the odds, costs, and benefits of going to court. It might have been a good *decision* to fight, but a bad *outcome* when you lost. Similarly, betting your life savings on the lottery, and winning, would represent a terrible *decision* but a terrific *outcome*.

From an American viewpoint, the Vietnam War and the associated negotiations clearly failed. In hindsight, we know the tragic outcome, with the North conquering the South two years after the

Paris Accords: atrocities, executions, forced "reeducation" camps, boat people, and the like. Only years later did the situation improve. Yet hindsight was not available at the time that choices had to be made. The wisdom of the decision to continue the war in the hope of an acceptable negotiated settlement ("peace with honor") depended on at least four key judgments by Nixon and Kissinger, each of which was hotly debated (and continues to be).

1. **VIETNAM WAS STRATEGICALLY SIGNIFICANT.** One core judgment concerned the nature and strategic significance of the Vietnam conflict itself. As just detailed, during much of the Cold War, many Americans believed that North Vietnamese aggression merely represented a local manifestation of a broader Communist strategy, orchestrated in Moscow and Peking, to confront the West worldwide. With the stakes posed this way in the era of "containment," a decisive Western response seemed imperative. Yet there were many dissenters at the time and later. For example, Colin Powell strongly critiqued this rationale in 1995. Having fought in Vietnam (and later serving as national security advisor, chairman of the Joint Chiefs of Staff, and secretary of state during the George W. Bush years), Powell stated, "Our political leaders had led us into a war for the one-size-fits-all rationale of anticommunism, which was only a partial fit in Vietnam, where the war had its own historical roots in nationalism, anti-colonialism, and civil strife beyond the East-West conflict."[158] If the war in Vietnam could be understood largely as a conflict, even a civil war, within and between rival Vietnamese players who had foreign patrons, then its broader strategic significance would have been far more limited.

2. **VIETNAM WAS VITAL TO U.S. CREDIBILITY ELSEWHERE.** Time and again, Kissinger returned to the argu-

ment that U.S. support for South Vietnam was important for the maintenance of American global credibility. "Not even the strongest critics in the mainstream of American life," Kissinger argued, "recommended immediate withdrawal in 1969. It would have shaken confidence in the United States in Asia, particularly Japan; during the entire period not *one* European leader urged on us the unconditional abandonment of the war we had inherited."[159] He went on to argue that, in 1969, there was little elite, allied, or popular support for immediate American withdrawal from Vietnam; widespread sentiment wanted "us to get out of Vietnam and yet it did not want defeat."[160]

In particular, Kissinger judged that withdrawing too rapidly from Vietnam and acceding to the North's demands to depose Saigon would cause Beijing to doubt U.S. resolve and power. He argued that the credible prospect of countervailing American force was a major factor that led China, facing a threatening Soviet Union that was massing troops on its border, to seek rapprochement with the United States: "I doubt our opening to China would have prospered after such a humiliation. China was inching toward us, after all, to find a counterweight to the growing Soviet threat on its borders."[161] Throughout his career, Kissinger had stressed the importance of credibility; its applicability in particular circumstances remains the subject of intense debate in foreign policy circles.[162]

3. **VIETNAMIZATION WOULD SUCCEED.** One such judgment: Nixon and Kissinger believed they had a plausible strategy for successful "Vietnamization" of the war. In principle, this would potentially have given Saigon the tools to defend itself from North Vietnam's aggression and would have permitted troops from the South to take over

the American ground role, with enhanced U.S. air support.[163] Vietnamization became something of a necessity because the president and his national security advisor had become convinced that total military victory was unattainable. Moreover, Nixon had pledged a reduction in American involvement, in part to sustain public support for the war effort.[164] Critics at the time judged Vietnamization to be futile; the merits of the policy continued to fuel debate both during and long after the war.[165] While Kissinger had doubts that Vietnamization could succeed given the rapid pace of American troop withdrawals, he indicated that he "went along with it because the other alternative of unconditional withdrawal . . . would have catastrophic consequences for the United States."[166]

4. **AN AGREEMENT COULD BE ENFORCED.** Finally, buoyed by Nixon's landslide victory in 1972, both Kissinger and Nixon assumed that a peace deal could be enforced—just as the massive 1972 North Vietnamese Spring Offensive had been blunted, by a combination of American airpower and South Vietnamese ground forces. This did not, of course, take into account the unanticipated effects of Watergate and subsequent congressional cutoffs of funds for the war. Yet, as we have demonstrated, without Watergate and its fallout, U.S. public opinion had decisively shifted against further American military action "even if North Vietnam were to try to take over South Vietnam."[167]

Conditional on these judgments at the time, and depending on the costs of doing so, the case for continuing the war until an acceptable agreement could be reached would have been more persuasive. But what if one or more of these assumptions were wrong? Suppose, for example, Vietnam was *not* strategically significant, that it was *not* vital to U.S. credibility elsewhere, that Vietnamization would *not* work, and/or an agreement to end the war could *not* be enforced. If so, the case for withdrawing much sooner would have been far stronger.

In hindsight (but also certainly according to many experts and laypeople at the time), we see that these premises were deeply flawed, with tragic results for those directly affected in the war, for U.S. domestic politics and society, and for American foreign policy more broadly. For purposes of analyzing the Vietnam negotiations, though, this chapter has provisionally assumed these underlying judgments to have been correct, though we count ourselves among the skeptics. Regardless of how one comes out on these assumptions, we believe a great deal can be learned from Nixon and Kissinger about the tight relationship between moves at and away from the table, about changing the game, and about strengthening a weak bargaining hand.

Yet, for its ultimate success, any negotiation depends on the quality of the assumptions that led to undertaking it in the first place. Brilliant tactics used to acquire a company whose value you have grossly overestimated will not go down as a triumph. Sophisticated legislative coalition building on behalf of a badly designed policy initiative will still be regarded as a failure. Even though, for analytic purposes, one might learn a great deal from studying the negotiating strategy and tactics in such cases, the outcome will inevitably reflect badly on the process.

Force and Diplomacy: Considerations of Ethics and Effectiveness

Viewing "negotiation" through a wide-angle lens, as Kissinger did, you see far beyond the face-to-face interaction with your direct counterpart. Inducing a "yes" by changing the game itself (the parties, issues, no-deal options, and the like) can often boost the chances of success far more than purely verbal means; this represents the central analytic theme of this chapter.

However, there can be a bloodless quality to phrases such as "changing the game to tilt the deal/no-deal balance in your favor." In more commonplace negotiations, threatening "no-deal" consequences may mean walking away and leaving the other side in the lurch, striking or imposing a lockout, placing a large order with your counterpart's hated rival, filing a lawsuit, or bringing an environmental group and zoning board into negotiations in order to thwart a competitor's building plans.

In the context of war or military actions, however, changing the game to "worsen the consequences of the other side's 'no'" may entail horrors: the fury of battle, suffering, death, destruction of property, environmental damage, and the future of peoples and countries. Especially in the saga of American involvement in Vietnam, Cambodia, and Laos, military force played a prominent role in tandem with negotiation. Actions of this kind should be assessed to determine whether they are both effective and ethical.

The more a proposed action entails violence, the greater the burden its advocates must shoulder to demonstrate effectiveness. After all, if a coercive measure to worsen the consequences of impasse won't work, there is no need to probe its ethics. Similarly, illegal and/or unethical actions should virtually always be ruled out of consideration without respect to their potential effectiveness. (Obvious gray areas include humanitarian interventions and some instances of civil disobedience.) Where judgments on these questions are murky, contested, or conflicting, as they often are in high-stakes cases, special care should be taken to evaluate proposed actions both for effectiveness and ethicalness.

The effectiveness of a threat to use force or the actual use of force as part of a negotiation depends on many factors, especially the credibility of the threatening party along with his or her capability to carry out the threat. Whether such a threat produces a "yes" also depends on whether the threat can be clearly communicated, the expected cost of the threat to the target relative to the cost of giving in to the demands of the threatening party, the target's confidence that agreeing to the threatening party's demand will really avoid the use of force, and the target's capacity and will to resist. Even with all these conditions satisfied, violence can produce seemingly irrational responses. It can backfire, leading to mutually destructive escalation. These factors have been extensively studied, generally under the heading of "coercive diplomacy."[168] (For a careful scholarly review of the effectiveness of coercive airpower in the Vietnam War, see Robert Pape's analysis, which essentially concludes that bombing was ineffective when the North relied primarily on guerrilla forces (early on) and much more effective when the North began to emphasize a conventional approach (e.g., the 1972 Spring Offensive).[169]

At a minimum, this work on coercive diplomacy makes abundantly clear that no simple equation connects amount of force with results. Blunting the massive North Vietnamese offensive in April 1972 almost surely turned the tide at the bargaining table in Paris. Yet the sheer extent of American military force focused on a small, poor region in Southeast Asia is remarkable. For example, almost 2.6 million U.S. troops served in South Vietnam; the tonnage of bombs dropped on North Vietnam exceeded that dropped on Germany, Japan, and Italy in World War II.[170] That this amount of force did not lead to outright victory should confound any naïve predictions about the effectiveness of raw power in producing desired outcomes.[171]

However, if force or the threat of force seems likely to generate results at the bargaining table, we must ask whether it would be ethical in the sense of being consistent with the relevant values, norms, and laws. As with coercive diplomacy, the ethics and legality associated with the use of force have been the subject of vast analysis, both legal and philosophical, and often with reference to the concept of a "just war."[172] Several questions can help one think through this issue:

1. How important are the interests involved?
2. Is there a legitimate justification (such as self-defense or a clear-cut treaty obligation)?
3. Are there nonviolent alternatives?
4. How extensive and serious are the consequences (especially in lives) of the application of force?
5. Will the proposed action affect uninvolved third parties?
6. Is the force to be employed, with its likely consequences, proportionate to the grievance to which it is addressed and/or the military goal to be sought?
7. In a country such as the United States, have legitimate, democratic processes been properly employed to authorize the use of force?

Nixon and Kissinger (as well as the North Vietnamese and Vietcong, for opposite reasons) saw military force as essential to their version of success at the negotiating table, and to advance the larger American foreign policy interests they saw as being at stake. Forceful actions include the 1969 secret bombing and May 1970 invasion of formally neutral Cambodia, renewed bombing of that country from January 1971, the bombing in North Vietnam and mining of the Haiphong harbor in response to the March 1972 offensive, and the "Christmas Bombing" in December 1972, before the final peace agreement was reached in January 1973. These are not mere listings with names and dates but violent actions that destroyed lives and convulsed countries.

As we detailed earlier in this chapter, Kissinger and Nixon judged these actions to be militarily essential, especially to cut North Vietnamese and Vietcong supply lines in Cambodia. Kissinger argued that, as such, they were integral to the American negotiating strategy as well: "Treating force and diplomacy as discrete phenomena caused our power to lack purpose and our negotiations to lack force."[173]

Opponents of the war, however, vigorously contested the wisdom of these massive military actions, which triggered intense domestic protest in the United States and damaged America's reputation in many quarters—in addition to the death and destruction they entailed. According to critics, these assaults into formally neutral countries were largely ineffective, provoked the North Vietnamese into further aggression within Cambodia, undermined the Cambodian government, and eventually resulted in the genocidal rule by the Khmer Rouge. Furthermore, issues of U.S. credibility were vastly overblown in what was essentially a civil war rather than a strategically important theater. Moreover, the critique continues, Nixon and Kissinger purposely misrepresented the extent and efficacy of their policies toward Cambodia and Laos, keeping many of their actions hidden from the American public.

The often vitriolic debate over the war's expansion and escalation continues unabated through this writing. This chapter examined these actions in terms of their effects on the negotiations, but this is too narrow a view. As the last section stressed, assessment of Kissinger's role, including his negotiating strategy and tactics, depends critically on the quality of key assumptions underlying his policies. These include the real nature of the conflict, credibility,

Vietnamization, enforceability of the agreement, and the larger foreign policy effects of American actions in Indochina. Though we reviewed them with care, it is not our purpose to evaluate such broader claims and counterclaims about Kissinger's actions in terms of their effectiveness and ethics.[174] Still, there is no doubt about the heavy costs, domestic and global, of opting for massive force as a tool of negotiation.

Multiparty Dexterity: Orchestrating Complex Negotiations

As Richard Neustadt, the great scholar of the American presidency, once trenchantly observed, "reality is not bilateral."[1] We have seen the multiparty reality of Kissinger's Rhodesian talks over majority rule. We have seen it in the Paris peace talks, which cannot properly be understood as a purely U.S.–North Vietnamese process—without even considering negotiations with contending factions *inside* the U.S. government. And some of Kissinger's negotiations that we have not examined, such as the talks leading to the 1975 Helsinki Accords, were overtly multilateral. Intended to reduce Cold War tensions and elevate human rights, the Helsinki negotiations can be analyzed only in terms of the *thirty-five* nations that took part. For a scholar whose early work dissected seventeenth- through nineteenth-century European balance-of-power politics, it is hardly surprising that Kissinger's approach to negotiation consistently displays sharp insight into multiparty dynamics, and coalition formation and dissolution.

Multiparty talks inherently distinguish themselves from purely bilateral negotiations given the possibilities for varying multiparty groupings (or "coalitions," as we'll sometimes say) to align in support of, or against, an agreement. In negotiations with only two parties, of course, coalitions are impossible; there is either a deal between the two or not. When three or more parties are involved, however, agreements may be possible between any two of the parties or, sometimes, among all three (or more), and these alignments often shift during the negotiations. If A, B, and C are jockeying for advantage, the result of their negotiations may be an A–B deal, an A–C deal, a B–C deal, an A–B–C deal, or no deal at all. As the number of parties increases, the number of possible alignments and agreements increases even faster. No wonder multiparty dexterity is of a wholly different order than more familiar two-party negotiations. The negotiator in such settings must envision which multiparty alignments ("coalitions") are likely, which are desirable, and which undesirable—and then figure out the negotiation strategy that is most likely to build or block them.

Recall, for example, the central coalitional dynamic of the Southern Africa negotiations that we analyzed in chapters 1 through 3. Start with the sheer number of parties: in addition to the Ford administration and its Republican critics of the initiative in Southern Africa, Kissinger catalogued them: "There were five front-line states, each with its own emphasis; internal groups competing with each other inside Rhodesia and Namibia; the government of South Africa; the authorities in Rhodesia; and the special position of Great Britain. Their purposes were partly overlapping, partly adversarial. But a change in the position of one party could send shock waves through the entire system and threaten to unravel what was being so painfully constructed."[2] From this welter of parties, Kissinger sequentially pieced together a tacit coalition whose members, collectively, pressured Ian Smith to accept black-majority rule.

As more recent negotiations underscore, one of the negotiating skills required to forge a sufficiently large coalition in favor of an agreement is multiparty dexterity. Consider the 196 parties who negotiated at the 2015 climate change talks in Paris. Further, many of the delegations in Paris were not monolithic, but represented diverse, often conflicting "internal" interests that had to be reconciled. For example, the U.S. delegation included four cabinet secretaries and high-level staff from multiple departments, not to mention the wide array of passionate nongovernmental organizations that sought to influence the talks. Similarly, the Iran nuclear negotiations that concluded an agreement in 2015 took place directly among France, Britain, Russia, China, Germany, the United States, and Iran; many other countries, such as Israel, Oman, and Saudi Arabia, played important indirect roles.

Henry Kissinger was at home in such multiparty negotiations. Ironically, the simplest such situation in which he played a vital role involved a "mere" three parties: the United States, China, and the Soviet Union. Yet this "merely" triangular negotiation had considerable significance for the world. We will examine its dynamics in some depth before moving to observations about Kissinger's approach to negotiation involving many more than three parties.

Triangular Negotiation

The United States, China, and the Soviet Union

During the two-decade period when the United States had no formal relations with China, the U.S.-Soviet superpower relationship was largely hostile and, in many important respects, frozen along a bilateral (U.S.-Soviet) axis. Along with Richard Nixon, however, Kissinger saw the possibility, via a carefully managed opening to China, of converting this bilateral superpower structure into a "triangular" one, with the United States at the apex of a U.S.-China-Soviet triangle. The Soviet Union's increasingly

threatening military action toward China offered a potential opening to bring this new structure into being.

This coalitional objective was informed by historical analogy.
Kissinger explained: "Since the Soviet Union was the only country
capable of dominating Asia, a tacit alliance to block Soviet expan-
sionism in Asia could be envisioned between the United States and
China (not unlike the Entente Cordiale between Great Britain and
France in 1904, and between Great Britain and Russia in 1907)."[3]

While historical insight offered some guidance, Kissinger and
Nixon were crystal clear on the rationale, in terms of American national interests at the time, for pragmatic, "triangular" moves: "We
agreed on the necessity of thwarting the geopolitical ambitions [of
the Soviet Union], but we had no reason to become involved in the
ideological dispute . . . If Moscow succeeded in humiliating Peking
and reducing it to impotence, the whole weight of the Soviet military effort could be thrown against the West. Such a demonstration
of Soviet ruthlessness and American impotence (or indifference—
the result would be the same) would encourage accommodation to
other Soviet demands from Japan to Western Europe, not to speak
of the many smaller countries on the Soviet periphery."[4]

In broad concept, therefore, triangular diplomacy potentially
had decisive advantages over the bilateral superpower relationship
that then existed between the Soviet Union and the United States.
But what did this mean as an objective in practice? Kissinger explained the structure of the triangular equilibrium that he and
Nixon aimed to bring into being: "[S]o long as China had more
to fear from the Soviet Union than it did from the United States,
China's self-interest would impel it to cooperate with the United
States. By the same token, China did not pursue its opposition to
Soviet expansionism as a favor to the United States, even though it
served both American and Chinese purposes. Impressed as Nixon
was by the clarity of thought of the Chinese leaders—especially of

Premier Zhou Enlai—he had no conceivable interest in placing the United States unambiguously on either side of the conflict between China and the Soviet Union. America's bargaining position would be strongest when America was closer to both communist giants than either was to the other."[5]

This core conception of how most advantageously to deal with the Soviets and the Chinese appears to have its origins in Kissinger's careful study of Otto von Bismarck's approach to Prussian survival in the center of a multipolar European continent. In a prescient 1968 essay, Kissinger wrote that Bismarck "proposed to manipulate the commitments of the other powers so that Prussia would always be closer to any of the contending parties than they were to each other. If Prussia managed to create a maximum of options for itself, it would be able to utilize its artificial isolation to sell its cooperation to the highest bidder."[6]

NEGOTIATING THE TRIANGULAR RELATIONSHIP: THE OPENING TO CHINA

It was not enough to recognize the situation that Kissinger hoped to bring about with the United States at the pivot point of the triangular relationship. Actually negotiating the dynamics of making this happen would be tricky. As Kissinger described the challenge, "Clearly, triangular diplomacy required agility. We had somehow not to flex our own muscles, but, as in judo, to use the weight of an adversary to propel him in a desired direction."[7]

Central to this agility was the American opening to China that stunned the rest of the world, not least the Kremlin. Yet this opening had its roots in the relationship between the United States and the Soviet Union. Early in the Nixon administration, the Soviets seemed to signal a willingness to begin negotiations on the mutual reduction of nuclear arsenals, which had reached frightening levels in the midst of the Cold War. For the first time in a generation, a

Strategic Arms Limitation Treaty (SALT) appeared to be conceivable.[8] Through their policy of détente, Kissinger and Nixon sought to reduce U.S.-Soviet tensions on a broad front, including with respect to nuclear arms. Progress on these complex negotiations ensued, partly through a secret "channel" involving Kissinger and Soviet ambassador Anatoly Dobrynin. (We discuss the potential roles of this kind of "channel" in greater depth in chapters 10 and 13.)

By late June 1971, a summit meeting between Nixon and Brezhnev appeared essential to bridge the final gaps for a SALT agreement. Yet, perhaps because the Soviets believed they had the bargaining edge or that Nixon was overly keen on the summit for domestic reasons, a "go slow" attitude seemed to prevail in Moscow. As Kissinger put it, "Moscow had been stalling for over a year on arrangements for a summit between Brezhnev and Nixon. By a sort of reverse linkage, it tried to make the high-level meeting dependent on a whole list of conditions."[9]

With the U.S.-Soviet talks in slow motion or stuck, Henry Kissinger stepped off a plane borrowed from the president of Pakistan and onto the tarmac in Beijing on July 9, 1971.[10] To keep his trip secret from reporters in Pakistan, a body double had been employed and (the actual) Kissinger was disguised in a black hat, sunglasses, and a dark raincoat. As the first senior American official to engage in talks with the Chinese government in two decades, he was greeted with warmth and hospitality, and was taken to the State Guesthouse to await the arrival of Premier Zhou Enlai.[11]

Background to Kissinger's China Trip: Mutual Hostility and Suspicion

By the time Kissinger became Richard Nixon's national security advisor in January 1969, the United States had been engaged in largely formulaic talks with the People's Republic of China (PRC) for a number of years.[12] Over the course of 134 sessions periodically held in Warsaw, U.S. support for an independent Taiwan, vehemently opposed by China, was publicly declared to be the reason for both sides' entrenchment, with the talks devolving to the sterile stating and restating of unchanging, incompatible positions on both sides.

An array of issues compounded and exacerbated the isolation of one nation from the other. The United States ideologically opposed the Communist leadership of China, and believed that the PRC was intent on spreading communism across the region. Chinese support for the North Vietnamese regime confirmed this view. The Cultural Revolution, a series of violent social and political policies implemented by PRC chairman Mao Zedong, further fed American fears that the Chinese leadership would sacrifice millions of its own people, and consequently people of other nations, to impose its vision of communism on the world.

In the Americans, Beijing saw an equally ideologically driven opponent, one willing to use brutal means to achieve its ends. Mao, Zhou, and other PRC leaders found support for their beliefs in the U.S. intervention in Vietnam, which to the Chinese leadership seemed to resemble U.S. involvement in the Korean War. Of course, massive Chinese intervention in that war had led to the rupture in diplomatic ties between the United States and China in the early 1950s.[13]

Widening Rift Between China and the Soviet Union: Could the United States Benefit?

During the 1950s and '60s, the foreign policy consensus in the United States envisioned a monolithic Communist bloc linking the

USSR and China, united in their opposition to Western democracies. However, relations between the PRC and the USSR had worsened in the early 1960s. The Soviet invasion of Czechoslovakia in August 1968, which caused serious concern in the United States, had also outraged the PRC, which believed it signaled the beginning of Soviet aggression against fellow Communist nations. Soviet justification for the move, announced in November 1968 as the "Brezhnev Doctrine," further confirmed Chinese suspicions by formally asserting the Soviet Union's right to intervene in Communist countries (possibly including China) in order to suppress opposition movements.[14]

In March 1969, mutual suspicion exploded into outright conflict between Chinese and Soviet forces in Siberia, along the Ussuri, the river marking the border between the two countries. Tensions escalated further when China counterattacked to signal that it would defend its borders. Intended to warn the Soviets off, the move had the opposite effect. The largest two Communist countries in the world were now locked in a military standoff with some 658,000 Soviet troops in forty modernized divisions confronting 814,000 Chinese troops along their mutual border. This tense standoff often erupted in military clashes, with significant casualties on both sides.[15] It later became apparent that Chairman Mao was concerned enough about the Soviet military threat to secretly move most of the Chinese government ministries out of Beijing.[16]

Pressured to declare an American stance on the Sino-Soviet split, Kissinger and Nixon reflected on what would be the right policy if the conflict between the two countries were to widen. Central among their objectives was constraining the expansion of Soviet influence. To that end, Kissinger and Nixon supported leaning in favor of the Chinese, something Nixon had already largely favored by 1969. Concerned about Soviet domination of China and signaling this to Mao, Kissinger stated, "Nixon took perhaps the most daring step of his presidency by warning the Soviet Union that the United States would not remain indifferent if it were to attack China."[17] Given that there was no formal Sino-U.S. relationship or official communication at the time, this was a striking message.

An Awkward Process of Coordination

Nixon and Kissinger scarcely understood that Mao was simultaneously attempting to signal a willingness to negotiate a significant thaw in relations between China and the United States. Heretofore, communication had often consisted of insults hurled at each other ("running dogs," "imperialists," "lackeys," "ideological fanatics," etc.). Coldly taking stock of the geopolitical situation, Mao feared war with the Soviets. He looked to the United States as a potential ally in a coalitional triangle. Like his American counterparts, Mao believed that a substantive, public agreement would offset the significant pressures against his regime, especially from the Soviets.

The two nations warily and somewhat blindly had approached each other. They had been so isolated from one another for so long that, in the various preliminary attempts by U.S. officials to arrange a high-level communication, the results were almost comic. For example, an American diplomat's (authorized) attempt at outreach at a fashion show in Warsaw caused his panicked Chinese counterpart to flee. Running away, the Chinese diplomat was pursued by the American, Walter Stoessel, who shouted his hope to establish a channel for high-level talks on behalf of the president of the United States.[18]

Kissinger realized that a limited number of secure interlocutors was needed for relaying a clearer message to the Chinese leadership. He identified Romania, a Communist country, and Pakistan as potential conduits through which to send messages to China. Neither nation was aligned with the United States, but both had contact with China and were not unconditional Soviet allies. In a series of preliminary exchanges, the United States communicated through Romania and Pakistan, and the PRC replied through Norway and Afghanistan.[19] Within a matter of months, a message came through from Premier Zhou, inviting the United States to send a representative to Beijing. A subsequent message conveyed an invitation to Nixon. Zhou wished to discuss Taiwan, but Nixon and Kissinger read more into his letter.[20]

They replied, testing to see if Zhou would be open to a broader agenda, and received positive signs. Anticipating ideological objections from Secretary of State William Rogers and a range of likely domestic opponents, Kissinger insisted on absolute secrecy. (We pause to note what an extraordinary, almost unthinkable, step it was for a national security advisor to embark on a negotiation of fundamental national importance without the knowledge of the secretary of state. In chapter 13 we will return in greater depth to the pros and cons of this kind of secrecy.) In early July, Kissinger boarded a plane with a handful of aides and Secret Service agents and set off on a "routine diplomatic mission" that would end in Pakistan.[21] With each stop, the press progressively lost interest, until Kissinger's entourage, only some of whom knew more than part of what was up, could secretly board the president of Pakistan's plane and slip into China on July 9.[22]

Negotiating with Zhou

Meeting with Zhou, Kissinger swiftly abandoned his prevailing assumption of Chinese hostility as his counterparts made great efforts to put him at ease. Initially concerned by the lack of scheduled time for negotiations, Kissinger realized that Mao and Zhou's approach was meant not to placate him, but rather to signal a willingness to learn more about each other, especially their fundamental views of the international system, after many years without direct communication.

In the formal negotiating sessions that followed, Kissinger and Zhou discussed the two most pressing issues, Taiwan and Vietnam, to learn whether talks could usefully proceed. Kissinger found an easy counterpart in Zhou. Both negotiated their most important issues largely by talking around them, linking them to major priorities they both knew to be most significant. Kissinger tested Zhou's desire to negotiate matters other than Taiwan, and received a favorable reply. Zhou would negotiate Taiwan but was not concerned by the order in which it and other issues would be negotiated; other issues could come first. Kissinger saw an opportunity to link potential Chinese concessions on Vietnam to potential U.S. concessions on Taiwan, dubbing Zhou's position "linkage in reverse."[23]

Kissinger came to understand the driving interest of his Beijing counterparts in coalitional terms: "The Chinese want to relieve themselves of the threat of a two-front war, introduce new calculations in Moscow about attacking or leaning on the PRC, and perhaps make the USSR more pliable in its dealing with Peking. Specifically from us they want assurances against US-USSR collusion."[24] Phrasing it more positively, Kissinger stressed Mao's "commitment to the creation of a *de facto* anti-Soviet coalition."[25]

As his visit came to a close, Kissinger drafted an agreement with Zhou, to be announced by the leaders of both nations. Knowing of Nixon's long-standing interest in China, Mao would extend an offer for a state visit. Richard Nixon would agree. For the first time in twenty years, the normalization of relations between the United States and the People's Republic of China was in prospect. On July 15, both nations made the stunning announcement.[26] As we will later explain, this "Nixon shock" enraged American anticommunists, deeply embarrassed U.S. officials and allies such as Japan that had been cut out of the process, and ultimately led to American recognition of China at the expense of Taiwan.

Kissinger immediately set about planning an interim trip, during which the significant details of a communiqué would be prepared in advance of Nixon and Mao's formal meeting. Returning to China in October, Kissinger proposed a relatively bland, formal unified statement on the shared positions of both nations. In return, he left blank the statement of a position on Taiwan, to signal a willingness to shift the American position in order to find agreement with the PRC. Zhou's reply was a firm rebuke. He demanded that each side state its positions, both common and conflicting, on key issues. Stunned at first, Kissinger realized that Zhou's demand would not substantively alter either side's position going forward, but could limit internal dissent from hard-liners.

The resulting "Shanghai Communiqué" had an unprecedented structure, completely unlike the relatively anodyne joint statements that often followed U.S.-Soviet meetings. Once the final terms were negotiated during Nixon's visit, Kissinger observed that the "Shanghai Communiqué . . . was to provide a road map for Sino-American relations for the next decade. The Communiqué had an unprecedented feature: more than half of it was devoted to stating the conflicting views of the two sides on ideology, international affairs, Vietnam, and Taiwan. In a curious way, the catalogue of disagreements conferred greater significance on those subjects on which the two sides agreed. . . . Stripped of diplomatic jargon, these agreements meant, at a minimum, that China would do nothing to exacerbate the situation in Indochina or Korea, that neither China nor the United States would cooperate with the Soviet bloc, and that both would oppose any attempt by any country to achieve domination of Asia. Because the Soviet Union was the only country capable of dominating Asia, a tacit alliance to block Soviet expansionism in Asia was coming into being."[27]

Four months later, Nixon and Kissinger followed the preliminary meeting with a statement on Taiwan, setting the stage for Nixon's state visit. Arriving in Beijing in late February, Nixon and Kissinger proceeded to the residence of Mao Zedong, and were greeted effusively by the ailing leader. Speaking in circuitous parables, questions, and statements, Mao invited a conversation with Nixon, signaling that no further agreement would be needed than the visit itself, should a formal agreement not be reached. In the long term, he conveyed, the two nations would draw together.

Nixon and Mao spoke in general terms while leaving the detailed negotiations to Kissinger and Zhao. Within days, the final Shanghai Communiqué was agreed upon at last, stating each side's positions on the issues, agreed positions, and a way forward on Taiwan.[28] (We will return in chapter 11 to some of the remarkable creativity that resulted in this agreed document.)

With carefully crafted ambiguities, the United States pledged to support the concept of "One China," significantly reduce support for Taiwanese independence groups, gradually reduce U.S. military personnel in Taiwan, and encourage regional peace and security.[29] Moreover, both sides agreed to move toward formal diplomatic ties and to avoid the pursuit of regional hegemony at all costs.[30]

Nixon's visit and the communiqué succeeded in achieving Kissinger's immediate goals, linking an agreement on Taiwan to a tacit agreement by the Chinese to moderate their support for the North Vietnamese. Both sides stood to gain by checking the aggression of the Soviet Union, and by doing so in a way that de-escalated a growing military crisis.

Agility in Coalitional Negotiations:
The Soviet Reaction

Despite the fact that "most Soviet experts had warned Nixon that improved relations with China would sour Soviet-American relations,"[31] Kissinger was less worried about this possibility. He judged that soured relations were less likely given Soviet concern about acting in a manner that would deepen a possible U.S.-Chinese alignment and the potential value to the USSR of improved relations with the United States. (Recall our assessment in the last chapter of the high expected value to Moscow of improved trade relations, and the top-level Soviet commitment to that economic result.) Despite dire predictions, Kissinger noted that "the opposite occurred. Prior to my secret trip to China, Moscow had been stalling for over a year on arrangements for a summit between Brezhnev and Nixon . . . then, within a month of my visit to Beijing, the Kremlin reversed itself and invited Nixon to Moscow.[32]

"Suddenly, the Moscow summit was not elusive. . . . Other negotiations deadlocked for months began magically to unfreeze: Berlin, for example, and the talks to guard against accidental nuclear war. . . . both these negotiations moved rapidly to completion within weeks of the Peking announcement."[33] More broadly, "the Soviet Union began to move energetically . . . to deal with the new international reality. . . . [I]t sought rapidly to improve its relations with Washington: It was suddenly anxious to create the impression that more serious business could be accomplished in Moscow than in Peking."[34]

To Kissinger, "agility" in negotiating this outcome involved balancing a number of tricky Chinese, Soviet, and domestic U.S. dynamics: "If we moved too quickly . . . the Chinese might rebuff the overture. If we moved too slowly, we might feed Chinese suspicions of Soviet-American collusion, which could drive them into making the best deal available with Moscow. As for the Soviets, we considered the Chinese option useful to induce restraint; but we had to take care not to pursue it so impetuously as to provoke a Soviet preemptive attack on China. And at home we had to overcome a habit of mind that [saw] the People's Republic either [as] an irreconcilable enemy or a put-upon country concerned only with . . . Taiwan."[35]

"In a period that was, in other respects, a high point of Soviet self-confidence and a low point of America's," Kissinger concluded, "the Nixon Administration managed to reshuffle the deck. It continued to see to it that general war proved too risky for the Soviets. After the opening to China, Soviet pressures below the level of general war became too risky as well, because they had the potential of accelerating the dreaded Sino-American rapprochement. Once America had opened to China, the Soviet Union's best option became seeking its own relaxation of tensions with the United States."[36]

Playing the "China Card": A Naïve Interpretation?

Observers of U.S. moves toward China were quick to interpret Kissinger's China initiative as "playing the China card" against the Soviets. In a fairly typical example, strategy professor Evelyn Goh asserted that "It was clear to Beijing that the American opening to China was motivated by its desire to play the 'China card' in order to motivate the Soviet Union to negotiate detente with the United States."[37]

While superficially appealing—after all, the United States was siding with the weaker of two contending parties (China) to balance the more aggressive one (the Soviet Union)—the coalitional rationale for the American approach to China was far subtler. In fact, Kissinger sharply criticized those who glibly opined about the administration and its so-called China card: "So the 'China card,' as it was often presented, was let us do something with China that annoys Russia and for which we can bargain. [Instead] our view was that the existence of the triangular relationship was in itself a form of pressure on *each* of them. And we carefully maneuvered so that we would try to be closer to each than they were to each other. . . . And one way we achieved that was by rather carefully informing each side what we were doing with the other. So that created its own pressures, but we added no threat. We treated our relationship with each as if it were the most natural event in the world and kept the other side informed, which also had the practical effect, actually, that it improved their confidence in us, at least to the extent that they could be reasonably sure that we were not planning any secret machinations."[38]

Of course, keeping each side exquisitely well informed about what the United States was doing with the other side was consistent with simple courtesy and an independent spirit of transparency. Yet the underlying message was both obvious and unnecessary to state explicitly, let alone couch in threatening terms, as Kissinger explained to those who might miss the point: "the mere existence of these American options gave us a bargaining weapon. So I was always concerned that, if we announced that China was a weapon against Russia, then it became a mortal conflict, and all the more so as we were also pursuing a policy of détente with the Soviet Union, and we wanted to give them a genuine option of improving their relations with us."[39]

When analyzing triangular diplomacy at the tactical level—how to play A against B and vice versa, which is certainly useful—it is easy to miss the broader strategic and structural motivations and consequences. While protecting American foreign policy interests, Kissinger always sought to reduce the probability of a devastating nuclear conflict. A new triangular relationship, properly configured, promised greater underlying global stability, along with other advantages: "We really wanted a world less likely to go to war," Kissinger explained. "And we also always had in mind that we wanted to settle the Vietnam War at the same time. And we didn't want little victories. What we wanted was a structural improvement."[40]

As we saw during our analyses of the disengagement agreements following the 1973 Arab-Israeli War and of the Paris peace talks, Henry Kissinger actively drew on the increasing stakes that China and the Soviet Union had in improving relations with the United States. As diplomatic and military supporters of North Vietnam, both China and the Soviet Union had to weigh, and chose to moderate, that support against the increasing value of relationships with the United States. Similarly, as Kissinger negotiated for a cease-fire during the 1973 Arab-Israeli War (and in disengagement accords among Egypt, Israel, and Syria), the Soviet Union was somewhat constrained in its response by the détente initiative and the benefits it promised. Not only was the "structural improvement" in the triangular U.S.–Soviet–Chinese relationship that Kissinger and Nixon negotiated valuable in and of itself, but it also proved to be an asset for addressing other key foreign policy interests.

From Three Parties to Many

Beyond the triangular negotiations just analyzed, Kissinger consistently sought to understand and act on the entire system of multiple parties and interests. As his biographer Walter Isaacson somewhat sardonically observed, "That type of thinking came naturally to someone who was both a brilliant conceptualizer and slightly conspiratorial in outlook, who could feel the connections the way a spider senses twitches in its web."[41] Kissinger offered a tactical example of adapting to this complexity: "Before formal positions could be advanced, it was necessary to reconnoiter the ground with all the parties and, even then, one had to be careful never to discuss the position of one side before committing the others—at least to some extent—lest concessions be pocketed and generate a new round of demands."[42]

Winning and Blocking Coalitions

While multiparty moves and countermoves can be complex, two fundamental negotiating tasks typically guide action. First, with a target agreement in mind, an advocate must build enough support among enough of the right parties to enable its adoption and implementation; we call this forging a "winning coalition." Frequently, however, opponents of a target agreement seek to prevent it from being adopted or implemented; we refer to a group of opponents able to accomplish this negative task as a "blocking coalition." For the advocate of agreement seeking to build a winning coalition, it is also necessary to thwart potential blockers.

Sequencing and Negotiation Campaigns

Building supportive coalitions and preventing or breaking adverse ones often depend on choosing the most promising sequence of approach: whom to approach first, next, and so on for the best chance of success. This can mean negotiating a series of subsidiary agreements that advantageously set the stage for achieving one's ultimate target deal. We have sometimes referred to such a series of negotiations as a "negotiation campaign," which is aimed at forging a "winning coalition" that enables the target deal to be reached.[43] We analyzed such campaigns in the Rhodesian and Vietnamese negotiations, where Kissinger aimed to achieve an ultimate "target deal" and then mapped backward from that target to identify and put in place the subsidiary agreements that, when negotiated, made the final desired result more likely.

Success, in these cases, depends on a thorough assessment of which parties tend to defer to which others and on the patterns of influence and antagonism among them.[44] Going through this process clarifies where to place one's negotiation emphasis first, next, and so on. In a simple everyday example, suppose Bob, from whom it would be tough to get agreement if he were approached directly, defers to Alice, who in turn pays strong attention to Kim, who is receptive to a good set of arguments for the deal you seek. The right sequence would be to persuade Kim to say yes, which would help with Alice, and in turn make an appeal to Bob far more likely to succeed.

Without reviewing the specifics, recall Figure 1.4, regarding Kissinger's planned strategy to persuade Rhodesia's Ian Smith to accept majority rule within two years. Collapsing a more complex sequence to its essence, the South Africans were key to the Rhodesians, while the British, Americans, and "Frontline" African states were keys to South African acquiescence. Figure 1.4 somewhat mechanically lays out this sequential strategy, which Kissinger later modified (Figure 7.1 here) as the situation evolved.

Similarly, as we described in chapter 6, Kissinger orchestrated a lengthy negotiation campaign to persuade North Vietnam's Le Duc Tho to agree to at least a minimally acceptable deal. Figure 7.2 reminds us of those sequential dynamics.

These two examples illustrate an important form of multiparty dexterity. Yet, beyond orchestrating sequential negotiation

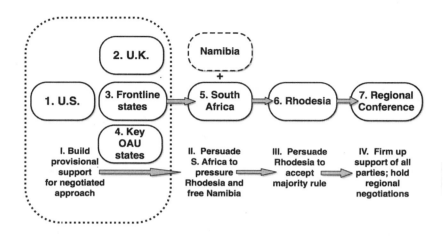

Figure 7.1: Kissinger's Initial Strategy to Achieve Majority Rule in Rhodesia

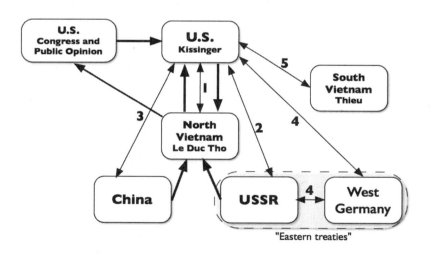

Figure 7.2: Kissinger's Negotiation Campaign for Agreement with North Vietnam

Note: Two-headed arrows imply direct negotiations; single-headed arrows imply pressure

(political, PR, diplomatic, military)

campaigns to build support for target agreements, a complementary set of skills is needed.

Blocking and Opposing Coalitions

An advocate for a target deal must effectively contend with potential opponents, sometimes referred to as "spoilers," who could block an agreement or its implementation. Several negotiating approaches exist for dealing with a possible blocking coalition: converting its members to your side by persuasive arguments; bringing them on board by meeting some of their key interests or making side payments; isolating and shaming them; sidestepping them; dividing and conquering them; or overwhelming them.

Negotiations that ignore or do not deal with potent blockers, however, often ends in failure. With respect to "left-out" spoilers, consider the 1919 Treaty of Versailles, which ended the state of war between Germany and the Allied Powers. Unlike the Congress of Vienna of roughly a century before, the defeated powers did not participate in the negotiations at the Paris Peace Conference. Kissinger observed: "Thus it happened that the peace concluding the war to end all wars did not include the two strongest nations of Europe—Germany and Russia—which, between them, contained well over half of Europe's population and by far the largest military potential. That fact alone would have doomed the Versailles settlement."[45]

As with this and earlier examples, Kissinger frequently looks to history for insight into coalitional dynamics that could lead to decisive opposing coalitions. He warned against the dominant power throwing its weight around in a manner that would stimulate smaller states to coalesce in opposition. He observed that "Bordering more neighbors than any other European state, Germany . . .

was stronger than any single neighbor but weaker than a coalition of all of them. . . . Ironically, Germany's attempt to break up these incipient coalitions by threats or blackmail before the First World War became a self-fulfilling prophecy that rendered the emergence of hostile coalitions almost inevitable."[46]

Kissinger drew a similar lesson from the Soviets' military buildup. "The generation governing the Soviet Union in the 1970s accumulated military and geopolitical power less as an expression of long-range geopolitical aims than as a substitute for them. Inevitably the pursuit of strength for its own sake frightened most of the noncommunist world and brought about a tacit coalition of all industrial nations plus China against the Soviet Union, which made its ultimate collapse inevitable."[47] More recently, China's aggressive actions in the South and East China Seas have worried neighboring countries, tending to drive them closer together. Russian invasions of Georgia and Ukraine (Crimea and Eastern Ukraine) in 2008 and 2014 produced a similar effect on European countries, who began to increase their defense spending in response.

Carefully assessing all the relevant parties made Kissinger keenly aware of how potential opposition could be aroused. In a Middle East context, he cautioned against "exploratory" discussions of sensitive possible negotiating moves in an environment where those discussions would leak: "Concessions difficult enough to sell to passionate publics on behalf of an actual deal became nearly unmanageable when part of a hypothetical agreement more than a year away."[48] Also, when he deemed it necessary to deal with all parties simultaneously, Kissinger was cautious about concluding any individual agreements, because "all the parties with nothing to gain would have an incentive to gang up on the leader most likely to proceed on his own."[49]

When evaluating the likely success of step-by-step versus comprehensive negotiations, Kissinger showed an acute awareness of the manner in which the dynamics might lead either to agreement or impasse depending on which parties were involved by what process. With respect to the most promising approach after the 1973 Arab-Israeli War, he reflected that "we had to make a basic strategic decision: Shall we go now for an overall settlement or continue the step-by-step? An overall effort has its advantages. Most importantly one can put everything on the table; one can argue the framework of final settlement with full knowledge of the objectives of all sides involved. But the disadvantages are that it would bring all the Arabs together, and when this happens the radical Arabs would have the upper hand. Then the Soviets would always be able to outbid whatever else was on the table and the radical Arabs would, of course, have to opt for what the Soviets had to offer. Of course, the Soviets would not make an offer in the interests of achieving peace but rather in the interest of assuring that there was no progress."[50] In short, under this set of circumstances, Kissinger saw a comprehensive process as enabling potential blockers.

Having forecast an impasse from the likely dynamics of a comprehensive approach, Kissinger contrasted it, for the 1973 case, with the very different process he structured to avoid these pitfalls. Notice that a significant aspect of his preferred process involved the parties that should *not* be involved: "First, we sought to break up the Arab united front. Also we wanted to ensure that the Europeans and Japanese did not get involved in the diplomacy; and, of course, we wanted to keep the Soviets out of the diplomatic arena. Finally, we sought a situation which would enable Israel to deal separately with each of its neighbors. We told the Israelis they could go to the Europeans if they wanted proclamations, but if they wanted progress toward peace they would have to come to us. Thus, the step-by-step process began. The step-by-step led to two disengagement agreements [Egyptian-Israeli and Syrian-Israeli]."[51]

In short, while Kissinger the dexterous multiparty negotiator was keenly focused on recruiting potential allies, he was equally aware of potential opponents, and of the process choices that might awaken or strengthen them.

★ ★ ★

Kissinger the negotiator was simultaneously Kissinger the analyst and architect of the structure and dynamics of coalitions in multiparty, multilevel situations. He paid close attention to which parties would need to agree in order to forge a sustainable winning coalition to advance his objectives. Through carefully sequenced negotiation campaigns, he built up such coalitions, both explicitly and tactically, in the Rhodesian and Vietnam cases. In this process, he was mindful of different ways that blocking and opposing coalitions might be activated to frustrate his objectives. With respect to China and the Soviet Union, he transformed the formerly bilateral U.S. focus into a triangular one, with America holding the advantageous pivot point. In the Middle East, given awareness of the risks of many parties in a comprehensive process, he opted for a sequential step-by-step approach with a small subset of the much larger group of parties that might have been involved. Overall, Kissinger was exquisitely aware of the complex dynamics of multiparty negotiations, at the not only tactical but also the strategic and structural levels.

Together with the characteristics we discuss in earlier chapters (being strategic, realistic, and game-changing), multiparty dexterity enabled Kissinger to "zoom out" as he sought to analyze and advantageously shape the larger context for individual bargaining encounters. Now the challenge becomes how, at the same time that one zooms out to the strategic level, to effectively "zoom in" to the people with whom one directly negotiates.

III

"Zooming In"

Introduction to Kissinger's Interpersonal Approach and Tactics

From Vietnam and Syria to China and Rhodesia, Henry Kissinger has stressed that "the secret of negotiations is meticulous preparation."[1] Other superb negotiators, such as James Baker, lived by this precept. Time and again, Kissinger's staff and counterparts attested to his fine-grained grasp of the issues. Former Israeli prime minister Golda Meir remarked on Kissinger's "fantastic capacity for dealing with the minutest of details of whatever problems he undertakes to solve." She continued: "He told me once that two years ago he had never heard of a place called [Q]uneitra. But when he became involved in negotiating the disengagement of the Syrian and Israeli forces on the Golan Heights, there wasn't a road, a house, or even a tree there about which he didn't know everything there was to know. As I said to him then, 'With the exception of the former generals who are now members of the Israeli cabinet, I don't think we have a single minister who knows as much about [Q]uneitra as you do.' "[2]

Beyond mastery of the issues, "meticulous preparation" to Kissinger meant developing clarity on his own interests and on the psychology, purposes, concerns, perceptions, relationships, political context, and culture of his opposite number(s). To prepare, he zooms out: envisioning a target agreement and provisional strategy, developing a realistic grasp of the deal/no-deal balance, often making game-changing moves to tilt that balance favorably.

And he zooms in: he cultivates an understanding of his individual counterparts and then customizes his interpersonal approach and tactics. In the negotiations we've discussed thus far, we have often seen glimmers of Kissinger the tactician. With Zhou Enlai, Kissinger opens with a broad philosophical statement of what he is trying to achieve before even broaching specific issues. In tough situations, such as negotiating with South Africa's John Vorster and Rhodesia's Ian Smith, Kissinger seeks simultaneously to be both empathetic and assertive. Whether focused on Sadat, Meir, Rabin, or Assad, he vividly paints the dire consequences of no-deal, confronting the reluctance to say yes with a characteristic challenge: "I know you don't like this, but what's the alternative?" He bluntly counters a hard accusation by Brezhnev; to a similar Chinese tirade at the bargaining table, Kissinger responds indirectly but firmly.

We've encountered a number of such actions in specific negotiations and counterparts. The next five chapters, however, analyze and illustrate several *classes* of interpersonal approaches and tactical choices that characterize Kissinger's approach. These often include:

- cultivating deep insight into "the other side" as individuals;
- building rapport and important relationships;
- making proposals and concessions;
- engaging in wordsmithing and "constructive ambiguity";
- bargaining tacitly;
- persisting and building momentum;
- employing "shuttles"; and
- opting for secrecy, a centralized process, and a dominant personal role.

For many people, tactics are the essence of negotiation. Some readers might find it odd that we put off a detailed discussion of Kissinger's tactical moves "at the table" to a point this late in the book, only after we have analyzed the ways in which he zooms out to the strategic level. Yet one of our core messages is that "Kissinger the negotiator" acts both away from and at the table (i.e., zooms out and zooms in) to induce the "yes" he seeks. Now, however, with the bigger picture in view, we zoom in to the conference room.

Clarifying the Real Nature and Purpose of a Negotiation

To gauge the best approach and tactics, Kissinger sought to clarify the real nature and purpose of the negotiations at hand. For example, he distinguished between negotiations that took place within a "legitimate international order" and those that took place with "revolutionary" powers.

As examples of negotiations within a "legitimate" order, one might imagine trade talks among the United States, Canada, and Mexico; burden-sharing bargaining within NATO; or negotiations to end a war between Peru and Ecuador. In such cases, issues of good faith and the willingness at least to explore mutually beneficial agreements color the approach to negotiations, which still may be very tough.

By contrast, a sophisticated negotiator dealing with a "revolutionary" power (e.g., Ayatollah Khomeini's Iran, the early Soviet Union, or Mao's China during the Cultural Revolution) may find standard negotiation approaches misplaced. Kissinger observed that in these situations, "diplomats can still meet but they cannot persuade each other. Instead, diplomatic conferences become elaborate stage plays which seek to influence and win over public opinion in other nations . . . They are less a forum for negotiation than a platform for propaganda."[3]

Obviously, negotiating to genuinely explore agreements calls for a radically different approach than negotiating to score (or avoid) propaganda points. Kissinger's Harvard and government colleague Fred Iklé, who served as director of the U.S. Arms Control and Disarmament Agency, highlighted other motives for negotiation than seeking agreement—he called them "side effects"—including gathering intelligence, influencing third parties, diverting the other side from using force, buying time, deceiving other governments, or maintaining contact to communicate on other matters.[4] Tactical choices obviously depend on the real purpose of the negotiation.

The stage of the negotiation process also influences choice of tactics. Well before the agenda has crystallized, especially in talks where mutual suspicion is high and prior communication limited or nonexistent, tactics for early meetings may have different goals from directly working out a deal. In 1971, for example, China and America did not recognize each other, had no diplomats in each other's capitals, had established no direct way to talk, and had not communicated officially for twenty years. Thus, when Kissinger made his secret visit to Beijing, the "underlying challenge . . . was to establish enough confidence to turn a first meeting into a process." The two problems that were "recognized as insoluble in the short term" were Taiwan and Vietnam. "The problem was how to put them aside."[5]

Choosing the most appropriate moves at the table, therefore, depends on analyzing the real nature of the negotiation at hand and whether it is in a preliminary or later stage. Given these assessments, the next five chapters of this book (chapters 9–13) help us drill down: How important are personal relationships in high-stakes negotiations? How much effort should I expend building rapport with my counterpart? Should I start high or more moderately? If a concession is required, when and how should I make it? Under what conditions should I keep the process secret? And so on. As we more systematically study Kissinger zooming in to the table itself, we will gain considerable insight into these and many other tactical choices.

9

Reading Counterparts

[Kissinger] was a tremendous strategist and conceptual thinker as a geopolitician. . . . He was a superb negotiator, one who was able to adjust his negotiating style to his interlocutors and their cultural history.

—WINSTON LORD[1]

[Kissinger displayed] an almost devilish psychological intuition, an instinct for grasping the hidden springs of character, of knowing what drives or what dooms another person. He was at his best as a face-to-face negotiator precisely because of this rare talent.

—STANLEY HOFFMANN[2]

In our experience, some negotiators gravitate to the general and strategic. Others focus on the specific and personal. Many fewer effectively maintain both perspectives. Thus far, we have elaborated Kissinger's highly developed capacity to "zoom out" to the broader picture, where we have characterized his approach to be strategic, realistic, prone to changing the game, and dexterous in multiparty situations. In tandem with this somewhat detached and analytical view, Kissinger consistently "zooms in" to his individual counterparts with highly customized personal and cultural insights. As the epigraphs that begin this chapter suggest—one by Winston Lord, longtime diplomatic colleague and admirer; the other by the late Stanley Hoffmann, Harvard colleague and fierce critic—Kissinger was unusually skilled at reading his negotiating counterparts and adapting his approach to each person with whom he dealt.

It would be too simple to write off this characteristic as innate. While other negotiators may not match Kissinger's psychological acuity, a great deal can be learned from his approach to zooming in on each interlocutor. Especially for those who regard negotiations mainly as dueling spreadsheets (or term sheets or legal briefs), it can be highly rewarding to cultivate the discipline to consciously assess and encompass the personal and psychological.

Our earlier account of Kissinger's Rhodesian negotiations suggests the value of combining these macro and micro perspectives and seeking to bring the two into productive alignment. With his broader sequential strategy as backdrop, recall Kissinger's intensive discussions with Tanzania's Julius Nyerere. Although the two men came from very different cultures, Kissinger simultaneously sought to understand Nyerere's perspectives and motivations and to build rapport on personal and geopolitical levels. Similarly, after intensively seeking to penetrate the mind-sets and interests of South African prime minister John Vorster and Rhodesian prime minister Ian Smith, Kissinger exhibited both empathy and assertiveness in his persuasive (and largely successful) efforts.

Time and again, we observe sharply etched portraits that Kissinger drew of his interlocutors with implications for how to negotiate most effectively with each. His behavioral and psychological insights derived from direct observation of those with whom he negotiated, from consultations with experts and others who had had direct contact with his counterparts, from research, from awareness of pivotal experiences and events that had shaped them, and from assessments of how political and institutional forces had left their marks.

It is one thing to suggest the importance of zooming in to understand one's negotiating counterparts. It is far more instructive to see what this means in practice. Thus we will review Kissinger's portrayals of several people with whom he negotiated, both foreign and within the U.S. government. (After all, "internal" negotiations are often as difficult as or more difficult than "external" ones.) Kissinger prepared some of these assessments in advance of the negotiations; others were also informed by later reflection.

Beyond Stereotypes: Understanding Individuals in Their Cultural and Political Contexts

We begin with Kissinger's very brief characterization of three important Chinese counterparts: "Mao, Zhou, and later Deng were all extraordinary personalities. Mao was the visionary, ruthless, pitiless, occasionally murderous revolutionary; Zhou, the elegant, charming, brilliant administrator; and Deng, the reformer of elemental convictions. The three men reflected a common tradition of painstaking analysis and the distillation of the experiences of an ancient country with an instinct for distinguishing between the permanent and the tactical."[3] While suggesting common "Chinese" characteristics, note how Kissinger avoids stereotypes by immediately differentiating among Mao, Zhou, and Deng.

In a continuation of the same passage, Kissinger broadly contrasts the "Soviet" style with the approach of the Chinese, whose "negotiating style was as different from that of their Soviet counterparts as was possible. Soviet diplomats almost never discussed conceptual issues. Their tactic was to select a problem of immediate concern to Moscow and to batter away at its resolution with a dogged persistence designed to wear down their interlocutors rather than to persuade them. The insistence and the vehemence with which Soviet negotiators put forward the Politburo consensus reflected the brutal discipline and internal strains of Soviet politics, and transformed high policy into an exhausting retail trade."[4]

This contrast of the Soviet negotiating style with that of the Chinese might seem to risk overreliance on national stereotypes. From time to time, Kissinger did indulge in broad national stereotyping (e.g., "to tell a Syrian not to haggle is like ordering a fish not to swim,"[5] and Thieu dealt in the "Vietnamese manner: indirectly, elliptically, by methods designed to exhaust rather than to clarify, constantly needling but never addressing the real issue."[6]) Yet, while culture, historical experience, and political structure certainly influence negotiating counterparts, and must be understood, Kissinger consistently highlighted striking differences among individuals who shared cultures and backgrounds. To see this more clearly, we turn to Kissinger's comparisons of two Soviet and two Chinese leaders with whom he had important negotiations.

Two Soviet Leaders: Dobrynin and Brezhnev

Consider how Kissinger characterized Anatoly Dobrynin, then Soviet ambassador to the United States: "Dobrynin . . . was a classic product of the Communist society. Born into a family of twelve children, and the first member of his family to go to a university, he had benefited from the system that he represented so ably. He was trained as an electrical engineer and seconded to the Foreign [Ministry] during the war. Whether he owed his flexibility to his training in a subject relatively free of deadening ideology, or to a natural disposition, he was one of the few Soviet diplomats of my acquaintance who could understand the psychology of others. . . . He knew how to talk to Americans in a way brilliantly attuned to their preconceptions. He too was especially skilled at evoking the inexhaustible American sense of guilt, by persistently but pleasantly hammering home the impression that every deadlock was our fault. [. . .] he understood that a reputation for reliability is an important asset in foreign policy. Subtle and disciplined, warm in his demeanor while wary in his conduct, Dobrynin moved through the upper echelons of Washington with consummate skill."[7]

In contrast to Kissinger's take on Dobrynin, consider a memo he wrote to help prepare President Gerald Ford deal effectively with Soviet general secretary Leonid Brezhnev. (Such memos were often group efforts, with input by area specialists, though they went to the president under his name.) In the memo, Kissinger offered trenchant assessments of Brezhnev's background, interests, political situation, habits, and personal negotiating style.[8] While referencing a stereotype in passing, Kissinger reminded Ford of the importance to Brezhnev of the upcoming meeting: "to be seen in the company of the U.S. President, or closeted with you in secret sessions fills a deep seated Russian need to be accepted as an equal."

Excerpts from Kissinger's preparatory memo further distinguished the general secretary from Ambassador Dobrynin: "Brezhnev is a mixture of crudeness and warmth . . . He has . . . love of physical contact—back slapping, bear hugs, and kisses . . . prides himself on being a sportsman . . . He vows he will never give up hunting, and he remains an avid soccer fan . . . He is given to incessant complaining to his colleagues about minor ailments, the workload . . . Brezhnev is a nervous man, partly because of his personal insecurity, partly for physiological reasons traced to his consumption of alcohol and tobacco, his history of heart disease and the pressures of his job. You will find his hands perpetually in motion, twirling his gold watch chain, flicking ashes from his ever-present cigarette. [World War II] remains an earth shaking experience for him. . . . He knows something of the human disaster of war—one should credit him with genuine abhorrence of

it, though, of course, he uses fear of war in others to obtain political ends. Brezhnev probably will remind you of a tough and
shrewd union boss, conscious of his position and his interests, alert
to slights. . . . He will try to flatter you . . . When he wants something, Brezhnev will be voluble in explaining how much in your
own interest a certain position is; he may intimate that it took a
great deal of effort to get his colleagues to agree to a concession . . .
He may stall interminably, but once he moves he will want things
settled at once."[9]

Reflecting on these characterizations, it is hard to take seriously
the many how-to manuals that purport to inform readers about
"negotiating with the Chinese," "negotiating with the Russians,"
or "negotiating with nationality X," manuals that ascribe uniform
characteristics to people of each nationality.[10] Of course, there are
central tendencies associated with different countries, but Kissinger's assessment reminds us that we negotiate with individuals, not
stereotypical cultural averages.

Two Chinese Leaders: Mao and Zhou

Kissinger's views of a pair of pivotal Chinese figures, Mao and
Zhou, help us zoom in even further. After Kissinger's two preliminary visits to China, he sought to prepare Nixon for his upcoming
trip to China on February 21, 1972, the first by an American president. Nixon was certain to deal primarily with Mao and Zhou.[11]

Kissinger's preparatory memo offered Nixon a comparative
overview of the two men, turning first to Mao: "A convenient
distinction between Mao and Zhou . . . is to cite the Chairman
as the philosopher and Zhou as the practitioner. Thus we can
think of Mao as the philosopher, the poet, the grand strategist, the
inspirer, the romantic. He sets the direction and the framework
and leaves the implementation to his trusted lieutenant. He can
be counted on to speak in broad, philosophic, historic terms and

leave the negotiations to Zhou. He will want to talk about the long view, the basic tides running in the world, where China and the U.S. are heading, with each other and with others."[12]

Turning to Zhou Enlai, Kissinger summarized his role and personality: "Zhou is the tactician, the administrator, the negotiator, the master of details and thrust and parry. His emphasis will be on the concrete substantive issues and he will invoke the Chairman's authority and prescience with what seems total sincerity. However, this distinction between the two men can be misleading. Zhou is perfectly at home on the philosophic plane, and he couches his tactical arguments in historical and conceptual terms . . . Zhou is clearly running China. He is the dominant figure in both the party and the government, and he steers both foreign and domestic policy."[13]

Leavening his initial characterization of Mao ("poet, philosopher," etc.), Kissinger reminded Nixon of the Chinese leader's toughness and the daunting challenges he had surmounted: "Mao can be as ruthlessly pragmatic as he is ideologically fanatic . . . after all, in the past half-dozen years, a whole string of his closest associates have been declared guilty of the most serious crimes and whisked out of sight—including two hand-picked heirs and his personal secretary. . . . [A]gain and again, [Mao] has faced one towering crisis after another—the annihilation campaigns of Chiang, Long March, Japanese invasion, civil war with the Nationalists, Korean War, Great Leap Forward, split with Moscow, Cultural Revolution, progressive Soviet encirclement. Surmounting such challenges requires vision as well as tactics . . . Mao's peasant background is evident in his direct and earthy humor, which he often used to ridicule or disarm opponents."[14]

Kissinger then offered Nixon more detailed advice, anticipating Zhou's approach to negotiation and making suggestions for how to deal with it most effectively. A number of excerpts from the preparatory memo are worth recounting to illustrate this point: "[Zhou] is charming, articulate and tough. . . . You can be sure that he has done his homework, not only on the issues, but also on America and you personally. . . . His negotiating style is extremely effective and requires finesse to counter. If he states a position in absolute terms, he will stick by it at least for awhile. He is not to be pressed if he is not ready to be pressed.

If, however, he is at all evasive or ambiguous—which is the usual case—this suggests room for exploration. In this case it is better to go at the issue circuitously rather than frontally. Either later in a meeting, or on an informal occasion, you could pick up the subject again and suggest another approach. He might then absorb this and come back subsequently with a new statement incorporating elements of what you said but presenting it as the Chinese view.

The indirect approach, the use of analogy, is typical of the Chinese in general and Zhou in particular. Almost everything he says, no matter how far it seems to stray from the subject at hand, is making a relevant point. This oblique style is not at all inconsistent with candor. Indeed, frankness was one of the dominant elements in our talks with Zhou and frankness would serve you well in your conversations.

Zhou can be extremely—and suddenly—tough. Both General Haig and I have been treated to withering blasts . . . You should not let such statements stand but rather respond very firmly, though non-abusively. If you start pulling back he will stay on the offensive."[15]

Finally, in contrast to dealing with the Soviets, Kissinger suggests the best approach to responding to "hard" statements from these Chinese leaders: "Zhou's firmness, however, is not the kind of brutalizing toughness which we have come to expect from the Russians, but rather a hardness and consistency of purpose derived from fifty years of revolutionary experience. . . .

Thus if Zhou (or Mao) makes hard statements, your response must be different than what you would use with the Russians. The latter can be met with tough language as well as tough substance. With the Chinese, it is important to counter strongly with one's own viewpoint, but in a way that reflects comprehension of their point of view. My own experience is that if you remain firm on principles but express yourself with restraint, they are likely to modify their rhetoric and address points of contention in a relatively realistic way. . . .

In sum, these people are both fanatic and pragmatic. They are tough ideologues who totally disagree with us on where the world is going, or should be going. At the same time, they are hard realists who calculate they need us because of a threatening Soviet Union, a resurgent Japan, and a potentially independent Taiwan. . . .

[Yet] . . . these leaders are in their seventies, and they surely want to reach certain goals before they depart the scene. . . . [the internal opposition to both men] underline[s] the great gamble that Mao and Zhou have taken in dealing with us and inviting you. Thus they will need to show some immediate results for *their* domestic audience."[16]

Elsewhere, Kissinger summed up the contrasting approaches of the Soviets and the Chinese: "The Soviets insist on their prerogatives as a great power. The Chinese establish a claim on the basis of universal principles and a demonstration of self-confidence that attempts to make the issue of power irrelevant."[17] The China of Mao and Zhou "had absorbed conquerors and had proved its inward strength by imposing its social and intellectual style on them. Its leaders were aloof, self-assured, composed. Brezhnev represented a nation that had survived not by civilizing its conquerors but by outlasting them . . . he sought to obscure his lack of assurance by boisterousness."[18]

Beyond the Soviets and the Chinese

Whether his interlocutor was Soviet (Dobrynin, Brezhnev), Chinese (Mao, Zhou, Deng), Vietnamese (Le Duc Tho), or from Southern Africa (Nyerere, Vorster, Smith) or elsewhere, Kissinger developed a granular sense of each individual as a person. This extended both to Middle Eastern counterparts and to those within the U.S. government. For example, Kissinger described Israeli prime minister Golda Meir: "She was a founder of her country. Every inch of land for which Israel had fought was to her a token of her people's survival; it would be stubbornly defended against enemies; it would be given up only for a tangible guarantee of security. She had a penetrating mind, leavened by earthiness and a mischievous sense of humor. She was not taken in by elevated rhetoric, or particularly interested in the finer points of negotiating tactics. She cut to the heart of the matter. She answered pomposity with irony and dominated conversations by her personality and shrewd psychology. To me she acted as a benevolent aunt toward an especially favored nephew, so that even to admit the possibility of disagreement was a challenge to family hierarchy producing emotional outrage. It was usually calculated."[19]

And since many negotiations have an extensive internal and domestic component, it is hardly surprising that Kissinger assessed his U.S. government colleagues, such as Secretary of State William Rogers, as carefully as his foreign counterparts.[20] For example, consider his characterization of Melvin Laird, then secretary of defense and a frequent "internal" negotiating counterpart. Note how the concise assessment sizes up not only Laird's personality but his experience and place in the political and bureaucratic environment of the time: "Having served on the Defense Subcommittee of the House Appropriations Committee for most of his sixteen years in the Congress, Laird knew his subject thoroughly before he took office. And Laird had an important constituency. Remaining influential in the Congress . . . Laird could be ignored by the President only at serious risk. And while Laird's maneuvers were often as Byzantine in their complexity or indirection as those of Nixon, he accomplished with verve and surprising goodwill what Nixon performed with grim determination and inward resentment. Laird liked to win, but unlike Nixon, derived no great pleasure from seeing someone else lose. There was about him a buoyancy and a rascally good humor that made working with him as satisfying as it could on occasion be maddening."[21]

It might be tempting to regard such observations as mere character sketches, undertaken almost for literary purposes. Yet close observation evidently served as a means of figuring out the most effective approach to dealing with the subject. In Laird's case, as with Chinese and Soviet leaders, Kissinger deployed psychological insight to generate negotiating advice: "Provided he was allowed some reasonable range for saving face by maneuvering to a new position without embarrassment, Laird accepted bureaucratic setbacks without rancor. . . . In working with him, intellectual arguments were only marginally useful and direct orders were suicidal. I eventually learned that it was safest to begin a battle with Laird by closing off insofar as possible all his bureaucratic or Congressional escape routes, provided I could figure them out, which was not always easy. Only then would I broach substance. But even with such tactics I lost as often as I won."[22]

Similarly, with respect to the Vietnam negotiations and his dealings with Le Duc Tho (which we describe in chapter 6), Kissinger observed that: "An experienced negotiator—which by this time, I was—develops a sixth sense for when the other side is ready to settle. The signals are usually matters of nuance: Some issues are not pressed to the absolute limit; some claims are marginally modified; the door to compromise is always kept tangentially ajar. None of these indicators appeared in the November round of [the Paris peace] talks; . . . One telltale sign was Tho's persistent refusal to let experts from both sides discuss the protocols . . . I repeatedly asked for North Vietnamese drafts . . . and said that our experts . . . were ready to negotiate on them immediately. Tho evaded each of our requests with the excuse that the North Vietnamese drafts were not ready. This was amazing in light of Hanoi's insistence three weeks earlier that we sign the basic documents by October 31."[23]

Of course, as we earlier established, North Vietnamese intransigence at the bargaining table was arguably driven by factors other than personalities (e.g., increasing American troop withdrawals, domestic U.S. opposition to the war).

There are many other telling examples of Kissinger's insight into individuals and how best to deal with each (e.g., Zhou Enlai,[24] Anwar Sadat,[25] Mao Zedong[26]). The prescriptive point, however, should be clear: in tandem with the capacity to "zoom out" to a strategic framework, effective negotiators should cultivate the habit of perceptively zooming in on their interlocutors so that, insofar as possible, the micro and macro can be brought into productive alignment.

Four Observations on Zooming In to Understand Your Counterpart

With these sketches in mind—of Dobrynin, Brezhnev, Mao, Zhou, Le Duc Tho, Meir, and Laird—we make four observations about Kissinger's practice of "zooming in."

- First, it is beyond our scope to assess the accuracy of Kissinger's portrayals. Assessments of negotiating counterparts can be only as good as the information and experience on which they are based. While Kissinger consulted the CIA and various China specialists (including Edgar Snow, Ross Terrill, John Fairbank, and even André Malraux)[27] to inform his preparatory memo on Mao and Zhou, the United States had had little official contact with China over the preceding twenty years. Kissinger's direct experience on which to base his assessment was limited to his two China trips in July and October prior to Nixon's visit. Little wonder that later scholars would offer significant correctives to the portrait that Kissinger painted, for example, of Mao in his preparatory memo.[28]

- Second, calibrating for limited available information and inevitable personal bias, we note the exquisite care Kissinger took to understand with whom he or the president would be dealing. As he put it with respect to Nixon's China visit, "I know of no Presidential trip that was as carefully planned," with voluminous briefing books on the issues, suggested talking points, and "lengthy analyses of the personalities."[29] These were not recitations of a few throwaway adjectives (e.g., "tough," "smart," "wily") plus simple biographical details (e.g., education, career trajectory). Instead, they were nuanced assessments of individuals and their formative experiences. Based on these assessments, Kissinger often spelled out recommendations for the most effective strategy and tactics. Even where information is scarce, this is an invaluable practice for effective negotiators.

- Third, while many of the descriptions we have cited were written after the fact and include later perspectives, we purposely cited Kissinger's more detailed analyses, which were written *in advance* of upcoming negotiations. The approach and focus of these preparatory assessments are consistent with those of the many after-the-fact sketches we have cited.

- Fourth, while the preceding four chapters on zooming out to the strategic, substantive, and analytic factors strike us as compelling—and for many negotiators, these factors constitute the central or sole focus of the process—Kissinger's extraordinary attention to the personal is instructive. The geopolitical (or financial or legal) chessboard, while absolutely necessary for effective negotiation, is normally insufficient for dealing successfully with the *people* on the other side of the table. The larger point here is the importance of deeply probing the psyche, history, perceptions, and motivations of your negotiating counterparts. In our jargon, the imperative is to "zoom in" to the person as well as to "zoom out" to the strategy and substantive analysis.

Factoring in Political Culture and Decision-Making Processes

As Kissinger's sketches suggest, it is not merely distinctive individual characteristics that matter. To avoid error, effective negotiators must understand the limits implied by their counterparts' cultural, political, and institutional contexts. This requires both awareness of gaps in one's knowledge and a determination to fill them. As Kissinger noted, "When I first came into office, there was no major country I understood less than Japan. Like most Americans, I admired its extraordinary recovery from the devastation of World War II. But I did not grasp Japan's unique character."[30] Indeed, after the 1973 Arab-Israeli War, Kissinger failed to persuade Japan's prime minister to follow American policy; in large part, the path Kissinger urged would have left Japan subject to a devastating oil embargo.

However, in later dealings, Kissinger refined his understanding

207

of the culture and decision-making processes faced when negotiating with senior Japanese officials. He noted that: "High office in Japan is not an entitlement to issue orders, much less to rule by decree; it basically confers the privilege of taking the lead in persuading one's colleagues. A Japanese prime minister is the custodian of national consensus, not the creator of it. Faced with American negotiators seeking to sway him on a personal level through the insistent reiteration of arguments or personal charm—as if the failure to agree were the result of incomprehension—the Japanese leader takes refuge in obscure evasions or, if pressed to the wall, implies the promise of something he cannot implement . . ."[31]

Kissinger continued, emphasizing the constraints that the Japanese consensus decision process imposes: "Summits between American presidents and Japanese prime ministers therefore all too frequently end in frustration. The American president asks for a decision—that is, an act of will to be imposed on reluctant colleagues or on a resistant bureaucracy. Since no modern Japanese prime minister has—or has ever had—that much authority, any acquiescence expresses at best a commitment to make an effort to persuade, not to command. Until the group relevant to the consensus (usually those who have to implement the decision) agrees that there is no alternative, the promise cannot be fulfilled. The single-mindedness of the consensus process is purchased at the cost of a seeming imperviousness to the sensibilities and views of foreigners and a languid pace in reaching decisions."[32]

Similarly, with respect to Israeli counterparts, that country's history and fragmented political system both carry strong implications for its leaders' approach to negotiation: "Because Israeli cabinets represent a coalition of competing personalities as well as parties, the opening Israeli position generally represents the sum of every key minister's preferences—especially when there is not a dominant Prime Minister, as was the case at the time of Rabin's first cabinet. Israeli negotiators modify their positions only after they have demonstrated to themselves and, above all, to their colleagues that there is no blood left to be squeezed out of the stone or, when there is a mediator—as there was during the shuttles—by saddling him with the blame for not having achieved their maximum position."[33]

With respect to the Sinai disengagement talks, Kissinger observed that: "extracting a concession from an Israeli government is usually a hair-raising enterprise. But one has to understand the dilemma. When you have a country 50 miles wide at its widest point and with a very narrow margin of survival, you cannot run risks. And when you are of the generation . . . who had with their own blood acquired every territory, you could understand . . . the reluctance. . . . But at any rate, Israel agreed in principle to a withdrawal some distance from the Suez Canal, but the Israeli cabinet is usually so divided, I don't think anybody has ever had a majority of more than four seats in parliament. . . . [T]hey never authorized their negotiators [with general instructions], so they had to have specific ones."[34]

It is easily possible to continue in this vein, reviewing other counterparts, cultures, and decision-making processes. But Stanley Hoffmann's observation seems apt: "One could cull a bestiary of negotiating styles" from Kissinger. We opened this chapter with shared views by Hoffmann and Winston Lord about Kissinger's insight into the interpersonal and cultural. However, this was not merely insight; together with a strategic overview, it guided Kissinger's negotiating approach. From an appreciative Winston Lord, "Kissinger had a sense of each of these negotiating styles [Chinese, Soviet, Israeli, Egyptian]. He was very good at trying to understand what the other side needed, as well as what we needed . . . He was never naive enough to base his negotiating style on personal likes or dislikes. He did this in terms of national self-interest. However, around the edges you can build up trust in some cases that help you get through some difficult points."[35]

Stanley Hoffmann's assessment of Kissinger's ability to zoom in on his counterparts mixes admiration for the technique with a critical edge. Hoffmann suggested that from Kissinger's memoir *White House Years* one could construct an "appendix to *The Prince*, on the art of diplomatic bargaining. For Kissinger's . . . gift is one that puts into practice his insights into personalities and cultures: it is the gift for the manipulation of power—exploiting the weaknesses and strengths of character of his counterparts, either by neutralizing them (if they were adversaries) or turning them into allies or accomplices by addressing their needs and playing on their fears of other countries."[36]

These observations suggest a far more general, if obvious, proposition. Beyond the strategic and analytical, your effectiveness as a negotiator can be dramatically enhanced by determination to develop a psychological understanding of your counterparts plus appreciation for their historical experiences and national and political cultures. Similarly, mapping the "behind-the-table" decision-making processes in which they are enmeshed (whether autocratic, coalitional among contending factions, a multilevel hierarchical procedure, or consensual) can usefully inform your approach.

There is an old saying that you are unlikely to find that for which you are not looking. Disciplining your negotiating approach to zoom in on your counterpart à la Kissinger will often yield nuggets of valuable insight well beyond the strategic and analytical.

10

Relationships and Rapport

Given the dominant image of Kissinger as a geopolitical grand-master moving pieces on the global chessboard in pursuit of what he saw as American interests, some may be surprised at the stress he places on developing personal relationships and rapport in negotiation. Predictably, Kissinger maintains the primacy of national interest over personal or relational considerations.[1] Yet national interest was not the whole story.

Kissinger observed that "Very often there arises a gray area where the national interest is not self-evident or [is] disputed . . ."[2] In such situations, Kissinger places a premium on the distinctive value of direct personal interactions with counterparts. Often, direct contact is key [because] "they have to have explained to them what is really being thought, which you can't put through cables."[3] In these interactions, building trust can pay off.[4]

Kissinger emphasizes the importance of developing and nurturing relationships *before* the needs of specific negotiations arise. Indeed, while our immediate focus will be on relationships with specific people, Kissinger built such relationships into an astonishingly large and varied network that extended far beyond official channels to include journalists, press, and television personalities, as well as cultural figures and academics. As Niall Ferguson shows, this carefully nurtured network proved to be a formidable asset.[5]

Along with former secretary of state George Shultz, who underscored the importance of "tending the diplomatic garden" for relationships to flourish, Kissinger observed that "It's very important to establish relationships before you need anything, so that there is a measure of respect in negotiations once they occur or when a crisis develops. When you travel as Secretary, . . . sometimes the best result is that you don't try to get a result but try to get an understanding for the next time you go to them."[6] Repeated personal contacts among leaders can help align goals and "keep the machinery of cooperation in working order."[7]

Such communication can sometimes be more effective when it takes place informally and outside the public eye. This can permit more wide-ranging exploration of possibilities and prevent potential political and bureaucratic opponents from prematurely mobilizing to block initiatives. A sometimes overlooked benefit of sustained private contact can be the positive effect it can have on relationships among the principals. A relationship of trust can lead counterparts to open up, unlocking useful information and insights. And a network of such relationships offers even greater value in complex negotiations.

Building a Relationship with Anatoly Dobrynin in the "Channel"

Relative to the conference rooms in which formal negotiations generally took place, a private channel proved especially important for Kissinger's dealings with his Soviet counterpart, Ambassador Anatoly Dobrynin. The secret "Channel," as it later came to be known, helped build a positive relationship between Kissinger and Dobrynin, which in turn facilitated important negotiations. It is worth examining this set of tactical choices (where, how, and under what conditions to meet) from each man's viewpoint.

Kissinger argued that "What the negotiator has to have, there has to be a channel in which the two sides can tell each other, at a minimum, what their thinking is, because you spend a lot of time in high office on the intentions of other countries. These other countries tell you accurately what their intentions are, and if you develop enough confidence in that, it facilitates the process of decision making. Of course it's possible that they fool you and it's possible that they tell you something, but they can do it only once, and then they've destroyed the channel. So what we could do through the Dobrynin channel was to permit the exploration of ideas."[8]

Dobrynin described his relationship with Kissinger and how communication between the two functioned logistically: "[T]he confidential [C]hannel between the leaders of both countries functioned continuously in the greatest secrecy. We used it by treating each other to breakfasts and lunches in private, but mostly I would visit Kissinger, entering the White House through the service gate. Our meetings there were usually held either in his office near the president's, or, when protracted negotiations on Vietnam and strategic arms limitation began, in the imposing and quiet ground floor Map Room from which Franklin Roosevelt used to address the nation by radio during the war. Later, as our contacts became more frequent and we met almost daily, the president ordered the installation of a direct and secure telephone line between the White House and the Soviet embassy for the exclusive use of Kissinger and me; we would just lift our receivers and talk, without dialing. . . .

Good personal relations with Kissinger were founded on our mutual desire to listen to and understand each other, and to seek some agreeable solution or compromise to our differences, all of which helped overcome or minimize our difficulties during our official contacts or negotiations. Of course we had rather heated discussions on some issues, but they never turned into personal confrontations. One factor, which I always valued, was Henry's keen sense of humor, which I always did my best to answer in kind. After all, humor helps to reach the heart as well as the mind of your partner."[9]

Kissinger gave numerous examples of how the Channel functioned in negotiations with the Soviets; for example, in the Strategic Arms Limitation Talks (SALT), he observed that "Whenever a deadlock persisted in these formal talks, the White House tended to interject itself through the Channel. Generally[,] Dobrynin and I would work out an agreement in principle on the stalemated issue; the delegations would then develop elaborate technical implementation and the textual language."[10]

Anatoly Dobrynin concurred on the importance of the Channel to the results of several U.S.–Soviet negotiations: "I can say with certainty that had it not been for that channel, many key agreements on complicated and controversial issues would have never been reached, and dangerous tension would not have been eased over Berlin, Cuba, or the Middle East. The basic agreements on the limitation of strategic arms, and finally, the most sensitive negotiations on the preparation of summit meetings would all go through our confidential channel."[11]

While the explicit focus in this section has been on the value (and limits) of building relationships in negotiation, the Kissinger-Dobrynin story adds secrecy into the mix. In this case, the private Channel fostered communication and a stronger relationship, which in turn helped produce highly valuable agreements in several highly contentious areas. Whether to negotiate secretly, for which Kissinger opted in several key negotiations, is a tactical choice with clear benefits but potentially significant costs—which we will explore in chapter 13.

Nurturing the Vital Relationship with the President/One's Superior

Having the confidence and backing of your superior self-evidently enhances your effectiveness as a negotiator. Your counterparts realize that you speak with authority and are unlikely to be overridden. Like James Baker with George H. W. Bush and Condoleezza Rice with George W. Bush, Kissinger enjoyed an unusually close relationship with President Nixon. In part, this resulted from their deeply compatible worldview and strategic orientation.

Kissinger explained: "My relationship with Nixon was unusual in the sense that he had appointed me out of the camp of his principal adversary within the Republican Party [Nelson Rockefeller], that I did not know him, when he appointed me was my first meeting with him, but that our thinking on the overall strategic necessities was so parallel that I could go abroad with the assurance that he would stand behind me. I can't think of one instance—there wasn't an instance—where he overruled me in a negotiation."[12]

Your relationship with your superiors is not something that can be taken for granted or assumed as a consequence of your formal position, even as secretary of state. Kissinger stressed that this relationship must be nurtured on an ongoing basis: "[T]he relationship of the president and the secretary is absolutely key. The State Department has a tendency to insist on its prerogative that it is exclusively entitled to conduct foreign policy. My view is that when you assert your prerogatives you've already lost the bureaucratic battle. I saw the president every day when we were both in town because I felt it was absolutely essential that we thought along the same lines. I was lucky. I had extraordinarily close relationships with the two presidents [Nixon and Ford whom] I served. In fact, if one looks at the history of the secretaries of state, it's rare. If they don't have a close relationship, they don't last."[13]

Kissinger may well have been referring obliquely to William P. Rogers, the often-ignored and sidelined secretary of state in the first Nixon administration, during which Kissinger served as national security advisor. Rogers, a former attorney general in the Eisenhower years and a very successful lawyer, had little experience in foreign affairs. In Kissinger's judgment, "Nixon considered Rogers's unfamiliarity with the subject an asset because it guaranteed that policy direction would remain in the White House . . . Few Secretaries of State can have been selected because of their President's confidence in their ignorance of foreign policy."[14] Given Nixon's legendary distrust of the State Department, Rogers's appointment greatly boosted the influence of the national security advisor and his White House staff. By September 1973, Kissinger had succeeded Rogers as secretary of state while simultaneously retaining his role as national security advisor.

With respect to negotiation, the role of a subordinate is not merely to act as an agent of his or her superior because the superior is too busy or otherwise unavailable. There are clear structural reasons for presidents or prime ministers not to negotiate personally, except for the resolution of the small set of issues they alone should address. As Kissinger explains, "[I]t is almost always a mistake for heads of state to undertake the details of a negotiation. They are then obliged to master specifics normally handled by their foreign offices and are deflected onto subjects more appropriate to their subordinates, while being kept from issues only heads of state can resolve. Since no one without a well-developed ego reaches the highest office, compromise is difficult and deadlocks are dangerous."[15] He continues: "[A]s a general negotiating rule, I think it is very dangerous for heads of state to meet unless they know the outcome pretty well, because they are people of strong egos and there's nobody to appeal to if it fails."[16]

Building Rapport with Counterparts

Whether building a relationship with the president or a negotiating counterpart, Kissinger could be charming. Although his rages were legendary, his personal style (well informed, sharp-witted, happy to share information and colorful anecdotes, sometimes flattering to his counterparts, and increasingly a celebrity) could constitute a formidable negotiation asset.

In his biography of Kissinger, Walter Isaacson describes Kissinger's particular charm, interviewing some journalists who dealt with him. One reporter noted, "[Kissinger] tells you what he thinks you want to hear, then asks what you think. It's very flattering." Isaacson elaborates: "Another tactic was intimacy. With an air of slight indiscretion and personal trust, neither totally feigned, Kissinger would share confidences and inside information. 'You always have the feeling that he's told you ten percent more than he has to,' said Barbara Walters. In social settings, or in offhand comments that he implicitly understood would remain off the record, he would be surprisingly revealing, especially in his descriptions of personalities."[17]

We have already heard from Winston Lord and Anatoly Dobrynin on the effectiveness of Kissinger's sense of humor, which could lighten the atmosphere and sometimes defuse tense moments. Humorous points and counterpoints were legion in Kissinger's dealings. During the 1972 Moscow Summit, the American photocopier broke down. "Knowing the KGB's reputation for Orwellian ubiquity," Kissinger quipped, "I asked Gromyko during a meeting in the elegant St. Catherine's Hall [*sic*] in the Kremlin whether he could have some copies made for us if we held certain documents up to the chandelier. Gromyko replied without missing a beat that unfortunately the cameras were installed by the tsars; they were adequate for photographing people but not documents."[18] British prime minister Ted Heath sharply clashed with Kissinger on important issues, including a refusal to let the United States use British bases in Cyprus to resupply Israel or to gather intelligence during the 1973 war. Yet Heath wryly remarked on Kissinger's "disarming way of handling people and a delightful, if somewhat unoriginal, sense of humor."[19]

Empathetically Identifying with Negotiating Counterparts

We have seen many examples of how consistently and closely Kissinger sought to understand the psychology and political context of his counterparts. This was not idle observation. After participating with Kissinger in countless negotiating sessions, Winston Lord commented, "When people talked to Kissinger, they had the feeling that he empathized with their point of view, even if they were ideologically at different poles. Whether they were conservatives or liberals, each one felt that Kissinger at least understood their point of view and may have been sympathetic with it."[20]

Frank Shakespeare, head of the U.S. Information Agency during the Nixon years, had a blunter assessment: "Kissinger can meet with six different people, smart as hell, learned, knowledgeable, experienced, of very different views, and persuade all six of them that the real Henry Kissinger is just where they are."[21] More pejoratively, Kissinger was said to be a "chameleon," casting "his words, acts, jokes, and style to appeal to his interlocutors of the moment. As he described the landscape they faced, he would stress to one side the hills and to the other the valleys."[22]

Of course, it is commonplace in negotiation and often useful to emphasize different aspects of a situation to different counterparts with different interests and perceptions. Coming across as empathetic and truly understanding the other's perspective can enhance communication, relationships, and progress in negotiation. *Empathy* can be a slippery term; when we use it, we don't mean sympathy or an emotional connection with the other. Instead, we mean the nonjudgmental demonstration that the empathizer truly understands, but does not necessarily agree with, the counterpart's perspective. If not overdone—and if combined with the ability to be assertive, as we have seen Kissinger to be in cases ranging from Southern Africa to the Soviet Union—this can be a valuable negotiating skill. It can lead counterparts to feel heard and can generate a sense of connection that can advance the process.

Genuine Empathy or Duplicity?

Yet this protean approach carries risks. It could lead Kissinger's counterparts to suspect that he was two-faced, especially if they compared notes and discovered seeming inconsistencies. Shimon Peres, who twice served as Israel's prime minister, is alleged to have remarked privately to Yitzhak Rabin, "With due respect to Kissinger, he is the most devious man I've ever met."[23] And Egypt's foreign minister Ismail Fahmy, no fan of Kissinger, was quoted as saying, "[Kissinger] always tried to hide his bias by cursing the Israelis and constantly making funny and unflattering remarks about the Israeli leaders to convince us that he was on our side.[24] . . . Unfortunately, his rather obvious ruses were fairly effective with Sadat."[25] (Of course, the Egyptian-Israeli accords Kissinger negotiated, regardless of how he came across, paved the way for a peaceful relationship, including Egypt's formal recognition of Israel in 1979, that has endured for decades.)

It is easy to lose credibility by lying or making conflicting statements to different people. According to Winston Lord, Kissinger sought to mitigate these risks. Lord noted that "Kissinger was very good at talking to different audiences, using different nuances . . . [But] you couldn't catch him in actually contradicting himself by comparing transcripts of interviews and speeches."[26] According to Walter Isaacson, Shimon Peres said that "If you didn't listen word by word, you could be carried away by what he said. . . . But if you listened word by word, he wasn't lying."[27] Isaacson affirmed that Kissinger was "careful to avoid outright duplicity and double-dealing," and quoted the former secretary of state as saying, "I may have kept things secret . . . but that's not the same as being deceitful."[28]

Many of his counterparts reflect positive views of Kissinger's personal approach to negotiation. Although British prime minister James Callaghan disagreed with Kissinger on a number of issues, Callaghan stated that "The flexibility and quickness of his mind gained him a reputation in some quarters for deviousness, and I therefore place on record that he never misled me in any of our joint enterprises."[29]

Anatoly Dobrynin reflected that "[Kissinger] was business-like and did not resort to ambiguities or avoid specific problems. When we later entered into serious negotiations, I learned that he could give you a big headache, but he was clever and highly professional."[30] Golda Meir ultimately lauded Kissinger, "whose efforts on behalf of peace in the area can only be termed superhuman. My own relationship with Henry Kissinger had its ups and downs. At times it became very complicated, and at times I know I annoyed and perhaps even angered him—and vice versa. But I admired his intellectual gifts, his patience and his perseverance were always limitless, and in the end we became good friends."[31] Even some who negotiated with Kissinger and ended up agreeing to terms they hated had positive words about his style and ability to connect. For example, Ian Smith bitterly underscored the isolation Rhodesia would face if he rejected the British-American plan. Smith lamented that "Kissinger was sympathetic . . . The case had been explained with superb clarity; the man had an obvious capacity for grasping a situation, analyzing it, and putting forward the pros and cons. Moreover, all of us had the refreshing feeling that it had been done with honesty and sincerity . . . Kissinger was absolutely straightforward and genuine."[32]

In tandem with developing an understanding for those with whom he negotiated, Kissinger generally sought to connect and build relationships with counterparts. Charm, flattery, and humor played roles, but a major factor was his effort to identify with the other side, demonstrating that he understood its interests and empathizing with its viewpoint. This form of empathy can be an invaluable asset, but with potentially mixed results depending on how it is pursued, and perceived. In this domain, perception trumps reality. If a counterpart suspects manipulation or deception, even if the strict truth does not support that view, the result may be wariness and suspicion rather than trust and a positive relationship. As Kissinger himself underscored, "The same negotiators meet over and over again; their ability to deal with one another is undermined if a diplomat acquires a reputation for evasion or duplicity."[33]

Yet while this chapter has focused on Kissinger's relationships and rapport with *individual* negotiating counterparts, such actions are part of a much larger story, brought to light by his biographer Niall Ferguson. About halfway through his work on Kissinger, Ferguson realized that it was not merely Kissinger's rapport with specific negotiating counterparts, but rather his "exceptional ability to build an eclectic network of relationships, not only to colleagues in the Nixon and Ford administrations, but also to people outside government: journalists, newspaper proprietors, foreign ambassadors, and heads of state—even Hollywood producers.[34] Developed at length in Ferguson's book, *The Square and the Tower*, Kissinger's capacity to forge emotional and intellectual connections in a vast network of his own construction was key to his formidable success as a negotiator.[35]

11

Proposals, Concessions, and "Constructive Ambiguity"

To settle on the right tactics, Kissinger stresses the importance of understanding the dynamics of the process. Almost poetically, he describes the uncertainties and intangibles that initially confront a negotiator and how the underlying situation will slowly be revealed: "The opening of a complicated negotiation is like the beginning of an arranged marriage. The partners know that the formalities will soon be stripped away as they discover each other's real attributes. Neither party can yet foretell at what point necessity will transform itself into acceptance; when the abstract desire for progress will leave at least residues of understanding; which disagreement will, by the act of being overcome, illuminate the as-yet-undiscovered sense of community and which will lead to an impasse destined to rend the relationship forever. The future being mercifully veiled, the parties attempt what they might not dare did they know what was ahead."[1]

Kissinger urges learning as much as possible about the situation before advocating one's own views, interests, or positions. In part, as we have highlighted, one learns through meticulous preparation. Yet even the best preparation yields incomplete understanding. As Kissinger explained, "Almost invariably I spent the first session of a new negotiation in educating myself. I almost never put forward a proposal. Rather, I sought to understand the intangibles in the position of my interlocutor and to gauge the scope as well as the limits of probable concessions."[2]

Making Proposals and Concessions:
How and When?

Many people think of negotiation as nothing more than haggling, not unlike at a bazaar: one side makes an initial extreme offer, and counteroffers follow. Concessions are slowly made in the hope that the parties may ultimately converge on a deal. Early in his career and later, reflecting on experience, Kissinger both characterized and critiqued the standard bargaining approach: "If agreement is usually found between two starting points, there is no point in making moderate offers. Good bargaining technique would suggest a point of departure far more extreme than what one is willing to accept. The more outrageous the initial proposition the better is the prospect that what one 'really' wants will be considered a compromise."[3]

He elaborated, cautioning about the risk of extreme demands: "One tactic—and indeed the traditional approach—is to outline one's maximum position and gradually retreat to a more attainable stance. Such a tactic is much beloved by negotiators eager to protect their domestic standing. Yet while it appears 'tough' to start with an extreme set of demands, the process amounts to a progressive weakening ushered in by the abandonment of the opening move. The other party is tempted to dig in at each stage to see what the next modification will bring and to turn the negotiating process into a test of endurance."[4]

Instead of tactical exaggeration, Kissinger counsels clearly conveying to the other side one's own objectives and underlying interests. He argues that failure to do so is an enemy of effective negotiation. Recall, for example, his early focus with South African prime minister John Vorster: "I began—as was my habit in almost all negotiations—with a philosophical discussion of what we were trying to achieve."[5]

Kissinger broadened this point to negotiations in general: "I made a considerable effort to leave no doubt about our fundamental approach. Only romantics think they can prevail in negotiation by trickery; only pedants believe in the advantage of obfuscation. In a society of sovereign states, an agreement will be maintained only if all parties consider it in their interest. They must have a sense of participation in the result. The art of diplomacy is not to outsmart the other side but to convince it either of common interests or of penalties if an impasse continues."[6] He continued: "[T]he wise diplomat understands that he cannot afford to trick his opponent; in the long run a reputation for reliability and fairness is an important asset. The same negotiators meet over and over again; their ability to deal with one another is undermined if a diplomat acquires a reputation for evasion or duplicity."[7]

★ ★ ★

Given a choice between the traditional bargaining approach and something very different, Kissinger expressed his clear bent: "[T]he preferable course is to make opening proposals close to what one judges to be the most sustainable outcome, a definition of 'sustainable' in the abstract being one that both sides have an interest in maintaining."[8]

Remaining close to what one judges to be the most sustainable outcome, rather than "starting high and conceding slowly," carries another potential benefit. It avoids one of the risks of developing a reputation for tactical "flexibility." Kissinger observed that

"American diplomacy . . . is urged to be 'flexible'; it feels an obligation to break deadlocks with new proposals—unintentionally inviting new deadlocks to elicit new proposals. These tactics can be used by determined adversaries in the service of a strategy of procrastination."[9] (Of course, by no means are all American diplomats susceptible to this risk.)

When Kissinger deviated from his own "anti-haggling" advice, however, Zhou Enlai unexpectedly jolted him back to what turned out to be a far more productive approach. Zhou urged negotiating on the merits rather than engaging in simple horse trading. In Kissinger's words, "While drafting the Shanghai Communiqué with Zhou Enlai, I at one point offered to trade an offensive phrase in the Chinese draft for something in the American version to which Zhou might object. 'We will never get anywhere this way,' he replied. 'If you can convince me why our phrase is offensive, I will give it to you.' "[10]

Of course, the extent to which this kind of joint problem-solving approach will be reciprocated depends on the other side. When one of us queried whether this method would have worked with his Soviet counterparts, Kissinger averred that, often, it would not have. More than he might have wished—for example, mediating between the Israelis and Syrians on a street-by-street basis in the Golan town of Quneitra after the 1973 war—he found himself in the role of the haggling rug merchant.

Kissinger generalized his advice on when to negotiate, how to formulate opening positions, and when to make concessions: "[T]he optimum moment for negotiations is when things appear to be going well. To yield to pressures is to invite them; to acquire the reputation for short staying power is to give the other side a powerful incentive for protracting negotiations. When a concession is made voluntarily it provides the greatest incentive for reciprocity. It also provides the best guarantee for staying power. In the negotiations that I conducted I always tried to determine the most reasonable outcome and then get there rapidly in one or two moves. This was derided as a strategy of 'preemptive concession' by those who like to make their moves in driblets and at the last moment. But I consider that strategy useful primarily for placating bureaucracies and salving consciences for it impresses novices as a demonstration of toughness.[11]

"Usually it proves to be self-defeating; shaving the salami encourages the other side to hold on to see what the next concession is likely to be, never sure that one has really reached the rock-bottom position. Thus, in the many negotiations I undertook—with the Vietnamese and others—I favored big steps taken when they were least expected, when there was a minimum of pressure, and creating the presumption that we would stick to that position. I almost always opposed modifications of our negotiating position under duress."[12]

Wordsmithing and "Constructive Ambiguity"

Evidently, the realist in Henry Kissinger regards actions and results, not words, as of supreme importance: "Statesmen prize steadiness and reliability in a partner, not a restless quest for ever-new magic formulas."[13] With respect to heads of state negotiating during summits, he cautions about the risk of merely papering over differences: "Deadlocks become difficult to break. Agreement may be achievable only by formulas so vague as to invite later disavowal or disagreement."[14]

Creative wordsmithing, however, can facilitate mutually beneficial results where clumsier formulations would result in impasse. Perhaps the most famous example of this comes from a U.S.-Chinese declaration that permitted more important joint interests to be pursued. During the negotiations over the opening to China, the thorniest issue involved the status of Taiwan, which claimed to be the legitimate government of the whole of China. At the same time, the People's Republic of China [the mainland] claimed that Taiwan was merely a rebellious province of the larger entity. Kissinger sharpened the negotiating challenge: "We needed a formula acknowledging the unity of China, which was the one point on which Taipei [the capital of Taiwan] and Peking agreed, without supporting the claim of either."[15]

To get past this issue, which had been a major contributor to total impasse in more than 130 prior U.S.-Chinese meetings in Warsaw, Kissinger modified an elegantly ambiguous formula with which both sides could live. This wordsmithing enabled U.S.-Chinese cooperation on a wide range of issues. The crucial sentences: "The United States acknowledges that all Chinese on either side of the Taiwan Straits maintain there is but one China. The United States Government does not challenge that position."[16]

Kissinger described the negotiation that followed his proposal on wording: "The Chinese asked for a recess at 11:35 p.m. At 4:45 a.m. we were given a new Chinese draft and by 5:30 a.m. Zhou returned. He and I refined the text for several more hours until at 8:10 a.m., concluding a nearly nonstop session of twenty-four hours, we had agreed on the main outline of what came to be known as the Shanghai Communiqué. It was an unusual document. Its explicit, sometimes brutal disagreements gave emphasis to the common positions—the concern with hegemony (a euphemism for Soviet expansionism), the commitment to normalize relations."[17] Kissinger later remarked, "I do not think anything I did or said impressed Zhou as much as this ambiguous formula with which both sides were able to live for nearly a decade."[18]

Consider a second example, involving the immediate aftermath of the 1973 Arab-Israeli War. Potential progress was stymied by contention over the wording of the letter of invitation to the formal negotiations; each party was trying to use the wording of the invitation to favorably influence the outcome of the planned negotiations. The process was stuck, in part over Palestinian participation in the talks on which the Arabs and Israelis had completely incompatible positions. If the parties did not come, there could be no headway on the issues.

Frustrated, Kissinger observed that "The debate over the letter of invitation could produce only deadlock, not progress. However the letter was phrased, it could not substitute for the actual negotiations. . . . As for the letter of invitation, I argued, it was essential to break out of the irrelevancies by which each party was trying to use the drafting exercise to foreordain the outcome before the conference was even assembled. If we were serious about disengagement first on the Egyptian and then on the Syrian front, the prime task was to . . . get on with the serious negotiation."[19]

Getting past the deadlocked and time-consuming debates on the wording of the invitation letter was clearly a worthy goal. But how, as a practical matter, to negotiate this desirable move forward? Kissinger explained: "I told Sadat, it might be best if we agreed on a . . . neutral formulation about other participants that made no explicit reference to the Palestinians at all—such as that [sic] 'the question of additional participants' would be discussed during the first stage of the conference. The Arabs could say that they would urge Palestinian participation at that point; Israel could say it would refuse—but all this would happen after the conference had opened."[20] (It worked, at least in the sense that the Geneva conference took place without Palestinian participation.)

A third example: during the Israeli-Egyptian disengagement talks, a particularly challenging question concerned control of the Cairo–Suez Road. This road led to Egypt's Third Army, which was at that point completely surrounded by Israeli forces. The Israeli cabinet had forced Prime Minister Golda Meir to refuse UN control of this road, which Sadat needed to send nonmilitary supplies to his encircled soldiers. However, Kissinger judged that "to ask Sadat to send nonmilitary supplies through Israeli checkpoints was a humiliation."[21]

In the face of Israeli refusal to turn over control of the road to the United Nations and of Egyptian refusal to submit to Israeli checkpoints on the road, how might creative wordsmithing lead to the desired substantive outcome? Kissinger explained: "The solution was to avoid the issue altogether by making the sort of compromise the acceptance of which marks a triumph of faith over substance. The checkpoints were placed under the United Nations; at the same time Israeli officers were permitted to participate 'to supervise the non-military nature of the cargo.' The Israelis could claim that the UN posts were there on sufferance on 'their' road; Egypt could insist that the UN presence effectively removed the road from Israeli control. The Israelis could point to the fact that their officers participated in the inspection; the Egyptians could argue that this was as part [sic] of a UN procedure. The fundamental fact was that there would now exist a mechanism for uninterrupted nonmilitary supply to the Third Army."[22]

Just words? Hardly. Innumerable examples of such creatively ambiguous diplomatic formulations dot Kissinger's negotiations. The common denominator is often a face-saving formulation that enables both sides to declare victory and move past previous blockages. Progress may result from direct engagement on previously blocked issues. Elliot Abrams, a veteran American negotiator, highlighted one of several uses of this concept: " '[C]onstructive ambiguity' is logically ugly but has been strategically effective. If all parties avoid talking about the one big conceptual issue on which they disagree, they can engage in countless practical ways."[23] Or creative ambiguity may buy enough time to improve relationships sufficiently to address the substance of deferred issues that earlier had been too contentious to negotiate.

Challenged by journalists on the correct interpretation of an ambiguous description he had used, Kissinger became testy: "For Christ's sake, leave everyone their face-saving formula! If it pleases the Israelis to consider it 'direct' if they are in the same room with Egyptians, and Sadat prefers to call this 'indirect' if somebody else is there, what the hell difference does it make?"[24] However, some constructively ambiguous "solutions" may blow up if they merely paper over fundamental disagreements that will soon surface.

Some observers view the tactic of constructive ambiguity with deep suspicion. For example, as Brookings Institution fellow Khaled Elgindy argued, "Whatever its virtues in other settings, in the context of Israeli-Palestinian negotiations, 'constructive ambiguity' has succeeded only in producing confusion and eroding trust between the parties. Throughout the Oslo process of [the] 1990s, disagreements over how to interpret various provisions led to endless delays as well as the renegotiation and outright lack of implementation of signed agreements."[25] While this indictment of constructive ambiguity is far too broad, it contains a core caution about fudging clashes that will not become amenable to resolution with the passage of time or the growth of relationships.

To those less familiar with the ways of effective negotiators and diplomats, it may seem absurd that "mere words" might block progress between parties with potentially shared interests in reaching a deal, sometimes one of a life-and-death character. Yet, as the examples just given illustrate, hallmarks of Kissinger's tactics at the table have been faith that apparently incompatible positions can be often bridged and the skill to do so with the use of creative wordsmithing and, potentially, constructively ambiguous solutions. So long as these formulations do not merely obscure, or worsen, an inevitable explosion, but instead create conditions that reduce the odds of a blowup and permit talks to proceed, constructive ambiguity can be a useful tactic.

Tacit Bargaining:
Agreement Without "Agreement"

In some cases, however, *any* words of agreement may be too costly to utter or formalize in an accord. However constructively ambiguous the proposed deal, it may be unacceptable if formally demanded. Former secretary of state George Shultz wisely noted bargaining situations in which a counterpart's view was "I can live with that as long as I don't have to agree to it, but if you make me agree to it, I won't be able to live with it."[26] Kissinger, too, understood the value of so-called tacit bargaining in obtaining de facto agreement on desirable results.[27]

By informally dealing with Jewish emigration from the Soviet Union via quiet, nonpublic back channels with Moscow, the Nixon administration was able to help increase the number of Jewish emigrants. In 1968, the Soviet Union permitted only four hundred Jews to leave the country to settle elsewhere, primarily in Israel and the United States. With détente and the slow improvement in U.S.-Soviet relations, Kissinger noted that the Nixon administration began raising the issue "in the presidential back-channel with the argument that Soviet actions would not pass unnoticed at the highest levels of the American government. The Kremlin began to respond to American 'suggestions,' especially after Soviet-American relations started improving. Each year, the number of Jewish emigrants rose, and by 1973 the annual figure reached 35,000. In addition, the White House regularly submitted to Soviet leaders a list of hardship cases—individuals who had been denied exit visas or whose families were separated, and some of whom were in prison. Most of these Soviet citizens were also permitted to emigrate. . . . *No formal requests were made and no formal responses were given* [emphasis added]."[28]

A similar tacit bargaining dynamic occurred in 1973 with respect to Egyptian president Anwar Sadat around the issue of reopening and clearing the Suez Canal. Kissinger judged that Sadat "could not accept a formal obligation to clear and reopen the Suez Canal. But he could tell me that if he could do so as his own decision—if Israel would only stop demanding it—he would begin clearance operations as soon as both armies had reached the lines foreseen in the disengagement agreement."[29] Thus, while Sadat bargained explicitly with Kissinger, he was induced to bargain tacitly with Israel.

Normally such tacit agreements can be potentially useful when a powerful internal or external stakeholder group or audience would oppose a formal deal, and would impose costs on a negotiator who agreed to one. A tacit agreement may yield the desired substance, if not the form, without many of the potential costs. Both constructive ambiguity and tacit agreements, when appropriate, enjoyed pride of place in Kissinger's tactical tool kit.

12

Persistence, Momentum, and Shuttle Diplomacy

Experienced negotiators know that few deals result simply from the brilliant insight or dramatic stroke. An intelligent strategy plus the willingness and ability on the part of the negotiator to grind away, pushing the process toward a conclusion, are often essential ingredients for a deal. Kissinger exemplified the kind of sustained negotiating drive needed to transform a strategic conception into a workable agreement. Along with many others, British prime minister Ted Heath noted Kissinger's "limitless capacity for hard work and an imperviousness to the strains of travel and long hours of negotiation."[1]

Persistence

Reaching agreements often took time and persistence: the SALT talks lasted over two years while the secret Paris peace talks went on for almost three—the public talks began earlier and took longer. Yet the intensity of negotiations during shorter periods could be extreme. For example, Israeli prime minister Yitzhak Rabin recalled the 1975 negotiations toward a second disengagement agreement with the Egyptians: "During those ten days, we held daylong—and occasionally nightlong—discussions. . . . Five hours might be spent discussing a stretch of sand one hundred meters long. It was a supreme test of our patience, persistence, and even our physical endurance. . . . [P]atiently, Kissinger inched his way forward between Sadat's difficulties and mine, between proclamations from each side that 'this is our final concession!' . . . The conclusive discussion on the bilateral issues was held on the night of August 31 and lasted until 6:00 a.m. As the hours wore on, participants on both sides dropped out of the discussions, so that by the end it had become a dialogue between Kissinger and me against a chorus of snores all around."[2]

In seeking to get an Israeli-Syrian deal, Harold Saunders described the negotiations with Kissinger as lasting thirty-five days with "26 round trips between Ben Gurion airport [Israel] and Damascus International. That meant 26 meetings with Hafez al-Assad. Most of those meetings averaged six hours. The pattern was to have a meeting in Jerusalem in the morning, rush to Ben Gurion airport, fly to Damascus arriving just before lunch."[3]

Negotiating Dynamics and "Momentum"

The willingness and ability to grind away can be essential, but to what precise purposes and to power what tactics? Kissinger commented on the dynamics of the negotiation process that could influence tactical choice: "In the course of every negotiation, a point is reached when the parties either conclude that they will eventually come together or that they are hopelessly deadlocked. In the former case, the negotiation gathers steam; individual issues are reconsidered in the light of imminent consensus. In the latter instance, though the process may drag on for some time, the negotiation is doomed because, from then on, the parties concentrate on shifting the blame for failure to each other."[4]

These positive or negative dynamics do not operate autonomously; the concerted action of astute negotiators can drive the momentum forward. Kissinger argued that "Speed . . . is often of the essence. Every negotiation reaches a critical point where it will move rapidly to a conclusion or lapse into stagnation. This is when the highest levels of government must engage themselves to overcome bureaucratic inertia."[5] When Kissinger used the term *momentum*, he meant a shared sense among the negotiators of accelerating movement toward, or away from, an agreement. And this perception can have the quality of a self-fulfilling prophecy.

Shuttle Diplomacy

One of Kissinger's best-known tactical devices for moving the parties closer together was the "shuttle," whereby he and his team would fly back and forth between the principals, carrying proposals, responses, and messages—which the shuttle team would often shape to enhance forward movement. The term *shuttle* was apparently invented by Kissinger's colleague Joseph Sisco, later undersecretary of state. After a foray to Jerusalem, Cairo, and back, Sisco shouted, "Welcome aboard the Egyptian–Israeli shuttle!"[6] (Given Kissinger's success with this novel tactic, various observers have called for "shuttles" as the proper approach in virtually all subsequent negotiations over Middle East peace.[7]) Geography permitted this kind of shuttle because the proximity of Cairo, Jerusalem, and Damascus made daily trips easily possible.

As practiced by Kissinger, the shuttle was a highly kinetic version of familiar diplomatic "proximity talks," in which the principals do not negotiate face-to-face, at least for the most part. Rather, a third party alternates between them, trying to coax an agreement from the process. (The Dayton talks to end the war in

Bosnia operated by this method, with Richard Holbrooke as the third party.)

Many factors can lead to the decision to keep the parties separate. For example, representatives of countries at war with each other or those that do not even recognize one another diplomatically may be completely unwilling even to meet. In such cases, indirect negotiations via a third party may be the only possible option. Or the key players might be willing to meet, but the chemistry between them could be toxic. For example, as President Carter mediated Camp David talks between Anwar Sadat and Menachem Begin, who had invariably ended up "locked in argument and continually antagonizing each other." Given this experience, Carter made sure these two men did not meet—though their cabins were scarcely a hundred yards from each other.

Separate meetings with each principal can help the mediator understand the real interests, convey the other side's priorities and hot buttons, and help shape proposals that have a better chance of acceptance. Since communication takes place through the mediator, shuttles offer the chance to influence, filter, and even buffer the communications between the principals to bring them closer together. If one party argued for making a harsh, one-sided demand, for example, the mediator might be able to moderate it or, at a minimum, warn the other side that a mere "bargaining position" or "opening gambit" was coming.[8] These process characteristics can greatly enhance the importance, scope, and role of the mediator, a consideration of which Kissinger was keenly aware.

While there are advantages to the mediator's keeping the parties apart, there can be disadvantages, too. It creates situations where only the mediator knows what is really going on. The parties lose the opportunity to assess each other's interests and concerns directly, to suggest options, and to figure out how to do business together. Although flare-ups may be avoided, miscommunication and lost opportunities may result.[9]

Shuttling, though, could be useful for other reasons. Foremost is building momentum and creating a sense of urgency. As Isaacson argues, the "whirlwind of publicity and the jet-powered pace of Kissinger's missions swept up the negotiators on each side and created a momentum that made last-minute breakthroughs more likely."[10] Kissinger elaborates that in a "shuttle, the presence of a high-level American mediator supplies the deadline and hence a sense of urgency. The parties have an incentive to consider what cost a stalemate might exact in terms of their relationship with the United States."[11]

Bruce van Voorst, a *Newsweek* correspondent who traveled on many Kissinger shuttles, stated, "My most powerful memories of those days involve the tremendous attention generated by Kissinger, both at home and abroad. The negotiators on both sides couldn't ignore his public drive for success."[12] Yitzhak Rabin judged that "Only by using shuttle diplomacy could [Kissinger] get both sides to create the atmosphere that in itself made agreement possible."[13] By this time, Kissinger's global celebrity added a key element to the process.

Beyond momentum and a sense of urgency, the shuttles could induce movement on each side that stimulated reciprocal movement by the other. Kissinger argued that "When the shuttles were effective, they were sustained because each party . . . was prepared to make slight adjustments in its position at each visit of the mediating team. This eased the atmosphere and encouraged the other party to make adjustments of its own. In this manner, the two sides narrowed the gulf between them."[14] When one side dug in its heels for a protracted time, however, Kissinger was clear that the shuttle would not be effective.[15] Moreover, if either or both sides suspected bias or a private agenda on the part of the mediator, the process could break down.

In short, Kissinger had a clear view of the characteristic dynamics of negotiation, especially the presence or absence of momentum. To shape these favorably, he often employed shuttle diplomacy. This device was quite successful in negotiations following the 1973 Arab-Israeli War, and Kissinger used variants elsewhere. However innovative or clever shuttle diplomacy might have been, though, it is worth underscoring that its success also depended on the almost Herculean stamina of Kissinger and his team.

13

Secrecy, Centralization, and a Dominant Personal Role

Guided by his own inclinations and Nixon's guarded nature, and/ or cool tactical choice, Kissinger frequently cloaked his most important negotiations in secrecy, operated through "back channels," and played a dominant personal role, supported by a very small staff. He dealt with Anatoly Dobrynin on SALT through the private White House Channel, with Zhou Enlai as part of a clandestine mission, with Yitzhak Rabin and Golda Meir separately from Foreign Minister Abba Eban, with Anwar Sadat covertly, and with Le Duc Tho confidentially in a secluded Paris villa. It was not merely the content of the discussions that was hidden, though. The fact that they were taking place at all also was often a closely guarded secret.

Either at Nixon's direction or with his encouragement, Kissinger's talks frequently bypassed colleagues who might have opposed an initiative, including Defense Secretary Melvin Laird, Secretary of State William Rogers, and the State and Defense bureaucracies. He circumvented Gerard Smith and his SALT experts in nuclear talks. Also, American allies, whether South Vietnam's president Thieu or the Japanese prime minister, could be brought into the process late, if at all.

Tactical Choices

Three tactical choices intermingle in these and similar cases; these choices are almost inseparable as we analyze their more general pros and cons:

1. Control of the negotiations tended to be centralized in the White House under Kissinger's tight direction (at least until he also took the role of secretary of state).
2. Both the fact of the negotiations and their content became a tightly held secret among the involved parties.
3. Kissinger personally assumed a dominant role in the process, with a relatively small team to support him.

Unsurprisingly, opting for centralized control, back channels, and a "Lone Ranger" approach offers a complex mix of costs and benefits. (For brevity, we will sometimes use "secrecy" as shorthand for the combination of these three tactical choices.)

Advantages of Secrecy in Negotiations

Secret talks have a long diplomatic pedigree. Cardinal Mazarin, who succeeded Richelieu and whose diplomacy led to the landmark Peace of Westphalia, cautioned diplomats in 1684: "Even if they are perfectly justified, reveal nothing of your political projects."[1] A few decades later, Louis XIV used François de Callières on important diplomatic missions. Arguing that secrecy was indispensable to success, de Callières warned that it "is easy to derail great initiatives if they are discovered too early."[2]

Preempting Likely Internal and External Opposition

These centuries-old admonitions resonate with many who cogently defend back channels in important cases. Earlier in this chapter, we saw a number of tangible benefits for U.S.-Soviet relations resulting from Kissinger's increasingly productive relationship with Dobrynin in the Channel. Winston Lord, later U.S. ambassador to China and someone who often accompanied Kissinger, argued for secrecy in connection with the initial China trip. Lord gave several reasons:

"The Chinese indicated that they wanted some degree of confidentiality as well . . . If it had been known in advance that Kissinger was going to China, first, you would have had the Washington bureaucracy weighing in with specific, and, in Kissinger's and Nixon's view, second level concerns, that we had to get this aspect of trade, cultural exchanges, or whatever. Or that we had to be careful about Russian sensitivities. This would have hamstrung the early discussions.

"Secondly, we would have had our allies weighing in, in advance, trying to bind us, whether this involved our South Vietnamese allies, the Japanese, or the Europeans making demands and limiting us in our discussions with the Chinese.

"Thirdly, there would have been a firestorm among the conservatives and many of the Republicans domestically in the U.S. about the President's even considering making this dramatic move toward China, causing an uproar. . . . All of this would also have put off the Chinese.

"Fourthly, all of this would have been exacerbated by the understandable anguish of our friends on Taiwan."[3]

Kissinger underscored the importance for his purposes of preempting both internal and external opposition, arguing that "a public mission would have set off a complicated internal clearance project within the U.S. government and insistent demands for consultations from around the world, including Taiwan (still recognized as the government of China). This would have mortgaged our prospects with Beijing, whose attitudes we were being sent to discover."[4] Beyond the China case, secrecy surrounding the negotiations themselves (not the contents of bargaining known to be ongoing) could prevent adverse publicity and opposition from domestic and international sources. Avoiding such publicity and opposition could facilitate tentative exploration and movement in a delicate process.

Sidestepping Bureaucratic Involvement

The tactical decision to keep talks secret was not Kissinger's sole prerogative. Richard Nixon entered office with a deep suspicion of the federal bureaucracy in general and the State Department in particular. Kissinger also reports that the president intensely disliked direct confrontation with cabinet officers with whom he disagreed. An example from fairly early in Nixon's first term may have accelerated the tendency to centralize the process in the White House and opt for secrecy. Working through standard Executive Branch policy channels, Kissinger and Nixon had arrived at a clear decision to link nuclear arms control talks with the Soviets to Middle East and Vietnam negotiations. Many in the State Department strongly preferred that these issues be dealt with separately, and took steps that, as a practical matter, would frustrate any meaningful linkage. Nixon and Kissinger's firm preference to link these issues was delayed and temporarily thwarted as a result of direct internal opposition, foot dragging, and a carefully orchestrated campaign of leaks to the press and Congress.[5]

However, Kissinger maintained that "the bureaucracy's victory was Pyrrhic. After yielding [i.e., temporarily abandoning linkage on this issue] . . . Nixon, buttressed by me, moved the conduct of negotiations more and more into the White House. While [Nixon's] preference for secrecy would have inclined him in this direction anyway, the bureaucracy's indiscipline accelerated it . . . There sprang into existence what came to be known in US-Soviet parlance as 'the Channel.' "[6]

Centralization of negotiations in the White House and secrecy suited both men, as Kissinger made clear: "Nixon also welcomed the secrecy because, among other reasons, it postponed an argument with his Secretary of State. I favored secrecy because it freed me from the necessity of living up to criteria set beforehand by the media and critics. When we gave briefings after the event, we would be able to do so in the context of whatever had been achieved, not what other people expected or desired or invented."[7]

Permitting Unhindered Exploration and Flexibility

Beyond circumventing potential opponents and keeping them in the dark, Kissinger stressed that secrecy and tight control of the policy apparatus offered negotiating flexibility and avoided cumbersome and formulaic processes. As an example, he cited the 134 fruitless U.S.-Chinese meetings in Warsaw in which the "main point . . . had been our relationship to Taiwan, a classic Catch-22 topic: no solution was conceivable so long as US-Chinese hostility persisted, and the hostility would not end so long as the Taiwan issue was unsettled. Other questions . . . were the hoary standbys . . . American claims to compensation for nationalized property and defaulted debts; Chinese efforts to recover assets in the United States, frozen after 1949 under the Trading with the Enemy Act; [etc.] . . . All the familiar themes were due for tedious rehearsal again at the 135th meeting."[8]

Relying on normal bureaucratic and diplomatic channels to address these essentially frozen issues frustrated genuine exploration of interests and joint possibilities. Each meeting called for "a statement that had been painfully cleared through the bureaucracy and among friendly countries. Our Ambassador would then read his statement; he received a reply no doubt produced by analogous procedures. The ambassadors' permitted discretion did not go beyond a few clarifying questions. At the next session they read out a response ponderously prepared anew in the respective capitals. It all took time and got nowhere."[9] Of course, there was nothing necessary about this formulaic rehash; the president could have ordered that a different approach be taken on a higher-level agenda, providing the Chinese counterparts could reciprocate. (This, in effect, was ultimately done, leading to Kissinger's China trip.)

While this represents a fairly extreme example, Kissinger found the interagency policy process ponderous and constraining, especially for genuinely new initiatives. He sought a much more flexible process: "I considered it essential to move the dialogue to a level where the negotiators could engage in some give-and-take and were sufficiently familiar with the thinking of their leaders to grasp the underlying strategy."[10] As Kissinger began to forge subtle linkages and manage delicate balances, the negotiating freedom offered by secrecy and a process centralized in the White House became increasingly irresistible.

Costs of Secrecy, Centralization, and Personal Dominance

Kissinger saw formidable advantages to a White House–centered, secret negotiating process that he personally dominated. Yet he and others were acutely conscious of a number of drawbacks.

Risks of Discovery

Most obviously, secret talks risk premature discovery. Blown cover can cause embarrassment, create awkwardness, and draw the potential wrath of parties who feel they have been wrongfully cut out. Revelation can energize opposition (internal, external, domestic, and international) on the grounds of secrecy as well as substance.

Inadequate Technical Understanding Due to Reduced Expert Input

Less dramatically, as Kissinger put it, "there was the problem of mastering the subject. My staff was too small to backstop two complex simultaneous negotiations."[11] Beyond Kissinger's practice of intensively studying the substance of a negotiation, however, he found somewhat surreptitious ways to generate input from various government agencies and bureaus. "The control of interdepartmental machinery served as a substitute. It enabled me to use the bureaucracy without revealing our purposes. I would introduce as planning topics issues that were actually being secretly negotiated. In this manner I could learn the views of the agencies (as well as the necessary background) without formally 'clearing' my position with them."[12]

In the opinion of some of his colleagues and subordinates, however, Kissinger's knowledge was stretched perilously thin, especially in highly technical negotiations. From the bureaucratic trenches, it is hardly surprising to hear this view. SALT delegation member Raymond Garthoff, often a critic, claimed that Kissinger had "developed a conviction that he did not need the government bureaucracy. A small personal staff, he felt, could skim the cream off the ponderous interagency staff studies that he ordered to keep the bureaucracy occupied. In this way, he thought, he could learn all he needed to know about a subject. . . . On some occasions, his penchant for going it alone prevented him from getting needed advice, and U.S. interests suffered as a consequence."[13]

Even some whom Kissinger admired offered similar critiques. Ambassador Gerard Smith, for example, was chief SALT negotiator and head of the Arms Control and Disarmament Agency. Though the two often disagreed, Kissinger described Smith as "dedicated, indefatigable, and shrewd," and as "one of those talented executives who serve successive administrations and epitomize the ideal of public service."[14] Also, on balance, Smith viewed Kissinger positively.[15]

Yet, in measured fashion, Smith chided Kissinger for not taking full advantage of government experts and for trying to shoulder too much of the burden: "no matter how able a presidential confidant may be, he cannot produce best results while simultaneously negotiating, as Kissinger was, a number of important issues."[16] A bit more pointedly, Smith described how experts and delegates became cynical, even disheartened, about their own supposed roles when major aspects of the deal were done "by the intervention of a presidential aide unsupported by a staff save a few White House officials whose military and arms control experience was modest."[17]

Risks of Confusion and Poor Coordination

Two tracks, a front channel and a secret back channel, inevitably led to some confusion, often on all sides. Smith observed that "Several covert back-channel negotiations deemed necessary by the President to break SALT deadlocks led to confusion and discontinuities in the U.S. negotiating posture . . . not much effort was made to enlighten the U.S. bureaucracy . . . I suspect that the Soviet delegation was also confused by this random process of high-level and somewhat erratic participation in a negotiating process that depended for progress on a painstaking process of developing and recording common understanding about complicated concepts."[18] He further claimed that the two-track approach and insufficient effort to inform those who had not been involved led to problems when the bureaucracy was called on to transform general terms reached in the private channel into precise, detailed agreements.[19]

Such criticisms were not limited to SALT. With respect to China, Kissinger acknowledged that "Senior officials who might have been conscious of China's concerns had been excluded from the opening to Peking. Hence, there was no one at State who felt fully responsible for the 'China account' or even fully understood its rationale—this was one of the prices paid for our unorthodox method of administration."[20] With respect to the Shanghai Communiqué, when the State Department, which had been kept in the dark, "demanded a host of changes" it was able to obtain some of them.[21]

William Bundy, a CIA and State Department official, noted with respect to U.S.-Israeli negotiations that, "at an early stage, Nixon and [Israeli prime minister] Golda Meir agreed to handle major matters via Kissinger and Rabin, leaving out Secretary Rogers and Foreign Minister Abba Eban. Yet the State Department remained very much involved . . . so that its frequent lack of information on what was passing on the White House circuit was frustrating as well as confusing."[22]

Similar confusions arose in talks over a Soviet guarantee of unfettered Western access to Berlin and enhanced political, economic, and cultural ties between East and West Germany. Kissinger observed "that the secret conclusion of the agreement among us, the Federal Republic [of Germany], and the Soviets dramatized the bureaucratic problem generated by our system of two channels. Somehow we had to see to it that our own State Department did not complicate matters. Moreover, the agreement had to be ratified in a Four-Power forum staffed by diplomats exquisitely conscious of their prerogatives as representatives of occupying powers. In addition, the speed with which the 'negotiation' had suddenly proceeded was mystifying to those who for a decade had been used to the rituals of stalemate . . . For the third time in three months a negotiation was being completed in which the regular bureaucracy had not participated, indeed, was unaware of its existence. There is no agreement that cannot be picked to death by professionals not involved in negotiating it."[23]

This situation led to what Kissinger described as a "serious quandary," one "that might force us to reopen issues settled already twice with the Soviets." The quandary was overcome only by a frenzied process, requiring President Nixon, who "had a genius for thinking up explanations for a fait accompli," to inform and graciously bring on board Secretary of State Rogers, who, along with the State Department, had been excluded.[24]

With a modicum of trust between the White House and State Department, a fairly common fix to such coordination problems involves designating a senior official from each "side" to accompany the chief negotiator. Not only does this prevent crossed signals, but it can also calm suspicions that otherwise could grow unchecked.

Risks of Contradiction and Sabotage

Such confusion led to other problems. For example, American arms control negotiators operating in the front channel sometimes made statements, innocently or manipulatively, that led to potent domestic demands for the negotiators to accept disadvantageous terms. As Kissinger lamented, "our secret style of negotiations left us vulnerable to these pressures; our critics did not know that we could do better."[25]

Outright sabotage was occasionally possible as well. In reflecting on an occasion in which the cover for secret talks with the

Egyptian foreign minister was blown, Kissinger's language became dramatic: "There is no fury like that of a Foreign Service Officer bypassed . . . The offended diplomat [who has somehow learned about secret talks] . . . can report his knowledge in regular channels, thus spreading it through the bureaucracy by means of the computerized distribution system. This will quickly churn out enough copies to explode any aspiration to secrecy."[26]

Risks of Being Whipsawed

Beyond inadvertent "friendly" miscues, adversaries could and did take advantage of the public front-channel/secret back-channel structure to whipsaw the American negotiators. For example, the North Vietnamese could trumpet their alleged flexibility and American alleged intransigence in order to stir up public, media, and congressional criticism of the U.S. government and its negotiators. In one case, Madame Binh, Vietcong delegate to the talks, publicly implied that a U.S. withdrawal and release of American POWs might be decoupled from other issues. This new "chance for peace" triggered widespread U.S. criticism of Nixon and Kissinger for not taking up the "offer."

Such domestic criticism frustrated Kissinger because Hanoi's actual positions in the secret channel took a much harder line and linked all the issues.[27] He believed that the odds of a deal were best via secret talks, yet "[w]e were constrained from demonstrating that the 'chance' was bogus . . . [secrecy] enabled our cynical adversaries to whipsaw us between a public position we dared not rebut and a private record we could not publish."[28] Such episodes led Kissinger to "wonder whether we paid too high a price for secrecy."[29]

Lack of Bureaucratic Support for Results

A further price came when Kissinger's secret talks bore fruit: "The procedures I developed enhanced decisiveness in negotiations, but they made it more difficult to develop a consensus behind the results."[30] This could fatally hamper the process of implementation. Moreover, secrecy and exclusion demoralized the "bureaucracy," which "reacted by accentuating the independence and self-will that had caused Nixon to bypass it in the first place."[31] Especially on the SALT talks, Kissinger observed that "we paid the price that negotiators, excluded from a process they consider their prerogative, are likely to take a harder position after the fact than when they conduct the talks themselves."[32] Such a hard line from the experts can help equip legislative and outside opponents with potent arguments against a deal that they might have supported had they been involved.

Bureaucratic Isolation

A cumulatively damaging consequence of Kissinger's frequent recourse to secrecy and White House control of negotiations was the increasingly widespread expectation within the government that the "real" negotiations would take place outside normal channels. After Kissinger's negotiating delegation had been kept in the dark, Gerard Smith reported that its "trust in its Washington authorities was never restored. Afterwards we always assumed that other contacts with the Soviets were taking place which we could not be trusted to know about—which proved to be the case."[33]

Kissinger ruefully reflected on this development: by 1973, various agencies "had discovered that the major negotiations took place without their knowledge. Hence I could be blamed for failure, or be made to bear the brunt of whatever controversy even success was sure to bring. Each department thereafter would stake out its maximum objective, whatever sense it made. If that pristine position was not achieved, the agencies were not responsible. The inevitable compromise that would be necessary for a solution, and which in normal procedures they would have urged, could now be blamed on inadequate vigilance by the negotiator. My position, in short, had become bureaucratically untenable . . . So it was that for the first time since I had come to government I was bureaucratically isolated."[34]

Allied Embarrassment and Unhappiness

Secrecy can pose considerable problems for American allies, especially if not handled with sensitivity. With respect to the opening to China, Kissinger reflected that "even with the perspective of nearly a decade[,] I do not know how the fundamental secrecy could have been avoided. The delicacy of the event and the uniqueness of the opportunity made it essential that the United States be in control of the context of its presentation."[35] Yet the Japanese prime minister, Eisaku Sato, "a staunch friend of the United States," was blindsided by Nixon's announcement of Kissinger's trip, as was the American ambassador to Japan, who heard the news on Armed Forces Radio. Considering that it was "particularly painful to embarrass a man [Sato] who had done so much to cement the friendship between our two countries," Kissinger wished he had at least sent an envoy a few hours before the announcement to brief Sato.[36] Similarly, British prime minister Heath displayed "lasting pique at not having been informed by Nixon in advance of the China gambit. He was particularly hurt because he had hitherto assumed that Nixon and he had a good relationship."[37]

Far more serious was the fact that South Vietnamese president Thieu, America's ally, did not participate in the secret Paris talks and felt badly misled as to their substance and direction. Kissinger indicated that Thieu "had authorized such secret talks at the Midway meeting and . . . was kept thoroughly briefed on my secret negotiations from the beginning."[38] How fully Thieu was informed or consulted is a matter of considerable disagreement.[39] After Kissinger and Le Duc Tho finally came to a tentative deal,

Kissinger did not initially share the full text with Thieu. When he did, Thieu soon became enraged: "Kissinger says I was always kept informed. Yes, I was informed—I was told what he chose to tell me. But I trusted my ally never to deceive me, make deals over my head and secretly sell my country out."[40] (As we earlier elaborated, both Nixon and Kissinger would vehemently deny this intent.)

Thieu's staunch opposition to the tentative deal would have presented major problems to Nixon, who absolutely did not want to be seen, domestically or internationally, as betraying South Vietnam. Getting Thieu's agreement required extreme American pressure, promises of support, and efforts (including the so-called Christmas Bombing of North Vietnam) to obtain changes from Hanoi to the deal sought by the South Vietnamese president.

Although Thieu ultimately acquiesced in the accords, many factors beyond the secrecy of the Paris talks drove this story. Arguably, had Thieu been involved and enjoyed the capacity to block progress along the way, agreement might never have been reached. Secrecy surrounding the Paris talks, and the fact that Thieu was excluded from what was a U.S.–North Vietnamese negotiation, helped avoid this outcome. Yet, in Kissinger's view, Thieu's outraged opposition was not fundamentally a matter of tactics, tact, or whether the talks were in front or back channels.

Instead, given incompatible national interests (the United States' imperative to end its involvement and South Vietnam's terror of abandonment to the North), the two parties were "doomed to collision." Kissinger ultimately concluded that "We failed early enough to grasp that Thieu's real objection was not to the terms but the fact of any compromise. Conflict between us and Thieu was built into the termination of the war on any terms less than Hanoi's total surrender."[41] It is hard for us to determine whether Kissinger's fatalistic assessment is correct. If it is, secrecy was likely necessary to agreement and unimportant to the denouement of the talks; if not, the manner by which the secrecy was handled and how a deal was unveiled to Thieu could have mattered greatly.

Evaluation of Secrecy, Centralization, and Kissinger's Personal Dominance

Henry Kissinger's negotiations were often very public and visible; think of the Middle East shuttles, Rhodesia, dealings with China after his initial trip, or the many negotiations associated with the fifteen covers of *Time* magazine on which he appeared. Yet, like many of his diplomatic predecessors back to the eighteenth century, he frequently opted for a dominant personal role in talks whose existence and substance both were hidden from broader view.

Secrecy permitted talks to proceed without arousing opposition from domestic, political, legislative, bureaucratic, or foreign sources whose interests or agendas might have clashed with Kissinger's purposes. By centralizing the process in the White House, Kissinger could move quickly, largely escaping what he often regarded as a cumbersome and irrelevant interagency process of consultation and clearance. Freedom from outside interference was especially important when talks were in a fragile, exploratory state or when Kissinger wanted to present agreement as a fait accompli. If talks were not public, Kissinger or Nixon could announce their results in a context that had not been shaped by others' expectations or agendas.

Yet secrecy, centralization, and personal dominance carried costs and risks to weigh against their potential advantages. A secret process could be discovered and denounced, embarrassing and angering parties who had been cut out or not informed. Although more sensitive handling could sometimes have mitigated the problem, key American allies could be humiliated if blindsided by news of talks or agreements.

Depending on the nature of the issue, secret negotiations could violate norms of transparency, democratic accountability, and legitimacy that many Americans held in high regard. After all, reacting to a long history of European diplomatic intrigue and deception, the very *first* of President Woodrow Wilson's famous Fourteen Points was "Open covenants of peace, openly arrived at, after which there shall be no private international understandings of any kind but diplomacy shall proceed always frankly and in the public view."

Kissinger would doubtless agree with many analysts who believe that, although the fact that negotiations are ongoing may be widely known, progress will be stymied if the actual discussions themselves take place in public. Even as idealistic a source as *Getting to Yes* would amend Woodrow Wilson's appealing point to read "open covenants, *privately* arrived at."[42]

Going it alone, in secret, meant losing the full advantages of the considerable expertise in various government agencies and departments. A front-channel/back-channel structure could lead to damaging confusion and contradiction on all sides, especially when the right hand does not know what the left hand is doing (or even that there *is* a left hand). Converting more general agreements reached in secret into detailed form could be challenging for those not party to the secret talks. Internal players could even sabotage the process. Cynical adversaries could and did publicly whipsaw U.S. negotiators who could only respond by blowing the cover of the private talks.

As the expectation grew that important negotiations would be handled directly by the White House, not by the relevant government departments, Kissinger found himself increasingly isolated. And when previously secret talks became public, resentful agencies could withhold active support or find ways to snipe at results.

Weighing all the factors, various observers come out very differently on whether Kissinger's centralized, back-channel tactics were wise. Stanley Hoffmann emphasizes the downsides: "frequent confusion when America's negotiators did not know the agreements in the making through the back channels; it also gave the Soviets opportunities to try to play one team against the other. It created deep resentments among American diplomats ignored or undercut by the White House. It even created suspicion in Moscow and Peking, for Soviet and Chinese diplomats wondered why the Americans wanted so much secrecy. It meant that vital decisions . . . were taken behind the backs or against the opposition of Secretaries Rogers and Laird."[43]

After attributing some of Kissinger's penchant for secrecy to "vanity," Walter Isaacson indicates that "Kissinger believed, with some justification, that in order to establish subtle linkages and calibrate delicate balances, he had to keep tight control over various strands of policy through back-channel machinations. In addition, he felt that he could better negotiate an opening to China if he kept the State Department in the dark, that he could more easily reach a settlement in Vietnam if he kept President Thieu uninformed, and that he could piece together an arms control accord if he circumvented Gerard Smith and his SALT experts."[44]

Kissinger's own assessment of these tactical choices is hedged but, on balance, positive, given the remarkable results. Freely admitting that "to individuals like Smith, it was unfair and demeaning"[45] and that "[i]t was demoralizing for the bureaucracy . . ."[46] Kissinger nevertheless came out clearly: "But it worked . . . In 1971 and 1972 these methods produced the SALT breakthrough, the opening to China, a Berlin agreement, the Peking and the Moscow Summits without any setback. The results should be judged on their merits, though I recognize a price was paid in the manner of their achievement."[47]

Intriguingly, however, he recognized both the unusual circumstances in which he and Nixon employed this approach and its disadvantages and limitations. As a general matter, he mused, "I do not consider this a procedure that can stand institutionalization."[48]

★ ★ ★

Clearly, when we move beyond Kissinger and the diplomacy of the 1970s, the decision to pursue secrecy in negotiation continues to be very much alive—although ubiquitous camera-equipped smartphones and pervasive social media render the task much more difficult. After all, the 2015 Iranian nuclear deal really began in earnest when facilitated by secret contacts in Oman between Deputy Secretary of State Bill Burns in 2012 and 2013. And secrecy in financial negotiations is extremely common, given concerns about market reaction, competitive advantage, and internal morale. On balance, then, are secret negotiations a good idea? Our review of Kissinger's use of the tactic, with its many potential pros and cons, suggests that the answer is a less-than-rousing "it depends."

Key Lessons on Negotiation from Henry Kissinger

Fascination led us to undertake this project. Having worked with and studied many of the world's most impressive negotiators, Henry Kissinger the negotiator appeared to be a breed apart. This conviction only strengthened as we read his many books, consulted countless sources, and interviewed him along with others who had observed him in the process. Recall Walter Isaacson's judgment of Kissinger as the "foremost American negotiator" of the twentieth century, or the recent survey we cited of 1,615 scholars in international relations across a wide variety of colleges and universities. This expert group overwhelmingly ranked Henry Kissinger as the most effective U.S. secretary of state over the last fifty years. Having done the research for this book, we're hardly surprised by these assessments. The pathbreaking agreements in which he was instrumental (with China, the Soviet Union, the Middle East, in Southern Africa, and elsewhere) suggested a distinctive approach to negotiation that we have sought to systematically articulate.

Accurately describing Kissinger's approach across multiple negotiations was our first goal. In doing so, we found a great deal to admire and several aspects to question. Though we became fascinated by how Kissinger actually handled these challenges during the Cold War–dominated diplomatic world of the 1970s, our real motivations were prescriptive and forward looking.

Of course, yesterday's bipolar U.S.–Soviet rivalry has given way to a multipolar reality, with countries such as China and India playing ever-larger roles. Nonstate actors such as ISIS and cross-border challenges ranging from climate change to financial flows play far greater roles in today's hyperconnected world. Yet, despite these changes, we have sought to extract enduring lessons for dealing productively with conflicts and forging agreements in challenging situations. It would be a mistake to take these lessons as primarily of historical interest, or to imagine them as mainly addressed to diplomats. As will soon become evident, we have formulated this chapter's prescriptions (which make no mention of their diplomatic origins) for current and future negotiators who must deal with legal and business topics as well as public and international ones. To apply these lessons, of course, the relevant factors (the proper context, the parties, how they see their interests, their alternatives to agreement, and so on) must be taken into account.

Given our decades-long experience as negotiators, researchers, and professors who teach this subject, we had already developed many prescriptions, which are reflected in a number of our other books, articles, and case studies.[1] So, beyond the negotiation advice that is readily available from our work and elsewhere, what special insights were sparked and illustrated by our examination of Kissinger's distinctive approach?

Expecting readers to take lessons from our accounts of Kissinger's negotiations, this chapter offers our answers to this question. We certainly did not discover a singular "Kissinger elixir" that dissolves barriers to agreement. Nor did we find each individual element of Kissinger's technique to be novel or unique among effective negotiators. Some elements are quite particular to Kissinger's approach; others, which he employed extensively, are more generic. Yet, when analyzed as parts of an overall approach to negotiation and illustrated as they actually played out in many tough cases of global significance, the advice found in this chapter should come alive and become highly valuable in practice.

From among the many possible lessons on negotiation that could be drawn from episodes we analyze in this book, we have selected fifteen as worthy of special mention.[2] By this point in the book, all should be more or less familiar and should deeply resonate with our case discussions in earlier chapters. Some episodes merit longer elaboration; a brief reminder suffices for others. We did not choose these lessons as a step-by-step method for negotiating. Rather, integrating the most relevant ones into your existing approach should greatly enhance your effectiveness. (At the conclusion of the chapter, we summarize each of these lessons for ease of reference.)

Our first three lessons are fairly broad. They highlight a central characteristic of Kissinger's effectiveness, stress the crucial role that underlying assumptions play in determining ultimate success, and emphasize the inadequacy of negotiation concepts and skills by themselves absent deep knowledge of the issues at stake. Subsequent advice fleshes out what "zooming out" and "zooming in" actually mean in practice.

LESSON 1: Zoom out to your strategy; zoom in to your counterpart—and continually bring both views into alignment.

Discussing various negotiations with Henry Kissinger and reading detailed accounts of these talks has gradually crystallized what for us stands out as a distinctive and valuable characteristic. Smoothly and repeatedly, Kissinger appears both to zoom out and to zoom in: out to his broader strategy and in to his counterpart, seeking to bring the macro and micro together to advance core interests. In planning as well as execution, these dual perspectives provide vital, complementary insights.

Many negotiators zoom out to the bigger picture and the broader strategy within which a given deal is situated. Ensuring that a well-thought-through strategy guides one's negotiations is a real strength, which we elaborated in part 2 of this book. Some big-picture negotiators, however, lack interpersonal effectiveness. This quality might seem unimportant to them, they may be arrogant, or they simply may not possess good "people skills."

Other negotiators zoom in to their counterparts, focusing on rapport, communication, trust, and relationships. Fostering emotional connection is also a real strength, which we elaborate in part 3 of this book. Some people-oriented negotiators, however, lack a strong strategic or analytic sense. It may seem unimportant to them, they may think of "negotiation" in purely interpersonal terms, or they may simply not possess good analytic and strategic skills.

Zooming out and zooming in both clearly underpin Kissinger's success. His capacity to zoom out to a carefully considered strategy certainly stands out as the most distinctive and familiar characteristic. Yet we judge that his closely aligned interpersonal focus was also key to his negotiating success. As we think back to his role in Southern Africa, we are struck by the tight relationship between his overall sequential strategy and the rapport he forged with leaders as different as Nyerere, Vorster, and Smith. Personal connections with Zhou and Dobrynin facilitated his triangular strategy with China and the Soviet Union. After the 1973 Arab-Israeli War, in seeking greater regional stability and reduced Soviet influence, Kissinger depended heavily on the affinity he had developed with Sadat, Meir, and Rabin. Across these and other negotiations, he brought the macro and micro together in service of his longer-term objectives.

Zooming out/zooming in should *not* be understood as a two-step procedure in which, after zooming out to the strategy, one then zooms in to the person—and is done. Rather, as the strategy clarifies and your counterparts are engaged, you will likely go back and forth between these twin perspectives, iteratively, as the negotiation evolves, nudging things forward toward your target agreement.

Whether this dual focus is deliberate or instinctive for Henry Kissinger is less important for prescriptive purposes than consistently asking whether your approach to negotiation incorporates both perspectives. If not, it is wise to discipline yourself to see things both ways. If, on reflection, you strongly incline toward either strategy or people, can you make a point of focusing on the neglected part of the equation? Or, if this feels as if it would be ineffective, can you partner with (or hire) someone with complementary skills?

LESSON 2: Evaluate and reevaluate your fundamental premises.

Ultimate negotiating success depends on the validity of your most basic assumptions, about the world, the situation, and your interests. Brilliant tactics based on bad assumptions or faulty understandings of your real interests will not go down as a triumph. A situation in which you cleverly surmount obstacles to negotiating a partnership with untrustworthy counterparts won't end well. Basing diplomacy in support of the 2003 Iraq War, for example on the existence (ultimately refuted) of weapons of mass destruction proved counterproductive. By the same token, insightfully pulling together diverse and unruly stakeholders in support of a complex real estate development that, after construction, turns out to contain a toxic waste dump will be regarded as a failure.

At a time when most Americans treated China as a fanatical and implacable enemy, Kissinger (together with Nixon) perceived that increasing hostility between China and the Soviet Union created a potentially transformative opening to favorably reshuffle the global cards. Based on this premise, savvy negotiation positioned the United States at a pivot point in a new triangular relationship in which each of the two major Communist adversaries was closer to America than it was to the other. As we have shown, beyond enhanced global stability, this strategic negotiation opened the door for Kissinger to negotiate dividends for American diplomacy both in Vietnam and in the aftermath of the 1973 Arab-Israeli War.

Yet Kissinger's view of the world was hardly infallible. Key assumptions underlying his Vietnam negotiations were contested at the time, and have been since. As we discussed at length, these premises included: that Vietnam was a major front in the Cold War rather than primarily a civil war among indigenous forces with foreign patrons; that a continued American commitment to the government of South Vietnam was vital to U.S. global credibility; that Vietnamization had a good chance of success; and that the United States would be willing and able to enforce the Paris Accords after its withdrawal. Even though, for analytic purposes, we believe that we learned a great deal from studying Kissinger's negotiating strategy and tactics in this case, the outcome inevitably reflects badly on the process.

We have certainly criticized Kissinger's dominant Cold War assumptions with respect to Southern Africa and Vietnam. Yet, regardless of how we might later assess the wisdom of Kissinger's premises, when we studied his negotiations, we took his overarching objectives and his worldview as initial givens for our analysis. Where those assumptions proved solid, his negotiations proceeded on firm foundations, and several became signal achievements. By contrast, a great negotiation strategy and brilliant tactics cannot save a fundamentally flawed project. Self-evident as it may sound, skeptically revisiting and reconfirming your basic assumptions about the deal you seek to achieve is essential to long-term success.

LESSON 3: Develop deep familiarity with the subject of your negotiation—and/or make sure that your team possesses this knowledge.

Join us in a brief thought experiment. Suppose Kissinger had developed his sophisticated approach to the process of negotiation over decades as a business development executive in the pharmaceutical sector. Had he suddenly been catapulted from pharma into the secretary of state's office, his effectiveness as a diplomatic negotiator would have been severely limited by his lack of knowledge about foreign affairs, at least until he had become deeply familiar with the policies and people in this new context. Indeed, without real awareness of a country's history, culture, economics, and politics (or of your counterparts), it is difficult to be an effective diplomatic negotiator. Kissinger's profound grasp of international relations, both historical and current, dramatically enhanced his negotiating abilities. His counterparts often remarked on his intensive drive to master new subjects along with his unusual capacity as a quick study. Where his understanding of the issues or regions was shakier (as with some highly technical nuclear topics in the SALT talks or with the politics of newly independent countries in Southern Africa), ensuring that his team possessed this knowledge was vital if good results were to be obtained.

Many books and seminars implicitly claim that knowledge of negotiation concepts and skills divorced from deep familiarity with the context in which this knowledge is to be employed will work wonders (example: the bestselling *You Can Negotiate Anything*[3]).

We doubt this claim, especially on issues about which you are an amateur. In addition, few would claim that subject matter expertise alone makes one an excellent negotiator. In our experience, the concepts and skills that Kissinger employed in diplomacy have great power when applied in areas where one already has considerable background. Ideally, you will find value in this approach in areas with which you are quite familiar; if you are negotiating on alien ground, be sure to get a map or include on your team people who have the relevant expertise.

It is hard to overstate the roles that good assumptions and domain knowledge play in successful negotiations. With these broad lessons in mind, the balance of our advice helps flesh out what we actually mean by zooming out to a strategic view along with zooming in to tactical and interpersonal factors.

LESSON 4: Take the long view.

Carefully analyze how the negotiation you currently contemplate relates to your long-term objectives. Each of the negotiations we have selected for fuller analysis in this book possessed longer-term significance for American foreign policy. Of course, by no means are all negotiations "strategic" in this sense. Nonstrategic deals would normally include buying a car or a house, working out a contract for cleaning services, renewing an uncontroversial agreement for educational exchange or scientific cooperation between friendly countries, or negotiating the fourth syndication season of a minor cable television show. Many of, if not most, such deals are transactional, with little broader significance (though the relationships that are enhanced or worsened in the process may be of larger concern).

Kissinger consistently criticized the all-too-common habit of analyzing negotiations on their "independent merits." For example, in

1969, he requested a major interagency analysis on China. Instead of the broader analysis he sought, the document he received "paid heavy attention to the conventional Chinese-American bilateral problems: Taiwan, admission to the United Nations, trade and travel, and . . . disarmament . . . All these concerns were treated as if they existed in a vacuum. No reference was made to the global implications of Sino-Soviet tensions and the opportunities for us in the triangular relationship. [The paper placed] excessive emphasis on China's ideology and alleged militancy; I thought the issue should be posed differently . . . Which of our problems with China were caused by its size and situation and which by its leadership? What did we want from China and how could we reasonably influence its decisions? How did we view the evolution of Sino-Soviet relations; how much could we influence them and which side should we favor?"[4]

Rather than focus on its immediate impact, Kissinger consistently asked how a given negotiation might fit into a larger puzzle. Given our review of several of his negotiations, the words that follow should resonate: "I attempted to relate events to each other, to create incentives or pressures in one part of the world to influence events in another. . . . I wanted to accumulate nuances for a long-range strategy. . . . I was more worried about results some years down the road."[5] When Kissinger envisioned a desirable agreement that would advance broader interests but that was currently out of reach, he would often conceive of moves that he might make ahead of time and across different issues or regions. Such moves would often generate a more promising setup for achieving his target deal.

A vital negotiation practice involves always asking whether a particular negotiation has longer-term significance. For example, in deciding the amount of financial and managerial resources that should be allocated to fighting or settling a lawsuit, a key judgment involves the legal and practical precedents that may be set. Settling the suit for less than it would cost to defend it might seem appealing if the focus is on this specific case. But such a settlement might act as a precedent that would invite many more similar suits in the future. Fighting it in court might cost more in the short run but lead to savings in the long run. Similarly, suppose you have recently developed a new technology and are negotiating with a high-profile customer that seeks a license to use it. If that customer is widely known to be tech savvy, it might be worth ultimately accepting discounted terms from that customer, if others would use this deal as a credible signal that your new technology is over the bar.

Credibility figures centrally into our discussion of taking the long view. The credibility you build or destroy in one negotiation often exerts profound effects in your later negotiations. Kissinger likened one's credibility with others to their perception of one's character. How much confidence do they have that you will actually do what you say you will do, refrain from what you rule out, make good on your promises, or carry out your threats? If the level of their confidence in your word is high, so is your credibility; the converse also is true. For this reason, maintaining and enhancing one's credibility is a vital asset in negotiation, whether personal or national. Credibility is hard to build but easy to lose. President Obama's failure to act when Syria violated his red line on using chemical weapons is thought to have diminished his later influence, in the Middle East and beyond. Likewise, President Trump's frequent contradictory statements on vital matters, both domestic and foreign, can lead counterparts to doubt his word.

LESSON 5: Adopt a wide-angle perspective.

Intimately related to taking the long view is examining the negotiation through what we've called a wide-angle lens. Should the negotiation at hand be dealt with on its own, or is there a bigger picture that should be taken into account? As you scan widely across other parties, issues, and regions, are there potential connections that could be usefully forged? One of the more striking features of Kissinger's approach was his consistent attention to discerning and acting on nonobvious but potentially crucial relationships, especially among negotiations involving the Soviet Union, China, Vietnam, the Middle East, and Southern Africa.

A wide-angle lens can be useful when focusing your entire attention on your immediate negotiating counterpart would put you at a disadvantage. A broader view may help you identify parties and issues that might be useful to include (or exclude) in the process. For example, had Kissinger sought to persuade Ian Smith to accept black-majority rule in a mano a mano encounter, he would almost certainly have failed. Instead, before dealing directly with Smith, a wide-angle analysis suggested the potential value of involving the British, the "Frontline" African states, other members of the Organization of African Unity, and South Africa in the process. In the Paris peace talks, Kissinger looked far beyond the North Vietnamese and Vietcong for leverage; he ultimately involved the Chinese, the Soviets, and, indirectly, the West Germans. Well after Kissinger's time in office, the United States sought to maximize its leverage in negotiating a nuclear deal with Iran, by combining forces with the other "P5+1" countries: France, Britain, Germany, Russia, and China, with Israel in the background.

As you prepare to negotiate, ask yourself if you've looked carefully beyond your immediate counterpart for others whose involvement may enhance your odds of success. To cite a small-scale example, with a corporation that may be a buyer of your product, suppose you will negotiate with one of that firm's procurement specialists, whose short-term incentives are to knock down whatever selling price you quote. Rather than focusing your attention solely on your procurement counterpart, have you quietly invested beforehand in building an alliance (not "negotiating") with the ultimate users in that organization over the real value of your product? If you've created an internal "champion," ideally someone who both truly sees your product's value and has some political clout, your later negotiation with the corporate buyer will be vastly easier.

LESSON 6: Be realistic: track the deal/no-deal balance.

With any negotiation in prospect, Kissinger clarified his side's interests as well as options in the event an agreement could not be struck. In parallel, having developed an understanding of the other side's interests, Kissinger routinely assessed how his counterparts might compare the value of a deal he had in mind to their no-deal alternatives. How does "yes" look to the other side relative to "no"? If a realistic assessment reveals that "no" seems to dominate "yes" for the other side, then one or both of two actions will be required to make an agreement possible (assuming you don't lower your own standards of acceptability). Your offer to them must be sweetened and/or the consequences of impasse worsened for the other side such that the deal/no-deal balance tips in favor of a deal. While this proposition may seem almost self-evident, it is common to hear calls for negotiation in situations where a bit of deal/no-deal analysis would reveal that "no" clearly dominates—and thus that the other side has no incentive to make a deal.

Tracking the deal/no-deal balance is a vital diagnostic tool that Kissinger almost instinctively employed. Indeed, when he contemplated negotiations over black-majority rule in Rhodesia, he immediately grasped what earlier British negotiators had not: that, if approached directly, Ian Smith would see impasse as preferable to a deal. Thus Kissinger concluded that a direct approach by itself would fail.

During the early years of the Paris peace talks, Kissinger was painfully aware of why the North Vietnamese resisted a deal: Le Duc Tho knew that U.S. involvement in the Vietnam War was increasingly unpopular with the American public and Congress, that Nixon was, in effect, unconditionally withdrawing American troops at a rapid pace, and that this withdrawal would strengthen Vietcong and North Vietnamese forces militarily while weakening the South. To open up space for a deal, Kissinger would need to tilt the deal/no-deal balance in a direction adverse to North Vietnam.

By contrast, even after twenty years of mutual hostility with no official communication, Kissinger and Nixon recognized the military threat from the Soviets that Mao's China increasingly faced. Without the United States as a counterweight, China's geopolitical situation promised to become ever direr. In addition to the joint gains that a better relationship with the United States might offer the two parties, China's worsening no-deal option arguably opened space for a mutually beneficial U.S.-Chinese agreement.

In characterizing Kissinger's approach to negotiation as "realistic" in terms of a keen focus on the deal/no-deal balance, we do not have in mind the "realist" or realpolitik school of foreign affairs. This approach interprets the international relations system as a set of rational state actors jockeying for and/or applying power in a perpetual state of conflict with one another. Instead, we urge a careful assessment of whether the most basic condition for a negotiated agreement is present—namely, that the possibility of a deal looks more appealing to the parties than impasse or worse.

Crudely put, assessing this balance is akin to asking whether you and your potential counterpart each have incentives to negotiate. If I have a terrific job and you approach me in an effort to get me to negotiate about taking an inferior one, "no" will immediately look better to me than "yes." If you are absolutely convinced you'll win big in court, my efforts at a modest out-of-court settlement are likely to fall flat. If a single consumer complains about a faulty product, its maker may well brush it off. But if that aggrieved consumer recruits an army of other disgruntled consumers and launches a social media campaign that goes viral, the negotiation may take an entirely different cast. In short, a realistic evaluation of the deal/no-deal balance gives a good initial read on the potential for negotiation and suggests where efforts toward agreement should be focused.

LESSON 7: Don't regard the elements of a negotiation as fixed; where useful, seek game-changing moves to favorably tilt the deal/no-deal balance.

If tracking the deal/no-deal balance is a useful diagnostic and a wide-angle lens offers a bigger picture within which to locate your specific deal, the next lesson follows directly: having analyzed the situation, you should consider changing the "negotiating game" in your favor. This means taking steps to "add" or "subtract" parties or issues that will shift the situation in your favor. Of course, skillful tactics within the situation as it initially presents itself is often the best option. Yet regarding the elements of a negotiation as fixed can be disadvantageous or even futile.

We have extensively discussed two cases where Kissinger changed the game: Rhodesia and Vietnam. As our examination of the deal/no-deal balance made clear, neither Ian Smith nor Le Duc Tho would have been likely to give Kissinger what he wanted if the negotiations had been limited to those two parties. It was game-changing moves to broaden each negotiation that offered the potential to favorably tilt the balance.

As we saw in the analysis of these cases, before approaching Smith, Kissinger secured American support. He then changed the Kissinger–Smith "game" to include the British, the Frontline States, other member states of the Organization of African Unity, and South Africa. Only by a complex sequence of such actions aimed at worsening the consequences of no-deal for Smith, plus some minority protections, did a zone of possible agreement open up. Reluctantly, "yes" finally looked better to Smith than "no."

In the Paris peace talks, Kissinger looked well beyond the North Vietnamese and Vietcong for leverage; he changed the U.S.–North Vietnamese "game" by involving the Chinese, the Soviets, and, indirectly, the West Germans. Meanwhile, by establishing a nominal "record of reasonableness" in the negotiation while Nixon steadily withdrew U.S. troops, he created enough "domestic space" to enable a powerful American and South Vietnamese response to the North's massive 1972 offensive. These moves paved the way for the 1973 accords (which, of course, failed two years later, after Watergate and a congressional cutoff of funds for Indochina).

LESSON 8: Evaluate the potential for a multifront negotiation campaign to achieve your target deal, paying special attention to the "home front."

In a number of cases, notably Rhodesia and Vietnam, Kissinger structured his game-changing moves as multifront "negotiation campaigns." Conceptually, a negotiation campaigner identifies an ultimate target deal, maps the full set of parties and their interests, groups the parties into similar "fronts," maps backward from the target to decide on the most promising sequential emphasis, and then orchestrates the campaign. While simple buy-sell negotiations sometimes call for small-scale negotiation campaigns, more complex dealmaking often requires a more ambitious campaign. Think of a large cross-border merger with regulatory approvals in multiple jurisdictions; gaining support for a major UN Security Council resolution; getting approval for a major infrastructure project with financial, political, environmental, and union fronts; and so on.

We note, however, that in both the Rhodesian and the Vietnamese negotiation campaigns, Kissinger's moves on "external" fronts were comparatively subtle and sophisticated. In each case, though Kissinger carefully maintained presidential backing, a vital requirement for success for any secretary of state, the broader domestic front proved problematic. The timing of Kissinger's advocacy for black-majority rule in Rhodesia badly damaged Gerald Ford among conservatives. Also, though a complex of factors fed U.S. public and congressional opposition to the Indochinese war, Nixon and Kissinger were ultimately unable to sustain support for enforcing the Paris agreements. These outcomes underscore the need for a strategy to sustain home front backing, whether nationally or in your home office.

LESSON 9: Develop multiparty insight and dexterity: coalition dynamics, sequencing, and information.

Many familiar negotiations appear as two-party affairs: a buyer and a seller dickering over price, a plaintiff and defendant settling out of court, a manufacturer and supplier working out a contract, or two nuclear powers structuring an arms control deal. Yet the bilateral façade often conceals greater complexity, whether in the form of diverse internal factions on each side, agents such as lawyers or bankers with their own agendas, or other interested parties that end up playing influential roles. Evidently, triangular diplomacy among the United States, the Soviet Union, and China cannot be understood in two-party terms. Also, though simplistic views of a negotiation such as the U.S. versus North Vietnam or Henry Kissinger dealing with Ian Smith might suggest bilateral interactions, the reality became decidedly multilateral.

Timing

A multiparty negotiator must keep at least three balls in the air, often more, seeking an advantageous and stable outcome. In the case of three parties, we saw that this involved much more than one party trying to play the others off against one another. Via triangular diplomacy, Kissinger was able to place the United States in a position where it had more options than either the Soviets or Chinese. This new structure lowered the overall risk of nuclear war and offered the United States advantages in other negotiations, including Vietnam and the disengagement agreements after the 1973 Arab-Israeli War. Yet recall how the process of reaching this new structure required careful timing as Kissinger discussed the dynamics: "If we moved too quickly . . . the Chinese might rebuff the overture. If we moved too slowly, we might feed Chinese suspicions of Soviet-American collusion, which could drive them into making the best deal available with Moscow. As for the Soviets, we considered the Chinese option useful to induce restraint; but we had to take care not to pursue it so impetuously as to provoke a Soviet preemptive attack on China."[6]

Separate or Combined?

When Kissinger sought disengagement agreements between the Egyptians and Israelis or, shortly after, between the Syrians and Israelis, he faced a different kind of tactical choice, one that is not present in pure two-party negotiations: whether to keep the parties apart and deal with each separately or to bring them together. Nominally, Kissinger played a mediating role between the protagonists, but the United States was a highly interested player, with various forms of clout in what was actually a three-party negotiation. Partly for political reasons—neither Egypt nor Syria recognized Israel—and partly for tactical reasons, Kissinger kept the parties separate during the negotiations. Beyond building momentum as the process quickened, this "shuttle" method permitted him to filter and manage the information flow, nudging each party toward a possible deal and defusing what could have been face-to-face blowups. Placing yourself in the middle offers advantages of this kind, but it has some drawbacks. It prevents the principals from directly communicating, learning firsthand about the other's perceptions and interests and potentially building a working relationship. It can also raise suspicions over whether the intermediary is shaping each side's perceptions on behalf of another agenda, perhaps raising the level of distrust.

Sequencing

In combination with decisions about combining or separating the parties and revealing information, notice how important sequencing choices were in the last few examples. In part to induce Soviet flexibility on various stalled issues, Kissinger and Nixon went to extraordinary lengths to conceal their approach to China, which had to come before subsequent dealings with the Soviets. Similarly, Kissinger undertook what he judged to be a (relatively) easier Israeli-Egyptian disengagement negotiation before a similar attempt with the Syrians (which was influenced by success with Egypt), which he judged had to come before an abortive attempt at a Jordanian deal.

When we discussed game-changing moves and negotiation campaigns, the sequential aspect was barely under the surface. Recall the multifront and multistage sequential negotiation campaign that led to the Paris Peace Accords. In fact, as the Rhodesian case study amply demonstrates, the essence of Kissinger's planned negotiation campaign was a carefully constructed sequence. In turn, before directly negotiating with Ian Smith, he needed a U.S. mandate, a promise of British involvement, Frontline State and selected OAU concurrence, and South African agreement. The sequence was deliberate, with each stage depending on prior stages as assets and allowing the negotiator to assess which parties' agreement (or opposition) would positively (or negatively) influence other parties.

Information Revelation

In a multiparty negotiation, knowing how much information should be revealed, and when, can be especially tricky. Full revelation to all parties may sound appealing on the grounds of transparency and inclusiveness. Yet sharing all information may stymie progress. For example, Kissinger gained private commitments from South African leader John Vorster to pressure the Rhodesians, and agreement from the British to call a regional conference. With these private commitments in his back pocket, he then negotiated with a number of African leaders, essentially saying, "If I could get commitments from the British and South Africans, would you agree to go along." Tanzania's Julius Nyerere, for example, believed such commitments to be unlikely—he said it would be a "miracle" if Kissinger obtained them—but agreed to support Kissinger's plan conditional on British and South African agreement. In Kissinger's view, had Nyerere and others been aware of these private agreements, they would have "pocketed them" and demanded more. Keeping them secret, pushed the process forward, but ran some risk of Kissinger being regarded as devious as the truth was later revealed.

Multiparty dexterity can take innumerable forms, but Kissinger demonstrated this quality across several of the negotiations we analyzed. Typically, across the many tactical choices such as information revelation or sequencing, the objective is to build a "winning coalition": enough of the right parties to support your target deal, actively or passively, to ensure its adoption, implementation, and sustainability. Along with building a winning coalition is the need to thwart the actual or potential blockers or spoilers. When many parties are involved in a negotiation, winning and blocking coalitions become the preoccupations of those seeking to orchestrate the process.

LESSON 10: Think strategically, act opportunistically.

Strategic concepts clearly guided Henry Kissinger's actions in the negotiations we have analyzed. He repeatedly stressed—to his team, to us, and in his writing—the importance of a strategy. Yet, as Kissinger's actions demonstrated, a negotiator should not regard a planned strategy as a fixed recipe to be meticulously followed, step by step, or as a blueprint to be methodically executed. The negotiating situation inevitably shifts and evolves, often unpredictably, or your understanding of the situation can alter. Moves and countermoves may create new opportunities or constraints. Changes can occur in the parties who are involved, their apparent alignments, their positions and interests, their no-deal options, the available information, the alternatives available to each side, the urgency for action, and so on. When the situation changes, it is time to reassess your strategy, then decide whether and how to adapt your approach in order to advance your interests.

In some cases, unexpected shifts may uncover possibilities for negotiation. For instance, as Nixon and Kissinger began to digest the implications of the Soviet military threat to China, the seemingly far-fetched option for fundamental negotiations to reshape the relationship opened up.

Shifts in the environment may also impede plans. In the Rhodesian case, for example, the U.S. Congress blocked Kissinger's initial plan to thwart Soviet and Cuban advances in Angola via covert action. While maintaining his objective, this shift caused him to switch to a purely diplomatic initiative based on a carefully crafted sequential strategy. Adding goals to his initial Cold War focus (including democratic principles such as majority rule and avoiding a regional race war), Kissinger's negotiations followed this new plan until, unexpectedly, the support he had supposedly garnered from the British and the Frontline States began to rapidly erode. Kissinger again adapted, upending the original sequence and traveling to London to get British assent in writing (and, later, to convince a surprised cabinet that had been kept out of the loop by a nervous prime minister).

Perhaps it is best to think of Kissinger-style negotiation less in terms of precise plans and more in terms of improvisational jazz around a central strategic theme. As different possibilities and impediments arise, often unexpectedly, act opportunistically to incorporate them into your strategic plan.

LESSON 11: Strive to understand your counterpart's perspective, and demonstrate this understanding as you build rapport and a relationship—while asserting your own needs and interests.

It may surprise those who envision Kissinger as mainly a geopolitical maestro that he so closely zoomed in on his counterparts as individuals. Though he did not believe that personal bonds trumped national interests, he still stressed relationships and rapport as useful negotiating tools. As we saw in the numerous insightful profiles that Kissinger crafted, he became an avid student of those with whom he dealt: their psychological tendencies, their personalities, their styles, and their histories.

Beyond their purely personal characteristics, Kissinger saw his counterparts as shaped by their politics and national culture. Thus Golda Meir had a distinctive individual approach to negotiation, but she embodied a fractious political tradition powerfully influenced by Israel's then-precarious existence and the tragic history of her people. The consensus nature of Japanese culture and governance sharply limited Prime Minister Eisaku Sato's personal freedom to make and implement decisions. Kissinger made many trenchant observations contrasting Chinese and Russian histories, cultures, and political systems. Yet, with few exceptions, he avoided national stereotypes, sharply distinguishing, for instance, Mao Zedong from Zhou Enlai and Anatoly Dobrynin from Leonid Brezhnev.

While he reported many of these assessments after the fact, we paid special attention to extensive memos he produced for Presidents Nixon and Ford as advance preparation for negotiations with individual Chinese and Soviet leaders. To generate this preparatory material, Kissinger relied on his own observations, extensive research by his staff, and consultations with outside experts. The care expended on this kind of groundwork, work that complemented his analysis of the issues and the broader strategy, offers a model for others who seek to best ready themselves for a challenging negotiation.

These assessments gave Kissinger important clues to the most effective negotiating approaches for zooming in on his individual counterparts; to the kinds of arguments to which they would be most receptive, their hot buttons and soft spots; as to the pressures and incentives that might have the greatest effect. Both friendly and critical observers generally credit Kissinger with developing unusually penetrating insight into his counterparts, which often translated into positive relationships and rapport.

Kissinger often conveyed to his counterpart his own nuanced understanding of the counterpart's perspective. For negotiation purposes, we refer to this activity as demonstrating "empathy." It is not the same as expressing agreement or sympathy but instead involves showing the other party your understanding of their perspective. It is a way of improving communication, building rapport, and enhancing relationships in negotiation.

In some cases, people with sharply divergent perspectives felt that Kissinger not only understood but agreed with each of them. This could have led to suspicion and distrust should they have compared notes. Kissinger risked being seen as a manipulative, even deceptive, chameleon. This was by no means a universal view, and by all accounts, he was careful not to contradict himself with different audiences. Nevertheless, the broader implication for negotiators is clear: empathy in negotiation can be quite useful, but you should take care not to develop a reputation as being two-faced.

Lest we leave the (unlikely) impression that Kissinger's primary personality trait is empathy, we stress that he often chose to be quite assertive about his perspectives and interests. Such assertiveness could carry a strong and unwelcome message, though it was sometimes delivered in a relatively low-key, even empathetic manner. Ian Smith, for example, had a positive view of the secretary of state, judging him to be "refreshingly honest, straightforward, and to the point,"[7] despite Kissinger's, in effect, asking Smith to sign what the Rhodesian described as his own "suicide note."[8] As we have stressed, there is no necessary tradeoff between empathy and assertiveness. In our experience, the most effective negotiators embody both traits.

Despite strenuous efforts to understand and connect with counterparts, Kissinger sometimes had antagonistic relations, for instance, with Le Duc Tho, Ismail Fahmy, and Nguyen van Thieu. This should hardly be surprising, as many factors beyond attempts at rapport can influence how one party relates to another in negotiation (e.g., interpersonal friction, sharply opposed core interests, and conflicting worldviews).

Reactions to Henry Kissinger, in particular, could have complex underpinnings. His bureaucratic rivalries were legion. He was universally seen as a brilliant man, but one who was sometimes arrogant and thin skinned. Still, his charm, humor, and capacity to draw in others were renowned. And of course, he figured centrally in many controversial U.S. policies that generated bitter animosity. These complicating factors notwithstanding, we emphasize the value to negotiators of expending real efforts to fathom the other side in order to build rapport and relationships—and to understand their real interests and priorities.

LESSON 12: Reconsider the traditional "start high, concede slowly" approach to negotiation.

Kissinger's preferred style of negotiation did not involve extreme offers followed by endless haggling. Before getting into specific issues, making proposals, or taking positions, he urged negotiators to listen, probe, and seek to understand with whom they were dealing and to develop a sense of the other side's real interests and context. Early in the process, he made the case that one should convey in broad strokes, almost philosophically, what one's overall objectives are for the negotiation. This makes good sense to us.

In Kissinger's view, making extreme opening offers and conceding slowly toward one's "real" limits, and only when forced to do so, converted negotiations into a lengthy test of wills and stamina. While useful to demonstrate "toughness" to a home audience, this process could take far longer than necessary and risks needless impasse. Rather than inviting a haggling process, a more productive approach (as with the negotiations over the Shanghai Communiqué) is to expend real effort in determining an outcome that will be genuinely sustainable among the parties. Then craft an initial proposal reasonably close to this point—and stick to it. While some room should be left for adjustment, developing a reputation for this kind of negotiation could be a long-term asset. Similarly, making concessions under pressure can simply invite more pressure. When concessions are necessary, it is better to make them somewhat unexpectedly, when they do not appear forced. This will magnify their impact.

Kissinger was not always able to stick to this preferred approach. The diplomatic equivalent of rug bazaar haggling certainly characterized some of his negotiations, especially toward their endgames. The numbers game in SALT, as well as the fate of Quneitra during the Syrian disengagement talks, offer examples, as did many of Kissinger's dealings with the Soviets. However, he consistently made the argument for a qualitatively different approach to bargaining.

In some cases, it was difficult or impossible to know early on what one's true limits were. For example, during the Paris talks, the U.S. position on the timing of withdrawal of its forces gradually shortened from a year to six months and then to four months—most likely as a result not of a tactical choice to haggle but of the evolving situation.

LESSON 13: Cultivate the fine art of wordsmithing; "constructive ambiguity" can be useful but carries risks; "tacit bargaining" can be a valuable option.

For an unsentimental negotiator who regarded the national interest as his lodestar, Kissinger was often able to move seemingly deadlocked negotiations forward with artful verbal formulations. Especially for situations in which the principals want to go ahead, at least to the next stage of negotiations, but are suspicious, or when negative constituencies stand in the way, elegant phrasing can offer a path forward. Ultimately, substance dominates words. Yet, in the right circumstances, carefully crafted words can offer the keys to unlock valuable substantive results.

While we offered various examples of where well-chosen words permitted otherwise blocked negotiations to proceed, perhaps the best example involves the Shanghai Communiqué. Both the mainland Chinese and those on Taiwan vehemently claimed to represent all of China; each insisted on the unity of the country. While maintaining its own relationship with Taiwan, the United States wanted to open relations with mainland China, but without conceding Beijing's claim to Taiwan. Simply agreeing to disagree would not have sufficed; the issue—which had blocked forward motion for years and threatened to continue to do so—was too important to key factions on each side. Hence the crucial negotiated sentence: "The United States acknowledges that all Chinese on either side of the Taiwan Straits maintain there is but one China. The United States Government does not challenge that position."[9] These artfully crafted, deliberately ambiguous words permitted U.S.-Chinese cooperation over the next decade.

Insisting too early on unambiguous resolution of such issues may simply produce an impasse. This may be the right outcome if the parties' core interests are incompatible and will remain so. Other than postponing the day of reckoning, which in some cases may be a virtue, there is no sense to be found in papering over truly fundamental differences. Yet "constructive ambiguity" produced by creative wordsmithing can prove invaluable. It can permit the process to go forward on a range of more tractable issues, with each side claiming "victory" on the too-contentious issue. If the other issues are resolved, the benefits of cooperation relative to conflict become more apparent, and the relationship strengthens, then there may be a more promising basis to tackle the tougher issue.

A closely related question for negotiators entails what one tells separate parties. Conveying inconsistent messages to different sides while hoping for "acoustic separation" can lead to grief if the inconsistency is later revealed. Lost trust, hurt credibility, and allegations of deceit can easily result. Yet stressing different aspects or characterizations of the same situation to different audiences can keep everyone in the game, perhaps long enough to develop a mutually valuable agreement.

In some cases, however, *any* words in an explicit agreement will be too many, yet a tacit agreement may produce the desired result. As détente took root, Jewish emigration from the Soviet Union (sought by the Nixon administration) was increasingly permitted, even though "No formal requests were made and no formal responses were given."[10] Anwar Sadat was quite willing to clear the Suez Canal after hostilities had ended if this action could be portrayed as his own independent decision and "if Israel would only stop demanding it."[11] Tacit agreements of this kind can be helpful when the *fact* of an agreement could be costly, perhaps activating opponents and prompting a negative response.

Well-chosen words and actions, then, can serve as useful tools for the sophisticated negotiator. With care, they can be artfully crafted or constructively ambiguous. They may emphasize different aspects of an issue to different parties or, by design, be completely absent from a tacit agreement.

LESSON 14: Opt for secrecy with great care; while sometimes vital, it can be a double-edged sword.

Henry Kissinger and Richard Nixon often opted for secrecy in negotiation, both about what was being discussed and even the fact that a negotiation was taking place. This choice was generally combined with centralization of negotiations in the White House and Kissinger's dominant role. As was the case with the opening to China, secrecy offers a major potential advantage: it can permit talks to proceed and options to be explored without alerting domestic, political, or allied opponents who might delay or block the initiative. If even holding negotiations would be controversial and they fail in secret, that fact may never become public. By centralizing the process in the White House, Kissinger could move quickly, avoiding what he often regarded as cumbersome interagency processes.

Secrecy is often employed in sensitive corporate talks over mergers or divestitures for similar reasons. Disclosure might signal that the entity is "in play," alert opponents who might block the deal (e.g., unions, government officials), lead to sharp price changes, or demoralize operating units. If agreement is reached in secret, however, it may well be a fait accompli once revealed.

Secret processes do carry several potential costs. First, they risk being discovered and denounced. This may embarrass and anger those who were sidelined, including close allies and high officials and agencies normally involved with the topics in question. If previously secret talks become public, resentful agencies may withhold active support and find ways to snipe at or even subvert results. Secret negotiations over public and diplomatic issues may also violate norms of transparency, democratic accountability, and legitimacy.

Going it alone, in secret, can also mean losing the advantages of the expertise that resides in excluded agencies and departments. Negotiating in a public front channel with secret back-channel talks under way could lead to damaging confusion and contradiction on all sides, especially when the right hand does not know what the left hand is doing (or even that there *is* a left hand). And if a widespread expectation develops that the only "real" talks are being held somewhere else, in secret, then normal negotiations may be hobbled by the belief that they are likely a sham.

Kissinger's experience aptly demonstrates both the advantages and disadvantages of opting for secrecy and a centralized process.

Reviewing it can usefully inform judgment about this important tactical choice.

LESSON 15: Be relentlessly persistent.

With an intellectual secretary of state such as Henry Kissinger, it is tempting to ascribe negotiating success to conceptual break-throughs. We have amply demonstrated how well-crafted strategies can surmount high barriers to agreement. Yet Kissinger's experi-ence, along with that of many top negotiators, reminds us that dogged persistence often provides the essential ingredient linking strategy with results. Whether it was the three years of the Paris talks, the two years toward the SALT agreement, or the twenty-six Tel Aviv–Damascus round trips in thirty-five days, the willing-ness to intelligently grind away, moving the disparate pieces of an agreement into alignment, must stand as one of the key lessons in negotiation from Henry Kissinger.

★ ★ ★

Reviewing these fifteen lessons from Henry Kissinger's negoti-ations, we observe that they apply well beyond the era when he served in government. True, much has changed: a Cold War–dominated, two-superpower world has become increasingly multi-polar; nonstate actors play more significant roles; and cross-border challenges ranging from climate change to organized crime and potentially destabilizing financial flows are on the increase. More generally, to employ Anne Marie Slaughter's useful mixed meta-phor, the global "chessboard" is now enmeshed in many connected webs.[12] Yet, looking with care over the negotiation lessons we have extracted, from the strategic to the tactical, we see that they are not specific to a particular diplomatic era, or even to diplomacy at all. To apply these general lessons, of course, the relevant circumstances (the context, the parties, how they see their interests, and so on) must properly be taken into account.

At the same time, effective diplomacy, then and now, requires far more than effective negotiation (e.g., representing one's home country, building mutual understanding and support for the policies of one's government, gathering and evaluating information, and developing insight into another country's culture, politics, and government). Though diplomacy encompasses much more than negotiation, negotiation remains an essential component. In this aspect, insights from Kissinger's dealmaking continue to offer useful guidance.

While diplomacy extends well beyond negotiation, negotiation obviously extends well beyond diplomacy, into business, finance, law, public policy, and elsewhere. Based on our research and experience in these realms, we can confidently assert that the strategic and tactical lessons extracted from Kissinger's high-level dealmaking offer valuable guidance. Despite their diplomatic origins in the world of almost a half century ago, these lessons can continue to inform the negotiators of today who seek worthy agreements in the face of complex and daunting challenges.

RECAP: Key Lessons from Kissinger the Negotiator

Core aspects of effective negotiation:

1. Zoom out to your strategy; zoom in to your counterpart—and continually bring both views into alignment.
2. Evaluate and reevaluate your fundamental premises.
3. Develop deep familiarity with the subject of your negotiation—or make sure that your team possesses this knowledge.

Zooming out to a strategic vantage:

4. Take the long view.
5. Adopt a wide-angle perspective.
6. Be realistic: track the deal/no-deal balance.
7. Don't regard the elements of a negotiation as fixed; where useful, seek game-changing moves to favorably tilt the deal/no-deal balance.
8. Evaluate the potential for a multifront negotiation campaign to achieve your target deal, paying special attention to the "home front."
9. Develop multiparty insight and dexterity: coalition dynamics, sequencing, and information.

Zooming in to the tactical and interpersonal aspects of the negotiation process:

10. Think strategically, act opportunistically.
11. Be both empathetic and assertive: strive to understand your counterpart's perspective, and demonstrate this understanding as you build rapport and relationships—while asserting your own needs and interests.
12. Reconsider the traditional "start high, concede slowly" approach to negotiation.
13. Cultivate the fine art of wordsmithing; "constructive ambiguity" can be useful but carries risks; "tacit bargaining" can be a valuable option.
14. Opt for secrecy with great care; while sometimes vital, it can be a double-edged sword.
15. Be relentlessly persistent.

Acknowledgments

We are grateful to Henry Kissinger for generously sharing his time, reflections, and insights, both at Harvard and in New York. We learned a great deal from him directly as well as from his extensive writings. Alex Green indefatigably and astutely did much of the background research for this project, drafted key segments and working papers, offered extensive editorial suggestions, and wrestled to the ground textual challenges from EndNote and Word. Eugene Kogan did considerable research on the Vietnam portion of this book, coauthored a working paper on this subject, and made helpful recommendations on the text. Nancy Buck, Jon Dorfman, David Lax, Paul Levy, Jan Martinez, David Sandberg, Alyza Sebenius, Isaac Sebenius, Zander Sebenius, Robert Toews, William Ury, and Michael Wheeler made countless useful suggestions, both fundamental and editorial, on earlier drafts. Their generous advice materially improved the book. Our editor, Sofia Groopman, insightfully sharpened our prose and ideas. The wise counsel and support of Jim Levine, our agent, have been indispensable. Without the help of Elizabeth Sweeny, Alison Hillegeist, Caryn Shelton-May, and our colleagues at the Program on Negotiation, especially Susan Hackley, James Kerwin, and Polly Hamlen, neither this book nor the flawlessly executed events of the American Secretaries of State Project would have been possible. Only spouses who have put up with, and encouraged, the truly endless demands of book projects know the full extent of our debt to them. To Nancy from Jim, to Dale from Bob, and to Libby from Nick, our profound gratitude.

Notes

Preface

1. Louis Harris, "Public's Appraisal of Henry Kissinger Remains High," Harris Poll press release, Aug. 19, 1974, http://media.theharrispoll.com /documents/Harris-Interactive-Poll-Research-PUBLICS-APPRAISAL -OF-HENRY-KISSINGER-REMAINS-HIGH-1974-08.pdf.

2. Walter Isaacson, *Kissinger: A Biography* (New York: Simon and Schuster, 1992), p. 549.

3. For a discussion, see Daniel Maliniak, Susan Peterson, Ryan Powers, and Michael J. Tierney, "The Best International Relations Schools in the World," *Foreign Policy*, Feb. 2, 2015, http://foreignpolicy .com/2015/02/03/top-twenty-five-schools-international-relations/. For a breakdown of the survey data by gender, political affiliation, etc., see "Who Was the Most Effective U.S. Secretary of State in the Last 50 Years?" (bar graph), TRIP Faculty Survey in United States, TRIP, Sept. 9, 2014, https://trip.wm.edu/charts/#/bargraph/37/1282.

4. Isaacson, *Kissinger*, p. 764.

5. This is a strong claim, which obviously risks falsification should the book or set of articles we have somehow missed turn up. Of course, the more general books about Kissinger are useful for describing his many specific negotiations, often in detail. Yet we have been unable to find extended analyses specifically about this facet of Kissinger's life and work in general. Kissinger himself, when asked, did not know of any such works. The closest treatments of Kissinger's general approach that we have found were written by T. G. Otte and Walter Isaacson. See T. G. Otte, "Kissinger," in *Diplomatic Theory from Machiavelli to Kissinger*, eds. Maurice Keens-Soper, G. R. Berridge, and T. G. Otte (New York: Palgrave, 2001), pp. 195–202;

and Isaacson, *Kissinger*. Both relatively brief accounts highlight several of Kissinger's negotiating characteristics without developing an overall analysis of his strategy and tactics. For example, Otte describes distinctive elements of what he calls Kissinger's approach to "diplomatic practice" as the use of "back channels," secrecy, linkage, trading concessions, step-by-step shuttle diplomacy, building on interim agreements, and summitry—all informed by a historical understanding of one's counterpart. Similarly, Walter Isaacson's biography contains a section (pp. 550–59) on Kissinger's "negotiating style" that describes his preference for reaching a target settlement directly, his emphasis on personal factors and relationships among leaders, his penchant for secrecy, statements intended to create desired impressions without actually lying, the value of "constructive ambiguity," shuttle diplomacy, and so on. Apart from these concise descriptions, the many negotiation-focused analyses of Kissinger's approach in particular cases have been quite useful for our purposes. Among the numerous sources we will cite throughout this book are Jeffrey Z. Rubin, *Dynamics of Third Party Intervention: Kissinger in the Middle East* (New York: Praeger, in cooperation with the Society for the Psychological Study of Social Issues, 1981); Tad Szulc, "How Kissinger Did It: Behind the Vietnam Cease-Fire Agreement," *Foreign Policy* 15 (Summer 1974); Edward R. F. Sheehan, "How Kissinger Did It: Step by Step in the Middle East," *Foreign Policy* 22 (Spring 1976): 3–70; W. Quandt, "Kissinger and the Arab-Israeli Disengagement Negotiations," *Journal of International Affairs* 9, no. 1 (Spring 1975): 33–48; Margaret MacMillan, *Nixon and Mao: The Week That Changed the World* (New York: Random House, 2007); and Janice Stein, "Structures, Strategies, and Tactics of Mediation: Kissinger and Carter in the Middle East," *Negotiation Journal* 1, no. 4 (Oct. 1985): 331–47.

6. Program on Negotiation, Harvard Law School, http://www.pon .harvard.edu/. Chaired by Professor James Sebenius since 2001, the

Great Negotiator Award program honors men and women from around the world who have overcome significant barriers to reaching agreements that have achieved worthy purposes. This initiative is sponsored by the Program on Negotiation, an active consortium of Harvard, MIT, and Tufts; and, more recently, on Harvard's Future of Diplomacy Project, https://www.belfercenter.org/project/future-diplomacy-project. Negotiation-oriented faculty from these universities do substantial advance research and case writing, bring the honoree to campus for at least a day of intensive videotaped interviews on his or her most challenging negotiations, and then extract his or her most valuable lessons in articles, course materials, and interactive video presentations. Since 2001, this project has honored the following people: Sen. George J. Mitchell, with special emphasis on his work in Northern Ireland leading to the Good Friday Agreement; Bruce Wasserstein, for his decades of financial dealmaking, with a special focus on his role at Lazard Asset Management; Special Trade Representative Charlene Barshefsky, in particular for her negotiations with China over intellectual property rights; Lakhdar Brahimi, special representative of the UN secretary-general, with special emphasis on his work to forge a post-conflict government in Afghanistan after 9/11; Ambassador Richard Holbrooke, for his negotiations leading to the Dayton Accords that ended the Bosnian War as well as his multiparty efforts to deal with unpaid U.S. dues to the United Nations; Colombian president and 2016 Nobel Peace Prize laureate Juan Santos, for his central role in forging an agreement between the government and the largest guerrilla group (the "FARC," or Revolutionary Armed Forces of Colombia), apparently, as of late 2017, ending a fifty-plus-year civil war in Colombia that had defied countless prior negotiation attempts, killed more than 220,000 people, and internally displaced over 5 million; the Honorable Stuart Eizenstat, for his negotiations over restitution of Holocaust-era assets in Switzerland and other European countries;

UN High Commissioner for Refugees Sadako Ogata, for her quiet negotiations on behalf of refugees and internally displaced persons in regions in places ranging from Iraq to the Balkans to Rwanda; the artists Christo and Jeanne-Claude for their negotiations to erect massive, controversial installations, from *Running Fence* in California to *The Gates* in New York City's Central Park, as well as wrapping Paris's Pont Neuf and Berlin's Reichstag; former Finnish president and Nobel Peace Prize laureate Martti Ahtisaari, in particular for his negotiation efforts leading to Kosovo's independence and the resolution of a decades-long bloody conflict between the government of Indonesia and the province of Aceh; former U.S. secretary of state James Baker, for his negotiations leading to the reunification of Germany within NATO, actions to forge the Gulf War coalition to eject Saddam Hussein from Kuwait, and diplomacy paving the road to the Madrid Conference; and Singapore's UN ambassador Tommy Koh, for his work chairing the Law of the Sea Negotiations, the Rio Earth Summit, the United States–Singapore Free Trade Agreement, and a number of other initiatives.

7. Our American Secretaries of State Project will use these many hours of interviews to produce a book and documentary films that analyze the leadership and negotiation approaches of the different secretaries over four decades with respect to the Soviet Union/Russia, China, and the Middle East. Future of Diplomacy Project, "Special Initiative—American Secretaries of State," Harvard Kennedy School American Secretaries of State website, http://www.belfercenter.org/american-secretaries-state/secretaries-state-interviews.

8. George P. Shultz, *Ideas and Action: Featuring the 10 Commandments of Negotiation* (Erie, PA: Free to Choose Press, 2010); and Program on Negotiation at Harvard Law School.

9. Kissinger's exact response: "When the various secretaries [of state] come here or when you put it together into a book, I don't think Baker could use my approach. And I couldn't use Baker's approach.

Baker is a very practical operator. And when you have a very concrete problem, you want Baker. And you don't want to get between Baker and an objective. I have a more structural approach. The period in which I served happened to have profound structural issues. Shultz is somewhere in between. And I wouldn't say that there is one absolute rule that you can apply in all conditions" (Program on Negotiation at Harvard Law School, Henry A. Kissinger, interview by R. Nicholas Burns, Robert Mnookin, and James K. Sebenius, Nov. 6, 2014).

10. Subsequently, we read several more of Kissinger's books and articles, along with invaluable additional sources, including the incomparable compilation by the Digital National Security Archive (DNSA), Kissinger Telephone Conversations: A Verbatim Record of U.S. Diplomacy, 1969–1977, George Washington University, Washington DC, http://proquest.libguides.com/dnsa/kissinger1, as well as numerous other sources that we later detail.

11. Henry Kissinger, *A World Restored: Europe After Napoleon* (New York: Grosset and Dunlap, 1964), pp. 287–89. Originally published as *A World Restored: Metternich, Castlereagh and the Problems of Peace, 1812–22* (London: Weidenfeld and Nicolson, 1957).

12. Anne-Marie Slaughter, *The Chessboard and the Web: Strategies of Connection in a Networked World* (New Haven, CT: Yale University Press, 2017).

13. William Burr, *The Kissinger Transcripts: The Top-Secret Talks with Beijing and Moscow* (New York: The New Press in conjunction with the National Security Archive, 1999); the Richard Nixon Presidential Library and Museum, Yorba Linda, CA, https://www.nixonlibrary.gov/; the Gerald R. Ford Presidential Library and Museum, Grand Rapids, MI, https://www.fordlibrarymuseum.gov/contact.aspx; Office of the Historian, *Foreign Relations of the United States*, U.S. Department of State (Government Printing Office: Washington, DC), https://history.state.gov/.

Introduction: Kissinger the Negotiator: A Story That Should Be Told

1.　This is obviously a strong claim, which we discuss and justify in note 1 of the preface.

2.　Although we initially thought we had originated this "zoom-out, zoom-in" terminology, others can appropriately claim credit. In particular, our Harvard Business School colleague Rosabeth Moss Kanter framed a major article in these terms; see her "'Zoom In, Zoom Out,'" *Harvard Business Review* 89, no. 3 (2011): 112–16. Also in 2011, Jim Collins and Morten Hansen used this phrase, in their case, with respect to strategy. See Jim Collins and Morten T. Hansen, *Great by Choice* (New York: Harper Business, 2011), pp. 113–21. And we suspect that we have omitted others who have used the phrase in other contexts.

3.　Henry Kissinger, *On China* (New York: Penguin Press, 2011); and Henry Kissinger, *World Order* (New York: Penguin Press, 2014). For a full list of his books, articles, and speeches, see "Henry A. Kissinger," http://henryakissinger.com/.

4.　The "intense confrontation" spawned a debate in the *New York Times* of Feb. 13, 2016. See Niall Ferguson and Todd Gitlin, "Henry Kissinger: Sage or Pariah?" *New York Times*, Feb. 13, 2016, http://www.nytimes.com/roomfordebate/2016/02/13/henry-kissinger-sage-or-pariah. Similarly, see the recent debate among ten historians, Nicholas Thompson et al., "Henry Kissinger: Good or Evil? 10 Historians Assess the Controversial Statesman's Legacy," *Politico*, Oct. 10, 2015, http://www.politico.com/magazine/story/2015/10/henry-kissinger-history-legacy-213237.

5.　Niall Ferguson, *Kissinger: Volume 1, 1923–1968: The Idealist* (New York: Penguin Books, 2015); Greg Grandin, *Kissinger's Shadow: The Long Reach of America's Most Controversial Statesman* (New York: Metropolitan Books/Henry Holt and Company, 2015).

6.　Beyond the books just mentioned, see biographical works such as Isaacson, *Kissinger*; Marvin L. Kalb and Bernard Kalb, *Kissinger* (Boston:

Little, Brown, 1974); Alistair Horne, *Kissinger: 1973, the Crucial Year* (New York: Simon and Schuster, 2009); Robert Dallek, *Nixon and Kissinger: Partners in Power* (New York: HarperCollins, 2007). The "Introduction" to Ferguson's *Kissinger: The Idealist* offers an entertaining and extensive *tour d'horizon* of writings about Kissinger. Complementing Ferguson's "survey," Alistair Horne offers a powerful "case for Henry Kissinger," while referencing and quoting his various critics. See Alistair Horne, "The Case for Henry Kissinger," *Independent*, Aug. 17, 2009, based on his 2009 book, *Kissinger: 1973*. Among the strongest critics are, for example, Christopher Hitchens, *The Trial of Henry Kissinger* (New York: Verso, 2001); Seymour M. Hersh, *The Price of Power: Kissinger in the Nixon White House* (New York: Summit Books, 1983); and William Shawcross, *Sideshow: Kissinger, Nixon, and the Destruction of Cambodia* (New York: Simon and Schuster, 1979).

7. As just noted, prominent detractors would include Grandin, *Kissinger's Shadow*; Hersh, *The Price of Power*; Hitchens, *The Trial of Henry Kissinger*; and Shawcross, *Sideshow*. Many highly critical chapters can be found in Walter Isaacson's biography. More recent echoes of these analyses can be found in articles by critics such as Zack Beauchamp, "The Obama Administration Is Honoring Henry Kissinger Today. It Shouldn't Be," *Vox*, May 9, 2016, http://www .vox.com/2016/5/9/11640562/kissinger-pentagon-award. Among his admirers, though hardly uncritical, would be Niall Ferguson, *Kissinger: The Idealist*; Horne, "The Case for Henry Kissinger"; Robert D. Kaplan, "Kissinger, Metternich, and Realism," *The Atlantic*, June, 1999; Josef Joffe, "In Defense of Henry Kissinger," *Commentary*, Dec. 1, 1992; President Obama's secretary of state John Kerry stated, "And Henry Kissinger . . . literally wrote the book on diplomacy; the Secretary whose exploits and expertise gave us the vocabulary of modern diplomacy, the very words "shuttle diplomacy" and "strategic patience"; and whose special insight into history has been an invaluable gift to every secretary who sat in that office on

mahogany row ever since the day that Henry left it." John Kerry, "Remarks at the U.S. Diplomacy Center Groundbreaking Ceremony," news release, Sept. 3, 2014, https://2009–2017.state.gov/secretary /remarks/2014/09/231318.htm.

8. James K. Sebenius, L. Alexander Green, and Eugene B. Kogan, "Henry A. Kissinger as Negotiator: Background and Key Accomplishments," Working Paper, No. 15–040, 2014 (revised Dec. 2016), Harvard Business School, Boston, MA.

9. Ferguson, *Kissinger: The Idealist*, p. 2. In 1973, Kissinger was number one in Gallup's "Most Admired Man" survey. Among secretaries of state, he alone appeared on Charlie Rose's television show almost forty times (this is not to mention the cameos on *Dynasty* and *The Colbert Report* and his role as animated characters on *The Simpsons* and *Family Guy*).

10. For further details, see "Henry A. Kissinger: Biography," at www .henryakissinger.com/biography.html.

11. For a complete listing, see "Henry A. Kissinger," www.henrya kissinger.com.

12. Kissinger, *A World Restored*; and Kissinger, *Nuclear Weapons and Foreign Policy* (New York: Harper, 1957).

13. *White House Years* (Boston: Little, Brown, 1979).

14. *Diplomacy* (New York: Simon and Schuster, 1994); Jussi M. Hanhimäki, *The Flawed Architect: Henry Kissinger and American Foreign Policy* (New York: Oxford University Press, 2004), p. 356.

15. Kissinger, *On China*. For further details, see "Henry A. Kissinger— Biography," www.henryakissinger.com/biography.html.

16. In particular, this latest book explores the evolution, interaction, and possible futures of divergent conceptions of "world order." These include the so-called Westphalian model, originating in Europe, of nominally equal sovereign states; the Chinese system envisioning the Middle Kingdon at its center, with outlying tributary states; an expansive Islamic idea of a world community, or *ummah*; and an American

order heavily informed by the supposedly universal ideals articulated by Woodrow Wilson, an order that both dominates the world and is under siege from many quarters. See Kissinger, *World Order*.

17. For summaries of several of these episodes, see James K. Sebenius, R. Nicholas Burns, Robert H. Mnookin, and L. Alexander Green. "Henry Kissinger: Negotiating Black Majority Rule in Southern Africa," Working Paper No. 17–051, Dec. 2016, Harvard Business School, Boston, MA. Of course, Kissinger himself offers detailed accounts of these and other negotiations in many works, especially Kissinger, *White House Years*; *Years of Upheaval* (Boston: Little, Brown, 1982); and *Years of Renewal* (New York: Simon and Schuster, 1999), as do many of the biographies and other sources already cited.

18. *White House Years*, p. 685.

19. Ibid., p. 695.

20. Note that, throughout, we have replaced the older transliteration "Chou" with the pinyin "Zhou" and "Mao Tse-Tung" with the pinyin "Mao Zedong" in quoted material.

21. Alec Gallup (2006). *The Gallup Poll: Public Opinion 2005*. Rowman & Littlefield. pp. 315–18.

22. Bureau of the Census, "Vietnam Conflict—U.S. Military Forces in Vietnam and Casualties Incurred: 1961 to 1972," Table 590, *Statistical Abstract of the United States, 1977* (Washington, DC: U.S. Department of Commerce, 1980), p. 369, https://www.gilderlehrman.org/history -by-era/seventies/resources/vietnam-war-military-statistics.

23. As quoted in Horne, *Kissinger: 1973*, p. 51.

24. For details, see A. B. Mutiti, "Rhodesia and Her Four Discriminatory Constitutions," *Présence Africaine*, Nouvelle série, No. 90 (2e Trimestre 1974): 261–75.

25. Below the surface of our narrative lurks a perennial methodological question often posed by international relations theorists, among other social scientists, who observe and analyze negotiations: Do, or even can, the actions of individual negotiators matter much to outcomes?

Aren't ultimate results really the produce of "structures" or "larger forces" (be they institutional, economic, cultural, historical, or whatever) inexorably working themselves out with human agency merely an "epiphenomena" or, more poetically, full of "sound and fury, signifying nothing"? A classic statement of this dilemma can be found in Alexander E. Wendt, "The Agent-Structure Problem in International Relations Theory," *International Organization* 41, no. 3 (1987): 335–70. In our analysis, we sidestep this deep issue, simply aligning ourselves with the view that individual agency can matter a great deal to outcomes and in shaping structures, while, obviously, existing structures constrain and shape agency. See the next note for a discussion; Audie Klotz et al., "Moving Beyond the Agent–Structure Debate," *International Studies Review* 8, no. 2 (2006): 355.

26. After all, for success in negotiation, each of us must necessarily act, as individuals and as members of teams, on the basis of our own interests and perceptions. It is therefore useful to view these events through Kissinger's eyes—as we must view our negotiation challenges through our own eyes. Analyzing events from the perspective of one player inevitably risks selective and self-serving perception. Yet, to be effective as negotiators, for us as for Kissinger, we must strive not to be prisoners of myopic or distorted views. At a minimum, we must incorporate an understanding of the context within which the negotiation takes place, including the likely perceptions, actions, and reactions of other players. As we study and recount Kissinger's dealings, we will keep these caveats in mind, often turning to other sources for corroboration of events.

27. For discussions of kinds of moves along with their psychological aspects, see, e.g., Leigh L. Thompson, *The Mind and Heart of the Negotiator*, 5th ed. (Boston: Pearson, 2012); Margaret Ann Neale and Max H. Bazerman, *Cognition and Rationality in Negotiation* (New York: Free Press; Toronto, 1991).

28. Thomas C. Schelling, *The Strategy of Conflict* (Cambridge: Harvard University Press, 1960); Thomas Schelling, *Arms and Influence* (New

Haven, CT: Yale University Press, 1966); David A. Lax and James K. Sebenius, *3-D Negotiation: Powerful Tools to Change the Game in Your Most Important Deals* (Boston: Harvard Business School Press, 2006). For the more technical foundations of negotiation analysis, including moves "away from the table," see James K. Sebenius, "Negotiation Arithmetic: Adding and Subtracting Issues and Parties," *International Organization* 37, no. 2 (Spring 1983): 281–316; James K. Sebenius, "International Negotiation Analysis," in *International Negotiation: Analysis, Approaches, Issues.* 2nd ed. Ed. Victor Kremenyuk (San Francisco: Jossey-Bass, 2002), pp. 229–52. A number of illustrative case studies of such moves can be found in Michael Watkins and Susan Rosegrant, *Breakthrough International Negotiation: How Great Negotiators Transformed the World's Toughest Post-Cold War Conflicts* (San Francisco, CA: Jossey-Bass, 2001).

Chapter 1: Crafting a Negotiating Strategy

1. Kissinger, *Years of Renewal*, p. 903.
2. Elizabeth Knowles, *Oxford Dictionary of Modern Quotations*, 3rd ed. (New York: Oxford University Press, 2008), p. 296.
3. Kissinger, *Years of Renewal*, p. 1011.
4. The quoted phrase is from ibid., p. 961.
5. *Time*, "Poised Between Peace and War," Oct. 11, 1976, p. 44.
6. *Observer*, "The Road to Zimbabwe," Sept. 26, 1976, p. 8.
7. Kissinger, *Years of Renewal*, p. 972.
8. Ibid., chaps. 26, 29, 30, 31, and 32.
9. We have drawn on far more detailed accounts of these remarkable negotiations, including Sebenius, Burns, Mnookin, and Green, "Henry Kissinger: Negotiating Black Majority Rule in Southern Africa"; Sue Onslow, "'We Must Gain Time': South Africa, Rhodesia, and the Kissinger Initiative of 1976," *South African Historical Journal* 56, no. 1 (2006): 123–53; William L. Bishop, "Diplomacy in Black and White:

America and the Search for Zimbabwean Independence, 1965–1980"
(PhD diss., Vanderbilt University, 2012); Stephen Low, "The Zimbabwe
Settlement, 1976–1979," in *International Mediation in Theory and Prac-
tice*, eds. Saadia Touval and I. William Zartman (Washington, DC:
Westview Press, 1985); Jamie Miller, *An African Volk: The Apart-
heid Regime and Its Search for Survival* (New York: Oxford University
Press, 2016); Andrew Novak, "Face-Saving Maneuvers and Strong
Third-Party Mediation: The Lancaster House Conference on Zim-
babwe-Rhodesia," *International Negotiation* 14, no. 1 (2009): 149–74;
and William E. Schaufele, "Interview with Ambassador William E.
Schaufele Jr.," Foreign Affairs Oral History Project, Nov. 19, 1994.
http://www.adst.org/OH%20TOCs/Schaufele,%20William%20
E.%20Jr.pdf; Ian Douglas Smith, *Bitter Harvest* (London: Blake, 2001);
Isaacson, *Kissinger*; Authors' interview with Ambassador Frank G.
Wisner, May 5, 2016; Marianne Spiegel, "The Namibia Negotiations
and the Problem of Neutrality," in Touval and Zartman, eds., *Inter-
national Mediation in Theory and Practice*; Mordechai Tamarkin, *The
Making of Zimbabwe: Decolonization in Regional and International Politics*
(Savage, MD: F. Cass, 1990); I. William Zartman, *Ripe for Resolution:
Conflict and Intervention in Africa* (New York: Oxford University Press,
1985); Grandin, *Kissinger's Shadow*; Andy DeRoche, *Kenneth Kaunda,
the United States and Southern Africa* (London: Bloomsbury, 2016).

10. "A Dr. K. Offer They Could Not Refuse," *Time* no. 108.14, Oct. 4,
1976, p. 43.

11. "Whites in Africa Fear Race War," *Morning Journal-Record*, Feb. 28,
1976, p. 7.

12. George F. Kennan, "Black Rule in Rhodesia: Some Implications,"
New York Times, May 2, 1976, p. E15.

13. Kissinger, *Years of Renewal*, pp. 917–18.

14. Anthony Lake, *The "Tar Baby" Option: American Policy Toward Southern
Rhodesia* (New York: Columbia University Press, 1976).

15. Isaacson, *Kissinger*, p. 822.

16. Kissinger, *Years of Renewal*, p. 925.

17. See, e.g., David R. Smock, "The Forgotten Rhodesians," *Foreign Affairs* 47, no. 3 (1969): 532; Sue Onslow, "A Question of Timing: South Africa and Rhodesia's Unilateral Declaration of Independence, 1964–65," *Cold War History* 5, no. 2 (2005): 129–59; Luise White, *Unpopular Sovereignty: Rhodesian Independence and African Decolonization* (Chicago: University of Chicago Press, 2015).

18. Kissinger, *Years of Renewal*, p. 915.

19. Alan Cowell, "Ian Smith, Defiant and Steadfast Symbol of White Rule in Africa, Is Dead at 88," *New York Times*, Nov. 21, 2007, p. A25.

20. Kissinger, *Years of Renewal*, p. 975.

21. Hanes Walton, *The African Foreign Policy of Secretary of State Henry Kissinger: A Documentary Analysis* (Lanham, MD: Lexington Books, 2007), p. 208.

22. Kissinger, *Years of Renewal*, p. 918.

23. Lax and Sebenius, *3-D Negotiation*, p. 21–34.

24. Kissinger, *Years of Renewal*, pp. 916–17.

25. Ibid., p. 917.

26. Gerald R. Ford, *A Time to Heal: The Autobiography of Gerald R. Ford* (New York: Harper and Row, 1979), p. 380.

27. This simplified diagram leaves out many figures that, in a fuller account of these negotiations, would be seen to have roles. Such figures would include Abel Muzorewa, Jomo Kenyatta, and the heads of a number of African states and their foreign ministers.

28. Kissinger, *Years of Renewal*, p. 918.

29. Ibid.

30. Ibid.

31. Ibid., pp. 918–19.

32. Ibid., p. 955. While part of the intended strategy, the French front receded in importance as the process unfolded.

33. Ibid., p. 921.

34. James K. Sebenius, "Beyond the Deal: Wage a 'Negotiation Campaign,'"

Negotiation Journal 13, no. 11 (2010): 1–4. For a fuller exposition in business contexts, see David A. Lax and James K. Sebenius, "Deal Making 2.0: A Guide to Complex Negotiations," *Harvard Business Review* 90, no. 12 (November. 2012): 92–100.

35. Kissinger, *Years of Renewal*, 903, 74–75; Schaufele, "Interview with Ambassador William E. Schaufele Jr.," p. 151.

36. Winston Lord, "Interview with Ambassador Winston Lord," Foreign Affairs Oral History Project, April 28, 1998, http://www.adst.org/OH%20TOCs/Lord,%20Winston.pdf.

37. Schaufele, "Interview with Ambassador William E. Schaufele Jr."

38. William Rogers, "Interview with Under Secretary William D. Rogers," Foreign Affairs Oral History Project, July 8, 1992, http://www.adst.org/OH%20TOCs/Rogers,%20William%20D.toc.pdf; Schaufele, "Interview with Ambassador William E. Schaufele Jr."

39. Association for Diplomatic Studies and Training, interview with Ambassador Frank G. Wisner, Foreign Affairs Oral History Project, March 22, 1998, http://www.adst.org/OH%20TOCs/Wisner,%20Frank%20G.toc.pdf; Schaufele, "Interview with Ambassador William E. Schaufele Jr."; Steven Low, "Interview with Stephen Low," Foreign Affairs Oral History Project, Dec. 5, 1997, http://adst.org/wp-content/uploads/2012/09/Low-Stephen.-1997-.toc_1.pdf; William D. Rogers interview; Kissinger, *Years of Renewal*, pp. 995–96.

40. For example, "Comments on Draft National Intelligence Estimate on Rhodesia," Memo, U.S. Department of State, Sept. 19, 1976; Donald B. Easum, "Nyerere and Obasanjo on Rhodesia, Report to Secretary of State Henry A. Kissinger, Nov. 23, 1976," U.S. Department of State, 1976; U.S. Department of State. "Secretary's Visit to Tanzania," Memcon, Wikileaks cable 1976DARES01504_b, dated March 25, 1976. https://wikileaks.org/plusd/cables/1976DARES01504_b.html; Ian Douglas Smith, "Smith Speech," Memcon. U.S. Department of State. Wikileaks Cable: 1976SECTO27255_b. Dated Sept. 21, 1976. https://wikileaks.org/plusd/cables/1976SECTO27255_b.html.

Chapter 2: From Strategy to Execution

1. Kissinger, *Years of Renewal*, p. 914.
2. Ford, p. 380.
3. Miller, *An African Volk*, p. 219. Onslow, "'We Must Gain Time,'" p. 130.
4. James Callaghan, "Rhodesia," Debate on March 22, 1976, U.K. House of Commons, vol. 908 cc29–45, http://hansard.millbanksystems .com/commons/1976/mar/22/rhodesia.
5. Kissinger, *Years of Renewal*, p. 925.
6. Ibid., pp. 916 and 925.
7. Ibid., pp. 932–33.
8. Ibid., p. 932.
9. David Martin, "Mwalimu Julius Kambarage Nyerere Remembered," undated blogpost, Southern Africa Research and Documentation Centre, http://www.sardc.net/en/mwalimu-julius-kambarage-nyerere -remembered-a-candle-on-kilimanjaro-by-david-martin/.
10. Herbert Howe, *Dancing on Cobwebs: American Diplomatic Participation in the 1976 Rhodesian Peace Process*, Pew Case Studies in International Affairs (Washington, DC: United States: Pew Charitable Trusts, 1988), p. 6.
11. Kissinger, *Years of Renewal*, p. 931.
12. Ibid., p. 936.
13. Ibid.
14. Ibid., p. 990.
15. Ibid., p. 992.
16. R. M. Kanter, "Zoom In, Zoom Out," *Harvard Business Review* 89, no. 3 (2011): 112–16. See also Jim Collins and Morten T. Hansen, *Great by Choice* (New York: Harper Business, 2011), pp. 113–21.
17. *Foreign Relations of the United States, 1969–1976, Volume XXVIII: Southern Africa*, eds. Myra F. Burton and Edward C. Keefer (Washington, DC: Government Printing Office, 2011), doc. 195. https:// history.state.gov/historicaldocuments/frus1969–76v28/d195; Michael T. Kaufman, "Chrome Ban Asked: Secretary, in Zambia, States

Africa Policy and Promises Aid. Kissinger to Press Rhodesia on Rule by Black Majority," *New York Times*, April 28, 1976, p. 1.

18. Senate Committee on Foreign Relations, Subcommittee on Multinational Corporations, *Multinational Corporations and United States Foreign Policy*, 93rd Congress, 1973, p. 77.

19. *Foreign Relations of the United States, 1969–1976*, Volume XXXVIII, Part 1, Foundations of Foreign Policy, 1973–1976, eds. Kristine L. Ahlberg and Alexander Wieland (Washington: Government Printing Office, 2012), Document 77. https://history.state.gov/historical documents/frus1969–76v38p1/d77 [accessed Dec. 20, 2017].

20. Kissinger, *Years of Renewal*, p. 939.

21. Kaufman, "Chrome Ban Asked."

22. Ibid., p. 942.

23. For example, Kissinger forged a relationship with the president of the Côte d'Ivoire, Félix Houphouët-Boigny, a former French senator who would act as a sounding board throughout the negotiations. See, e.g., "Message for President Houphouët-Boigny," Wikileaks cable 1976SECTO27213_b, dated Sept. 20, 1976, https://wikileaks .org/plusd/cables/1976SECTO27213_b.html; also, Kissinger, *Years of Renewal*, p. 939.

24. Kissinger, *Years of Renewal*, p. 943.

25. Ibid., pp. 946–47.

26. Ibid., p. 950.

27. Ibid., p. 952.

28. Ibid., pp. 953–54.

29. Ibid. Consistent with their support, the ministers agreed to provide only one channel for supplying weapons to the Rhodesian opposition, thereby limiting the ability of the Cubans to traffic arms through the region.

30. Marvin Kalb, *First Line Report*, CBS Radio, May 4, 1976.

31. Piero Gleijeses, "A Test of Wills: Jimmy Carter, South Africa, and the Independence of Namibia," *Diplomatic History* 34, no. 5 (2010): 862.

32. Kissinger, *Years of Renewal*, p. 940.

33. Ibid., p. 983.

34. Ibid., pp. 967–68.

35. Ibid., p. 983.

36. Walton, *The African Foreign Policy of Secretary of State Henry Kissinger*, pp. 71 and 73.

37. Kissinger, *Years of Renewal*, 921–22; Walton, *The African Foreign Policy of Secretary of State Henry Kissinger*, 73.

38. Kissinger, *Years of Renewal*, pp. 921–22.

39. Ibid., p. 956.

40. Ibid., p. 961.

41. Ibid.

42. United Nations Security Council, Resolution 385, Adopted by the United Nations Security Council at Its 1885th Meeting, S/RES/385, 1885, Jan. 30, 1976.

43. Onslow, "'We Must Gain Time,'" p. 131.

44. Onslow writes that the combined military demands of South West Africa and Rhodesia created "a growing security predicament" and substantial "potential dangers for South African national security." Onslow, "'We Must Gain Time,'" pp. 126–27. Also see pp. 29–30, 40–41.

45. Ibid., p. 140. During his Sept. 4, 1976, meeting with Kissinger, Vorster noted South Africa's reliance on laborers from Mozambique, saying, "We employ hundreds of thousands of laborers from Mozambique, from Lesotho." In U.S. Department of State, "Memcon with B. J. Vorster, Zurich, Switzerland," Sept. 4, 1976, located in Kissinger Telephone Conversations, http://search.proquest.com.ezp-prod1.hul.harvard.edu/docview/1679067316?accountid=11311.

46. Onslow, "'We Must Gain Time,'" pp. 129–30. Onslow quotes Vorster in an Aug. 3, 1976, cabinet meeting as having "concluded: 'We receive icy winds, economically and politically, from the front. We must not become panic stricken, or take crisis decisions.'" See Onslow, "'We Must Gain Time,'" p. 140. Miller, *An African Volk*, pp. 208–13 details

increases in SADF [South African Defence Force] military spending in the aftermath of the Angola intervention.

47. Kissinger, *Years of Renewal*, p. 958.

48. In Kissinger, *Years of Renewal*, p. 995. Kissinger notes that Kaunda was eager to see Nkomo's ascent over that of Mugabe, who was referred to as one of "the boys with the guns." The phrase is often attributed to Nyerere, who purportedly backed Mugabe. In a September 6, 1976, meeting with Callaghan and British foreign secretary Anthony Crosland, Kissinger characterized Vorster's inclination to support Nkomo. Kissinger told the UK delegation that Vorster hoped that "Rhodesia will be a Zambia, not a Mozambique," on his border. In U.S. Department of State, "Southern Africa," Memcon, Foreign and Commonwealth Office, London, Sept. 24, 1976, located in Kissinger Telephone Conversations. Kissinger concluded this conversation by noting that Vorster agreed that leadership by "Nkomo shouldn't be made a precondition" of negotiations, but that Vorster still felt that "the blacks, when they come around to a negotiation, may come back to Nkomo." Kissinger's assessment, however, was that Nkomo had already "slipped." U.S. Department of State, "Southern Africa," Memcon, Foreign and Commonwealth Office, London, Sept. 24, 1976, located in Kissinger Telephone Conversations.

49. Vorster's détente initiative is described in detail in chapter 4 of Miller, *An African Volk*; Onslow, pp. 125–26 provides a brief summary of this initiative.

50. South Africa had launched a series of disastrous military incursions into Angola during the political instability that began with the departure of the Portuguese. By framing the Angola initiative as fundamentally anti-communist, Miller argues that the South Africans gave opponents the opportunity to do the same, and to leverage that opposition against an already isolated South Africa. This resulted in rising regional tensions that made "Vorster's task in seeking a Rhodesian settlement . . . more difficult in 1976 than it had been in 1974–

75." Whereas a settlement could be looked upon as "an opportunity," writes Miller, "By 1976, it was a necessity. He [Vorster] was caught between the urgency of producing a settlement before regional tensions escalated and the regional imperative of avoiding Smith's replacement by radicals who might provide safe havens for revolutionary cadres bent on the Republic's overthrow, or even invite military support on their behalf from extracontinental powers." Miller, *An African Volk*, p. 223. More broadly, see Miller, chapters 5, 6, and 7.

51.   It was the stated position of the South African government to remain neutral in the affairs of foreign nations. This was, of course, not the case in the covert invasion of Angola in 1975. However, South African public opinion and the stated public position of the government was such that an overt break with Smith would have been a shock. As such, Onslow notes that Vorster was "loathe" to be seen undermining the "official position" of the government by publicly breaking with Smith. See Onslow, "'We Must Gain Time,'" pp. 128–30. Miller documents Vorster's bind in detail in chapter 7 of *An African Volk*. In a September 4, 1976, meeting with Kissinger, Vorster described the Victoria Falls interaction [the location of key talks in Vorster's détente initiative] with Smith as follows: "At the bridge, I spoke with Kaunda about his economic difficulties, his problems with getting his copper out. I said, 'You know the only way you can get it out is over Rhodesian railways.' He said, 'Yes, I thought about it. Suppose I do, and use Smith's railways, and at the last minute he cuts me off? I'll be in a worse situation than before.' So we went to Smith in the other coach. He said he would do it. I said, 'The snag is his fear you might cut him off at an awkward moment. I tell you now—in front of Kaunda—that if you give an undertaking and ditch it, I'll ditch you, and in public.' You can ask Kaunda." U.S. Department of State, "Memcon with B. J. Vorster."

52.   Miller, *An African Volk*, details the lengthy, fraught relationship between Vorster and Smith; for examples, see pp. 142, 148, 157, and,

more broadly, pp. 119–61 and 225–59. Despite Vorster's strong line against Smith at Victoria Falls, in the same September 4, 1976, conversation with Kissinger, he was more circumspect about his ability to publicly play a role in Smith's undoing, telling Kissinger that "we cannot be seen to be deposing Ian Smith. The Rhodesians can depose him but not us." U.S. Department of State, "Memcon with B. J. Vorster."

53. Kissinger, *Years of Renewal*, p. 964; "No NP [National Party] prime minister had ever met an American secretary of state." Miller, *An African Volk*, p. 221.

54. Kissinger, *Years of Renewal*, p. 964; Vorster's acceptance of an offer to meet with Kissinger was by no means preordained. Vorster blamed Kissinger, in particular, for South Africa's disastrous attempted military intervention in Angola the year before. Miller notes that the sense of betrayal was overstated by the South Africans, but also notes, by way of Vorster's remarks to *Newsweek* at the time, that it was deeply felt. Vorster: "US Secretary of State Henry Kissinger had urged the SADF [South African Defence Force] incursion into Angola and then failed to provide the necessary back-up." Miller, *An African Volk*, pp. 201–2. As a result, he writes, "Vorster was skeptical about working with Washington again after Angola." It was the combination of Kissinger and Ford's overtures and meetings between Kissinger and South African ambassador Roelof "Pik" Botha that persuaded him to do so. Miller, *An African Volk*, p. 219.

55. Kissinger, *Years of Renewal*, p. 966; Sue Onslow, "'Noises Off': South Africa and the Lancaster House Settlement 1979–1980," *Journal of Southern African Studies* 35, no. 2 (2009): 490. Miller links rising domestic black opposition in South Africa to the failed Angola intervention, noting that South Africa's efforts confirmed a growing sense among South African blacks that the South African government was not committed to any substantive reform. Miller, *An African Volk*, pp. 203–5.

56. Kissinger, *Years of Renewal*, p. 969.

57. Ibid. p. 968.

58. Ibid.

59. Ibid.

60. Ibid., p. 959.

61. Ibid., p. 969.

62. Ibid.

63. Ibid., p. 959.

64. See Robert H. Mnookin, Scott R. Peppet, and Andrew S. Tulumello, *Beyond Winning: Negotiating to Create Value in Deals and Disputes* (Cambridge, MA: Belknap Press/Harvard University Press, 2000); For a fuller treatment, see Robert H. Mnookin, Scott R. Peppet, and Andrew S. Tulumello, "The Tension Between Empathy and Assertiveness," *Negotiation Journal* 12, no. 3 (1996): 217–30.

65. Kissinger, *Years of Renewal*, pp. 970–72.

66. Onslow, "'We Must Gain Time,'" p. 148.

67. Kissinger, *Years of Renewal*, p. 973.

68. Ibid., p. 979.

69. Ibid., p. 980.

70. Ibid.

71. Ibid.

72. Ibid., p. 985.

73. Ibid., pp. 986–87.

74. Ibid., p. 991.

75. Ibid.

76. Ibid., p. 992.

77. Onslow, "'We Must Gain Time,'" p. 146.

78. Ibid., p. 142.

79. Ibid., p. 143.

80. Ibid., p. 128. Ian Douglas Smith, *The Great Betrayal: The Memoirs of Ian Douglas Smith* (London: Blake Publishing Ltd, 1997), p. 196.

81. Onslow, "'We Must Gain Time,'" p. 144; Henry Kamm, "Rhodesian Drama Engrosses South Africa," *New York Times*, March 22, 1976, p. 3;

Robin Wright, "Vorster and Smith Hold Talks on Kissinger's Africa Shuttle," *Washington Post*, Sept. 15, 1976, p. A10.

82. Smith, *The Great Betrayal*, pp. 198–99.

83. Ibid., p. 200.

84. Kissinger, *Years of Renewal*, p. 998.

85. Smith, *The Great Betrayal*, pp. 201–2.

86. Ibid., pp. 203 and 207.

87. Ken Flower, *Serving Secretly: An Intelligence Chief on Record: Rhodesia into Zimbabwe, 1964 to 1981* (London: J. Murray, 1987), p. 170.

88. See Mnookin, Peppet, and Tulumello, *Beyond Winning: Negotiating to Create Value in Deals and Disputes*; For a fuller treatment, see Mnookin, Peppet, and Tulumello, "The Tension between Empathy and Assertiveness."

89. Smith, *The Great Betrayal*, pp. 207 and 209.

90. Smith, *Bitter Harvest*, pp. 202–3.

91. Abel Tendekayi Muzorewa, *Rise Up and Walk: An Autobiography*, ed. Norman E. Thomas (London: Evans Books, 1978), p. 208.

92. Kissinger, *Years of Renewal*, pp. 985–87.

93. Ibid., p. 1006.

94. Ibid., pp. 1007–8.

95. Ibid., p. 1011. For a detailed transcript of Kissinger's presentation to the British cabinet, see U.S. Department of State, "Southern Africa," Memcon, Number 10 Downing Street, London, Sept. 23, 1976, in Kissinger Telephone Conversations.

96. Ibid., p. 1011.

97. Smith, *The Great Betrayal*, p. 210.

98. Authors' interview with Ambassador Frank G. Wisner, May 5, 2016.

99. For an elaboration, see Onslow, "'We Must Gain Time,'" p. 123.

100. Flower, *Serving Secretly*, p. 152.

101. Muzorewa, *Rise Up and Walk*, p. 208.

102. Schaufele, "Interview Ambassador William E. Schaufele Jr.," p. 177.

103. Henry Kissinger, personal communication with authors, Aug. 31, 2017.

104. Kissinger, *Years of Renewal*, pp. 1013–14.

105. James K. Sebenius, "Level Two Negotiations: Helping the Other Side Meet Its "Behind-the-Table" Challenges," *Negotiation Journal* 29, no. 1 (2013): 7–21.

106. Robert H. Mnookin and Ehud Eiran, "Discord 'Behind the Table': The Internal Conflict Among Israeli Jews Concerning the Future of Settlements in the West Bank and Gaza," *Journal of Dispute Resolution* 1 (2005): 11–44.

107. Isaacson, *Kissinger*, p. 691.

108. "Rhodesia's Alternatives," *Washington Post*, Nov. 2, 1976.

Chapter 3: The Outcome of the Southern African Campaign and Insights into Effective Negotiation

1. These sources are provided in notes 15–19 for this chapter.

2. Gleijeses, "A Test of Wills"; Sue Onslow, "South Africa and the Owen/Vance Plan of 1977," *South African Historical Journal* 51, no. 1 (2004).

3. "Zimbabwe's Landslide Leader," *Christian Science Monitor*, March 5, 1980.

4. Dan Van Der Vat, "Ian Smith, 88, Politician," *Globe and Mail*, Nov. 21, 2007.

5. Donald G. McNeil Jr., "Joshua Nkomo of Zimbabwe Is Dead at 62," *New York Times*, July 2, 1999; Paul Jackson, "The Civil War Roots of Military Domination in Zimbabwe: The Integration Process Following the Rhodesian War and the Road to Zanla Dominance," *Civil Wars* 13, no. 4 (2011): 385–89.

6. "List of Countries by Past and Projected Gdp (Nominal) Per Capita," Wikipedia, https://en.wikipedia.org/w/index.php?title=List_of_Countries_by_past_and_projected_GDP_(nominal)_per_capita&oldid=711796013.

7. Daniel Compagnon, *A Predictable Tragedy: Robert Mugabe and the Collapse of Zimbabwe* (Philadelphia: University of Pennsylvania Press,

2011), pp. 254–60; "Zimbabwe: Mugabe Booed over Economic Crisis," *Africa Research Bulletin: Economic, Financial and Technical Series* 52, no. 8 (2015).

8. "Twilight in Pretoria," *New York Times*, Feb. 5, 1989.

9. Kenneth R. Dombroski, "South Africa After Apartheid," *Journal of Democracy* 17, no. 3 (2006): 43–57.

10. Gretchen Bauer, "Namibia in the First Decade of Independence: How Democratic?" *Journal of Southern African Studies* 27, no. 1 (2001): 33–55; Robert Rotberg, "Namibia's Nationhood," *Christian Science Monitor*, March 20, 1990.

11. James Callaghan, "Leader's Speech," Labour Party Conference, Sept. 28, 1976, Blackpool. http://www.britishpoliticalspeech.org/speech-archive.htm?speech=174.

12. Onslow, "'We Must Gain Time'"; also Bishop, "Diplomacy in Black and White"; Perhaps the harshest take on Kissinger's negotiations in Southern Africa is that of Greg Grandin, who while conceding that "in order to preempt another triumph for Castro, Kissinger helped negotiate the surrender of Rhodesia's white supremacist government," he quickly asserted, "This about-face notwithstanding, the damage was done. Kissinger left behind him a terrorist infrastructure that would be rebooted by the New Right" (Grandin, *Kissinger's Shadow*, p. 122).

13. A concise summary of the various rationales for "failure" is in Watts; See, e.g., various assertions in Gleijeses; Low, "The Zimbabwe Settlement, 1976–1979"; Bishop; Tamarkin.

14. This claim recurs in writings about Kissinger's tactics in these negotiations. For example, Onslow, in "'We Must Gain Time,'" cites Kissinger's "mendacity" (p. 148) and writes that he "deliberately deceived the Rhodesians" (p. 152). Or this: "Kissinger negotiated in Southern Africa with a sense of urgency but did so with a certain disregard for specific details that allowed him to deceive and to lie in order to obtain his stated objectives" (Arrigo Pallotti and Corrado Tornim-

beni, *State, Land and Democracy in Southern Africa* [London: Routledge, 2015], pp. 107–8).

15. Low, "Interview with Stephen Low."

16. Lord, "Interview with Ambassador Winston Lord."

17. Jeffrey Davidow, *A Peace in Southern Africa: The Lancaster House Conference on Rhodesia, 1979*, Westview Special Studies on Africa (Boulder, CO: Westview Press, 1984), p. 21.

18. Authors' interview with Ambassador Frank G. Wisner, May 5, 2016.

19. Schaufele recalled his earlier assessment (made prior to Kissinger's Rhodesian initiative) "'If we achieve majority rule in Rhodesia and the independence of Namibia, South Africa weakens itself, because it will have less protection, so to speak, from black power. Then we can go after apartheid.'" He later added that "if Namibia and Rhodesia both gained their independence and majority rule, South Africa may have opened the route to its own emancipation, so to speak. That's what happened, essentially" (Schaufele, "Interview with Ambassador William E. Schaufele Jr.").

20. Talleyrand's maxim is widely cited, but with respect to Kissinger's initiative in Southern Africa at the time, see C. L. Sulzberger, "Policy and Politicians," *New York Times*, May 12, 1976, p. 41.

21. Isaacson, *Kissinger*, pp. 691–92.

22. Kissinger, *Years of Renewal*, p. 1015.

23. Ibid., p. 918.

24. Schaufele, "Interview with William Schaufele Jr.," pp. 170–71.

Chapter 4: Strategic: Big-Picture Negotiating

1. Kissinger, "Transcript of the American Secretaries of State Project: Henry A. Kissinger."

2. Kissinger, *Diplomacy*, p. 738.

3. For some of the press reaction to Kissinger's 1970 statements foreshadowing his strategy, see Murrey Marder, "U.S. Seeking to Oust Soviet

Units in Egypt: U.S. Seeks Soviet Pullback in Mideast," *Washington Post*, July 3, 1970, pp. A1 and A4; or the op-ed "On 'Expelling' the Russians from the Mideast," *Washington Post*, July 7, 1970, p. A14.

4. Kissinger, *Diplomacy*, pp. 738 and 740.

5. More specifically, an analysis in *Security Studies* "shows the strong role of detente on Soviet behavior during the 1973 Middle East crisis . . . Without the carrot of increased expected U.S.-Soviet trade, Moscow would have been more likely to have intervened actively in the Arab-Israeli dispute, and the probability of a dangerous superpower clash would have been that much greater." Dale C. Copeland, "Trade Expectations and the Outbreak of Peace: Détente 1970–74 and the End of the Cold War, 1985–91," *Security Studies* 9, nos. 1–2 (Autumn 1999–Winter 2000): 37.

6. Kissinger, *White House Years*, p. 31.

7. Ibid.

8. Jeffrey Goldberg, "World Chaos and World Order: Conversations with Henry Kissinger," *The Atlantic*, Nov. 10, 2016, https://www .theatlantic.com/international/archive/2016/11/kissinger-order-and -chaos/506876/.

9. Horne, *Kissinger: 1973*, p. 30. Similarly, as his colleague Winston Lord observed, Kissinger was "a tremendous strategist and conceptual thinker. . . . He was also a terrific tactician in terms of implementing this strategy. He was a superb negotiator" (Lord, "Interview with Ambassador Winston Lord," p. 97).

10. Henry Kissinger, *The Necessity for Choice* (New York: Harper and Brothers, 1961), pp. 4–5.

11. Goldberg, "World Chaos and World Order."

12. Henry Kissinger, "A Path out of the Middle East Collapse," *Wall Street Journal*, Oct. 16, 2015. https://www.wsj.com/articles/a-path-out-of -the-middle-east-collapse-1445037513.

13. Kissinger, "Transcript of the American Secretaries of State Project: Henry A. Kissinger."

14. Harold Saunders, cited in "On the Road Again—Kissinger's Shuttle Diplomacy," Moments in U.S. Diplomatic History, Association for Diplomatic Studies and Training, http://adst.org/2016/03/on-the-road-again-kissingers-shuttle-diplomacy/.

15. Ibid.

16. Kissinger, "Transcript of the American Secretaries of State Project: Henry A. Kissinger." An important summary of the opening to China, along with primary source documents and analysis can be found in Burr, *The Kissinger Transcripts*. A searchable database of the documents contained in that volume can be found at The Kissinger Telephone Conversations.

17. Kissinger, *Diplomacy*, p. 719.

18. Kissinger, "Transcript of the American Secretaries of State Project: Henry A. Kissinger."

19. Chapter 6 will explore this in more detail. But for the curious at this stage, here are some of the key conflicting views: Marvin and Bernard Kalb offered a positive assessment: "On June 15 [1972], President [Nikolai] Podgorny flew to Hanoi. The North Vietnamese, feeling betrayed by Russia's hospitality to Nixon, were nevertheless dependent on Moscow as the chief supplier of their war matériel, and they listened carefully to Podgorny's message. It was simple but fundamental: he suggested it was time to switch tactics, time for serious negotiations with the United States. The risk, he argued, would not be critical; after all, Nixon seemed serious about withdrawing, and the new U.S. position no longer demanded a North Vietnamese troop pullout from the south. . . . It was a new vocabulary for the Russians—the first time they had so openly committed their prestige to a resumption of negotiations. It clearly reflected the Soviet conclusion that the advantages of dealing with Washington on such matters as trade, credits, and SALT were important enough for Moscow to lend Nixon a hand in settling the Vietnam war" (Kalb and Kalb, *Kissinger*, pp. 336–37). By contrast, Alistair Horne, in his generally admiring account of Kissinger's

diplomacy, indicates that "Both Nixon and Kissinger placed great hope in using their opening to China[,] as well as détente with Moscow, to put pressure on North Vietnam . . . As far as Vietnam was concerned, however, the success with either of these communist behemoths was sorely limited—the line being from Moscow and Beijing: 'we won't interfere with Vietnam's affairs'; though the flow of Soviet arms was reduced" (Horne, *Kissinger: 1973*, p. 155). Winston Lord, who was directly involved in the negotiations with China, the Soviets, and the North Vietnamese, observed that "we thought that by our dealing with both giants in the Communist world we would have some psychological impact on Hanoi. This showed Hanoi that Moscow and Beijing cared more about their bilateral relations with the U.S. than they did about their relations with Hanoi. They wouldn't snub Hanoi, but psychologically this would help to isolate Hanoi, e.g., holding summits in Beijing and Moscow while we had some of our meetings with Hanoi in the winter and spring of 1972, in the middle of Hanoi's offensive in South Vietnam. Neither Moscow nor Beijing went so far as to cut off aid to North Vietnam or really lean on Hanoi. However, both Moscow and Beijing had a stake in our trying to get the Vietnam War behind us. . . . We believed that both Russia and China talked to Hanoi and suggested to North Vietnam that, in its own self-interest, they ought to settle for a military solution. . . . We were fairly confident that Moscow and Beijing made this kind of argument to Hanoi, in their own self-interests of moving ahead with us" (Lord, "Interview with Ambassador Winston Lord"). Similarly, see, e.g., chap. 19 of Isaacson, *Kissinger*.

20. For an extended analysis, see Sebenius, "Negotiation Arithmetic: Adding and Subtracting Issues and Parties," pp. 281–316.

21. For an elaboration, see, e.g., chap. 15, Lax and Sebenius, *3-D Negotiation*.

22. Saunders, in "On the Road Again."

23. Stephen A. Walt, "The Credibility Addiction." *Foreign Policy*, Jan. 26, 2015, http://foreignpolicy.com/2015/01/06/the-credibility-addiction

-us-iraq-afghanistan-unwinnable-war/; Kissinger, *White House Years*, p. 228. For a fuller guide to the still-simmering debate over the importance of credibility in international relations and negotiations, start with its most famous exponent: Schelling, *The Strategy of Conflict*; and Schelling, *Arms and Influence.* Then consult Christopher Fettweiss, "Credibility and the War on Terror," *Political Science Quarterly* 122, no. 4 (2007–2008); Robert J. McMahon, "Credibility and World Power: Exploring the Psychological Dimension in Postwar American Diplomacy," *Diplomatic History* 15 (Fall 1991).

24. Kissinger, *White House Years*, p. 1304. Kissinger repeatedly returns to the argument that the U.S. support for South Vietnam was important for the maintenance of the American global credibility. See, e.g., Kissinger, *White House Years*, pp. 109, 292, 307, 311, 324, and 1038.

25. Kissinger, "Transcript of the American Secretaries of State Project: Henry A. Kissinger."

26. For a fuller discussion of the Syrian "red line" issue, both pro and con, see Jeffrey Goldberg, "The Obama Doctrine," *The Atlantic*, April 2016, http://www.theatlantic.com/magazine/archive/2016/04/the -obama-doctrine/471525/.

27. Philip Rucker, Sean Sullivan, and Paul Kane, "The Great Dealmaker? Lawmakers Find Trump to Be an Untrustworthy Negotiator," *Washington Post*, Oct. 23, 2017, https://www.washingtonpost .com/politics/the-great-dealmaker-lawmakers-find-trump-to-be -an-untrustworthy-negotiator/2017/10/22/7709aea8-b5d4–11e7-be 94-fabb0f1e9ffb_story.html?utm_term=.208fb983dd4b. See also Jeffrey Frankel, "Deal-maker Trump Can't Deal," *Views on the Economy and the World* (blog), Aug. 28, 2017, https://www.belfercenter.org /publication/deal-maker-trump-cant-deal.

28. Goldberg, "World Chaos and World Order: Conversations with Henry Kissinger."

29. James K. Sebenius, "Negotiating Lessons from the Browser Wars," *MIT Sloan Management Review* 43, no. 4 (Summer 2002): 43–50.

Chapter 5: Realistic: Tracking the Deal/No-Deal Balance

1.   Kissinger, *Diplomacy*, p. 709.

2.   Ibid., p. 710.

3.   Ibid., p. 714.

4.   Robert H. Mnookin, *Bargaining with the Devil: When to Negotiate, When to Fight* (New York: Simon and Schuster, 2010).

5.   Kissinger, "Transcript of the American Secretaries of State Project: Henry A. Kissinger."

6.   This is hopelessly oversimplified for international relations scholars, for whom *neorealism* might be a more apt term for what we are *not* describing when we use the term *realistic*. If you must, see David Allen Baldwin, *Neorealism and Neoliberalism: The Contemporary Debate* (New York: Columbia University Press, 1993).

7.   Kissinger, *Diplomacy*, p. 712.

8.   Kissinger, *White House Years*, p. 130.

9.   For a careful elaboration of the concept of interests in negotiation, see chap. 5, pp. 69–84, in Lax and Sebenius, *3-D Negotiation*.

10.   Niall Ferguson made the case that, for Henry Kissinger, being a "realist" need not in practice mean being "amoral," the opposite of "idealist," or indifferent to principle. For example, Kissinger variously argued that "South Vietnam's right to self-determination was worth U.S. lives" and that the case for freedom should be intrinsic and not based on any material superiority of capitalism. Kissinger further held that an "idealistic" insistence on a pure form of morality can lead to inaction in the face of evil, whereas a realistic approach might more effectively challenge it. See, generally, Niall Ferguson, *Kissinger: The Idealist*, and his "The Meaning of Kissinger: A Realist Reconsidered," *Foreign Affairs* 94, no. 5 (Sept./Oct. 2015): 134–43.

11.   Kissinger, *World Order*, p. 134.

12.   This popular piece of jargon originates in Roger Fisher, William Ury, and Bruce Patton's *Getting to Yes: Negotiating Agreement Without Giving*

In, 2nd ed. (New York: Penguin Press, 1991). For greater analytic depth (and the much older pedigree of the concept in negotiation), see James K. Sebenius and David A. Lax, "The Power of Alternatives or the Limits to Negotiation," *Negotiation Journal* 1, no. 2 (1985): 77–95. In essence, the orientation described in this paragraph reflects what philosophers would call a "consequentialist" approach that evaluates negotiations by their effects (in terms of the parties' interests) on outcomes of concern, both for a deal or no deal (rather than on one's views of the act of negotiation itself, whether theological, psychiatric, or realistic).

13. Kissinger, "Transcript of the American Secretaries of State Project: Henry A. Kissinger."

14. Isaacson, *Kissinger*, p. 568.

15. Perhaps the most glaring "failure" was the sustainability of the Paris Peace Accords to end the Vietnam War, which we analyze in chapter 6. Kissinger did not reach a SALT II agreement, for reasons related to our extended discussion of secrecy in chapter 13. He unsuccessfully sought Japanese concurrence with U.S. Middle East policy during the oil embargo after the 1973 Middle East War, an episode we briefly assess in chapter 9. The 1973 "Year of Europe" was, in theory, a set of initiatives that was supposed to lead to a comprehensive reformulation of NATO and economic arrangements between the United States and Western Europe. Ideally, this would have reduced the burdens of American military support, lowered trade tariffs, and articulated a clear mutual defense and cooperation strategy. Unfortunately, as Kissinger clearly acknowledged, as "mere" national security advisor, he was ill-placed to effectively negotiate with Europe's top national leaders. Moreover, the intended scope of agreement was huge, and Kissinger was preoccupied in 1973 with developing the opening to China, encouraging détente and arms control with the Soviets, ending the Vietnam War, and dealing with the 1973 Arab-Israeli War. As a result, these talks received intermittent American emphasis. By the

time Nixon began to face the endgame of Watergate, none of the four major European leaders with whom Kissinger negotiated remained in power." See Kissinger, *Years of Upheaval*, pp. 128–95, 700–46; Isaacson, *Kissinger*, pp. 557–58; and "The Year of Europe? *Foreign Affairs* 52, no. 2 (Jan. 1974): 237–48.

16. This effort followed the breakaway from Pakistan of East Pakistan, later Bangladesh, with horrific human rights violations and hundreds of thousands of deaths in that country, largely caused by Pakistan's military. The muted response of the United States, in part given Pakistan's key role in the negotiations with China, heightened charges, especially against Kissinger, of callously elevating geopolitics over human rights. Indian military assistance to East Pakistan/Bangladesh led to India's war with Islamabad. For a summary, see chap. 18 of Isaacson, *Kissinger.*

17. Warren H. Donnelly, "Pakistan's Nuclear Activities: A Chronology of Four Eras," in *United States Congressional Research Service* (Washington, DC: Environment and Natural Resources Policy Division/Library of Congress, 1987), p. 22.

18. Had the United States been on better terms with India at the time, it is at least conceivable, though a long shot, that it might have brokered an agreement between the two adversaries that would have prevented further proliferation.

19. United Nations, "Treaty on the Non-Proliferation of Nuclear Weapons," United Nations Office for Disarmament Affairs, March 5, 1970, New York, p. 21, http://disarmament.un.org/treaties/t/npt; William Burr, "The United States and Pakistan's Quest for the Bomb," in *The Nuclear Vault Briefing Book 333*, National Security Archive, George Washington University, http://nsarchive.gwu.edu/nukevault /ebb333/.

20. *The Economist*, "The Spider's Stratagem," Jan. 3, 2008, http://www .economist.com/node/10424283.

21. Tariq Ali, *The Duel: Pakistan on the Flight Path of American Power* (New York: Scribner, 2008), pp. 110–13.

22. Peter Tzeng, "Nuclear Leverage: US Intervention in Sensitive Technology Transfers in the 1970s," *The Nonproliferation Review* 20, no. 3 (2013): 479.

23. Ibid.

24. Ibid, p. 480.

25. Shirin Tahir-Kheli, *The United States and Pakistan: The Evolution of an Influence Relationship* (New York: Praeger Publishers, 1982), p. 90.

26. Tariq Ali, *The Duel: Pakistan on the Flight Path of American Power*, p. 110. Among the innumerable references to this exchange, see Benazir Bhutto, *Daughter of the East* (London: Hamish Hamilton, 1988), p. 86. Kissinger reportedly denies having said this; see Shahid-ur-Rahman, *Long Road to Chagai* (Islamabad: Print Wise, 1999): 101, quoted in Rizwana Karim Abbasi's July 2010 doctoral thesis at the University of Leicester, "Understanding Pakistan's Nuclear Behaviour (1950s–2010): Assessing the State Motivation and Its International Ramifications (a Three Models Approach)," at https://lra.le.ac.uk /bitstream/2381/27568/1/2010abbasirkdsocsci.pdf. However, Peter Tzeng, "Nuclear Leverage," p. 480, cites related wording by Kissinger "in a meeting with Pakistani Ambassador Sahabzada Yaqub Khan on September 11. Secretary Kissinger emphasized that if Jimmy Carter won the upcoming election, then the new administration 'would like nothing better than to make a horrible example of somebody[,]'" citing U.S. Department of State, "The Pakistan Nuclear Reprocessing Issue," Folder: "Nodis Memcons Sept. 1976/2," National Archives and Records Administration, U.S. Department of State, College Park, MD.

27. *Wall Street Journal*, "Kissinger Talks in Pakistan Again Show Problems of Curbing Nuclear-Arms Flow," Aug. 10, 1976, p. 8.

28. Tzeng, "Nuclear Leverage," pp. 480–81.

29. Ibid.

30. Ibid., p. 481.

31. For much greater analytic detail, see Eugene B. Kogan, "Coercing

Allies: Why Friends Abandon Nuclear Plans," PhD diss., Brandeis University, 2013.

32. Akhilesh Pillalamarri, "Pakistan's Nuclear Weapons Program: 5 Things You Need to Know," *The National Interest*, April 21, 2015, http://nationalinterest.org/feature/pakistans-nuclear-weapons-program-5-things-you-need-know-12687?page=2.

33. Hussein had engaged in "as many as five hundred hours of secret talks with Israeli leaders" by 1974, according to Kissinger, *Years of Renewal*, p. 356; Under American pressure, Israel, too, had shown support for Jordan, massing troops along the Golan Heights and preparing to offer military support to Jordan in 1970, following the invasion of hundreds of Syrian tanks, which were ultimately repelled by the Jordanian army. Dennis Ross, *Doomed to Succeed: The U.S.-Israel Relationship from Truman to Obama* (New York: Farrar, Straus, and Giroux, 2015), pp. 115–18; Kissinger, *Years of Upheaval*, pp. 847–48.

34. Kissinger, *Years of Upheaval*, pp. 847–48.

35. Ibid., p. 847.

36. Kissinger, *Years of Renewal*, p. 352. According to a 2017 survey, historians' views of Kissinger's approach to the Palestinians range widely. James R. Stocker summarizes it: On one end, some historians see the US contacts with the Palestinians as part of what might be called a policy of "ambiguous flexibility." In order to avoid antagonising Arab states and their publics, the United States had to be seen as moving towards recognition of Palestinian rights. So contacts with the PLO [Palestinian Liberation Organization] might have pleased one side of the equation. However, Israel did not recognise the validity of Palestinian claims to territory under Israeli control, and wanted to keep the PLO out of any negotiations, even as they gained increasing legitimacy. Thus, Kissinger was forced to be circumspect about these contacts. At the same time, his policy was not intentionally designed to harm the Palestinians. Edward Sheehan, for instance, wrote that Kissinger "was not innately hos-

tile to Palestinian aspirations, but he had little sympathy for their liberation movement."

Steven Spiegel argues that Kissinger generally hoped to increase US influence through "interim agreements that skirted the fundamental questions," such as the role of the Palestinians. For William Quandt and Kathleen Christison, this was in part because Kissinger was "blind" to the importance of the Palestinian issue.

At the other end of the scale, many assert that Kissinger did not just seek to ignore the Palestinians: he actively sought to help repress them. In this interpretation, which might be called "strategic delay," contacts with the PLO placated Arab leaders, but more importantly, they bought time, excluding the PLO from peace negotiations indefinitely, in the hope that an alternative solution to the Palestinian issue might appear, such as Jordan agreeing to act as a representative of the Palestinian people. For Salim Yaqub, Kissinger's policy was motivated by a desire "to shield Israel from pressure to withdraw from all or most of the territory it had occupied in the 1967 Arab-Israeli War." Douglas Little argues that Kissinger and Nixon's "disdain" for the Palestinian Fedayeen coloured their views. Paul Chamberlin maintains that US policy had a strong ideological component: Nixon and Kissinger sought to foster an anti-Palestinian coalition in the Middle East, comparing the Palestinian militants to "American student radicals" as "part of the same transnational challenge to order and state authority." Jeremi Suri relates this issue to Kissinger's ethnic background, claiming that his policy towards the Middle East was the product of a "well-considered worldview of a German Jew seeking to protect cherished values—and his heritage—from political extremes." In these accounts, Kissinger seems irrevocably opposed to any diplomatic move towards the recognition of the Palestinian groups, especially the PLO.

Kissinger's memoirs contain evidence that could support both of these interpretations (see James R. Stocker, "A Historical Inevitability?

Kissinger and US Contacts with the Palestinians [1973–76]," *The International History Review* 39, no. 2 [2017]: 316–37).

37. Kissinger, *Years of Renewal*, pp. 352.

38. Kissinger, *Years of Upheaval*, pp. 1141–42.

39. Ibid., p. 1138.

40. Ibid., pp. 358–59.

41. Kissinger, *Years of Upheaval*, p. 1139.

42. Ibid., p. 978.

43. Nathan Thrall, *The Only Language They Understand* (New York: Henry Holt and Company, 2017), p. 44. For Kissinger's articulation of Middle East policy regarding the PLO, Jordan, Israel, Egypt, and Syria in the days following the Syrian-Israeli Disengagement Accords, see U.S. Department of State, "Meeting with Moshe Dayan and Ambassador Simcha Dinitz," Memcon, U.S. Department of State, June 8, 1974, in Kissinger Telephone Conversations.

44. Kissinger, *Years of Upheaval*, p. 1139.

45. Kissinger, *Years of Renewal*, p. 358.

46. Gerald R. Ford and King Hussein, "Joint Statement Following Discussions with King Hussein of Jordan," news release, Aug. 18, 1974, http://www.presidency.ucsb.edu/ws/index.php?pid=4454.

47. Kissinger, *Years of Renewal*, p. 361.

48. "Israeli Parliament Approves Pact over Right-Wing Bloc Objections," *Boston Globe*, May 31, 1974, p. 26.

49. Kissinger, *Years of Upheaval*, pp. 1139–40.

50. Clinton Bailey, *Jordan's Palestinian Challenge, 1948–1983: A Political History* (Boulder, CO: Westview Press, 1984), pp. 71–72.

51. L. Carl Brown, "The Endgame," in *The October War*, ed. Richard B. Parker (Gainesville: University Press of Florida, 2001), pp. 234–35.

52. Edward R. F. Sheehan, "How Kissinger Did It: Step by Step in the Middle East," *Foreign Policy* 22 (Spring, 1976): 47.

53. In *Years of Upheaval* (p. 1141), Kissinger states, "Torn between our analysis and objective conditions, I played for time, keeping both the

Egyptian and Jordanian options open—finally committing to neither—hoping that circumstance might resolve our perplexities." Others allege a Machiavellian calculation in which Kissinger schemed to
undermine the Jordanian option." See Avi Shlaim, *Lion of Jordan: The
Life of King Hussein in War and Peace* (New York: Alfred A. Knopf,
2008), pp. 376–80.

54. The preceding paragraph draws from Kissinger, *Years of Renewal*, p. 383.

55. Kathleen Christison says that "Kissinger repeatedly indicates, moreover, that he believed that including the Palestinians would complicate
matters. Against the judgment of most of his Middle East ambassadors, he concluded that engaging the PLO in the peace process would
radicalize the process because the Palestinians, he shuddered, would
'raise all the issues the Israelis can't handle' (p. 1053). This memoir,
more than many similar self-serving political reminiscences, is a testa-
ment to political myopia and the persistence of a mind-set even in the
face of evidence that contradicts it." Kathleen Christison, "Kissinger:
Years of Renewal (Review)," *Journal of Palestine Studies* 29, no. 1
(1999/2000), http://www.palestine-studies.org/jps/fulltext/40756.
Similarly, Hanhimäki has argued, "Kissinger's failure to take action
on the issue of the Palestinians 'would continue to mar any efforts at a
comprehensive solution to one of the world's most volatile areas." See
Hanhimäki, *The Flawed Architect*, p. 331.

Chapter 6: Game Changing: Shaping the Deal/No-Deal Balance

1. Kissinger, "Transcript of the American Secretaries of State Project:
Henry A. Kissinger."

2. Of course, much academic writing on negotiation is perfectly consistent with Kissinger's view, most notably the standard prescriptive
advice to build up one's no-deal options, or BATNA, "best alternative to a negotiated agreement." For the acronym, see Fisher, Ury, and Patton, *Getting to Yes*. For negotiation analytic work that addresses these

issues, see, e.g., Lax and Sebenius, *3-D Negotiation*; and David A. Lax and James K. Sebenius, "3-D Negotiation: Playing the Whole Game," *Harvard Business Review* 81, no. 11 (2003). Beyond negotiation, scholarship consistent with Kissinger's approach can be found in the work of international relations researchers on "coercive diplomacy" and other eclectic scholars loosely grouped together as "negotiation analysis." See G. A. Craig and A. L. George, *Force and Statecraft: Diplomatic Problems of Our Time* (New York: Oxford University Press, 1995); Schelling, *The Strategy of Conflict*; and Schelling, *Arms and Influence*.

3. See, e.g., Thompson, *The Mind and Heart of the Negotiator*; Neale and Bazerman, *Cognition and Rationality in Negotiation*.

4. Jeffrey Z. Rubin, "Editor's Introduction," *Negotiation Journal* 1, no. 1 (1985): 5.

5. Kissinger, *The Necessity for Choice*, p. 170.

6. Henry A. Kissinger, "U.S. Naval Academy Forrestal Lecture," Annapolis, MD, 2007, Speeches and Public Statements, http://www.henryakissinger.com/speeches/041107.html.

7. Kissinger, *The Necessity for Choice*, p. 170.

8. Kissinger, *On China*, pp. 221–22.

9. Kissinger, "Transcript of the American Secretaries of State Project: Henry A. Kissinger"

10. Ibid., p. 10.

11. Goldberg, "World Chaos and World Order: Conversations with Henry Kissinger."

12. In 2017, filmmakers Ken Burns and Lynn Novick produced a widely acclaimed, eighteen-hour public television series on this war, which attests to its continuous importance and the fascination it still holds for an American (Vietnamese and other) audience. Ken Burns and Lynn Novick, *The Vietnam War*, documentary, PBS, Walpole, NH: Florentine Films, 2017. A sampling would include: Fredrik Logevall's *Embers of War: The Fall of an Empire and the Making of America's Vietnam* (New York: Random House, 2012), and his *Choosing War: The Lost Chance*

for Peace and the Escalation of War in Vietnam (Berkeley: University of California Press, 1999); David Halberstam, *The Best and the Brightest* (New York: Random House, 1972); Michael Maclear, *Vietnam: The Ten Thousand Day War* (New York: Methuen, 1981); Stanley Karnow, *Vietnam: A History* (New York: Penguin, 1984); Michael Lind, *The Necessary War: A Reinterpretation of America's Most Disastrous Military Conflict* (New York: Free Press, 1999).

13. Throughout this chapter, we provide explicit sources for many of the dates of events associated with the Vietnam War. Where we do not cite sources, we generally rely on the detailed timeline of the war put together by Philip Gavin, "United States in Vietnam, 1945–1975: Comprehensive Timelines with Quotes and Analysis," http://www .historyplace.com/unitedstates/vietnam/index.html; or see Philip Gavin, *The Fall of Vietnam*, World History Series (New York: Lucent Press, 2003).

14. A divided, and thus dependent, Vietnam was arguably in China's interest. See, Kissinger, *Diplomacy*, p. 635. For example, historian Adam Ulam argues that "For China . . . the [1954 Geneva] settlement represented an unqualified diplomatic success. Continued fighting would have meant the probability of American bases and soldiers on China's frontiers. Now there would be a Communist buffer state, and the very incompleteness of Ho Chi Minh's success would make him more dependent on China than would otherwise be the case." See Adam B. Ulam, *Expansion and Coexistence: The History of Soviet Foreign Policy, 1917–67* (New York: Praeger, 1968), p. 553.

15. Kissinger, *Diplomacy*, p. 639.

16. Ibid., p. 653. Kennedy authorized sending 500 troops and advisors to Vietnam in May 1961, increasing the American presence to 900 advisors.

17. Fox Butterfield, "Nguyen Van Thieu Is Dead at 76; Last President of South Vietnam," *New York Times*, Oct. 1, 2001, p. A1.

18. Jeffrey Record, *The Wrong War: Why We Lost in Vietnam* (Annapolis, MD: Naval Institute Press, 1998).

19. A number of scholars argue that the Johnson administration used the Gulf of Tonkin incident, whatever actually occurred, as a pretext for unleashing the war in Indochina. See, e.g., Edwin Moise, *Tonkin Gulf and the Escalation of the Vietnam War* (Chapel Hill, North Carolina: University of North Carolina Press, 1996). For a review of the issues of fact, law, and policy relating to the Gulf of Tonkin Resolution and its subsequent application to the president's power to make war in Vietnam, see William W. Van Alstyne, "Congress, the President, and the Power to Declare War: A Requiem for Vietnam," *University of Pennsylvania Law Review* 121, no. 1 (1972): 1–28. The controversy over this incident continued decades after the war ended; see, e.g., Scott Shane, "Vietnam Study, Casting Doubts, Remains Secret," *New York Times*, Oct. 31, 2005, p. A1.

20. "Deployment of a limited but significant Soviet military presence into North Vietnam has unquestionably sharpened the already bitter Sino-Soviet competition for influence in Hanoi . . . has put Hanoi in a better position to take an independent stance and to play one Communist partner off against the other" (Central Intelligence Agency, "Status of Soviet and Chinese Military Aid to North Vietnam," *Special Report*, Sept. 1965, p. 5, https://www.cia.gov/library/readingroom /docs/DOC_0000652931.pdf). Evidence of the Sino-Soviet tension on this issue can be seen by way of several incidents. China unenthusiastically agreed to allow the Soviet aid to be transported by rail through Chinese territory. See Brantly Womack, *China and Vietnam: The Politics of Asymmetry* (New York: Cambridge University Press, 2006), p. 177. For example, Adam Ulam references an instance in 1965 wherein Beijing declined Moscow's request to allow four thousand Soviet troops to pass through Chinese territory and to establish air bases in China in order to transport war suppliies for the North Vietnamese. See Ulam, *Expansion and Coexistence*, p. 705. Many other disputes between the two Communist giants took place over supplies to North Vietnam. For example, the Chinese refused a Soviet request

for an "air corridor" across China to supply the North. For details, see Central Intelligence Agency, "The Sino-Soviet Dispute on Aid to North Vietnam (1965–1968), Sept. 30 1968 [formerly top secret, released in May 2007], Directorate of Intelligence, https://www.cia .gov/library/readingroom/docs/esau-37.pdf.

21. Michael Lee Lanning and Dan Cragg, *Inside the VC and the NVA: The Real Story of North Vietnam's Armed Forces* (New York: Fawcett Columbine, 1992), p. 119.

22. Womack, *China and Vietnam*, p. 176.

23. Lanning and Cragg, *Inside the VC and the NVA*, p. 119; Ulam, *Expansion and Coexistence*, p. 699; William H. Mott IV, *Soviet Military Assistance: An Empirical Perspective* (Westport, CT: Greenwood Press, 2001), p. 239.

24. For details and further sources, see, e.g., Nicholas Khoo, "Breaking the Ring of Encirclement: The Sino-Soviet Rift and Chinese Policy Toward Vietnam, 1964–1968," *Journal of Cold War Studies*, Vol. 12, No. 1, Winter 2010, pp. 3–42.

25. Mott IV, *Soviet Military Assistance*, p. 239.

26. Ulam, *Expansion and Coexistence*, p. 741.

27. Womack, *China and Vietnam*, p. 177; Mott IV, *Soviet Military Assistance*, p. 240.

28. Throughout the conflict, the U.S. and South Vietnamese governments insisted that the Vietcong were simply a tool of the North, while the Communists and many antiwar activists treated the Vietcong as a purely indigenous insurgency.

29. Arthur J. Dommen, *The Indochinese Experience of the French and Americans: Nationalism and Communism in Cambodia, Laos, and Vietnam* (Bloomington: Indiana University Press, 2001), p. 636.

30. Alan Taylor, "The Vietnam War, Part I: Early Years and Escalation," *The Atlantic*, March 30, 2015.

31. Bureau of the Census, "Vietnam Conflict—U.S. Military Forces in Vietnam and Casualties Incurred: 1961 to 1973 Figure No. 428."

32. James H. Willbanks, cited in "Tet 1968: Turning Point," May 15, 2012, FootNotes, Foreign Policy Research Institute, http://www .fpri.org/article/2012/05/tet-1968-the-turning-point/.

33. Joseph A. Fry, "Unpopular Messengers: Student Opposition to the Vietnam War," in *The War that Never Ends: New Perspectives on the Vietnam War*, ed. David L. Anderson and John Ernst (Lexington, KY: University of Kentucky, 2007), p. 227.

34. While not directly pertinent to an analysis of Kissinger's approach to these negotiations, it is worth noting that a Jan. 2, 2017, article in the *New York Times* described recently uncovered documents that appear to confirm a long-held suspicion of Richard Nixon's involvement. Many people believe that then-candidate Nixon attempted to disrupt and derail negotiations led by President Lyndon Johnson to end the Vietnam War in the run-up to the 1968 presidential elections. Specifically, Nixon appears to have maintained a secret channel of communication to the South Vietnam regime in order to persuade its leaders to resist Johnson's peace negotiations in the expectation of a better deal under a Nixon administration. See Peter Baker, "Nixon Tried to Spoil Johnson's Vietnam Peace Talks in '68, Notes Show," *New York Times*, Jan. 2, 2017, https://www.nytimes.com/2017/01/02/us/politics/nixon -tried-to-spoil-johnsons-vietnam-peace-talks-in-68-notes-show.html ?mcubz=2&_r=0; Philip Habib, who was involved in the Johnson- era talks, offers more details. See Philip Habib, "Cursed Is the Peace- maker," Association for Diplomatic Studies and Training, http:// adst.org/oral-history/fascinating-figures/philip-habib-cursed-is -the-peacemaker/; Kissinger, however, was an advisor to Nixon's Re- publican rival, Nelson Rockefeller, until August of that year. He was not a formal member of Nixon's team until after the November elec- tion. Normally among Kissinger's most fierce detractors, sociologist Todd Gitlin, in reviewing Niall Ferguson's recent Kissinger biogra- phy, noted that "Ferguson also, to my eyes, makes mincemeat of the charge that Kissinger, by relaying inside information about the 1968

Paris negotiations that Lyndon Johnson was sponsoring, helped sabotage those talks and therefore to elect Richard Nixon." See Todd Gitlin, "The Servile Fanatic: Niall Ferguson's Grotesque but Telling New Biography of Henry Kissinger," *Tablet*, Oct. 28, 2015, http://www.tabletmag.com/jewish-news-and-politics/194356/niall-ferguson-henry-kissinger. For Niall Ferguson's analysis, see Ferguson, *Kissinger: The Idealist*, pp. 791–97.

35.   Richard M. Nixon, "Address Accepting the Presidential Nomination at the Republican National Convention in Miami Beach, Florida." American Presidency Project, Aug. 8, 1968. http://www.presidency.ucsb.edu/ws/?pid=25968.

36.   Richard Nixon, *RN: The Memoirs of Richard Nixon* (New York: Grosset and Dunlap, 1978), p. 349.

37.   Written in 1968 but published in January 1969; the source is Henry Kissinger, "The Viet Nam Negotiations," *Foreign Affairs* 47, no. 2 (1969): 216.

38.   On the importance of credibility of security commitments to Kissinger, see *White House Years*, p. 1304; Kissinger repeatedly returns to the argument that the U.S. support for South Vietnam was important for the maintenance of the American global credibility. See, e.g., pp. 109, 292, 1038; Of course, as we indicated in chapter 5, the scholarly debate over the importance of credibility in international relations and negotiations continues. See Fettweiss, "Credibility and the War on Terror"; McMahon, "Credibility and World Power"; Walt, "The Credibility Addiction."

39.   Kissinger, *White House Years*, p. 1304.

40.   Ibid., p. 259. Nguyen Van Thieu, Nguyen Cao Ky, and Tran Van Huong were, respectively, South Vietnam's president, vice president, and prime minister.

41.   Kissinger, *White House Years*, pp. 1030–31.

42.   Ibid., p. 282; In fact, Le Duc Tho made repeatedly clear that "even if we [the U.S.] withdrew, Hanoi would stop fighting only if there were

a political settlement" that included the overthrow of the Thieu government. See Kissinger, *White House Years*, p. 444.

43. North Vietnamese foreign minister Nguyen Co Thach declared, "The breakthrough point for the negotiation and leading to ceasefire, it was in the beginning of October 1972. On October the 8th, '72, Le Duc Tho put a very new proposal. That means we have dropped the demand for the dissolution of the Thieu government." See Thach, "Interview with Nguyen Co Thach."

44. Kissinger, *White House Years*, p. 237.

45. For simplicity, we often loosely combine the North Vietnamese and Vietcong forces in the discussion. However, there were two types of Communist forces fighting in South Vietnam: first, Vietcong insurgents and some regulars, directed in part by Hanoi since May 1959, and second, regular North Vietnamese troops first deployed in September 1964. Kissinger first raised the issue for mutual (U.S. and North Vietnamese) withdrawal from South Vietnam during his April 4, 1970, meeting with Le Duc Tho. It was understood that the Vietcong would remain within South Vietnam, whose government would have to confront this force. As early as September 1965, Kissinger noted that the "only outcome is [a] limited one . . . in which VC have some kind of role." In any event, Kissinger assessed that "in many areas government survives only by means of a tacit agreement with the Vietcong whereby both sides coexist without getting into each other's way." See Ferguson, *Kissinger: The Idealist*, pp. 683 and 63. "In some areas the civil government was in cahoots with the Vietcong," Kissinger pointedly observed (Ferguson, *Kissinger: The Idealist*, p. 668).

46. Richard M. Nixon, "Address to the Nation on Vietnam," American Presidency Project, Nov. 3, 1969, http://www.presidency.ucsb.edu/ws/?pid=2303.

47. Kissinger, *White House Years*, pp. 258–59; Kissinger, *Years of Renewal*, p. 468.

48. Kissinger, *White House Years*, p. 437.

49. Ibid., pp. 440–48, esp., p. 445. Kissinger's suggested sixteen-month

schedule seemed to contradict an earlier proposal by Nixon: "The North Vietnamese said it was unacceptable because it differed from the proposal of twelve months in the President's November 3 speech. (I had used sixteen months because it was the only precise schedule that existed in the Pentagon and reflected the technical assessment of how long it would take us to withdraw our 400,000 remaining men and their equipment.) When I explained that the schedule was illustrative only and that the deadline would of course be made to coincide with Presidential pronouncements, it was rejected because Hanoi supported the 'correct and logical' deadline of six months put forward by the NLF" (*White House Years*, p. 445). Seeking to induce Hanoi to compromise, Kissinger told Le Duc Tho that the United States did not require the North Vietnamese to withdraw their troops publicly—that is, the United States would not make an effort to humiliate Hanoi. See Kissinger, *White House Years*, p. 443. Yet Hanoi repeatedly denied having troops within South Vietnam. See Szulc, "How Kissinger Did It," p. 25.

50. For an account of these and related events, see Isaacson, *Kissinger*, pp. 269–70.

51. U.S. Department of Defense, "'Casualty Status': U.S. Military Operations 2003 to Present," Washington, DC: Government Printing Office, https://www.defense.gov/casualty.pdf.

52. For a summary of poll results on whether it was a mistake to send U.S. troops to Vietnam, see William L. Lunch and Peter W. Sperlich, "American Public Opinion and the War in Vietnam," *Western Political Quarterly* 32, no. 1 (1979): 25. See the whole article (pp. 21–44) for a much fuller discussion. Even though most Americans judged the war to be a mistake, support for "the way President Nixon is handling the Vietnam situation" was at 50 percent in the wake of the Cambodian invasion. See Andrew Z. Katz, "Public Opinion and Foreign Policy: The Nixon Administration and the Pursuit of Peace with Honor in Vietnam," *Presidential Studies Quarterly* 27, no. 3 (1997): 500–501.

53. Kissinger, *White House Years*, p. 291.

54. Kissinger, *Diplomacy*, p. 689.

55. "Vietnam Conflict—U.S. Military Forces in Vietnam and Casualties Incurred: 1961 to 1973 Figure No. 428."

56. Kissinger, *White House Years*, p. 275.

57. Ibid., p. 444.

58. Ibid., p. 275.

59. Vernon A. Walters, *The Mighty and the Meek: Dispatches from the Front Line of Diplomacy* (London: St Ermin's Press, 2001), p. 518. (Cited in Horne, *Kissinger: 1973, The Crucial Year*, p. 51.)

60. Kissinger, *White House Years*, p. 260.

61. Kissinger, *Years of Upheaval*, p. 86.

62. See Sebenius, "Beyond the Deal," p. 2; Lax and Sebenius, "Deal Making 2.0."

63. Of course, actions associated with some of these fronts built on aspects of the negotiations begun under President Johnson.

64. Of course, how the war would have ended in this hypothetical case, and its battlefield consequences, would have depended on unknowable North and South Vietnamese responses—vis-à-vis each other and departing American forces.

65. Kissinger, *White House Years*, p. 436.

66. We will later return to the prospects for successful Vietnamization.

67. Kissinger, *White House Years*, p. 1108.

68. Ibid., pp. 976 and 1018.

69. Robert B. Semple Jr., "Nixon Urges Supervised Truce in Vietnam, Cambodia and Laos and a Wider Peace Conference," *New York Times*, Oct. 8, 1970, p. 1.

70. Kissinger, *White House Years*, pp. 980–81.

71. Kissinger, *Years of Upheaval*, p. 86. When leaving office, President Dwight Eisenhower warned President John Kennedy that the situation in Laos was "the most important problem facing the U.S." Quoted in Ferguson, *Kissinger: The Idealist*, p. 585.

72. See the review by Col. Thomas E. Hanson, "A Raid Too Far: Operation Lam Son 719 and Vietnamization in Laos and Invasion of Laos, 1971," *Military Review* (2015): 124–26.

73. Rachel Halliburton, "Henry Kissinger's World Order: The Outer Edge of What Is Possible," *Independent*, Sept. 26, 2014, http://www.independent.co.uk/news/world/politics/henry-kissingers-world-order-the-outer-edge-of-what-is-possible-9752563.html.

74. Kalb and Kalb, *Kissinger*, p. 172, also p. 58; Ferguson, *Kissinger: The Idealist*, pp. 36–37; Kissinger, *White House Years*, p. 486; Kissinger, *Years of Upheaval*, p. 35.

75. Kissinger, *White House Years*, pp. 262 and 311.

76. Ibid., p. 1017; *Foreign Relations of the United States, 1969–1976, Volume VII, Vietnam, July 1970–January 1972.* Ed. David Goldman and Erin Maha. Washington, DC: Government Printing Office, 2010. Doc. 207. https://history.state.gov/historicaldocuments/frus1969–76v07/d207. This concession was not made public; nor was its precise relation to Nixon's putatively temporary offer of a year earlier.

77. Kissinger, *White House Years*, p. 1035.

78. Ibid., p. 441.

79. Ibid., p. 442.

80. Ibid., p. 1100.

81. Kissinger notes that the Cambodia and Laos operations in 1970 and 1971, respectively, aimed to disrupt the timetable of this offensive. *White House Years*, p. 1099.

82. Kissinger, *White House Years*, p. 1101.

83. Ibid., p. 1103.

84. Ibid., pp. 1043–44. This was, Kissinger noted, an improvement by one month on the last secret offer Nixon had made to Le Duc Tho.

85. Kissinger, *White House Years*, pp. 1043–6.

86. Ibid., p. 1045.

87. Ibid., p. 1109.

88. Ibid., p. 1306.

89. Ibid., p. 1178. "A blockade [by intercepting ships, as opposed to mines], in contrast, would produce daily confrontations with the Soviets. Every time a ship was stopped we would see a repetition of the drama of the Cuban missile crisis; our challenge and the Soviet reaction to it would have to be acted out over and over again, probably on television. The danger of some slip or of a pretext for serious incident would be too great." See Kissinger, *White House Years*, p. 1179.

90. Lewis Sorley, "Courage and Blood: South Vietnam's Repulse of the 1972 Easter Offensive," *Parameters* 29 (1999): 38–56.

91. Apart from Lewis Sorely's assessment (ibid.) of how the offensive was blunted by U.S. and South Vietnamese forces, see also the text and extensive notes in Robert A. Pape Jr., "Coercive Air Power in the Vietnam War," *International Security* 15, no. 2 (Fall 1990): 103–46.

92. Katz, "Public Opinion and Foreign Policy," p. 498.

93. Kissinger, *White House Years*, p. 1190.

94. Hence Kissinger writes about the "ideological truce" and "ideological armistice" with China. See Kissinger, *On China*, pp. 270 and 284. As he wrote in 1966, "Tactical intransigence and ideological vitality should not be confused with structural rigidity." Quoted in Ferguson, *Kissinger: The Idealist*, p. 726; Kissinger "began to discern that, despite its obviously revolutionary character, the People's Republic of China could also be brought into the pale of the balance of power" (Ferguson, *Kissinger: The Idealist*, p. 704).

95. Kissinger, *White House Years*, p. 167.

96. Central Intelligence Agency, "The Evolution of Soviet Policy in the Sino-Soviet Border Dispute," April 28, 1970, (declassified May 2007), pp. 31–38; "Strategic Survey: The Sino-Soviet Dispute," *International Institute for Strategic Studies* 70, no. 1 (1969): 100–102.

97. Kissinger, *White House Years*, p. 171.

98. Kissinger, *On China*, p. 218.

99. This information and quotations in this paragraph are from ibid., p. 219.

100. Ibid., p. 250.

101. Thach, "Interview with Nguyen Co Thach." The exact question he was asked was "Could you be a little more precise about how the Chinese changed their position after Kissinger's trip in July of 1971? Did they stop sending aid or did they put pressure on you to negotiate?"

102. As just indicated, North Vietnamese foreign minister Nguyen Co Thach alluded to the importance of Chinese pressure on North Vietnam after Kissinger's 1971 visit. Kissinger argues that linkage played an important role in restraining Beijing's reactions to the American actions against North Vietnam: "Peking . . . demonstrated that it had its priorities straight. In a conversation with me in New York on May 16 [1972], UN Ambassador Huang Hua repeated the official line that China stood behind its friends. But he did not demur when I pointed out that we had warned Peking at least half a dozen times of our determination to react strongly if Hanoi sought to impose a military solution. Nor did our actions in Vietnam prevent Huang Hua from encouraging a visit by me to Peking in June. We had not only achieved a free hand in Vietnam; we would be able to continue at the same time the construction of the larger design of our foreign policy." See, Kissinger, *White House Years*, p. 1197. It was "certainly true," Kissinger recently clarified, that China did not assist the United States in the actual negotiations with the North Vietnamese, but Beijing's contribution was to "isolate Hanoi": "China played a role in the atmosphere that was created—not in pressing them [Hanoi] on specific points." See *The Week That Changed the World*, dir. Michael Trinklein, YouTube (2012), https://www.youtube.com/watch?v=qoHAPj9O5c0.

103. Kissinger, *Diplomacy*, pp. 730–31.

104. Kissinger, *White House Years*, p. 1116, and also p. 13. Kissinger elaborated on this logic of isolating an adversary by comparing it to chess: "One elementary lesson for students of chess is that, in choosing among moves, one can do worse than to count the number of squares dominated by each choice. Generally, the more squares a player dominates,

the greater his options and the more constrained become those of his opponent. Similarly, in diplomacy, the more options one side has, the fewer will be available to the other side and the more careful it will have to be in pursuing its objectives. Indeed, such a state of affairs may in time provide an incentive for the adversary to seek to end his adversarial role." See Kissinger, *Diplomacy*, p. 719. Or, as Kissinger put it elsewhere, "the demonstration of options is almost always an asset." See Kissinger, *White House Years*, p. 725. He echoed this in his interview with Harvard's American Secretaries of State Project, when discussing the triangular relationship he devised between the United States, the Soviet Union, and China: "the mere existence of these American options gave us a bargaining weapon." See Kissinger, "Transcript of the American Secretaries of State Project: Henry A. Kissinger."

105. Kissinger uses the term *stake* on a number of occasions when discussing the dynamics of combining pressure and incentives in devising détente with the Soviet Union and rapprochement with China. For example, see Kissinger, *Diplomacy*, pp. 714 and 740; Kissinger, *White House Years*, pp. 192, 1164–65, 1200; Kissinger tried to remain on guard against permitting the U.S. interest in détente and rapprochement to be used by Moscow and Beijing as levers to rein in American policy in Vietnam. America would not "permit itself to become emotionally dependent on relations with the Soviet Union." See Kissinger, *Diplomacy*, p. 712.

106. Kissinger, *White House Years*, pp. 528–34. Background: This was the case because, after World War II, the four Allied powers (the United States, Soviet Union, France, and Britain) maintained military control over Germany. As a democratic West German state emerged alongside a pro-Communist, Soviet-backed East German state, tensions had mounted between the two, with the status of Berlin as its focus. For a fuller analysis see, David M. Keithly, *Breakthrough in the Ostpolitik: The 1971 Quadripartite Agreement* (Boulder, CO: Westview, 1986). The

three non-Soviet powers retained military control over West Berlin, while the Soviets walled off East Berlin. West Berliners were not recognized as citizens of the Bonn-based Federal Republic of Germany ("West Germany"); see Kissinger, *White House Years*, pp. 529–34, 824. Throughout the 1960s, with Berlin surrounded by East German territory and supported by vulnerable supply lines from the West, the West Germans and Allies refused to settle significant territorial disputes and wartime claims with the Soviets. Without a settlement, the Soviets' ability to trade, especially with West Europeans, was severely restricted.

107. West Germany and USSR (Treaty of Moscow, Aug. 1970); West Germany and Poland (Treaty of Warsaw, Dec. 1970); United States, Soviet Union, France, and United Kingdom (Four Power Agreement, Sept. 1971); United States, Soviet Union, France, and United Kingdom (Transit Agreement, May 1972); West Germany and East Germany (Basic Treaty, Dec. 1972); West Germany and Czechoslovakia (Treaty of Prague, Dec. 1973). See "Germany, a Country Study," 1996, Federal Research Division, Library of Congress, Washington, DC.

108. Kissinger, *Diplomacy*, p. 737. Also see Kissinger, *White House Years*, p. 533. Initially skeptical of Brandt's initiative, Nixon and Kissinger came to see his diplomacy as advantageous by linking Brandt's negotiations to the separate U.S.-Soviet negotiations over Berlin (see Kissinger, *White House Years*, pp. 530–34), as well as creating additional linkage with Soviet policy in Vietnam. Kissinger wrote, "Nixon and his advisers . . . came to accept Ostpolitik as necessary even while they believed that Brandt—unlike Adenauer—never had an emotional attachment to the Atlantic Alliance" (Kissinger, *Diplomacy*, p. 735).

109. In that memo, Hal Sonnenfeldt framed the issue explicitly: "[W]e need to be clear about the extent to which we wish to make what happens in Vietnam, and the Soviet role with regard to it, a determinant of what happens next in US-Soviet relations . . . we need to be clear about the extent to which our substantive positions on other issues

should be influenced by whatever the Soviets may do for us regarding Vietnam." See *Foreign Relations of the United States, 1969–1976, Volume XIV: Soviet Union October 1971–May 1972*, eds. David C. Geyer, Nina D. Howland, Kent Sieg, and Edward C. Keefer (Washington DC: Government Printing Office, 2006): Document 125, https://history .state.gov/historicaldocuments/frus1969–76v14/d125.

110. *Foreign Relations of the United States, 1969–1976, Volume XL, Germany and Berlin, 1969–1972*, eds. David C. Geyer and Edward C. Keefer (Washington DC: Government Printing Office, 2008), "356. Editorial Note," https://history.state.gov/historicaldocuments/frus1969 –76v40/d356.

111. In particular, see pp. 25–39 of Dale C. Copeland, "Trade Expectations and the Outbreak of Peace: Détente 1970–74 and the End of the Cold War, 1985–91," *Security Studies* 9, nos. 1–2 (Autumn 1999– Winter 2000).

112. Ibid, pp. 29–31.

113. Kissinger, *White House Years*, pp. 1114, 1150.

114. Ibid., p. 1117.

115. Ibid., p. 1189.

116. Kissinger later explained the actual timing of this concession: "With respect to leaving North Vietnamese troops in South Vietnam, that proposal was already implicit in October 1970, when we offered a cease-fire in place. That was not coupled with any proposal for the withdrawal of North Vietnamese troops. It was made explicit in our secret proposal of May 1971. It was publicly repeated in January, I believe, 1972[,] in the sense that our peace program did not call for the withdrawal of the troops, and only called for a cease-fire so that we did not make an additional concession on the presence of the North Vietnamese troops in October 1972." For a discussion, see Szulc, "How Kissinger Did It," pp. 36–37.

117. However, knowing how keen Nixon was on the summit, the Soviets could hold hostage the prospect of the summit in return for reduced

U.S. demands for pressure by Moscow on Hanoi. Both sides could play the linkage game with an event (the summit) that both wanted. Kissinger, *White House Years*, p. 1145. This point about which way linkage between Vietnam and the summit actually functioned is extensively discussed in chapter 19 of Isaacson, *Kissinger*.

118. Kissinger, *White House Years*, p. 1120.

119. Ibid., p. 1135.

120. Kalb and Kalb, *Kissinger*, pp. 336–37.

121. For example, journalist Alistair Horne, in his generally admiring account of Kissinger's diplomacy, indicated that "Both Nixon and Kissinger placed great hope in using their opening to China[,] as well as détente with Moscow, to put pressure on North Vietnam . . . As far as Vietnam was concerned, however, the success with either of these communist behemoths was sorely limited—the line being from Moscow and Beijing: 'we won't interfere with Vietnam's affairs'; though the flow of Soviet arms was reduced." See Horne, *Kissinger: 1973*, p. 155. Winston Lord, who was directly involved in the negotiations with China, the Soviets, and the North Vietnamese, observed that "we thought that by our dealing with both giants in the Communist world we would have some psychological impact on Hanoi. This showed Hanoi that Moscow and Beijing cared more about their bilateral relations with the U.S. than they did about their relations with Hanoi. They wouldn't snub Hanoi, but psychologically this would help to isolate Hanoi, e.g. holding summits in Beijing and Moscow while we had some of our meetings with Hanoi in the winter and spring of 1972, in the middle of Hanoi's offensive in South Vietnam. Neither Moscow nor Beijing went so far as to cut off aid to North Vietnam or really lean on Hanoi. However, both Moscow and Beijing had a stake in our trying to get the Vietnam War behind us. . . . We believed that both Russia and China talked to Hanoi and suggested to North Vietnam that, in its own self-interest, they ought to settle for a military solution" (Lord, "Interview with Ambassador Winston Lord," p. 271).

122. Isaacson, *Kissinger*, p. 422. Anatoly Dobrynin provides additional evidence on the Soviet decision not to cancel the 1972 Moscow Summit in view of the mining and bombing of Haiphong harbor: "the agreements with the Federal Republic of Germany were to be ratified several days before Nixon's arrival, and a cancellation of the summit could exacerbate relations and block ratification, giving weight to the arguments to the ultraright in West Germany who opposed the agreements. Moscow was fully aware of this. Moreover, it also realized that refusing to receive Nixon would complicate our relations with the American administration for a long period, putting off the summit indefinitely, jeopardizing the ABM and SALT agreements, and promoting another round of the arms race." See Anatoly Dobrynin, *In Confidence: Moscow's Ambassador to America's Six Cold War Presidents (1962—1986)* (New York: Random House, 1995), p. 248.

123. Kissinger, *White House Years*, p. 1345 and also see p. 17.

124. Kissinger, "Transcript of the American Secretaries of State Project: Henry A. Kissinger." However, this was strictly a private reaction: "negotiators must not betray emotion; it becomes a weapon in the hands of the other side." See Kissinger, *White House Years*, p. 659. Furthermore, as the negotiations were nearing conclusion in January 1973, Kissinger confided in Nixon: "The slightest hint of eagerness could prove suicidal." See Kissinger, *White House Years*, p. 1464 and also p. 438, on the dangers of giving an "unnecessary impression of eagerness" in a negotiation.

125. Nixon and Kissinger originally raised the possibility of high-level U.S.-North Vietnam contacts with Thieu during a meeting at Midway Atoll in the Pacific on June 8, 1969. "Thieu agreed," Kissinger remembered, "provided he was informed about any political discussions." See Kissinger, *White House Years*, p. 274. Alexander Haig, Kissinger's military aide, also briefed Thieu on July 3, 1972. See Kissinger, *White House Years*, p. 1310. While keeping Thieu generally informed, Kissinger clearly preferred to keep Thieu away from

the specifics of the negotiation because of the need to dissociate the military (withdrawal) and political (structure of South Vietnamese government) aspects of the negotiation. Writing in 1969, Kissinger had stated, "The United States . . . should concentrate on the subject of the mutual withdrawal of external forces and avoid negotiating about the internal structure of South Viet Nam for as long as possible. . . . The participation of Saigon and the NLF [in earlier negotiations] raised issues . . . that would have been better deferred; it made discussion of the internal structure of South Viet Nam hard to avoid." See Kissinger, "The Viet Nam Negotiations," p. 232.

126. Kissinger, *White House Years*, p. 282.

127. The issue of who told what to whom and when has been the subject of conflicting accounts; see e.g., Isaacson, *Kissinger*, or chaps. 31 and 32 of Kissinger, *White House Years*.

128. Kissinger, *White House Years*, pp. 1319, 1327.

129. The threats were communicated on Oct. 22, 24, 28, Nov. 10, 29, Dec. 17, 1972, and Jan. 5, 16, 17, and 20, 1973. See ibid., pp. 1382, 1396, 1402, 1412, 1426, 1459, 1462, 1469–70.

130. The assurances were communicated on Oct. 19, 24, 28, Nov. 14, 29, 1972, and Jan. 5, 14, and 21, 1973. See Kissinger, *White House Years*, pp. 1369, 1396, 1402, 1412, 1426, 1462, 1470. "American air power was thus always seen as an essential deterrent to the resumption of all-out war. Nixon gave assurances on this score to South Vietnamese President Nguyen Van Thieu to persuade Thieu to accept the Paris Agreement" (Kissinger, *Years of Upheaval*, 303).

131. Kissinger, "Transcript of the American Secretaries of State Project: Henry A. Kissinger."

132. Ibid.

133. Kissinger, *White House Years*, p. 1411.

134. In Kissinger's words,

"We failed early enough to grasp that Thieu's real objection was not to the terms but the fact of *any* compromise. Conflict between us and Thieu was built into the termination of the war on any terms less than Hanoi's total surrender. By definition[,] sovereignty cannot be divided. Any outcome that left Thieu in less than total control of his entire territory was therefore for him a setback. He might not be able to change the balance of power on the ground, but this was a far cry from accepting it as a legal obligation. He had gone along with various compromise offers suggesting the contrary, not out of conviction, but as the price for continued American support. We had sustained our backing for Saigon in America by a series of proposals—all of which he had accepted—designed to prove our willingness to walk the extra mile. But the cumulative impact of these proposals—cease-fire in place, new elections, American withdrawal—all amounted to giving Saigon a legal status different from Hanoi's. This is what rankled deeply" (Kissinger, *White House Years*, p. 1393).

This was the same situation as before 1968 when, as Clark Clifford, Lyndon Johnson's secretary of defense, said, "The South Vietnamese did not want to end the war—not while they were protected by over five hundred thousand American troops and a gold flow of money." Quoted in Douglas Brinkley, *Tour of Duty: John Kerry and the Vietnam War* (New York: William Morrow, 2004), p. 131. Or, as Kissinger assessed during his own negotiations with Thieu in 1972, the South Vietnamese "were not satisfied with survival; they wanted a guarantee that they would prevail." See Kissinger, *White House Years*, pp. 1323–24. Yet this stood in direct opposition to the U.S. objectives: "We had to fight the war and simultaneously strengthen the South Vietnamese to survive without us—in other words, to make ourselves dispensable" (*White House Years*, p. 232). Indeed, Kissinger argued in that same work that "we had no duty to them to guarantee them a total victory that we were unable to define, whose achievement required an open-ended commitment extending over many years more, and that we had publicly forsworn for the past three years" (p. 1349).

In the following passages, Kissinger reflects on the barriers to a negotiated agreement between the two Vietnams, and the cultural differences that prevented the United States from promptly grasping the seriousness of these obstacles:

"Our constant search for some compromise formula illuminated the cultural gap between us and the Vietnamese because the very concept of compromise was alien to both Vietnamese parties.

We had no way of understanding the primeval hatred that animated the two sides. They had fought each other for a generation. They had assassinated each other's officials, tortured each other's prisoners. The chasm of distrust and mutually inflicted suffering was unbridgeable by goodwill or the sort of compromise formulas toward which Americans incline. Each Vietnamese party saw in a settlement the starting point of a new struggle sometime in the not too distant future. Every deliberately vague formula I put forward was tested by each side to determine to what extent it represented an opportunity to inflict a humiliation on the despised opponent. And both sides were marvelously subtle and ingenious in changing phraseology to score such victories, particularly in the Vietnamese language with its finely shaded meanings quite beyond our grasp" (Kissinger, *White House Years*, p. 1325).

135. Thach, "Interview with Nguyen Co Thach."
136. Kissinger, *White House Years*, pp. 1416–22, 1428–43.
137. "I had come to Paris on December 4 with instructions from Nixon to settle. Le Duc Tho had kept me there ten days, our longest negotiating session ever, and each day we seemed farther away from an agreement. . . . Each day several issues that we thought had been settled in the agreement emerged again in loaded North Vietnamese drafts of either the understandings or the protocols. Le Duc Tho would then yield on most of these in a long day of negotiation, but made sure that enough were left over, or new ones reopened, to prevent a conclusion. . . . This was the insoluble problem over which we began the Christmas bombing five days later." See Kissinger, *White House Years*, pp. 1444–45.

138. For an overview, see Stephen E. Ambrose, "The Christmas Bombing," *MHQ: The Quarterly Journal of Military History* 4 (Winter 1992): 8–17. The efficacy of this campaign, along with that of earlier air campaigns, in terms of the negotiating objectives, was carefully evaluated by Robert A. Pape, Jr., and found to be generally effective. See Pape, "Coercive Air Power in the Vietnam War," pp. 103–46. The specific reference behind this efficacy claim in the text is at p. 141; see also Kissinger, *White House Years*, pp. 1448, 1459. The destructive capacity of this bombing campaign (called Operation Linebacker II) was larger than that of all the bombs used against North Vietnam from 1969 to 1971. At the time, Vietnam veteran John Kerry was "flabbergasted" (in the words of historian Douglas Brinkley) by the "monstrous brutality" of the bombing campaign, and Senate Majority Leader Mike Mansfield called the attacks a "Stone Age tactic." See Brinkley, *Tour of Duty*, pp. 425–28. Kissinger offers a very different view of the actual bombing and its effects on the negotiations. See *White House Years*, pp. 1446–57.

139. For specifics of the changes, see Kissinger, *White House Years*, pp. 1461–62. Douglas Brinkley agrees that the "Christmas bombings had worked" in forcing Hanoi to negotiate at least some changes. See Brinkley, *Tour of Duty*, p. 427.

140. Kissinger, *White House Years*, pp. 1469–70. One of Nixon's brutal letters to Thieu reflects the strain between the two nominal allies: On Jan. 16, 1973, he wrote, "I have therefore irrevocably decided to proceed to initial the Agreement on Jan. 23, 1973, and to sign it on Jan. 27, 1973, in Paris. I will do so, if necessary, alone. In that case I shall have to explain publicly that your Government obstructs peace. The result will be an inevitable and immediate termination of U.S. economic and military assistance which cannot be forestalled by a change of personnel in your government." Quoted in Kissinger, *White House Years*, p. 1469.

141. Kissinger, "Transcript of the American Secretaries of State Project: Henry A. Kissinger."

142. See, for example, Herring, *America's Longest War: The United States in Vietnam, 1950–1975*, 5th ed. (Boston: McGraw-Hill, 2014), p. 334, and Dallek, *Nixon and Kissinger*, p. 468.

143. Kissinger, "Transcript of the American Secretaries of State Project: Henry A. Kissinger."

144. Kissinger, *Diplomacy*, p. 696.

145. Kissinger, *Years of Upheaval*, p. 327; In the same work, Kissinger notes, "I was fighting a desperate but losing struggle against the Pentagon's desire to redeploy air and naval forces out of Southeast Asia in order to devote scarce funds to the procurement of new weapons" (p. 329).

146. Lunch and Sperlich, "American Public Opinion and the War in Vietnam," p. 25.

147. Kissinger, *Years of Renewal*, p. 546.

148. Horne, "The Case for Henry Kissinger."

149. Kissinger, "Transcript of the American Secretaries of State Project: Henry A. Kissinger."

150. Kissinger, "U.S. Naval Academy Forrestal Lecture."

151. Goldberg, "World Chaos and World Order."

152. Kissinger, *White House Years*, p. 1102.

153. Kissinger, "Transcript of the American Secretaries of State Project: Henry A. Kissinger."

154. Rachel Halliburton, "Henry Kissinger's World Order."

155. Morton A. Kaplan and Abram Chayes, *Vietnam Settlement: Why 1973, Not 1969?*, Rational Debate Series (Washington, DC: American Enterprise Institute Press, 1987).

156. For example, Roger Morris, then of the National Security Council, resigned over the Cambodia invasion of April 1970, indicating that the invasion was a "betrayal of the president's pledge to seek an honorable and just peace in Vietnam. I knew that that peace was within our grasp. I was intimately involved in the negotiations. I knew that the other side was ready to agree, that we were ready to agree, and that the Cambodian invasion really destroyed all of that. Devastated it for years

to come. And literally cost tens of thousands of American lives, hundreds of thousands of Vietnamese lives." From BBC4, "The Trials of Henry Kissinger," YouTube. https://youtu.be/DwGtctUYhRI; or, in the view of the BBC's David Taylor, "Once in office [Nixon] escalated the war into Laos and Cambodia, with the loss of an additional 22,000 American lives—quite apart from the lives of the Laotians, Cambodians and Vietnamese caught up in the new offensives—before finally settling for a peace agreement in 1973 that was within grasp in 1968." David Taylor, "The Lyndon Johnson Tapes: Richard Nixon's 'Treason,'" *BBC News Magazine* (2013). Published electronically March 22, 2013, http://www.bbc.com/news/magazine-21768668.

157. Kissinger continues "Not even the strongest critics in the mainstream of American life recommended immediate withdrawal in 1969 . . . Above all, Hanoi had made clear repeatedly that the war could not be ended—or our prisoners released—even by our unilateral withdrawal." Kissinger, *White House Years*, p. 286.

158. Colin L. Powell and Joseph E. Persico, *My American Journey* (New York: Random House, 1995), p. 149.

159. Kissinger, *White House Years*, p. 286.

160. "[E]very poll showed that unilateral withdrawal was rejected by crushing majorities. The public was as ambivalent as the government planners: It wanted us to get out of Vietnam and yet it did not want defeat." Kissinger, *White House Years*, p. 286.

161. Kissinger, *White House Years*, p. 286. As we've just noted, Kissinger made this point even more emphatically elsewhere in his writing: "Peking had no interest in a demonstration that the United States was prepared to dump its friends," Kissinger stated, "in its long-range perspective of seeking a counterweight to the Soviet Union, Peking in fact had a stake in our reputation for reliability." Kissinger, *White House Years*, p. 1304.

162. As previously mentioned in note 43 for this chapter, Kissinger repeatedly returns to the argument that the U.S. support for South Vietnam was important for the maintenance of American global credibility.

See, for example, Kissinger, *White House Years*, pp. 109, 292, and 1038. As we indicate in chapter 4, the debate over the importance of credibility in international relations and negotiations continues; for examples, see Fettweiss; McMahon; Walt.

163. For the importance of the Vietnamization program along with its military and political components, see, e.g., Gregory A. Daddis, "American Military Strategy in the Vietnam War, 1965–1973," *Oxford Research Encyclopedia of American History*, Oxford Research Encyclopedia of American History (New York: Oxford University Press, 2015).

164. Nixon, *RN*, p. 349; Kissinger, "The Viet Nam Negotiations," p. 216; With respect to policymakers' understanding of the constraints on what U.S. power could achieve, see Lawrence W. Serewicz, *America at the Brink of Empire: Rusk, Kissinger, and the Vietnam War* (Baton Rouge: Louisiana State University Press, 2007), p. 10.

165. See, e.g., Eugene McCarthy, "Topics: The Failure of Vietnamization by Any Name," *New York Times*, Aug. 1, 1970. A major offensive test of the Vietnamization strategy, a ground invasion of Laos in 1971 by Vietnamese troops, suggested the weaknesses of this approach. See the review by Hanson, "A Raid Too Far"; or, later, see Scott Sigmund Gartner, "Differing Evaluations of Vietnamization," *Journal of Interdisciplinary History* 29, no. 2 (1998).

166. Kissinger, "Interview with Henry Kissinger, April 17, 1982," *Vietnam: A Television History*, WGBH (1982), https://www.digitalcommonwealth.org/search/commonwealth-oai:dv141j297.

167. As we've just noted, after the Paris Agreement was signed in January 1973, a Gallup poll reported that an overwhelming 79 percent of the public opposed the reintervention of American military troops in Vietnam even "if North Vietnam were to try to take over South Vietnam" (Lunch and Sperlich, "American Public Opinion and the War in Vietnam," p. 25).

168. The classic works on this topic are Schelling's, *The Strategy of Conflict* and *Arms and Influence*. Substantial advances were made in Robert

J. Art and Patrick M. Cronin, *The United States and Coercive Diplomacy* (Washington, DC: United States Institute of Peace Press, 2003); George Alexander and William Simons, *The Limits of Coercive Diplomacy*, 2nd Rev. Ed. (Boulder, CO: Westview Press, 1994); Paul Gordon Lauren, Gordon A. Craig, and Alexander L. George, *Force and the Limits of Military Might* (New York: Cambridge Unviersity Press, 2002); Lawrence Freedman, ed. *Strategic Coercion: Concepts and Cases* (Oxford: Oxford University Press, 1998).

169. Pape, "Coercive Air Power in the Vietnam War."

170. CNN, "Vietnam War: Fast Facts," July 1, 2013, http://www.cnn.com /2013/07/01/world/vietnam-war-fast-facts/.

171. Of course, the strategy and tactics used in the application of force are as important as its total magnitude. For a summary, see, e.g., Daddis, "American Military Strategy in the Vietnam War, 1965–1973."

172. For the classic treatment of the ethics of the use of force, see Michael Walzer, *Just and Unjust Wars: A Moral Argument with Historical Illustrations*, 5th ed. (New York: Basic Books, 2015). For a complementary discussion, see the special section on "Just War and Its Critics," *Ethics and International Affairs* 27, no. 1 (2013): 1–114. See also David P. Fidler, "Just and Unjust Wars: The Uses of Coercion," *Daedalus* 145 (2016): 37–49. A helpful legal treatment of these issues can be found in Michael W. Reisman, "Criteria for the Lawful Use of Force in International Law," *Yale Journal of International Law* 279 (1985), http:// digitalcommons.law.yale.edu/fss_papers/739. For an accessible introduction to key principles of international law and the use of force, see, e.g., Christine Gray, *International Law and the Use of Force* (Oxford: Oxford University Press, 2001). For help in thinking through a wider set of ethical issues in negotiation, an excellent compendium of articles was edited by Carrie Menkel-Meadow and Michael Wheeler, eds., *What's Fair? Ethics for Negotiators* (Hoboken, NJ: Jossey-Bass/Wiley, 2010).

173. Kissinger, *White House Years*, p. 48.

174. Interested readers may wish to review prominent arguments against his

use of force in Indochina and on the implications for American foreign policy. For prominent critiques of the Nixon administration's Cambodia policies, see Hersh, *The Price of Power*; Hitchens, *The Trial of Henry Kissinger*. Probably the most influential critique of the Nixon administration's Cambodia policy has been Shawcross (about which, see below within this note). Walter Isaacson has a more moderate, but still critical view: "Although the North Vietnamese had violated Cambodia's neutrality, their camps had not yet disrupted the lives of the Cambodian peasants and fishermen. But that delicate balance began to falter when the American bombing campaign caused the communist camps to disperse over a larger area. The bombing may not have been the main cause of Cambodia's plunge toward chaos a year later, but it did not make Sihanouk's balancing act any easier." See Isaacson, *Kissinger*, p. 177. Judging far more harshly than Isaacson, Greg Grandin says, "Kissinger didn't create the Khmer Rouge, but his mad and illegal bombing of Cambodia created the conditions where the most genocidal, militant faction of a broad and diverse insurgency could seize control of first the insurgency and then the state." See Greg Grandin, "Henry Kissinger's 'Mad and Illegal' Bombing: What You Need to Know About His Real History—and Why the Sanders/Clinton Exchange Matters," *Salon*, Feb. 12, 2016, http://www.salon.com/2016/02/12/henry_kissingers_mad_and _illegal_bombing_what_you_need_to_know_about_his_real_history _and_why_the_sandersclinton_exchange_matters/. Similarly, see Todd Gitlin, "Kissinger Was a Courtier to Atrocity," *New York Times*, Feb. 13, 2016, https://www.nytimes.com/roomfordebate/2016/02/13 /henry-kissinger-sage-or-pariah/kissinger-was-a-courtier-to-atrocity ?mcubz=2. Unsurprisingly, among the most extensive explanations and justifications of Kissinger's actions can be found in the three volumes of his memoirs: Kissinger, *White House Years*; *Years of Upheaval*; and *Years of Renewal*. A number of pros and cons of Kissinger's record in Vietnam and beyond are summarized in Thompson, *Henry Kissinger: Good or Evil?*; While we have cited numerous critics, Kissinger's actions in Indochina also find strong support in many quarters. For examples, see Robert D. Kaplan, "In Defense of Henry Kissinger," *Atlantic*, May 2013; Joffe, "In Defense of Henry Kissinger"; Robert D. Blackwill, "In Defense of Kissinger," *National Interest* (Jan.–Feb. 2014), http://nationalinterest.org/article/defense-kissinger-9642; Niall Ferguson, "The Kissinger Diaries: What He Really Thought About Vietnam," *Politico*, Oct. 10, 2015, http://www.politico.com/magazine/story/2015/10/henry-kissinger-vietnam-diaries-213236; Kaplan, "Kissinger, Metternich, and Realism." Indeed, some initially harsh critics later became ambivalent. For example, William Shawcross's highly influential 1979 book, *Sideshow: Kissinger, Nixon and the Destruction of Cambodia*, found particular fault with Kissinger's actions, as well as those of the Nixon administration and the South Vietnamese regime. In that book, Shawcross singled them out for what he saw as their disproportionate responsibility for later atrocities in Cambodia. In 1995, however, Shawcross substantially moderated his earlier critique. He noted that his initial analysis was unbalanced, and specifically that he had not sufficiently taken into account the brutality of the North Vietnamese regime. He said, "Indeed those of us who opposed the American war in Indo-China should be extremely humble in the face of the appalling aftermath: a form of genocide in Cambodia and horrific tyranny in both Vietnam and Laos. Looking back on my own coverage for the *Sunday Times* of the South Vietnamese war effort of 1970–75, I think I concentrated too easily on the corruption and incompetence of the South Vietnamese and their American allies, was too ignorant of the inhuman Hanoi regime, and far too willing to believe that a victory by the communists would provide a better future. But after the communist victory came the refugees to Thailand and the floods of boat people desperately seeking to escape the Cambodian killing fields and the Vietnamese gulags. Their eloquent testimony should have put paid to all illusions" (William Shawcross, "Shrugging Off Genocide," *Times* [London], Dec. 19, 1994, p. 16).

Chapter 7: Multiparty Dexterity: Orchestrating Complex Negotiations

1. Richard E. Neustadt, *Alliance Politics* (New York: Columbia University Press, 1970), p. 5.
2. Kissinger, *Years of Renewal*, p. 972.
3. Kissinger, *Diplomacy*, p. 728.
4. Kissinger, *White House Years*, pp. 764–65.
5. Kissinger, *Diplomacy*, p. 729.
6. Kissinger, "The White Revolutionary: Reflections on Bismarck," pp. 912–13.
7. Kissinger, *White House Years*, pp. 764–65.
8. Ibid., p. 132.
9. Kissinger, *Diplomacy*, p. 731.
10. Kissinger, *On China*, p. 237.
11. Ibid., p. 238.
12. Kissinger, *Diplomacy*, p. 772.
13. Kissinger, *White House Years*, p. 685.
14. Ibid., p. 166.
15. "Strategic Survey: The Sino-Soviet Dispute."
16. Kissinger, "Transcript of the American Secretaries of State Project: Henry A. Kissinger"; Kissinger, *On China*, p. 220.
17. Kissinger, *Diplomacy*, p. 723.
18. Ibid., p. 223.
19. Kissinger, *On China*, pp. 225–26.
20. Ibid., pp. 230–31.
21. Ibid., pp. 233–34.
22. Kissinger, *White House Years*, p. 740.
23. Kissinger, *On China*, p. 249.
24. Kissinger, *White House Years*, p. 765.
25. Kissinger, *Years of Renewal*, p. 150.
26. Kissinger, *White House Years*, pp. 758–59.
27. Ibid.; *Diplomacy*, p. 728.

28. Kissinger, *White House Years*, pp. 1084–87.

29. Kissinger, *On China*, p. 271.

30. Ibid., p. 270.

31. Kissinger, *Diplomacy*, pp. 730–31.

32. Ibid.

33. Kissinger, *White House Years*, pp. 766–67.

34. Ibid.

35. Ibid., pp. 177–78.

36. Kissinger, *Diplomacy*, p. 730.

37. Evelyn Goh, *Constructing the U.S. Rapprochement with China, 1961–1974* (Cambridge: Cambridge University Press, 2004), p. 231. Or, in a standard text: "President Nixon and National Security Assistant Henry Kissinger opted for triangular diplomacy. They would play the 'China card' to win concessions from Moscow and the 'Soviet card' to influence China" (Walter Clemens, *Dynamics of International Relations* [London: Rowman and Littlefield, 2004], p. 254).

38. Kissinger, "Transcript of the American Secretaries of State Project: Henry A. Kissinger."

39. Ibid.

40. Ibid., p. 5.

41. Isaacson, *Kissinger*, p. 166.

42. Ibid.

43. See Sebenius, "Beyond the Deal."

44. James K. Sebenius, "Sequencing to Build Coalitions: With Whom Should I Talk First?" in *Wise Choices: Decisions, Games, and Negotiations*, eds. Richard Zeckhauser, Ralph Keeney, and James Sebenius (Boston, MA: Harvard Business School Press, 1996). See also chapter 7 in Lax and Sebenius, *3-D Negotiation*.

45. Kissinger, *Diplomacy*, p. 231.

46. Kissinger, *Years of Renewal*, p. 616.

47. Ibid., pp. 263–64.

48. Ibid., p. 1028.

49. Ibid.

50. Henry Kissinger, "Kissinger Memorandum: 'To Isolate the Palestinians': Meeting with Jewish Leaders," Memcon, June 15, 1975, New York, http://www.merip.org/mer/mer96/kissinger-memorandum -isolate-palestinians.

51. Ibid.

Chapter 8: Introduction to Kissinger's Interpersonal Approach and Tactics

1. Kissinger, *White House Years*, p. 733.

2. Golda Meir, *My Life* (New York: G.P. Putnam's Sons, 1975), p. 442.

3. Henry A. Kissinger, *Nuclear Weapons and Foreign Policy: Abridged Edition* (New York: W.W. Norton, 1969), pp. 44–45.

4. Fred Iklé, *How Nations Negotiate* (New York: Harper and Row, 1964).

5. Kissinger, *On China*, pp. 247–48.

Chapter 9: Reading Counterparts

1. Lord, "Interview with Ambassador Winston Lord," p. 97.

2. Stanley Hoffmann, "The Case of Dr. Kissinger," *New York Review of Books*, Dec. 6, 1979, http://www.nybooks.com/articles/1979/12/06 /the-case-of-dr-kissinger/.

3. Kissinger, *Diplomacy*, p. 727.

4. Ibid.

5. Kissinger, *Years of Upheaval*, p. 1099.

6. Ibid.

7. Ibid., p. 140.

8. Henry A. Kissinger, "Memorandum to the President: Leonid Brezhnev: The Man and His Style," U.S. Department of State, Gerald Ford Presidential Library, 1974, https://www.fordlibrarymuseum.gov /library/exhibits/vladivostok/brezhnev.pdf.

9. Ibid.

10. For a number of references to such manuals, plus suggested correctives, see, e.g., James K. Sebenius, "The Hidden Challenge of Cross-Border Negotiations," *Harvard Business Review* 80, no. 3 (2002); "Assess, Don't Assume, Part I: Etiquette and National Culture in Negotiation," Harvard Business School Working Paper, No. 10–048, Dec. 2009; "Assess, Don't Assume, Part II: Negotiating Implications of Cross-Border Differences in Decision Making, Governance, and Political Economy," Harvard Business School Working Paper, no. 10–050, Dec. 2009.

11. Henry A. Kissinger, "Memo from the President's Assistant for National Security Affairs (Kissinger) to President Nixon," *Foreign Relations of the United States, 1969–1976*, U.S. Department of State, Feb. 19, 1972, pp. 672–77.

12. Ibid., p. 673.

13. Ibid., pp. 674–75.

14. Ibid.

15. Ibid., pp. 675–76.

16. Ibid., pp. 675–77.

17. Kissinger, *White House Years*, p. 1056.

18. Ibid., p. 1138.

19. Ibid., p. 370.

20. Ibid., pp. 27, 28.

21. Ibid., p. 33.

22. Ibid.

23. Henry Kissinger, *Ending the Vietnam War: A History of America's Involvement in and Extrication from the Vietnam War* (New York: Simon and Schuster, 2003), pp. 394–95.

24. Ibid., pp. 710 and 745–46.

25. Kissinger, *Years of Upheaval*, pp. 647–48.

26. Ibid., pp. 1061, 1065–66.

27. Kissinger, *White House Years*, p. 1051.

28. William C. Kirby, "A Note on the 40th Anniversary of Nixon's Visit to China," *Cross Currents: East Asian History and Culture Review* 2 (March 2012); Kissinger, "Memorandum to the President: Leonid Brezhnev."

29. Kissinger, *White House Years*, p. 1051.

30. Kissinger, *Years of Upheaval*, p. 735.

31. Henry A. Kissinger, *Does America Need a Foreign Policy?* (New York: Simon and Schuster, 2002), pp. 121–22.

32. Ibid., p. 122.

33. Kissinger, *Years of Renewal*, p. 387.

34. Kissinger, "Transcript of the American Secretaries of State Project: Henry A. Kissinger."

35. Lord, "Interview with Ambassador Winston Lord," pp. 97–98.

36. Hoffmann, "The Case of Dr. Kissinger."

Chapter 10: Relationships and Rapport

1. For example, he and President "Nixon relied neither on personal relations nor on the conversion of the Soviets but on a balancing of incentives as a way of making the Kremlin more malleable." Kissinger, *Diplomacy*, p. 730. His colleague Winston Lord noted that Kissinger was "never naive enough to base his negotiating style on personal likes or dislikes. He did this in terms of national self-interest" (Lord, "Interview with Ambassador Winston Lord").

2. Henry A. Kissinger and Hillary Clinton, interview by Jon Meacham, Jan. 4, 2009.

3. Ibid.

4. His colleague Winston Lord, after noting that Kissinger took national interest as primary, nonetheless stated that "around the edges you can build up trust in some cases that help you get through some difficult points" (Lord, "Interview with Ambassador Winston Lord").

5. Niall Ferguson, "The Secret to Henry Kissinger's Success," *Politico*, January 20, 2018, https://www.politico.com/magazine/story/2018/01/20/henry-kissinger-networking-216482; and Niall Ferguson, *The Square and the Tower: Networks and Power, from Freemasons to Facebook*, New York: Penguin, 2017.

6. Ibid.

7. John D. Montgomery, "The Education of Henry Kissinger," *Journal of International Affairs* 29, no. 1 (1975): 5.

8. Kissinger, "Transcript of the American Secretaries of State Project: Henry A. Kissinger."

9. Dobrynin, *In Confidence*, pp. 200–201.

10. Kissinger, *White House Years*, p. 1216.

11. Dobrynin, *In Confidence*, pp. 200–201.

12. Kissinger, "Transcript of the American Secretaries of State Project: Henry A. Kissinger."

13. Jon Meacham. "Hillary Clinton, Kissinger on Sec. of State Job."

14. Kissinger, *White House Years*, p. 26.

15. Kissinger, *Diplomacy*, p. 230.

16. Kissinger, "Transcript of the American Secretaries of State Project: Henry A. Kissinger."

17. Isaacson, *Kissinger*, p. 557.

18. Kissinger, *White House Years*, p. 792.

19. Edward Heath, *The Course of My Life: My Autobiography* (London: Hodder and Stoughton, 1998), p. 244.

20. Lord, "Interview with Ambassador Winston Lord," p. 87.

21. Halliburton, "Henry Kissinger's World Order."

22. Isaacson, *Kissinger*, pp. 553–56.

23. Ibid., p. 554.

24. Ibid., p. 553.

25. Ibid., pp. 553, 554.

26. Lord, "Interview with Ambassador Winston Lord," p. 87.

27. Isaacson, *Kissinger*, p. 554.

28. Isaacson explained more fully that "a study of [Kissinger's] words— even the transcripts of relatively unguarded conversations—shows him phrasing his remarks carefully so as not to contradict directly what he was telling someone else. He would withhold information and even allow a listener to be misled—which comes close to the definition of

deceit. But he seldom resorted to unadorned lying in his negotiating efforts" (*Kissinger*, p. 554).

29. James Callaghan, *Time and Chance* (London: Collins, 1987), pp. 358–59.

30. Dobrynin, *In Confidence*, pp. 200–201.

31. Meir, *My Life*, p. 442.

32. Smith, *The Great Betrayal*, pp. 203–4.

33. Kissinger, *White House Years*, p. 791.

34. Ferguson, "The Secret to Kissinger's Success."

35. Ferguson, *The Square and the Tower.*

Chapter 11: Proposals, Concessions, and "Constructive Ambiguity"

1. Kissinger, *Years of Upheaval*, p. 214.

2. Ibid.

3. Kissinger, *The Necessity for Choice*, p. 205.

4. Kissinger, *On China*, pp. 270–71.

5. Kissinger, *Years of Renewal*, p. 969.

6. Kissinger, *Years of Upheaval*, p. 214.

7. Kissinger, *White House Years*, p. 791.

8. Kissinger, *On China*, pp. 270–71.

9. Ibid., pp. 221–22.

10. Kissinger, *Diplomacy*, p. 727.

11. There can be exceptions to this nominally general advice. For example, a haggling style may be useful to persuade key members of Congress or a skeptical ally that you have held out for the best possible deal.

12. Kissinger, *White House Years*, 436–37.

13. Kissinger, *Years of Upheaval*, p. 685.

14. Ibid., p. 286.

15. Kissinger, *White House Years*, p. 783.

16. Ibid. Kissinger acknowledged that "In fairness I must say that I adapted it from a State Department planning document for negotiations, which aborted in the Fifties" (p. 783).

17. Ibid.
18. Ibid.
19. Ibid., pp. 767, 769.
20. Ibid., p. 770.
21. Kissinger, *Years of Upheaval*, pp. 641–42.
22. Ibid.
23. James Fallows, "Elliott Abrams on Hypocrisy," *The Atlantic*, Sept. 19, 2011.
24. Isaacson, *Kissinger*, p. 556.
25. Khaled Elgindy, "When Ambiguity Is Destructive," Jan. 22, 2014, *Brookings* (blog), https://www.brookings.edu/opinions/when-ambiguity-is-destructive/.
26. Shultz, *Ideas and Action*, p. 100.
27. The term originates in the work of Schelling, *The Strategy of Conflict*.
28. Kissinger, *Diplomacy*, p. 753.
29. Kissinger, *Years of Upheaval*, p. 825.

Chapter 12: Persistence, Momentum, and Shuttle Diplomacy

1. Heath, *The Course of My Life*, p. 244.
2. Yitzhak Rabin, *The Rabin Memoirs* (Berkeley: University of California, 1996), pp. 272–74.
3. Saunders, "On the Road Again."
4. Kissinger, *Years of Renewal*, p. 406.
5. Kissinger, *White House Years*, p. 803.
6. Isaacson, *Kissinger*, p. 546. Isaacson also noted that "The first known use of shuttle in this context was in a *New York Times* story, Jan. 11, 1974, by Bernard Gwertzman, which referred to Kissinger's 'unorthodox bit of shuttle diplomacy'" (p. 813).
7. The following is a small set of examples of such proposals, recommending shuttles for, respectively, Secretaries of State John Kerry, Warren Christopher, and James Baker: Bruce van Voorst, "Silent Shuttle," *Foreign Policy*, July 26, 2013, http://foreignpolicy.com/2013/07/26/silent-shuttle/;

Anthony Lewis, "A Christopher Shuttle?" *New York Times*, Dec. 3, 1993, A33; and "The Baker Shuttle," *Washington Post*, May 14, 1991, A18.

8. Much of this and the previous paragraph is paraphrased, directly quoted from, or inspired by David A. Hoffmann, "Mediation and the Art of Shuttle Diplomacy," *Negotiation Journal* 27, no. 3 (2011): 268–70.

9. In legal disputes, some mediators essentially engage in shuttle diplomacy and separate the disputants while others primarily ask that the parties and mediators work in the same room. Proponents of each method claim benefits. Compare G. Friedman and Jack Himmelstein, *Challenging Conflict: Mediation Through Understanding* (Chicago: American Bar Association, 2008), which emphasizes the benefits of having disputants work together; and Hoffmann, "Mediation and the Art of Shuttle Diplomacy," emphasizing the advantages of a mediator caucusing separately with disputants.

10. Isaacson, *Kissinger*, p. 559.

11. Kissinger, *Years of Renewal*, p. 390.

12. van Voorst, "Silent Shuttle."

13. Quoted in Isaacson, *Kissinger*, p. 559.

14. Kissinger, *Years of Renewal*, pp. 406–7.

15. See, e.g., ibid., pp. 394–95.

Chapter 13: Secrecy, Centralization, and a Dominant Personal Role

1. Attributed to Cardinal Jules Mazarin (passage translated by James K. Sebenius), *Bréviaire des politiciens* (1684; Paris: Arlèa, 1996).

2. François de Callières, *De la manière de négocier avec les souverains*, ed. Alain Pekar Lempereur (passage translated by James K. Sebenius) (1716; Geneva: Droz, 2002), p. 69. Other historical observations on secrecy in diplomacy can be found in Aurélien Colson, "The Ambassador, Between Light and Shade: The Emergence of Secrecy as the Norm for International Negotiation," 2007, ESSEC Business

School, Institute for Research and Education on Negotiation, No.
DR07023.

3.   Lord, "Interview with Ambassador Winston Lord," pp. 98–99.

4.   Kissinger, *On China*, p. 236.

5.   A detailed account of these actions from Kissinger's point of view can
       be found in *White House Years*.

6.   Kissinger, *White House Years*, p. 138.

7.   Ibid., p. 1125.

8.   Ibid., p. 684.

9.   Ibid., p. 686.

10.   Ibid.

11.   Ibid., p. 805.

12.   Ibid.

13.   Raymond L. Garthoff, "Negotiating SALT," *The Wilson Quarterly* 1,
       no. 5 (1977).

14.   Kissinger, *White House Years*, p. 147.

15.   Gerard C. Smith, *Doubletalk: The Story of the First Strategic Arms Limita-
       tion Talks* (Garden City, NY: Doubleday and Co., 1980), p. 1.

16.   Ibid., p. 466.

17.   Ibid., p. 235.

18.   Ibid., p. 466.

19.   Smith noted that this problem could be exacerbated when back-chan-
       nel negotiations sometimes used only Soviet interpreters. "[I]n the
       absence of an American interpreter's verbatim notes, one cannot pre-
       pare the fullest possible record of negotiating exchanges. In a number
       of cases, no record was made available to SALT officials as to what
       transpired in the back channel . . . unavailability of significant portions
       of the record can be a substantial handicap" (*Doubletalk*, p. 467). Of
       course, better use of interpreters can be remedied; it is not an inherent
       flaw in secret negotiations, unless truly discreet interpreters cannot
       be found.

20. Kissinger, *White House Years*, p. 865.

21. Stanley Hoffmann, "The Case of Dr. Kissinger."

22. William P. Bundy, *A Tangled Web: The Making of Foreign Policy in the Nixon Presidency* (New York: Hill and Wang, 1998), p. 128.

23. Kissinger, *White House Years*, pp. 831–32.

24. Ibid.

25. Ibid., p. 816.

26. Kissinger, *Years of Upheaval*, pp. 224–25.

27. Kissinger, *White House Years*.

28. Ibid., p. 1025.

29. Ibid. He went on, however, to state that "There is no doubt that in 1971 secrecy enabled Hanoi to whipsaw us; the question whether more openness would have stopped this or produced an even earlier stalemate must remain in the realm of conjecture" (p. 1020).

30. Kissinger, *White House Years*, p. 805.

31. Ibid.

32. Ibid., pp. 1229–30.

33. Smith, *Doubletalk*, p. 235.

34. Kissinger, *Years of Upheaval*, p. 264.

35. Kissinger, *White House Years*, p. 762.

36. Ibid.

37. Horne, *Kissinger: 1973*, p. 112.

38. Kissinger, *White House Years*, p. 282.

39. There are many, more detailed, accounts of who told what to whom than are relevant here; see, e.g., chap. 20 of Isaacson, *Kissinger*; or chaps. 31 and 32 of Kissinger, *White House Years*.

40. *Der Spiegel*, "The Americans Betrayed Us: Interview with Nguyen Van Thieu" 50, no. 33, Dec. 10, 1979, pp. 197–213, https://www.cvce.eu/content/publication/1999/1/1/20035c62-a1c8-44ab-9721-273749085ae4/publishable_en.pdf.

41. Kissinger, *White House Years*, p. 1393.

42. Fisher, Ury, and Patton, *Getting to Yes*, p. 36.

43. Stanley Hoffmann, "The Case of Dr. Kissinger."

44. Isaacson, *Kissinger*, pp. 762–63.

45. Kissinger, *White House Years*, p. 822.

46. Ibid., p. 806.

47. Ibid.

48. Ibid., p. 822.

Conclusion: Key Lessons on Negotiation from Henry Kissinger

1. See especially Robert H. Mnookin, Scott R. Peppet, and Andrew S. Tulumello, *Beyond Winning: Negotiating to Create Value in Deals and Disputes* (Cambridge, MA: Belknap Press/Harvard University Press, 2000); as well as David A. Lax and James K. Sebenius, *The Manager as Negotiator: Bargaining for Cooperation and Competitive Gain* (New York: Free Press, 1986); Lax and Sebenius, *3-D Negotiation*.

2. Throughout this book, we have paid very close attention to what Kissinger actually does in negotiation as well as the words he uses to describe his views on the subject. Where we have judged it to be more useful, we have often couched our analysis in our own terms, rather than Kissinger's. For example, though he never employed phrases such as "deal/no-deal balance," "negotiation campaign," or "empathy and assertiveness," we believe they accurately characterize important elements of his approach. In crystallizing this chapter's advice, we continue to use our own terms where they seem to communicate an idea best.

3. Herb Cohen, *You Can Negotiate Anything* (New York: Bantam, 1982).

4. Henry Kissinger, *White House Years*.

5. Ibid., p. 31.

6. Ibid., pp. 177–78.

7. "Ian Smith, News Conference, October 25, 1976."

8. Isaacson, *Kissinger*, p. 690.

9. Kissinger, *White House Years*, p. 783. Kissinger acknowledged that "In fairness I must say that I adapted it from a State Department planning document for negotiations, which aborted in the Fifties."

10. Kissinger, *Diplomacy*, p. 753.

11. Kissinger, *Years of Upheaval*, p. 825.

12. Anne-Marie Slaughter, *The Chessboard and the Web*.

Bibliography

Abbasi, Rizwana Karim. "Understanding Pakistan's Nuclear Behaviour (1950s–2010): Assessing the State Motivation and Its International Ramifications (a Three Models Approach)." PhD diss., University of Leicester, 2010. https://lra.le.ac.uk/bitstream/2381/27568/1/2010abbasirkdsocsci.pdf.

Ali, Tariq. *The Duel: Pakistan on the Flight Path of American Power.* New York: Scribner, 2008.

Ambrose, Stephen E. "The Christmas Bombing." *MHQ: The Quarterly Journal of Military History* 4 (Winter 1992): 8–17.

Art, Robert J., and Patrick M. Cronin. *The United States and Coercive Diplomacy.* Washington, DC: United States Institute of Peace Press, 2003.

Bailey, Clinton. *Jordan's Palestinian Challenge, 1948–1983: A Political History.* Boulder, CO: Westview Press, 1984.

Baker, Peter. "Nixon Tried to Spoil Johnson's Vietnam Peace Talks in '68, Notes Show." *New York Times*, Jan. 2, 2017. https://www.nytimes.com/2017/01/02/us/politics/nixon-tried-to-spoil-johnsons-vietnam-peace-talks-in-68-notes-show.html?mcubz=2&_r=0.

Baldwin, David Allen, ed. *Neorealism and Neoliberalism: The Contemporary Debate.* New York: Columbia University Press, 1993.

Bauer, Gretchen. "Namibia in the First Decade of Independence: How Democratic?" *Journal of Southern African Studies* 27, no. 1 (2001): 33–55.

Beauchamp, Zack. "The Obama Administration Is Honoring Henry Kissinger Today. It Shouldn't Be." *Vox*, May 9, 2016. http://www.vox.com/2016/5/9/11640562/kissinger-pentagon-award.

Bhutto, Benazir. *Daughter of the East.* London: Hamish Hamilton, 1988.

Bishop, William Lowrey. "Diplomacy in Black and White: America and the Search for Zimbabwean Independence, 1965–1980." PhD diss., Vanderbilt University, 2012.

Blackwill, Robert D. "In Defense of Kissinger." *National Interest* (Jan.–Feb. 2014). http://nationalinterest.org/article/defense-kissinger-9642.

Boston Globe. "Israeli Parliament Approves Pact over Right-Wing Bloc Objections." May 31, 1974, p. 26.

Brinkley, Douglas. *Tour of Duty: John Kerry and the Vietnam War*. New York: William Morrow, 2004.

Brown, L. Carl. "The Endgame." In *The October War*. Ed. Richard B. Parker. Gainesville: University Press of Florida, 2001.

Bundy, William P. *A Tangled Web: The Making of Foreign Policy in the Nixon Presidency*. New York: Hill and Wang, 1998.

Burr, William, ed. *The Kissinger Transcripts: The Top-Secret Talks with Beijing and Moscow*. New York: The New Press in conjunction with the National Security Archive, 1999.

———. "The United States and Pakistan's Quest for the Bomb." In *The Nuclear Vault Briefing Book 333*. National Security Archive, George Washington University. http://nsarchive.gwu.edu/nukevault/ebb333/.

Butterfield, Fox. "Nguyen Van Thieu Is Dead at 76; Last President of South Vietnam." *New York Times*, Oct. 1, 2001, p. A1.

Callaghan, James. "Leader's Speech." Labour Party Conference, Sept. 28, 1976, Blackpool. http://www.britishpoliticalspeech.org/speech-archive.htm?speech=174.

———. "Rhodesia." Debate on March 22, 1976. UK House of Commons. Vol. 908 cc29–45. http://hansard.millbanksystems.com/commons/1976/mar/22/rhodesia.

———. *Time and Chance*. London: Collins, 1987.

Callières, François de. *De la manière de négocier avec les souverains*. Ed. Alain Pekar Lempereur. [Passage translated by James K. Sebenius.] 1716; repr. Geneva: Droz, 2002.

Central Intelligence Agency. "The Evolution of Soviet Policy in the Sino-Soviet Border Dispute," April 28, 1970 (declassified May 2007).

———. "The Sino-Soviet Dispute on Aid to North Vietnam (1965–1968). Directorate of Intelligence. Sept. 30, 1968 [formerly top secret; released in May 2007]. https://www.cia.gov/library/readingroom/docs/esau-37.pdf.

―――. "Status of Soviet and Chinese Military Aid to North Vietnam." Office of Current Intelligence Special Report, Sept. 1965 [formerly top secret; released in Sept. 2001]. https://www.cia.gov/library/reading room/docs/DOC_0000652931.pdf.

Christison, Kathleen. "Kissinger: Years of Renewal (Review)." *Journal of Palestine Studies* 29, no. 1 (1999/2000). http://www.palestine-studies.org /jps/fulltext/40756.

Clemens, Walter. *Dynamics of International Relations.* London: Rowman and Littlefield, 2004.

CNN Library. "Vietnam War: Fast Facts." CNN, July 1, 2013. http://www .cnn.com/2013/07/01/world/vietnam-war-fast-facts/.

Cohen, Herb. *You Can Negotiate Anything.* New York: Bantam, 1982.

Collins, Jim, and Morten T. Hansen. *Great by Choice.* New York: Harper Business, 2011.

Colson, Aurélien. "The Ambassador, Between Light and Shade: The Emergence of Secrecy as the Norm for International Negotiation." *International Negotiation* 13, no. 2 (2008): doi: 10.1163/157180608X320199.

Compagnon, Daniel. *A Predictable Tragedy: Robert Mugabe and the Collapse of Zimbabwe.* Philadelphia: University of Pennsylvania Press, 2011.

Copeland, Dale C. "Trade Expectations and the Outbreak of Peace: Détente 1970–74 and the End of the Cold War, 1985–91." *Security Studies* 9, nos. 1–2 (Autumn 1999–Winter 2000): 15–58.

Cowell, Alan. "Ian Smith, Defiant and Steadfast Symbol of White Rule in Africa, Is Dead at 88." *New York Times,* Nov. 21, 2007, p. A25.

Craig, G. A., and A. L. George. *Force and Statecraft: Diplomatic Problems of Our Time.* New York: Oxford University Press, 1995.

Daddis, Gregory A. "American Military Strategy in the Vietnam War, 1965–1973." *Oxford Research Encyclopedia of American History.* New York: Oxford University Press, 2015.

Dallek, Robert. *Nixon and Kissinger: Partners in Power.* New York: Harper-Collins, 2007.

Davidow, Jeffrey. *A Peace in Southern Africa: The Lancaster House Conference on Rhodesia, 1979.* Westview Special Studies on Africa. Boulder, CO: Westview Press, 1984.

DeRoche, Andy. *Kenneth Kaunda, the United States, and Southern Africa.* London: Bloomsbury, 2016.

Der Spiegel. "The Americans Betrayed Us: Interview with Nguyen Van Thieu," vol. 50, no. 33, Dec. 10, 1979, pp. 197–213. http://www.cvce.eu /content/publication/1999/1/1/20035c62-a1c8-44ab-9721-27374 9085ae4/publishable_en.pdf.

Dobrynin, Anatoly. *In Confidence: Moscow's Ambassador to America's Six Cold War Presidents (1962—1986).* New York: Random House, 1995.

Dombroski, Kenneth R. "South Africa After Apartheid." *Journal of Democracy* 17, no. 3 (2006): 43–57.

Dommen, Arthur J. *The Indochinese Experience of the French and Americans: Nationalism and Communism in Cambodia, Laos, and Vietnam.* Bloomington: Indiana University Press, 2001.

Donnelly, Warren H. "Pakistan's Nuclear Activities: A Chronology of Four Eras." 1987. U.S. Congressional Research Service. Environment and Natural Resources Policy Division. Library of Congress, Washington DC, p. 22.

Easum, Donald B. "Nyerere and Obasanjo on Rhodesia, Report to Secretary of State Henry A. Kissinger." Wikileaks cable 1976STATE286831_b. Dated Nov. 23, 1976.

The Economist. "The Spider's Stratagem." Jan. 3, 2008. http://www.economist .com/node/10424283.

Elgindy, Khaled. "When Ambiguity Is Destructive" (blogpost). *Brookings,* January 22, 2014. https://www.brookings.edu/opinions/when-ambiguity -is-destructive/.

Fallows, James. "Elliott Abrams on Hypocrisy." *The Atlantic,* Sept. 19, 2011. https://www.theatlantic.com/international/archive/2011/09/elliott -abrams-on-hypocrisy/245319/.

Ferguson, Niall. "The Kissinger Diaries: What He Really Thought About Vietnam." *Politico*, Oct. 10, 2015. http://www.politico.com/magazine /story/2015/10/henry-kissinger-vietnam-diaries-213236.

———. *Kissinger: Volume 1, 1923–1968: The Idealist*. New York: Penguin Books, 2015.

———. "The Meaning of Kissinger: A Realist Reconsidered." *Foreign Affairs* 94, no. 5 (Sept./Oct. 2015): 134–43.

———. "The Secret to Henry Kissinger's Success," *Politico*, Jan. 20, 2018. https://www.politico.com/magazine/story/2018/01/20/henry-kissinger -networking-216482.

———. *The Square and the Tower: Networks and Power, from Freemasons to Facebook*. New York: Penguin, 2017.

Ferguson, Niall, and Todd Gitlin. "Henry Kissinger: Sage or Pariah?" *New York Times*, Feb. 13, 2016. http://www.nytimes.com/roomfordebate/2016 /02/13/henry-kissinger-sage-or-pariah.

Fettweiss, Christopher. "Credibility and the War on Terror." *Political Science Quarterly* 122, no. 4 (2007–2008): 607–33.

Fidler, David P. "Just and Unjust Wars: The Uses of Coercion." *Daedalus* 145 (Fall 2016): 37–49.

Fisher, Roger, William Ury, and Bruce Patton. *Getting to Yes: Negotiating Agreement Without Giving In*. 2nd ed. New York: Penguin, 1991.

Flower, Ken. *Serving Secretly: An Intelligence Chief on Record: Rhodesia into Zimbabwe, 1964 to 1981*. London: J. Murray, 1987.

Ford, Gerald R. *A Time to Heal: The Autobiography of Gerald R. Ford*. New York: Harper and Row, 1979.

Ford, Gerald R., and King Hussein. "Joint Statement Following Discussions with King Hussein of Jordan." News release, Aug. 18, 1974, http://www .presidency.ucsb.edu/ws/index.php?pid=4454.

Foreign Relations of the United States, 1969–1976, Volume XXXVIII, Part 1, Foundations of Foreign Policy, 1973–1976. Ed. Kristine L. Ahlberg and Alexander Wieland. Washington, DC: Government Printing Office, 2012. Doc. 77. https://history.state.gov/historicaldocuments/frus1969–76v38p1/d77.

Foreign Relations of the United States, 1969–1976, Volume VII, Vietnam, July 1970–Jan. 1972. Ed. David Goldman and Erin Maha. Washington, DC: Government Printing Office, 2010. Doc. 207. https://history.state.gov /historicaldocuments/frus1969–76v07/d207.

Foreign Relations of the United States, 1969–1976. Volume XIV: Soviet Union, Oct. 1971–May 1972. Ed. David C. Geyer, Nina D. Howland, Kent Sieg, and Edward C. Keefer. Washington, DC: Government Printing Office, 2006. Doc. 125. https://history.state.gov/historicaldocuments/frus1969 –76v14/d125.

Foreign Relations of the United States, 1969–1976. Volume XXVIII: Southern Africa. Ed. Myra F. Burton and Edward C. Keefer. Washington, DC: Government Printing Office, 2011, doc. 195. https://history.state.gov /historicaldocuments/frus1969–76v28/d195.

Foreign Relations of the United States, 1969–1976. Volume XL: Germany and Berlin, 1969–1972. Ed. David C. Geyer and Edward C. Keefer. Washington, DC: Government Printing Office, 2008, p. 356, "Editorial Note." https://history.state.gov/historicaldocuments/frus1969–76v40 /d356.

Foreign Relations of the United States, 1981–1988, Volume XLI: Global Issues II. Ed. Alexander O. Poster. Washington, DC: Government Printing Office. https://history.state.gov/historicaldocuments/frus1981-88v41.

Frankel, Jeffrey. "Deal-maker Trump Can't Deal." *Views on the Economy and the World* (blog), Aug. 28, 2017. https://www.belfercenter.org/publication /deal-maker-trump-cant-deal.

Freedman, Lawrence, ed. *Strategic Coercion: Concepts and Cases.* Oxford: Oxford University Press, 1998.

Friedman, G., and Jack Himmelstein. *Challenging Conflict: Mediation Through Understanding.* Chicago: American Bar Association, 2008.

Fry, Joseph A. "Unpopular Messengers: Student Opposition to the Vietnam War." In *The War that Never Ends: New Perspectives on the Vietnam War.* Ed. David L. Anderson and John Ernst. Lexington: University Press of Kentucky, 2007.

Future of Diplomacy Project. "Special Initiative—American Secretaries of State." Harvard Kennedy School Belfer Center for Science and International Affairs. http://www.belfercenter.org/american-secretaries-state /secretaries-state-interviews.

Gallup, Alec. *The Gallup Poll: Public Opinion 2005.* Rowman & Littlefield. pp. 315–18. 2006.

Garthoff, Raymond L. "Negotiating SALT." *Wilson Quarterly* 1, no. 5 (Autumn 1977): 76–85.

Gartner, Scott Sigmund. "Differing Evaluations of Vietnamization." *Journal of Interdisciplinary History* 29, no. 2 (Autumn 1998): 243–62.

Gavin, Philip. *The Fall of Vietnam.* World History Series. New York: Lucent Press, 2003.

———. "United States in Vietnam, 1945–1975: Comprehensive Timelines with Quotes and Analysis," http://www.historyplace.com/unitedstates /vietnam/index.html.

George, Alexander L., and William Simons. *The Limits of Coercive Diplomacy.* 2nd rev. ed. Boulder, CO: Westview Press, 1994.

The Gerald R. Ford Presidential Library and Museum. Grand Rapids, MI. https://www.fordlibrarymuseum.gov/contact.aspx.

"Germany, a Country Study." 1996. Federal Research Division. Library of Congress, Washington, DC, 1996.

Gillespie, Mark. "Americans Look Back at Vietnam War." Gallup News Service, Nov. 17, 2000, http://www.gallup.com/poll/2299/americans -look-back-vietnam-war.aspx.

Gitlin, Todd. "Kissinger Was a Courtier to Atrocity." *New York Times,* Feb. 13, 2016. https://www.nytimes.com/roomfordebate/2016/02/13 /henry-kissinger-sage-or-pariah/kissinger-was-a-courtier-to-atrocity ?mcubz=2.

———. "The Servile Fanatic: Niall Ferguson's Grotesque but Telling New Biography of Henry Kissinger." *Tablet,* Oct. 28, 2015. http://www .tabletmag.com/jewish-news-and-politics/194356/niall-ferguson-henry -kissinger.

Gleijeses, Piero. "A Test of Wills: Jimmy Carter, South Africa, and the Independence of Namibia." *Diplomatic History* 34, no. 5 (2010): 853–91.

Goh, Evelyn. *Constructing the U.S. Rapprochement with China, 1961–1974.* Cambridge: Cambridge University Press, 2004.

Goldberg, Jeffrey. "The Obama Doctrine." *The Atlantic*, April 2016. http://www.theatlantic.com/magazine/archive/2016/04/the-obama-doctrine/471525.

———. "World Chaos and World Order: Conversations with Henry Kissinger." *The Atlantic*, Nov. 10, 2016. https://www.theatlantic.com/international/archive/2016/11/kissinger-order-and-chaos/506876/.

Grandin, Greg. "Henry Kissinger's 'Mad and Illegal' Bombing: What You Need to Know About His Real History—and Why the Sanders/Clinton Exchange Matters." *Salon*, Feb. 12, 2016. http://www.salon.com/2016/02/12/henry_kissingers_mad_and_illegal_bombing_what_you_need_to_know_about_his_real_history_and_why_the_sanders-clinton_exchange_matters/.

———. *Kissinger's Shadow: The Long Reach of America's Most Controversial Statesman.* New York: Metropolitan Books/Henry Holt and Company, 2015.

Gray, Christine. *International Law and the Use of Force.* Oxford: Oxford University Press, 2001.

Habib, Philip. "Cursed Is the Peacemaker." Association for Diplomatic Studies and Training. http://adst.org/oral-history/fascinating-figures/philip-habib-cursed-is-the-peacemaker/.

Halberstam, David. *The Best and the Brightest.* New York: Random House, 1972.

Halliburton, Rachel. "Henry Kissinger's World Order: The Outer Edge of What Is Possible." *Independent*, Sept. 26, 2014. http://www.independent.co.uk/news/world/politics/henry-kissingers-world-order-the-outer-edge-of-what-is-possible-9752563.html.

Hanhimäki, Jussi M. *The Flawed Architect: Henry Kissinger and American Foreign Policy.* New York: Oxford University Press, 2004.

Hanson, Col. Thomas E. "A Raid Too Far: Operation Lam Son 719 and Vietnamization in Laos and Invasion of Laos, 1971." *Military Review* (Jan.–Feb. 2015): 124–26.

Harris, Louis. "Public's Appraisal of Henry Kissinger Remains High." Harris Poll press release, Aug. 19, 1974. http://media.theharrispoll.com /documents/Harris-Interactive-Poll-Research-PUBLICS-APPRAISAL -OF-HENRY-KISSINGER-REMAINS-HIGH-1974–08.pdf.

Heath, Edward. *The Course of My Life: My Autobiography.* London: Hodder and Stoughton, 1998.

Herring, George C. *America's Longest War: The United States in Vietnam, 1950–1975*, 5th ed. Boston: McGraw-Hill Education, 2014.

Hersh, Seymour M. *The Price of Power: Kissinger in the Nixon White House.* New York: Summit Books, 1983.

The History Place. "United States in Vietnam 1945–1975: Comprehensive Timelines with Quotes and Analysis." http://www.historyplace.com /unitedstates/vietnam/index.html.

Hitchens, Christopher. *The Trial of Henry Kissinger.* New York: Verso, 2001.

Hoffmann, David A. "Mediation and the Art of Shuttle Diplomacy." *Negotiation Journal* 27, no. 3 (2011): 263–309.

Hoffmann, Stanley. "The Case of Dr. Kissinger." *New York Review of Books*, Dec. 6, 1979. http://www.nybooks.com/articles/1979/12/06/the-case -of-dr-kissinger/.

Horne, Alistair. "The Case for Henry Kissinger." *Independent*, Aug. 17, 2009. http://www.independent.co.uk/news/world/americas/the-case -for-henry-kissinger-1773365.html.

———. *Kissinger: 1973, the Crucial Year.* New York: Simon and Schuster, 2009.

Howe, Herbert. *Dancing on Cobwebs: American Diplomatic Participation in the 1976 Rhodesian Peace Process.* Pew Case Studies in International Affairs. Washington, DC: Pew Charitable Trusts, 1988.

Iklé, Fred. *How Nations Negotiate.* New York: Harper and Row, 1964.

Isaacson, Walter. *Kissinger: A Biography.* New York: Simon and Schuster, 1992.

Jackson, Paul. "The Civil War Roots of Military Domination in Zimbabwe: The Integration Process Following the Rhodesian War and the Road to Zanla Dominance." *Civil Wars* 13, no. 4 (2011): 371–95.

Joffe, Josef. "In Defense of Henry Kissinger." *Commentary*, Dec. 1, 1992. https://www.commentarymagazine.com/articles/in-defense-of-henry-kissinger/.

"Just War and Its Critics." *Ethics and International Affairs* 27, no. 1 (April 2013): 1–114.

Kalb, Marvin. *First Line Report.* CBS Radio, May 4, 1976.

Kalb, Marvin L., and Bernard Kalb. *Kissinger.* Boston: Little, Brown, 1974.

Kamm, Henry. "Rhodesian Drama Engrosses South Africa." *New York Times*, March 22, 1976, p. 3.

Kanter, R. M. "Zoom In, Zoom Out," *Harvard Business Review* 89, no. 3 (2011): 112–16.

Kaplan, Morton A. and Abram Chayes. *Vietnam Settlement: Why 1973, Not 1969?* Rational Debate Series. Washington, DC: American Enterprise Institute Press, 1987.

Kaplan, Robert D. "In Defense of Henry Kissinger." *The Atlantic*, May 2013. https://www.theatlantic.com/magazine/archive/2013/05/the-statesman/309283/.

———. "Kissinger, Metternich, and Realism (Parts 1 and 2)." *The Atlantic*, June 1999. https://www.theatlantic.com/magazine/archive/1999/06/kissinger-metternich-and-realism/377625/ and https://www.theatlantic.com/past/docs/issues/99jun/9906kissinger2.htm.

Karnow, Stanley. *Vietnam: A History.* New York: Penguin, 1984.

Katz, Andrew Z. "Public Opinion and Foreign Policy: The Nixon Administration and the Pursuit of Peace with Honor in Vietnam." *Presidential Studies Quarterly* 27, no. 3 (Summer 1997): 496–513.

Kaufman, Michael T. "Chrome Ban Asked: Secretary, in Zambia, States Africa Policy and Promises Aid. Kissinger to Press Rhodesia on Rule by Black Majority." *New York Times*, April 28, 1976, p. 1.

Keithly, David M. *Breakthrough in the Ostpolitik: The 1971 Quadripartite Agreement.* Boulder, CO: Westview, 1986.

Kennan, George F. "Black Rule in Rhodesia: Some Implications." *New York Times*, May 2, 1976, p. E15.

Kerry, John. "Remarks at the U.S. Diplomacy Center Groundbreaking Ceremony." News release, Sept. 3, 2014. https://2009–2017.state.gov /secretary/remarks/2014/09/231318.htm.

Khoo, Nicholas. "Breaking the Ring of Encirclement: The Sino-Soviet Rift and Chinese Policy Toward Vietnam, 1964–1968." *Journal of Cold War Studies* 12, no. 1 (Winter 2010): 3–42.

Kirby, William C. "A Note on the 40th Anniversary of Nixon's Visit to China." *Cross Currents: East Asian History and Culture Review* 2 (March 2012). https://cross-currents.berkeley.edu/e-journal/issue-2/note-40th -anniversary-nixon-s-visit-china.

Kissinger, Henry. "Comments on Draft NIE on Rhodesia." Wikileaks cable 1976SECTO27189_b. Dated Sept. 19, 1976. https://wikileaks.org/plusd /cables/1976SECTO27189_b.html.

———. *Diplomacy.* New York: Simon and Schuster, 1994.

———. *Does America Need a Foreign Policy?* New York: Simon and Schuster, 2002.

———. *Ending the Vietnam War: A History of America's Involvement in and Extrication from the Vietnam War.* New York: Simon and Schuster, 2003.

———. "Henry A. Kissinger." http://henryakissinger.com/.

———. "Henry A. Kissinger—Biography." www.henryakissinger.com /biography.html.

———. "Interview with Henry Kissinger, 1982." *Vietnam: A Television History.* WGBH (1982). https://www.digitalcommonwealth.org/search /commonwealth-oai:dv141j297.

———. "Kissinger Memorandum: 'To Isolate the Palestinians': Meeting with Jewish Leaders." Memcon, June 15, 1975, New York. http://www. merip.org/mer/mer96/kissinger-memorandum-isolate-palestinians.

———. "Memo from the President's Assistant for National Security Affairs (Kissinger) to President Nixon, Feb. 19, 1972." *Foreign Relations of the United States, 1969–1976.* Washington, DC: Government Printing Office, 2006, pp. 672–77.

————. "Memorandum to the President: Leonid Brezhnev: The Man and His Style." Memorandum, U.S. Department of State. Gerald Ford Presidential Library, 1974, https://www.fordlibrarymuseum.gov/library/exhibits/vladivostok/brezhnev.pdf.

————. "Message for President Houphouët-Boigny." Wikileaks cable 1976SECTO27213_b. Dated Sept. 20, 1976. https://wikileaks.org/plusd/cables/1976SECTO27213_b.html.

————. *The Necessity for Choice.* New York: Harper and Brothers, 1961.

————. *Nuclear Weapons and Foreign Policy.* New York: Harper, 1957.

————. *Nuclear Weapons and Foreign Policy: Abridged Edition.* New York: W. W. Norton, 1969.

————. *On China.* New York: Penguin Press, 2011.

————. "A Path out of the Middle East Collapse." *Wall Street Journal*, Oct. 16, 2015. https://www.wsj.com/articles/a-path-out-of-the-middle-east-collapse-1445037513.

————. "Transcript of the American Secretaries of State Project: Henry A. Kissinger." Interview with R. Nicholas Burns, Robert Mnookin, and James K. Sebenius, Nov. 6, 2014.

————. "U.S. Naval Academy Forrestal Lecture." Annapolis, MD, April 11, 2007. Speeches and Public Statements. http://www.henryakissinger.com/speeches/041107.html.

————. "The Viet Nam Negotiations." *Foreign Affairs* 47, no. 2 (Jan. 1969): 211–34.

————. *White House Years.* Boston: Little, Brown, 1979.

————. "The White Revolutionary: Reflections on Bismarck." *Daedalus* 97, no. 3 (Summer 1968): 888–924.

————. *World Order.* New York: Penguin Press, 2014.

————. *A World Restored: Europe After Napoleon.* New York: Grosset and Dunlap, 1964.

————. *A World Restored: Metternich, Castlereagh, and the Problems of Peace, 1812–22.* Boston: Houghton Mifflin, 1957.

————. *Years of Renewal.* New York: Simon and Schuster, 1999.

————. *Years of Upheaval*. Boston: Little, Brown, 1982.

The Kissinger Telephone Conversations: A Verbatim Record of U.S. Diplomacy, 1969–1977. Digital National Security Archive. George Washington University, Washington DC. http://proquest.libguides.com/dnsa/kissinger1.

Klotz, Audie, Cecelia Lynch, Jeffrey T. Checkel, and Kevin C. Dunn. "Moving Beyond the Agent-Structure Debate." *International Studies Review* 8, no. 2 (2006): 355.

Knowles, Elizabeth. *Oxford Dictionary of Modern Quotations*. 3rd ed. New York: Oxford University Press, 2008.

Kogan, Eugene B. "Coercing Allies: Why Friends Abandon Nuclear Plans." PhD diss., Brandeis University, 2013.

Lake, Anthony. *The "Tar Baby" Option: American Policy Toward Southern Rhodesia*. New York: Columbia University Press, 1976.

Lanning, Michael Lee, and Dan Cragg. *Inside the VC and the NVA: The Real Story of North Vietnam's Armed Forces*. New York: Fawcett Columbine, 1992.

Lauren, Paul Gordon, Gordon A. Craig, and Alexander L. George. *Force and the Limits of Military Might*. New York: Cambridge University Press, 2002.

Lax, David A., and James K. Sebenius. "Deal Making 2.0: A Guide to Complex Negotiations." *Harvard Business Review* 90, no. 12 (Nov. 2012): 92–100.

————. *The Manager as Negotiator: Bargaining for Cooperation and Competitive Gain*. New York: Free Press, 1986.

————. "3-D Negotiation: Playing the Whole Game." *Harvard Business Review* 81, no. 11 (Nov. 2003): 65–74.

————. *3-D Negotiation: Powerful Tools to Change the Game in Your Most Important Deals*. Boston, MA: Harvard Business School Press, 2006.

Lewis, Anthony. "A Christopher Shuttle?" *New York Times*, Dec. 3, 1993, p. A33

Lind, Michael. *The Necessary War: A Reinterpretation of America's Most Disastrous Military Conflict*. New York: Free Press, 1999.

"List of Countries by Past and Projected GDP (Nominal) Per Capita." Wikipedia. https://en.wikipedia.org/w/index.php?title=List_of_Countries_by_past_and_projected_GDP_(nominal)_per_capita&oldid=711796013.

Logevall, Fredrik. *Choosing War: The Lost Chance for Peace and the Escalation of War in Vietnam*. Berkeley: University of California, 1999.

———. *Embers of War: The Fall of an Empire and the Making of America's Vietnam*. New York: Random House, 2012.

Lord, Winston. "Interview with Ambassador Winston Lord." Foreign Affairs Oral History Project, April 28, 1998. http://www.adst.org/OH%20TOCs/Lord,%20Winston.pdf.

Low, Stephen. "Interview with Stephen Low." Foreign Affairs Oral History Project, Dec. 5, 1997. http://adst.org/wp-content/uploads/2012/09/Low-Stephen.-1997-.toc_1.pdf.

———. "The Zimbabwe Settlement, 1976–1979." In *International Mediation in Theory and Practice*. Ed. Saadia Touval and I. William Zartman. Washington, DC: Westview Press, 1985.

Lunch, William L., and Peter W. Sperlich. "American Public Opinion and the War in Vietnam." *Western Political Quarterly* 32, no. 1 (1979): 21–44.

Maclear, Michael. *Vietnam: The Ten Thousand Day War*. New York: Methuen, 1981.

MacMillan, Margaret. *Nixon and Mao: The Week that Changed the World*. New York: Random House, 2007.

Maliniak, Daniel, Susan Peterson, Ryan Powers, and Michael J. Tierney. "Best International Relations Schools in the World." *Foreign Policy*, Feb. 2, 2015. http://foreignpolicy.com/2015/02/03/top-twenty-five-schools-international-relations/.

Marder, Murrey. "U.S. Seeking to Oust Soviet Units in Egypt: U.S. Seeks Soviet Pullback in Mideast." *Washington Post*, July 3, 1970, pp. A1 and A4.

Martin, David. "Mwalimu Julius Kambarage Nyerere Remembered." Undated. *Knowledge for Development* (blog). Southern Africa Research and Documentation Centre. http://www.sardc.net/en/mwalimu-julius-kambarage-nyerere-remembered-a-candle-on-kilimanjaro-by-david-martin/.

Mazarin, Cardinal Jules [passage translated by James K. Sebenius]. *Bréviaire des politiciens*. 1684; reprint. Paris: Arlèa, 1996.

McCarthy, Eugene. "Topics: The Failure of Vietnamization by Any Name." *New York Times*, Aug. 1, 1970, p. 22.

McMahon, Robert J. "Credibility and World Power: Exploring the Psychological Dimension in Postwar American Diplomacy." *Diplomatic History* 15 (Fall 1991): 455–71.

McNeil, Donald G., Jr., "Joshua Nkomo of Zimbabwe Is Dead at 62." *New York Times*, July 2, 1999, p. C17.

Meacham, Jon. "Hillary Clinton, Kissinger on Sec. of State Job." *Newsweek*, Jan. 4, 2009. http://www.newsweek.com/hillary-clinton-kissinger-sec -state-job-75525.

Meir, Golda. *My Life*. New York: G.P. Putnam's Sons, 1975.

Menkel-Meadow, Carrie, and Michael Wheeler, eds. *What's Fair? Ethics for Negotiators*. Hoboken, NJ: Jossey-Bass/Wiley, 2010.

Metternich, Clemens von. *The Autobiography, 1773–1815*. Garden City, NY: Welwyn, 2007.

Miller, Jamie. *An African Volk: The Apartheid Regime and Its Search for Survival*. New York: Oxford University Press. 2016.

Mnookin, Robert H. *Bargaining with the Devil: When to Negotiate, When to Fight*. New York: Simon and Schuster, 2010.

Mnookin, Robert H., and Ehud Eiran. "Discord 'Behind the Table': The Internal Conflict Among Israeli Jews Concerning the Future of Settlements in the West Bank and Gaza." *Journal of Dispute Resolution* 1 (2005): 11–44.

Mnookin, Robert H., Scott R. Peppet, and Andrew S. Tulumello. *Beyond Winning: Negotiating to Create Value in Deals and Disputes*. Cambridge, MA: Belknap Press/Harvard University Press, 2000.

———. "The Tension Between Empathy and Assertiveness." *Negotiation Journal* 12, no. 3 (1996): 217–30.

Moise, Edwin. *Tonkin Gulf and the Escalation of the Vietnam War*. Chapel Hill: University of North Carolina Press, 1996.

Montgomery, John D. "The Education of Henry Kissinger." *Journal of International Affairs* 29, no. 1 (1975): 49–62.

Morning Journal-Record. "Whites in Africa Fear Race War." Feb. 28, 1976, p. 7.

Mott, William H., IV. *Soviet Military Assistance: An Empirical Perspective.* Westport, CT: Greenwood Press, 2001.

Mutiti, A. B., "Rhodesia and Her Four Discriminatory Constitutions." *Présence Africaine*, Nouvelle série no. 90 (2ᵉ Trimestre 1974): 261–75.

Muzorewa, Abel Tendekayi. *Rise Up and Walk: An Autobiography.* Ed. Norman E. Thomas. London: Evans Books, 1978.

Neale, Margaret Ann, and Max H. Bazerman. *Cognition and Rationality in Negotiation.* New York and Toronto: Free Press, 1991.

Neustadt, Richard E. *Alliance Politics.* New York: Columbia University Press, 1970.

New York Times. "Twilight in Pretoria." *New York Times*, Feb. 5, 1989, p. E24.

Nixon, Richard M. "Address Accepting the Presidential Nomination at the Republican National Convention in Miami Beach, Florida." American Presidency Project, Aug. 8, 1968. http://www.presidency.ucsb.edu /ws/?pid=25968.

———. "Address to the Nation on Vietnam." American Presidency Project, Nov. 3, 1969. http://www.presidency.ucsb.edu/ws/?pid=2303.

———. *RN: The Memoirs of Richard Nixon.* New York: Grosset and Dunlap, 1978.

Novak, Andrew. "Face-Saving Maneuvers and Strong Third-Party Mediation: The Lancaster House Conference on Zimbabwe-Rhodesia." *International Negotiation* 14, no. 1 (2009): 149–74.

Observer. "The Road to Zimbabwe." Sept. 26, 1976, p. 8.

Onslow, Sue. "'Noises Off': South Africa and the Lancaster House Settlement 1979–1980." *Journal of Southern African Studies* 35, no. 2 (2009): 489–506.

———. "A Question of Timing: South Africa and Rhodesia's Unilateral Declaration of Independence, 1964–65." *Cold War History* 5, no. 2 (2005): 129–59.

———. "South Africa and the Owen/Vance Plan of 1977." *South African Historical Journal* 51, no. 1 (2004): 130–58.

———. "'We Must Gain Time': South Africa, Rhodesia and the Kissinger Initiative of 1976." *South African Historical Journal* 56, no. 1 (2006): 123–53.

Otte, T. G. "Kissinger." In *Diplomatic Theory from Machiavelli to Kissinger.* Ed. Maurice Keens-Soper, G. R. Berridge, and T. G. Otte. New York: Palgrave, 2001.

Pallotti, Arrigo, and Tornimbeni, Corrado. *State, Land, and Democracy in Southern Africa.* London: Routledge, 2015.

Pillalamarri, Akhilesh. "Pakistan's Nuclear Weapons Program: 5 Things You Need to Know." *The National Interest*, April 21, 2015. http://national interest.org/feature/pakistans-nuclear-weapons-program-5-things-you -need-know-12687?page=2.

Powell, Colin L., and Joseph E. Persico. *My American Journey.* New York: Random House, 1995.

Program on Negotiation at Harvard Law School. http://www.pon.harvard.edu/.

Quandt, W. "Kissinger and the Arab-Israeli Disengagement Negotiations." *Journal of International Affairs* 9, no. 1 (1975): 33–48.

Rabin, Yitzhak. *The Rabin Memoirs.* Berkeley: University of California Press, 1996.

Rahman, Shahid ur. *Long Road to Chagai.* Islamabad: Print Wise, 1999.

Record, Jeffrey. *The Wrong War: Why We Lost in Vietnam.* Annapolis, MD: Naval Institute Press, 1998.

Reisman, Michael W. "Criteria for the Lawful Use of Force in International Law." Yale Faculty Scholarship Series 739. *Yale Journal of International Law* (1985). http://digitalcommons.law.yale.edu/fss_papers/739.

Richard Nixon Presidential Library and Museum. Yorba Linda, CA. https:// www.nixonlibrary.gov/.

Rogers, William D. "Interview with Under Secretary William D. Rogers." Foreign Affairs Oral History Project, July 8, 1992. http://www.adst.org /OH%20TOCs/Rogers,%20William%20D.toc.pdf.

Ross, Dennis. *Doomed to Succeed: The U.S.-Israel Relationship from Truman to Obama*. New York: Farrar, Straus, and Giroux, 2015.

Rotberg, Robert. "Namibia's Nationhood." *Christian Science Monitor*, March 20, 1990, p. 19.

Rubin, Jeffrey Z. *Dynamics of Third Party Intervention: Kissinger in the Middle East*. New York: Praeger, in cooperation with the Society for the Psychological Study of Social Issues, 1981.

———. "Editor's Introduction." *Negotiation Journal* 1, no. 1 (1985): 5–8.

Rucker, Philip, Sean Sullivan, and Paul Kane. "The Great Dealmaker? Lawmakers Find Trump to Be an Untrustworthy Negotiator." *Washington Post*, Oct. 23, 2017. https://www.washingtonpost.com/politics/the-great-dealmaker-lawmakers-find-trump-to-be-an-untrustworthy-negotiator/2017/10/22/7709aea8-b5d4–11e7-be94-fabb0f1e9ffb_story.html?utm_term=.ba98764241d3.

Saunders, Harold. "On the Road Again—Kissinger's Shuttle Diplomacy." Moments in U.S. Diplomatic History. Association for Diplomatic Studies and Training. http://adst.org/2016/03/on-the-road-again-kissingers-shuttle-diplomacy/.

Schaufele, Jr., William E. "Interview with Ambassador William E. Schaufele, Jr." Foreign Affairs Oral History Project, Nov. 19, 1994. http://www.adst.org/OH%20TOCs/Schaufele,%20William%20E.%20Jr.pdf.

Schelling, Thomas C. *Arms and Influence*. New Haven, CT: Yale University Press, 1966.

———. *The Strategy of Conflict*. Cambridge, MA: Harvard University Press, 1960.

Sebenius, James K. "Assess, Don't Assume, Part I: Etiquette and National Culture in Negotiation." Harvard Business School Working Paper, No. 10–048, Dec. 2009, Boston.

———. "Assess, Don't Assume, Part II: Negotiating Implications of Cross-Border Differences in Decision Making, Governance, and Political Economy." Harvard Business School Working Paper, no. 10–050, Dec. 2009, Boston.

———. "Beyond the Deal: Wage a 'Negotiation Campaign'." *Negotiation Journal* 13, no. 11 (2010): 1–4.

———. "The Hidden Challenge of Cross-Border Negotiations." *Harvard Business Review* 80, no. 3 (2002): 76–85.

———. "International Negotiation Analysis." In *International Negotiation: Analysis, Approaches, Issues.* 2nd ed. Ed. Victor Kremenyuk. San Francisco: Jossey-Bass, 2002, pp. 229–52.

——— "Level Two Negotiations: Helping the Other Side Meet Its 'Behind-the-Table' Challenges." *Negotiation Journal* 29, no. 1 (2013): 7–21.

———. "Negotiating Lessons from the Browser Wars." *MIT Sloan Management Review* 43, no. 4 (Summer 2002): 43–50.

———. "Negotiation Arithmetic: Adding and Subtracting Issues and Parties." *International Organization* 37, no. 2 (Spring 1983): 281–316.

———. "Sequencing to Build Coalitions: With Whom Should I Talk First?" In *Wise Choices: Decisions, Games, and Negotiations.* Ed. Richard Zeckhauser, Ralph Keeney, and James Sebenius. Boston, MA: Harvard Business School Press, 1996.

Sebenius, James K., R. Nicholas Burns, Robert H. Mnookin, and L. Alexander Green. "Henry Kissinger: Negotiating Black Majority Rule in Southern Africa." Harvard Business School Working Paper No. 17–051, Dec. 2016, Boston.

Sebenius, James K., Laurence A. Green, and Eugene B. Kogan. "Henry A. Kissinger as Negotiator: Background and Key Accomplishments." Harvard Business School Working Paper No. 15–040, 2014, rev. Dec. 2016, Boston.

Sebenius, James K., and David A. Lax. "The Power of Alternatives or the Limits to Negotiation." *Negotiation Journal* 1, no. 2 (1985): 77–95.

Semple, Robert B., Jr. "Nixon Urges Supervised Truce in Vietnam, Cambodia, and Laos and a Wider Peace Conference." *New York Times*, Oct. 8, 1970, p. 1.

Serewicz, Lawrence W. *America at the Brink of Empire: Rusk, Kissinger, and the Vietnam War.* Baton Rouge: Louisiana State University Press, 2007.

Shane, Scott. "Vietnam Study, Casting Doubts, Remains Secret." *New York Times*, Oct. 31, 2005, p. A1.

Shawcross, William. "Shrugging Off Genocide." *Times* (London), Dec. 19, 1994, p. 16.

———. *Sideshow: Kissinger, Nixon, and the Destruction of Cambodia*. New York: Simon and Schuster, 1979.

Sheehan, Edward R. F. "How Kissinger Did It: Step by Step in the Middle East." *Foreign Policy* 22 (1976): 3–70.

Shirin, Tahir-Kheli. *The United States and Pakistan: The Evolution of an Influence Relationship*. New York: Praeger Publishers, 1982.

Shlaim, Avi. *Lion of Jordan: The Life of King Hussein in War and Peace*. New York: Alfred A. Knopf, 2008.

Shultz, George P. *Ideas and Action: Featuring the 10 Commandments of Negotiation*. Erie, PA: Free to Choose Press, 2010.

Slaughter, Anne-Marie. *The Chessboard and the Web: Strategies of Connection in a Networked World*. New Haven, CT: Yale University Press, 2017.

Smith, Gerard C. *Doubletalk: The Story of the First Strategic Arms Limitation Talks*. Garden City, NY: Doubleday and Co., 1980.

Smith, Ian Douglas. *Bitter Harvest*. London: Blake, 2001.

———. *The Great Betrayal: The Memoirs of Ian Douglas Smith*. London: Blake Publishing Ltd, 1997.

———. News Conference, Oct. 25, 1976. https://youtu.be/6gZx6Nda2tM.

———. "Smith Speech." Wikileaks cable 1976SECTO27255_b. Dated Sept. 21, 1976. https://wikileaks.org/plusd/cables/1976SECTO27255_b.html.

Smock, David R. "The Forgotten Rhodesians." *Foreign Affairs* 47, no. 3 (1969): 532.

Sorley, Lewis. "Courage and Blood: South Vietnam's Repulse of the 1972 Easter Offensive." *Parameters* 29 (Summer 1999): 38–56.

Spiegel, Marianne. "The Namibia Negotiations and the Problem of Neutrality." In *International Mediation in Theory and Practice*. Ed. Saadia Touval and I. William Zartman. Washington, DC: Westview Press, 1985.

Steel, Ronald. *Walter Lippmann and the American Century*. Boston: Little, Brown and Company, 1980.

Stein, Janice. "Structures, Strategies, and Tactics of Mediation: Kissinger and Carter in the Middle East." *Negotiation Journal* 1, no. 4 (1985): 331–47.

"Strategic Survey: The Sino-Soviet Dispute." *International Institute for Strategic Studies* 70, no. 1 (1969): 66–72 and 100–102.

Sulzberger, C. L. "Policy and Politicians," *New York Times*, May 12, 1976, p. 41.

Szulc, Tad. "How Kissinger Did It: Behind the Vietnam Cease-Fire Agreement." *Foreign Policy* 15 (1974): 21–69.

Tamarkin, Mordechai. *The Making of Zimbabwe: Decolonization in Regional and International Politics*. Savage, MD: F. Cass, 1990.

Taylor, Alan. "The Vietnam War, Part I: Early Years and Escalation." *The Atlantic*, March 30, 2015. https://www.theatlantic.com/photo/2015/03/the-vietnam-war-part-i-early-years-and-escalation/389054/.

Taylor, David. "The Lyndon Johnson Tapes: Richard Nixon's 'Treason.'" *BBC News Magazine* (2013). Published electronically March 22, 2013. http://www.bbc.com/news/magazine-21768668.

Thach, Nguyen Co. "Interview with Nguyen Co Thach, 1981." *Vietnam: A Television History; Peace Is at Hand (1968–1973)*. WGBH (Feb. 24, 1981). https://www.digitalcommonwealth.org/search/commonwealth-oai:dv141t68k.

Thompson, Leigh L. *The Mind and Heart of the Negotiator*. 5th ed. Boston: Pearson, 2012.

Thompson, Nicholas et al. "Henry Kissinger: Good or Evil?" *Politico*, Oct. 10, 2015. http://www.politico.com/magazine/story/2015/10/henry-kissinger-history-legacy-213237.

Thrall, Nathan. *The Only Language They Understand*. New York: Henry Holt and Company, 2017.

Time. "A Dr. K. Offer They Could Not Refuse." Vol. 108, no. 14, Oct. 4, 1976, p. 43.

———. "Poised Between Peace and War." Oct. 11, 1976, p. 44.

The Trials of Henry Kissinger. Directed by Eugene Jarecki. BBC4 (2002). YouTube. https://youtu.be/DwGtctUYhRI.

Tzeng, Peter. "Nuclear Leverage: US Intervention in Sensitive Technology Transfers in the 1970s." *The Nonproliferation Review* 20, no. 3 (2013): 473–92.

Ulam, Adam B. *Expansion and Coexistence: The History of Soviet Foreign Policy, 1917–67.* New York: Praeger, 1968.

United Nations. "Treaty on the Non-Proliferation of Nuclear Weapons," United Nations Office for Disarmament Affairs, March 5, 1970, New York. http://disarmament.un.org/treaties/t/npt.

United Nations Security Council. Resolution 385 Adopted by the United Nations Security Council at Its 1885th Meeting. S/RES/385. 1885, Jan. 30, 1976.

U.S. Census Bureau. "Vietnam Conflict—U.S. Military Forces in Vietnam and Casualties Incurred: 1961 to 1972." Table 590: Statistical Abstract of the United States, 1977. U.S. Department of Commerce, 1980, Washington, DC. https://www.gilderlehrman.org/history-by-era/seventies/resources/vietnam-war-military-statistics.

U.S. Department of Defense. " 'Casualty Status': U.S. Military Operations 2003 to Present." Washington, DC: Government Printing Office, ND. https://www.defense.gov/casualty.pdf.

U.S. Department of State. "Meeting with Moshe Dayan and Ambassador Simcha Dinitz." Memcon, U.S. Department of State, June 8, 1974. In the Kissinger Telephone Conversations: A Verbatim Record of U.S. Diplomacy, 1969–1977. Digital National Security Archive. George Washington University, Washington DC. http://proquest.libguides.com/dnsa/kissinger1.

———. "Memorandum of Conversation Between Henry Kissinger and Xuan Thuy, Paris," May 31, 1971. In Ed. David Goldman and Erin Mahan, *Foreign Relations of the United States, 1969–1976.* Washington, DC: Government Printing Office, 1971. https://history.state.gov/historical/documents/frus1969–76v07/d207.

————. "The Pakistan Nuclear Reprocessing Issue." Folder: "Nodis Memcons, Sept. 1976/2." National Archives and Records Administration. U.S. Department of State, College Park, MD.

————. "Secretary's Visit to Tanzania." Wikileaks cable 1976DARES 01504_b. Dated, March 25, 1976. https://wikileaks.org/plusd/cables /1976DARES01504_b.html.

————. "Southern Africa." Memcon. Number 10 Downing Street, London, Sept. 23, 1976. In the Kissinger Telephone Conversations: A Verbatim Record of U.S. Diplomacy, 1969–1977. Digital National Security Archive. George Washington University, Washington DC. http://proquest .libguides.com/dnsa/kissinger1.

————. "Southern Africa." Memcon. Foreign and Commonwealth Office, London. Sept. 24, 1976. In the Kissinger Telephone Conversations: A Verbatim Record of U.S. Diplomacy, 1969–1977. Digital National Security Archive. George Washington University, Washington DC. http:// proquest.libguides.com/dnsa/kissinger1.

————. "Memcon with B. J. Vorster, Zurich, Switzerland." Sept. 4, 1976. In the Kissinger Telephone Conversations: A Verbatim Record of U.S. Diplomacy, 1969–1977. Digital National Security Archive. George Washington University, Washington DC. http://search.proquest.com .ezp-prod1.hul.harvard.edu/docview/1679067316?accountid=11311.

Van Alstyne, William W. "Congress, the President, and the Power to Declare War: A Requiem for Vietnam." *University of Pennsylvania Law Review* 121, no. 1 (1972): 1–28.

Van Der Vat, Dan. "Ian Smith, 88 Politician." *Globe and Mail*, Nov. 21, 2007, p. S10.

van Voorst, Bruce. "Silent Shuttle." *Foreign Policy*, July 26, 2013. http:// foreignpolicy.com/2013/07/26/silent-shuttle/.

The Vietnam War. Documentary. Directed by Ken Burns and Lynn Novick. PBS. Walpole, NH: Florentine Films, 2017.

The Wall Street Journal. "Kissinger Talks in Pakistan Again Show Problems of Curbing Nuclear-Arms Flow." Aug. 10, 1976, 8.

Walt, Stephen. "The Credibility Addiction." *Foreign Policy*, January 26, 2015. http://foreignpolicy.com/2015/01/06/the-credibility-addiction-us -iraq-afghanistan-unwinnable-war/.

Walters, Vernon A. *The Mighty and the Meek: Dispatches from the Front Line of Diplomacy*. London: St. Ermin's Press, 2001.

Walton, Hanes. *The African Foreign Policy of Secretary of State Henry Kissinger: A Documentary Analysis*. Lanham, MD: Lexington Books, 2007.

Walzer, Michael. *Just and Unjust Wars: A Moral Argument with Historical Illustrations*. 5th ed. New York: Basic Books, 2015.

Washington Post. "The Baker Shuttle." May 14, 1991, p. A18.

———. "On 'Expelling' the Russians from the Mideast." July 7, 1970, p. A14.

———. "Rhodesia's Alternatives." Nov. 2, 1976, p. A8.

Watkins, Michael, and Susan Rosegrant. *Breakthrough International Negotiation: How Great Negotiators Transformed the World's Toughest Post-Cold War Conflicts*. San Francisco, CA: Jossey-Bass, 2001.

Watts, Carl. "Ripe for Settlement? Kissinger's Attempted Mediation of the Rhodesian Conflict." 22. http://www.academia.edu/3878573/Ripe_for _settlement_Kissinger_s_Attempted_Mediation_of_the_Rhodesian _Conflict.

The Week That Changed the World. Directed by Michael Trinklein. YouTube (2012). https://www.youtube.com/watch?v=qoHAPj9O5c0.

Wendt, Alexander E. "The Agent-Structure Problem in International Relations Theory." *International Organization* 41, no. 3 (1987): 335–70.

White, Luise. *Unpopular Sovereignty: Rhodesian Independence and African Decolonization*. Chicago: The University of Chicago Press, 2015.

"Who Was the Most Effective U.S. Secretary of State in the Last 50 Years?" TRIP Faculty Survey in United States, Feb. 9, 2014. https://trip.wm.edu /charts/#/bargraph/37/1282.

Willbanks, James H. "Tet 1968: Turning Point." Foreign Policy Research Institute, May 15, 2012. http://www.fpri.org/article/2012/05/tet-1968 -the-turning-point/.

Bibliography

Association for Diplomatic Studies. Interview with Ambassador Frank G. Wisner. Foreign Affairs Oral History Project, March 22, 1998. http://www.adst.org/OH%20TOCs/Wisner,%20Frank%20G.toc.pdf.

Wisner, Frank G. Authors' interview with Ambassador Frank G. Wisner, May 5, 2016.

Womack, Brantly. *China and Vietnam: The Politics of Asymmetry.* New York: Cambridge University Press, 2006.

Wright, Robin. "Vorster and Smith Hold Talks on Kissinger's Africa Shuttle." *Washington Post*, Sept. 15, 1976, p. A10.

"Z." "The Year of Europe?" *Foreign Affairs* 52, no. 2 (Jan. 1974): 237–48.

Zartman, I. William. *Ripe for Resolution: Conflict and Intervention in Africa.* New York: Oxford University Press, 1985.

"Zimbabwe: Mugabe Booed over Economic Crisis." *Africa Research Bulletin: Economic, Financial and Technical Series* 52, no. 8 (2015): 20957B–C. doi:10.1111/j.1467–6346.2015.06619.x

"Zimbabwe's Landslide Leader." *Christian Science Monitor*, March 5, 1980, p. 24.

Index

About the Authors

JAMES K. SEBENIUS specializes in analyzing and advising corporations and governments on their most challenging negotiations. He is the Gordon Donaldson Professor of Business Administration at Harvard Business School, where he founded the Negotiation unit and now teaches advanced negotiation to students and senior executives. Formerly on the faculty of Harvard's Kennedy School, he chairs the Harvard-MIT-Tufts Great Negotiator Award program. Sebenius also serves as the director of the Harvard Negotiation Project at Harvard Law School and vice chair for practice-focused research at the Program on Negotiation. He wrote *Negotiating the Law of the Sea*, and coauthored (with David Lax) *3-D Negotiation* and *The Manager as Negotiator*, both widely used in negotiation courses in the United States and abroad. He also cofounded Lax Sebenius LLC, an active negotiation strategy firm that advises leading companies and governments worldwide on their most challenging negotiations. He has worked at Blackstone Group, and has also served with the U.S. State and Commerce Departments. He holds a BA summa cum laude from Vanderbilt, an MS from Stanford's Engineering School, and a PhD in business economics from Harvard.

R. NICHOLAS BURNS is the Roy and Barbara Goodman Family Professor of the Practice of Diplomacy and International Relations at the Harvard Kennedy School of Government. He is the director of the Future of Diplomacy Project and faculty chair for the Programs on the Middle East and on India and South Asia. For his government service, he received the Secretary of State's

Distinguished Service Award. Burns is director of the Aspen Strategy Group, senior counselor at the Cohen Group, and serves on the board of directors of Entegris Inc. He is a member of former Secretary of State John Kerry's Foreign Affairs Policy Board and serves on the boards of numerous nonprofit organizations, including the Council on Foreign Relations and Special Olympics International. He is a member of the American Academy of Arts and Sciences, the Order of St John, and Red Sox Nation. Professor Burns has received twelve honorary degrees as well as a BA from Boston College and an MA from the Johns Hopkins School of Advanced International Studies.

ROBERT H. MNOOKIN is the Samuel Williston Professor of Law at Harvard Law School, the chair of the Program on Negotiation at Harvard Law School, and the director of the Harvard Negotiation Research Project. A leading scholar in the field of conflict resolution, Professor Mnookin has applied his interdisciplinary approach to negotiation and conflict resolution to a remarkable range of problems, both public and private. Professor Mnookin has written or edited ten books. In his most recent book, *Bargaining with the Devil: When to Negotiate, When to Fight*, Mnookin explores the challenge of making critical decisions. His book *Beyond Winning: Negotiating to Create Value in Deals and Disputes* is used throughout the world to instruct lawyers how to negotiate more constructively. Professor Mnookin graduated from Harvard College and Harvard Law School, served as a law clerk to Supreme Court justice John M. Harlan, and practiced law in San Francisco. Prior to his appointment to Harvard Law School's faculty, he taught for many years at Stanford and Berkeley, serving as a founder and director of the Stanford Center on Conflict and Negotiation, an interdisciplinary group focused on overcoming barriers to the negotiated resolution of conflict.

HENRY KISSINGER (foreword) is an American diplomat and political scientist. He served as national security advisor and later, concurrently, as U.S. secretary of state in the administrations of Presidents Richard Nixon and Gerald Ford. For his actions negotiating the cease-fire in Vietnam, Kissinger received the 1973 Nobel Peace Prize. Since the end of his term, his advice has been sought by world leaders, including subsequent U.S. presidents.